Medical Pluralism in the Andes

Medical Pluralism in the Andes is the first major collection of anthropological approaches to health in the Andes for over twenty years. Written in tribute to Libbet Crandon-Malamud's pioneering work on Andean medicine, this readable, extensively illustrated and instructive book reflects the diversity of approaches in medical anthropology that have evolved during the past two decades. The thirteen essays from leading experts cover subject areas including gender, ethnicity and health seeking, common illnesses and remedies, nutrition, alternative therapies and healer roles and practices, and how children are socialized into popular medical beliefs and practices. Almost all previously unpublished, and reliant on extensive individual fieldwork, they offer a detailed and rounded explanation of the multiple issues affecting the health of local populations in Peru, Ecuador, and Bolivia. Essays include:

- Kathryn S. Oths on musculoskeletal injury among Andean potato farmers
- Christine Greenway's "Healing Soul Loss: The Negotiation of Identity in Peru"
- Ann Miles on the healing industry in Ecuador
- Margaret A. Graham on food, health, and identity in the rural Andes
- Joseph William Bastien's "Sucking Blood or Snatching Fat," on Chaga's disease in Bolivia
- Ann C. Larme and Thomas Leatherman on women's health, work, and reproduction in Southern Peru
- Bonnie Glass-Coffin on Shamanism and belief in Peru.

Libbet Crandon-Malamud's profound influence on the subject is recalled in a reprint of her celebrated article "Changing Times, Changing Symptoms," on processsess of resort to health care integrally linked to change in social and economic status, while Joan Koss-Chioino and Hans Baer contribute commentary on her life and work. Capturing the intricacies of health practice within the fascinating context of Andean social history, cultural tradition, community, and folklore, *Medical Pluralism in the Andes* is a remarkable and intimate chronicle of Andean culture and everyday life.

Joan D. Koss-Chioino is Professor of Anthropology and affiliate of the Women's Studies Department at Arizona State University. She is also Visiting Professor of Psychiatry and Neurology at Tulane Medical Center in New Orleans, Research Professor of Psychology at George Washington University, and author of *Women as Healers, Women as Patients* (1992) and *Working with Latino Youth* (1999). **Thomas Leatherman** is Professor and Chair in the Department of Anthropology at the University of South Carolina, Columbia. **Christine Greenway** is affiliated with the University of Washington.

Theory and Practice in Medical Anthropology and International Health
A series edited by *Susan M. DiGiacomo*
University of Massachusetts, Amherst

Medical Pluralism in the Andes

Edited by Joan D. Koss-Chioino,
Thomas Leatherman, and Christine
Greenway

with a foreword by June Nash

Routledge
Taylor & Francis Group

LONDON AND NEW YORK

First published 2003 by Routledge
2 Park Square, Milton Park, Abingdon, Oxon, OX14 4RN

Simultaneously published in the USA and Canada
by Routledge
270 Madison Ave, New York NY 10016

Routledge is an imprint of the Taylor & Francis Group

Transferred to Digital Printing 2007

Typeset in Times New Roman by
Newgen Imaging Systems (P) Ltd, Chennai, India

British Library Cataloguing in Publication Data
A catalogue record for this book is available from the British Library

Library of Congress Cataloging in Publication Data
Medical pluralism in the Andes / edited by Joan Koss-Chioino, Thomas Leatherman, and
Christine Greenway; with a foreword by June Nash.
    p. cm. – (Theory and practice in medical anthropology and international health)
Includes index.
    1. Medical anthropology – Andes Region. 2. Medicine – Andes Region. 3. Social medicine –
Andes Region. 4. Medical care – Andes Region. 5. Indians of South America – Health and hygiene –
Andes Region. 6. Indians of South America – Medicine – Andes Region. 7. Public health – Andes
Region. I. Koss-Chioino, Joan. II. Leatherman, Thomas L. III. Greenway, Christine. IV. Series.

RA650.55.A47 M43 2002
306.4'61'098–dc21   2002075186

ISBN 0-415-29918-7 (hbk)
ISBN 0-415-29920-9 (pbk)

This book is a tribute to Libbet Crandon-Malamud and all spirited women

Andean fieldsites

Contents

List of Illustrations

Tables

Contributors

June Nash is Distinguished Professor Emeritus at the City University of New York. She has carried out research in Bolivia, Mexico, Guatemala and the US. Her books include: *We Eat the Mines and the Mines Eat Us: Dependency and Exploitation in Bolivian Tin Mines*; *In the Eyes of the Ancestors: Belief and Behavior in a Mayan Community*; *From Tank Town to High Tech: The Clash between Community and Industrial Cycles*; *Crafts in the World Market: Impact of Global Exchange on Middle American Artisans*; edited books on *Sex and Class in Latin America* with Helen Safa; *Women, Men and the International Division of Labor* with Patricia Fernandez Kelly, *Women and Change in Latin America Women* with Helen Safa. Her latest book is *Mayan Visions: The Quest for Autonomy in an Age of Globalization* based on forty years of intermittent field work in Mesoamerica. She has received the Conrad Arensberg award, the C. Wright Mills award for *We Eat the Mines*, and the Distinguished Service award from the American Anthropological Association.

Hans A. Baer is Professor in the Department of Sociology and Anthropology at the University of Arkansas at Little Rock. He has been a visiting professor at Humboldt University in Berlin, University of California, Berkeley, and Arizona State University. Baer has done research on Mormonism, African–American religion and religious healing, medical pluralism in the United States and Great Britain, and sociopolitical and religious life in East Germany both before and after the unification. He has published nine books and over 100 book chapters or journal articles.

In the area of medical anthropology, his books include *Encounters with Biomedicine: Case Studies in Medical Anthropology* (Gordon and Breach, 1987); *Critical Medical Anthropology* (with Merrill Singer) (Baywood, 1995); *Medical Anthropology and the World System: A Critical Perspective* (Bergin & Garvey, 1997); and *Biomedicine and Alternative Healing Systems in America: Issues of Class, Race, Ethnicity, and Gender* (University of Wisconsin Press, 2001).

Joseph William Bastien first went to Bolivia in 1963 as a Maryknoll Mission priest, where he worked among the Aymaras in La Paz and Las Penas until 1969, when he left the priesthood to study anthropology at Cornell. He returned to Bolivia in 1973 to study their rituals and understand Andean religion, published in *Mountain of the Condor (1978)*. Andean religion is very concerned with health and sickness, so he became involved with herbal, ritual, and bio-medical curing among Aymaras, Quechuas, and Kallawayas. He's presently involved with the study of how to control Chagas' disease in Latin America, published in *Kiss of Death: Chagas' Disease in the Americas* (2001). He also maintains a website on this disease: www.uta.edu/chagas

Bonnie Glass-Coffin received her PhD in anthropology from UCLA in 1992. She has conducted extensive field-work with female shamans (called *curanderas*) and has studied the transformation of healing practices in Northern Peru over the last 500 years. Her recently published book, *The Gift of Life: Female Spirituality and Healing in Northern Peru* (University of New Mexico, 1998) describes the results of this research. In addition to her book, she has published in scholarly journals such as Ethnohistory and the Journal of Ritual Studies. Her work has been reported on in local, regional, and national newspapers and magazines, and she was invited to write an opinion piece for The Chronicle of Higher Education (1994) on "Anthropology, Shamanism, and the 'New Age.'" Currently, she is Associate Professor of Anthropology and Anthropology Program Director at Utah State University, where she has been employed since 1993.

Margaret A. Graham (PhD Michigan State University, 1991) is Assistant Professor of Anthropology in the Department of Anthropology & Sociology at Santa Clara University. As a biocultural anthropologist, she is primarily interested in the biological consequences of social change and economic factors on the health and nutrition of women and children in Latin America. Her research among smallholders in Puno, Peru examined the link between agricultural production and food consumption by focusing on seasonal changes in household diets and their consequences for preschooler nutritional status. Her publications appear in *Social Science and Medicine, Ecology of Food and Nutrition*, and the *Journal of Tropical Pediatrics*. She is expanding her interests in health and poverty to urban contexts specifically with low-income Mexican Americans in San Jose, California.

Christine Greenway conducted field work in Mollomarca, Peru in the south central Peruvian Andes under the auspices of a Fulbright grant for fifteen months in 1983–4. Subsequent research periods have occured in 1986, 1987, 1997, and 2000. She received her PhD in 1987 from the University of Washington and taught anthropology at Holy Cross College from 1990–7 where she received tenure. She is currently affiliated with the University of Washington.

Joan D. Koss-Chioino, PhD is Professor of Anthropology and affiliate of the Women's Studies Department at Arizona State University. She is also Visiting Professor of Psychiatry and Neurology at Tulane Medical Center in New

Orleans and Research Professor of Psychology at George Washington University. She developed the Program in Medical Anthropology at A.S.U. and works at the interface between anthropology, psychiatry, and psychology. Her primary interest is the treatment of illness and emotional disorders – whether traditional, alternative, or psychotherapeutic – in Latino cultures in the US, Latin America, Spain, and Thailand. Currently she is completing analyses of a treatment study with Mexican American youths and families in Arizona and has recently begun a study of emotions and mood regulation among women in Andalucia, Spain. Her publications include: *Women as Healers, Women as Patients: Mental Health Care and Traditional Healing in Puerto Rico* (Westview Press, 1992), *Working With Culture: Psychotherapeutic Interventions with Ethnic Minority Children and Adolescents*, editor, with Luis A. Vargas (Jossey Bass, 1992) and *Working With Latino Youth: Culture, Development and Context* (1999), with Luis A. Vargas as coauthor.

Anne C. Larme, PhD is a medical anthropologist who has conducted research on ethnomedicine in highland Peru and in Mexico before specializing in diabetes and health care among US Hispanics, and the process of research translation among health professionals. She currently teaches family practice residents and conducts research in the Department of Family and Community Medicine at the University of Texas Health Science Center at San Antonio.

Thomas Leatherman is Professor and Chair in the Department of Anthropology at the University of South Carolina, Columbia. His work has focused on relationships between health and class in contexts of social and economic change in Latin America (Peruvian Andes; Mexico), and in Coastal South Carolina. His Andean research focused on illness, social relations, and household production in farming–herding households in Southern Peru. His publications include *Building a Biocultural Synthesis: Political Economic Perspectives on Human Biology* (edited with Alan Goodman 1998). Recent research has been conducted on barriers to prenatal care among poor and minority women in South Carolina, and on the effects of tourism-led development on food commoditization, diet, and nutrition in Mayan Communities of the Yucatan (Mexico).

Lauris A. McKee has worked in the Andean region of Ecuador since 1975. She received her BA from George Washington University, and her MA and PhD from Cornell University. She was a Research Associate in Cornell's International Population Program from 1981–5, and taught at Franklin and Marshall College from 1985 to 1996. Her research interests include ethnomedicine, psychological anthropology, population dynamics, and gender-socialization. Among her publications are: "Men's rights/women's wrongs: domestic violence in Ecuador," in *To Have and to Hit*, D. A. Counts, J. K. Brown and J. C. Campbell, eds. 1999; "Women's work in rural Ecuador: multiple resource strategies and the gendered division of labor," in *Women and Economic Change: Andean Perspectives*, A. Miles and H. Buechler, 1997;

Nuevos Investigaciones Antropológicas Ecuatorianas, L. McKee and S. Argüello, eds., 1988; "Ethnomedical treatment of children's diarrheal illnesses in the highlands of Ecuador," In *Social Science and Medicine*, v. 25(10), 1987; and guest editor of and contributor to a special issue of *Medical Anthropology* titled "Child survival and sex differentials in the treatment of children," v. 8(2),1984. At present, she lives in Ithaca, NY.

Ann Miles is an Associate Professor of Anthropology and Women's Studies at Western Michigan University. She works primarily in the southern Ecuadorian highland city of Cuenca where she has had two research foci. Dr. Miles is a medical anthropologist interested primarily in the symbolic analysis of the cultural meanings of medical systems and medical commodities. She has published on these topics in *Social Science and Medicine, Medical Anthropology Quarterly* and *Body and Society*. Dr. Miles has also researched and written on rural to urban and transnational migration, globalization, and changing notions of family, gender, and identity in Cuenca. In the last few years her interest in migration and health has led to some preliminary research among migrant farm workers in the West Michigan area.

Kathryn S. Oths (PhD Case Western Reserve, 1991) is a medical anthropologist with an area specialization in Latin America. Her interests in health beliefs and practices cross-culturally include: medical treatment choice; reproductive health; musculoskeletal therapies; and, gender, ethnicity and health. Her work has been conducted using a combination of traditional anthropological methods and quantitative research designs. Oths has carried out research on practitioner–patient interactions in a chiropractic clinic, health seeking behavior in highland Peru, the social value of food in Brazil, psychosocial factors in low birth weight in the southern United States and domestic violence on which she has published articles in leading journals.

Laurie J. Price has been carrying out intermittent field work in Ecuador since her dissertation research in the early 1980s. Her research in Latin America has focused on medical pluralism, the household and narrative management of illness, and the use of biomedical pharmaceuticals. In the US, she has studied the management and prevention of chronic illness, especially arthritis and AIDS. Price is an Associate Professor of Anthropology at California State University at Hayward, California. For the past twelve years she has taught applied anthropology, ethnographic methods, anthropological theory, medical anthropology, and life history at Northern Arizona University. She is very interested in furthering dialogue between applied and academic anthropologists, and was Program Chair for the Society for Applied Anthropology annual meetings in 2000.

Foreword

Those of us who knew Libbet Crandon are gratified by the recognition of her life and her work by young scholars who have dedicated this volume to her memory. In an age when so much anthropology has become self-indulgent and narcissistic, Libbet's work stands out as a substantive contribution, forged in the finest traditions of holistic ethnography and theoretically informed anthropology. While many scholars have abandoned serious ethnography and class analyses, Libbet has delved deeper to illumine the dialectical relationship between class and ethnicity and how this relationship can be embedded in a variety of interacting medical systems and strategies. With a multitude of case studies in her book, *From the Fat of Our Souls*, she demonstrates how the people she studied negotiate new identities through illness and their choice of cures, thus resituating themselves in social and class hierarchies. The cases, fascinating in themselves, provide key insights into medical metaphors that affect a broad range of political and social behaviors.

The central theme in Libbet Crandon's work is the disclosure of classist and racist paradigms and how people reject the structures that generate and affirm them. She utilizes Foucault's historical analysis of the cultural construction of madness and Susan Sontag's metaphorical analysis of master diseases as means of restructuring social relations in order to ground her own pluricultural analysis of disease and its treatment in the village of Kachitu, Bolivia. She vividly portrays and documents how it is that the Aymara patients with whom she worked refused to go silent into the dark abyss of death. She shows how, even in their confrontation with their own mortality, they utilize their own resources and the resources of their families to influence the destiny that they must face.

Libbet played out some of the same principles she had discovered with the Aymara in the context of her own battle with cancer and her knowledge of the immanence of her own death. She drew on her analyses of the multifarious strategies that enter into Aymara curing as she confronted the inevitable time limit on her life. Even after she became aware that the progress of her disease was irreversible, she negotiated a major change in her professional career, taking on a new job at the University of Arkansas, while continuing to advise the students she left behind at Columbia University. During her short tenure at Arkansas she galvanized students of different class backgrounds with her dynamic approach to medical knowledge and health care delivery. As the founding director of the Program in Women's Studies, she sought to bridge the gap between the academy and the community through novel multiracial forums that invited the active participation of local intellectuals and activists. Libbet mobilized a state-wide network of college professors who, while often marginalized at their own institutions, were energized by meeting others doing innovative teaching on gender issues. Hers was a holistic vision of the field of Women's Studies and the role of university academics.

Libbet's attendance at the 1994 American Anthropological Association annual meetings where she was a discussant for the papers of some of the contributors of this volume was an affirmation of her life work and her commitment to young scholars engaged in the ethnographic enterprise. Colleagues and students had an opportunity to relive memories with Libbet at a special fiesta arranged by Loy Carrington and Kay Warren. It was a lively session, filled with the kinds of reflexive wisdom and insights into human nature that characterize Libbet's work.

This volume is a testament to Libbet's commitment to expanding the horizons of the field by attending in new and creative ways to the universal problematic that characterizes the human condition.

June Nash, Distinguished Professor Emeritus
City College and Graduate Center of the City University of New York

Preface

Every work and every event has its unique history. The history of this book began in 1994 when Christine Greenway and Ann Larme organized a session at the annual meetings of the American Anthropological Association on Health and Medicine in the Andean region. They invited Joan Koss-Chioino to be the discussant but she asked that they contact Libbet Crandon-Malamud, who, as an Andean scholar, was a more appropriate choice. They did and Libbet came to discuss their work, even though by that time she was confined to a wheelchair and in fact dying of complications of breast cancer. After her death early in 1995, we (Christine and Joan) decided to hold another symposium at the AAA annual meetings in 1996, entitled "The Andes as a Context for Studies in Medical Anthropology: A tribute to Libbet Crandon-Malamud." This symposium was meant to honor and remember Libbet whose work, particularly in Bolivia, introduced new themes and innovative ideas into the rich corpus of anthropological studies of the Andean region. Although not all of the contributors to that symposium are in this book, and some new contributors have been recruited, all of the authors have been engaged in an extended process of interchange of ideas and understandings of Andean medicine as reflections of the themes Libbet raised in her work. These themes are the warp of the tapestry we attempt to weave in this book, topics metaphorically described by Libbet in *From the Fat Of Our Souls: Social Change, Political Process and Medical Pluralism in Bolivia*.[1]

At first glance what one notices about the book, *From the Fat of Our Souls*, are the marvelous drawings of textile designs expertly executed by Libbet's daughter Anna, when she was still a teenager. They remind us that the heart and soul of Andean culture is reflected in multidimensional thematic weaves that have been recycled through many millennia, in the midst of periods of rapid cultural change and chaotic political and economic upheavals. These themes, as reiterated by Libbet, are: insatiable hunger, vulnerability, victimization, and exploitation. They "emerged from four integral components of the national political economy which have become entrenched institutions in Bolivian society."[2] These components include race, unequal access to economic resources, unequal participation in entrenched political structures and antagonism between Indian and non-Indian. In the historical context that she studied, the four themes are expressed in medical behaviors such as etiological perspectives, diagnosis and treatment choice. One or more of the four themes appear in all of the chapters in the current book, albeit in different historical, geographical, and sociopolitical contexts.

The four themes, and their expression within national political and social structures, are pervasive in Andean reality and appear in local worlds throughout the region. They are reflected in each of the chapters, in part by design, but mostly because these themes have emerged in the studies of the authors who have contributed to the book. Libbet's work was characterized by intense immersion in the field and a deep knowledge of Andean peoples as individuals as well as social actors coping with economic, sociopolitical, and environmental challenges. Congruent with her personal and intellectual traditions, the case studies in this book are based on long-term intensive field work and describe health and illness in particular social and environmental contexts.

The book initiates its exploration of Andean medical pluralism through a multidimensional examination of the Andean context in the first chapter by Ann Miles and Thomas Leatherman. Because an important feature of Libbet's commitment to the "new" ethnographic genre was to include self reflection in her texts, Joan Koss-Chioino then introduces Libbet Crandon by describing and reflecting upon her role in the field. She asks the question, "Who was Libbet and how did the Bolivian villagers see her?" The related issues of the links between the life experience of the ethnographer and the questions she asks are addressed, as well as why she reports particular observations. In the following chapter we have then included a reprinted article by Libbet, "Changing Times, Changing Symptoms: The Effects of Modernization on *Mestizo* Medicine in Rural Bolivia" in which she initiated her consideration of the dynamics between identity and medicine, later more fully developed in her book *From the Fat of Our Souls*. The first section concludes with Hans Baer's analysis of Libbet's contributions to a critical analysis of medical pluralism in which he cogently reviews her work as an intellectual journey that foreshadows the development of the theoretical perspective in medical anthropology that has been labeled "critical medical anthropology."

Part two, Choices, changing times, and medical pluralism, includes case studies that address the themes of medical pluralism in the context of culture change and competing medical choice. Scholars have long noted the variety of traditional treatment choices such as bonesetting, herbal remedies, and spiritual cures available to patients in the Andes. The first case study by Kathy Oths explores a type of healer rarely discussed in the literature, bonesetters. Her analysis of the bodily manipulations practiced by these therapists is grounded in the exploration of the literal physical burdens borne by Andean peasants in the current exploitative, political-economic system. The second chapter in this section by Christine Greenway focuses on how the strategies and narratives used by healers in healing ceremonies reconfigure and challenge the borders between ethnic and class identities. The narratives used by healers foment change in the perception of identity and social status. The final case study in this section by Anne Miles, describes very recent work (1999) in Cuenca, Ecuador in the midst of a worsening economic crisis. She views urban *curanderos* as innovative entrepreneurs who combine the symbols and meanings of traditional and modern medicine. In doing so, they compete for success and legitimacy in the market, demonstrating Libbet's conclusion that medical choice can be used to gain access to secondary resources.

In *Part three, Andean bodies: metaphors and medicine*, Lauris McKee orients her discussion around how *mestizo* children are socialized into the prevailing medical beliefs and practices in Ecuador. She answers questions that could be raised (implicit in Libbet's work) about how people learn the meanings that relate to social status and power inherent in medical choices and practices. However, she also effectively explores the theme of personal vulnerability in two related senses: in terms of bodily distress and illness, and socially, as a result of political and economic exploitation. In her chapter, Margaret Graham treats us to a description and analysis of the dietary choices found among Peruvian farmers who are also seasonal wage laborers exposed to prestigious packaged foods. She shows the intimate connections between food, ideas of identity and status, and notions of health, illness and vulnerability. The last chapter in this section, by Joseph Bastien, deals with a contemporary public health problem, Chagas' Disease, that is clearly rooted in poverty, inadequate housing, and faulty understanding of the etiology of the disease. This chapter is an excellent discussion of the difficulties in reconciling the biomedical and indigenous ideas of causality.

In *Part four, Gender, power, and health,* The first chapter by Anne Larme and Tom Leatherman analyzes the problem of gender and health in the context of work across communities in Peru. A reproductive illness, *sobreparto*, a socially negotiated diagnosis, allows women respite from some of their role obligations. Laurie Price then explores case studies in which the Ecuadorian urban men dominate medical choices made by female relatives. In response, the women use subtle means to recoup that power and enhance their own status in the family and community. The negotiation of power between the sexes takes place in the medical arena. The final chapter by Bonnie Glass-Coffin returns us to the reflective mode as she reviews her problematic relationship to her major participant/healer. The theme of negotiating power and identity is particularly salient here, as the ethnographer tries to cope with the changes in her social status and its effect upon a healer who has become increasingly sensitive to unequal power relationships.

Joan D. Koss-Chioino
Christine Greenway

Notes

1 Crandon-Malamud, *From the Fat of Our Souls: Social Change, Political Process and Medical Pluralism in Bolivia*, University of California Press, 1991.
2 Crandon-Malamud, *From the Fat of Our Souls*, p. 46.

Part I

Introduction: Andean medical studies and the contribution of Libbet Crandon-Malamud

Chapter 1

Perspectives on medical anthropology in the Andes

Ann Miles and Thomas Leatherman

Plate 1.1 Central Plaza of Ancoraimes, Bolivia (Photograph by Mauricio Mamani, 2000).

This volume emerged from an effort over the past decade to update and share knowledge about health and healing in the Andes. At the time that most of the contributors to this volume conducted their fieldwork, there was only one edited collection of medical anthropology in the Andes, *Health in the Andes*, published by the American Anthropological Association.[1] Much of the work found in that volume occurred in the 1960s and 1970s, in very different political, economic, as well as theoretical contexts from the 1980s and early 1990s when most of the research represented in this volume was carried out. The pace of major transformations in Andean economies and societies has accelerated since the 1970s, due to agrarian reform and the monetization of rural economies, social resistance movements and revolutions, rural to urban migration and the rapid growth in urban sectors, hyperinflation, neoliberal structural adjustment policies, privatization and increasing poverty, transnational migrations and increasing globalization. Since the late 1970s and 1980s, there have also been major shifts in anthropological theory, Andean ethnography, and medical anthropology away from ecological and "Andeanist" orientations and towards theoretical frameworks which seek to incorporate multiple layers of analyses, including a concern for political economy and post-colonial structures and processes and how they intersect with varied understandings of the body, sickness, health, and healing. This volume reflects some of the real and theoretical shifts that have occurred in the past decades but, as is the case in many such volumes, it is playing catch-up. In the past decade we have witnessed little real improvement in the economic, social, and health conditions in the Andes. The results of the structural violence of poverty, political unrest, and social inequality have been dramatically played out in epidemics of cholera and dengue fever, in ever-increasing rates of HIV-AIDS and in the development of multidrug-resistant strains of TB.[2] Much work, anthropological and otherwise, still needs to be done.

The purpose of this chapter is to review themes central to the contexts of health in the Andes and to explore the intellectual paths that have led to the emergence of the perspectives on Andean medical anthropology that are represented in this volume. To be sure, it is a sketchy background given the diversity of Andean histories, environments, societies, cultures, medical systems, and anthropological writings that could be addressed. Yet, much like a good symphony, themes in medical anthropology of the Andes emerge and re-emerge and are elaborated upon, refined, and enhanced over time. Indeed, by laying bare our own intellectual history, if only partially, it becomes clear that Libbet Crandon-Malamud, to whom this volume is dedicated, was uniquely positioned in Andean medical anthropology and her work was pivotal to the development of the theoretical perspectives represented in this volume.

Health in the Andes

The original publication that influenced and inspired so much subsequent work, *Health in the Andes*, resulted from three symposia held at the American Anthropological Association Meetings in Los Angeles in 1978 on nutrition, medicine, and morbidity. The broad topics include the intersection of environment and biology, cultural and social factors in health and healing and applied aspects of health, disease, and the provision of health care.[3] The volume's central focus is on health maintenance and an evaluation of Andean notions of well being, and it was divided into the three sections – environment, ethnomedicine, and health improvement. In fact, the three thematic sections of the volume on the role of the environment, ethnomedical conceptions, and the delivery of health services remain central to Andean medical anthropology until the present time, albeit with very different approaches and orientations.

The themes of environment and adaptation dominate many of the papers[4] in *Health in the Andes*, reflecting the overall importance of ecological perspectives and community studies in anthropology in the 1960s and 1970s.[5] The key factors shaping Andean environments were altitude and verticality, which researchers viewed as both a stressor and a resource for biological, behavioral, and cultural adaptations. Dominant themes in Andean ethnography from this period include the importance of reciprocity (especially in labor, but also in gender roles, and ritual practice), complementarity (of production strategies, ecological zones, and later gender roles) and social cooperation and exchange. These themes also provided important organizing principles for ecologists interested in micro-environmental use and technological adaptation. The characteristics of Andean peoples that came to dominate much of the discussion in Anthropology was their knowledge and use of micro-environments, the incredible range of technological innovations that they employed, and the formalized systems of labor exchange they developed.[6] While these themes are described most clearly and consistently as features of social organization, especially the organization of production, they are also found in the ideology and practice of local medical systems and beliefs. In 1978, Bastien's, *Mountain of the Condor*[7] examined Andean cosmology and ritual and the theme of reciprocity linking it to medical beliefs and the treatment of illness in an Andean *ayllu* in Bolivia. Indeed, he argued that ecological features such as mountains are sites of ancestor spirits and hence spiritual power, and they are, therefore, important in health, illness, and healing. Later, in 1985, Bastien elaborated further on the connection between environment, community, and the body as he describes how the local mountains and their surrounding waterways become a "topographical-hydraulic model of physiology," or, in other words, an environmental metaphor that residents of Qollahuaya used to understand and explain how the human body functions in illness and in health.[8]

The second and third thematic areas of *Health in the Andes*, ethnomedicine and the delivery of health care, while seemingly distinct, were not seen by the volume's editors as wholly separate from each other, or from ecological considerations. They argue that understanding ethnomedical conceptions is crucial to the delivery of health services as Stein's selection highlights, but also that, as the editors state in their introduction to Buechler's chapter, "all rituals are involved with ecological and social processes."[9] For the most part, studies of ethnomedicine in the 1970s often entailed describing the symptoms, treatment, and moral dimensions for what at the time were called "folk illnesses" or "culture-bound syndromes." However, in addition to describing the etiology of different maladies such as *susto, mal aire,* or *shongo naney,*[10] researchers of ethnomedicine grappled with trying to understand what folk illness could tell us about the relationship between culture, illness, and biology. Were folk illnesses "real" in the biomedical sense, or were they psychosocial in origin? If they were in fact biomedically "real" as Stein argued for a case of *shongo naney* in 1981, then the job of the anthropologist is clear. "Anthropologists should study the ways in which Andean folk medicine can be integrated with Western medicine so that cognitively, culturally, and socially both systems fit into Andean patterns and enhance health maintenance."[11] In other words, understanding folk illness in biomedical terms will assist in the delivery of western health services. If, however, "culture-bound syndromes" cannot be linked to biomedically understood conditions, then something else altogether is going on. Then, it must be, as Libbet Crandon-Malamud points out her 1983 article "Why Susto,"[12] that "culture plays a role in the existence of an illness, its expression, and its treatment ... there is value in understanding the syndrome in its indigenous terms.[13] By asking the question "why susto?" and not "what is susto?" Crandon stresses the importance of social differences in the appearance, symptomatology, and expression of illness.

While community studies generally were very much the norm in Andean ethnography until the 1980s there were, as has been pointed out many times, some very real problems associated with this general orientation. Indeed, in 1994, Orin Starn argued that the ecologically oriented community studies of the 1960s and 1970s in the Andes tended to erect analytical boundaries around populations and cultures that were more apparent than real, and that they neglected the importance of interregional and national processes in the lives of these rural communities. Frozen ethnographically in space and time, rural Andean peoples were frequently portrayed in a static way that tended to emphasize tradition over change. Andean peasants were noted for resisting change by insulating themselves from outsiders rather than seeking articulation with regional and national economic and political processes. The prevailing picture of Andean societies then was of stable adaptations girded and upheld by persistent cultural traditions. The few studies in medical anthropology suffered from similar weaknesses. In ecological and biocultural studies of population adaptation, the Andean environment was seen to challenge populations through the combined stresses of altitude (hypobaric hypoxia), cold, high solar radiation, rugged terrain with poor soils, and low primary energy productivity. These conditions made it a marginal environment at best and the limitations and constraints imposed by the physical environment were the critical forces shaping local social organization of production, human adaptation, and health.

Similarly, there was a good deal of ethnographic work in the 1970s on myth and ritual in the Andes with much of it focusing on describing collective world views and the continuities in Andean ceremonials between the past and present.[14] Studies of Shamanism and *curanderismo* demonstrated how ancient ideas were embedded in the current healing practices,[15] or emphasized the categorization of healers and healing technologies, and the continuity of "tradition" in folk illnesses and treatments over time. Yet, while the search for continuity from past to present oriented much rural analysis, anthropologists working in urban areas in the 1970s described a different phenomena unfolding. Both Press, working in Bogota, Colombia, and Buechler in La Paz, Bolivia, take note not of continuity in medical beliefs and practices, but eclecticism and variability. As early as 1971, Press critiqued previous "peasant inspired" studies in Latin America which sought to categorize healers by type and argued that by doing so we were in danger of stereotyping, and therefore reifying, them and their work. In contrast, he argued for more flexibility in our perceptions of healers and demonstrated that urban *curanderos* embrace "heterogeneity in healer style and curative resources"[16] in order to accommodate patients with diverse physical and social needs. Buechler, writing in 1981, notes that throughout the course of an illness, patients in the city often avail themselves of a wide range of varied practitioners. Working primarily with migrants to the city he argues that rural and urban differences become blurred and ultimately meaningless as both healers and patients move freely back and forth between the rural and urban contexts, altering both medical and social milieus as they do so. Once considered "peasants in cities," as the numbers of rural to urban migrants increased, their influence on the city and the country became undeniable.

As ideas about the constructed and contested nature of culture took center stage in social theory in the 1980s, Andean ethnographers[17] were influenced by trends in political economy and feminist anthropology. Their work reflected an increasing concern for the political unrest, exploitation, poverty, and social differentiation which was in fact so much a part of the Andean reality. Situating communities in historical contexts, they drew attention to such issues as the centuries of external domination, the 150 years of international wool trade, the growing impact of drug trafficking, the market penetration and monetization of rural economies, agrarian reforms which failed to meet their promise, and the increasing feminization of agriculture. Andean history was marked not only by continuity, resilience, and adaptation, but also by centuries of domination by outsiders who became insiders and controlled access to labor and resources and who created and perpetuated patterns of social relations that economically and politically marginalized large segments of the population. Anthropologists became increasingly cognizant not only of the internal differences within "communities" based on social race, class, or gender but also the ways in which global and regional forces shaped local level realities. Indeed, it was clear that the adaptive capacity of Andean peoples was in fact limited by material and social inequalities that were local, national, and global in their origins.[18]

Not surprisingly, medical anthropology too began a reformulation of perspectives in the 1980s, looking to broaden the contexts of research and restructure key theoretical concepts such as adaptation. This was spurred on by numerous critiques from critical medical anthropology,[19] including concerns about static reductionist models which tended to reify cosmopolitan biomedicine by naturalizing social phenomena, and the failure of previous models to address the role of historical and contemporary social relations in shaping perceptions of health and sickness. Bodies, the manifestation and expression of bodily distress, and understandings of effective treatment are understood to be informed not only by "culture" and/or "biology" but also by social and political relations. Discussions of the "embodiment" or the inscription on the body of social inequalities created a theoretical emphasis that sought to unravel the complex interactions between the individual, social, and political bodies.[20] In the Andes, then, we saw the emergence in the 1980s of a medical anthropology which considered the importance of differences in the localized etiology of illness. For example, a number of articles emphasized the particular social roles played by women in indigenous and *mestizo* households and the connections between gender roles, family, community, and illness.[21] Crandon-Malamud's, *From the Fat of Our Souls*,[22] a study of medical pluralism in a Bolivian community, argued that in this medical pluralistic environment, medicine was a resource through which people negotiated and expressed cultural identity and political and social power. It was the first book length ethnography on medical anthropology in the Andes to emerge since Bastien's work on ritual in 1978 and it took on social inequality as a primary theme.

Andean medical anthropology in the 1990s

To be sure, the themes of reciprocity and exchange, complementarity and cooperation, and historical tradition and beliefs which guided early efforts are still found in contemporary Andean ethnography and medical anthropology. Greenway,[23] for example, argues that ties of reciprocity to nature, society, and cosmos are critical to healing rituals which restore balance to body and soul. Bastien states that "reciprocal obligations provide Andean ethnomedicine with a perpetuating structure of prestation and counterprestation between the person cured and the specialist" that is central to the healing process.[24] And Tousignant,[25] Finerman,[26] and Oths[27] have all noted that when reciprocal relations between kin are unsatisfying or unfulfilled, women, in particular, experience certain kinds of afflictions. However, the themes of reciprocity and complementarity no longer dominate or constrain interpretations of Andean life, but they are placed in contexts that recognize how global histories shape local realities, how access to social and material resources influence levels of health and possibilities for adaptation, and how the practices of reciprocity themselves shift and change through time. Leatherman,[28] for example, notes from his research in southern Peru that while the ideology of labor reciprocity is central to most individuals' descriptions of how they might deal with illness during critical production periods, social networks and reciprocal labor relations were diminished in contexts of the monetization of labor markets. This echoes other research on the disappearance of reciprocity with the increase of monetization in the Andes, due to factors of prestige, time, cash availability, and a tendency towards the increasing "individualization" of households.[29] Indeed, a theme of individual containment of health problems[30] and the reluctance to seek outside help in illness[31] as a result of the modern capitalist economy is seen in a number of Andean health studies.

Throughout the 1990s, discussions of the environment were less prominent in Andean medical anthropology, but they did not disappear altogether. Indeed, the environment itself is analyzed now as a locus of historic and contemporary class and/or ethnic contestation – one that impacts upon access to resources of individuals or groups and, therefore, affects health and choices in health care. So, for example, Crandon-Malamud argued in 1991 that the class differences in Kachitu, which figure so prominently in her analysis of medical pluralism, were at least in part an outcome of intra-regional trading made necessary by an ecology that promoted dependency between ecological zones. Those who were able to wrest control over the movement of goods and produce became economically and socially prominent. Similarly, Suárez-Torres and López-Paredes,[32] focusing on modern development policies in Ecuador argue that "nature" is used for the accumulation of capital by a few, thus creating a scarcity of resources and therefore, poverty and poor health for others.

As discussed above, one of the most important thematic questions that guided Bastien and Donahue's volume was the ethnographic documentation of the "compatibility or incompatibility between Andeans' traditional medical systems and health maintenance."[33] "Health maintenance" here was clearly a western construct based on biomedical determinants of health and/or disease. In particular, the authors asked how particular beliefs, rituals and practices serve to promote or, conversely, compromise the health of Andeans. Indeed, some practices, they argued, were shown to cause harm or, at the very least, inhibited the delivery of biomedical treatment. In contrast, many medical anthropologists in the 1980s and 1990s have self-consciously moved away from placing biomedically oriented value judgments on the ethnomedical ideas or health practices even when their goal is to assist in the delivery of biomedically based health or nutrition interventions. Instead, those concerned with the provision of needed health or nutrition services emphasize the importance of health care workers understanding that power inequities, poverty, or landlessness can play a role in creating and perpetuating intracultural diversity in health, health care, and illness within even a single community.[34]

Current themes in medical anthropology, and in Andean medical anthropology, recognize biomedicine as an ethnomedical representation of western systems of knowledge and while a dominant and often hegemonic force, it is also just one alternative from which individuals might choose. Moreover, the choice of one or more forms of healing within broadly pluralistic health systems reflects not degrees of rationality, but degrees of negotiation among myriad social forces including (or not) perceived efficacy of treatment. Medical systems in the Andes are pluralistic and they incorporate a variety of indigenous specialists including *curanderos*, bone setters, herbalists, and midwives (among others) who practice among a population that also avails itself of biomedical practice ranging from self-care with the use of pharmaceuticals[35] to tertiary care hospitals. Indeed, pluralism is only increasing in the Andes as new practices are continually being introduced, sometimes driven by practitioners seeking new healing techniques and sometimes by more obviously commercial considerations.[36] Indeed, by the late 1990s, Korean ginseng, American vitamins, Chinese herbs, and packaged Amazonian roots could be found in regional markets throughout the Andes. The options, it seems, just keep on growing. However, the issue of the compatibility between medical ideologies and systems or treatment options, which was once such a concern for scholars, no longer seems a relevant issue to anthropologists.

We now recognize that patients create their compatibility which can shift and change over time.

Despite the often dominant nature of biomedicine as a state-supported apparatus, it is clear that indigenous healers and medical systems remain strong, both for their perceived efficacy and expertize and for the expressions of cultural identity they represent. Ethnomedicine can be an important source for revaluing cultural identity and a symbolic means of resisting the penetration of western capitalist ideology and social relations.[37] Indeed, social influence can be created, maintained, increased, or lost by controlling access to knowledge about health, medicines, and treatments.[38] Several chapters in this volume illustrate the flexibility and creativity of healers today who make use of the products, symbols, and ideologies of multiple healing traditions, including biomedicine to augment and revalue their practices. New forms of healing rituals and healers are continually emerging as healers avail themselves of different medical epistemologies and practices, for pragmatic as well as commercial reasons. The degree of pluralism seen in Andean health systems is in large part due to the negotiation of illness by local agents. This greater recognition of agency among participants in health systems is a key theme reflected in more recent medical anthropology in the Andes and the role of gender, class, and power in this negotiation is well recognized. Individuals are enmeshed in webs of social relations that influence their experience and options, and they act from multiple motives – or motives that can change over time. In so doing, they construct and reconstruct the pluralistic health systems in which they participate.

Summary

While ecology and adaptation dominated earlier perspectives on health, research in the 1980s and 1990s adopted a broader framework that recognizes the role of macro-political and economic factors in structuring local environments, and the importance of social relations in shaping and health. This shift followed developments in Andean ethnography,[39] biological studies,[40] and in critical medical anthropology.[41] These new perspectives have led Andean medical anthropologists to expand their earlier definitions of environment and adaptation to acknowledge the multifaceted ways that social, economic, and political forces shape the nature of Andean life.

The Andean landscape, described in this volume is supernatural, social, political, economic, rural, urban, global, and local. The environment shifts, emerges, affects, and shapes health, as do the constructions of self, identity, family, and community of the inhabitants of these multiple landscapes. Social relationships, economic disparities, infrastructure limitations, and cosmological beliefs impact peoples lives and health status in various convergent and conflicting ways. The previous, narrow notion of environment then has had to be construed and analyzed more broadly in contemporary medical anthropological work in the Andes. It adds to previous assessments of environment and landscape a significant cultural dimension – one that recognizes both symbolic, but also real power. The inhabitants of Andean villages and cities are no longer viewed as passive and suspicious victims of supernatural and harsh environmental constraints, rather they are resilient, persistent, and engaged in maintaining their well being in a complex setting through a variety of means. Yet, we must not overstate the case. Andeans are up against tremendous odds in their attempts to maintain health because of the very same political, economic, environmental, and social conditions imposed by inequality and poverty.

The chapters in this volume represent a contribution to Andean health research in that they call for Andean scholars to move beyond rigid paradigms such as "adaptation," "reciprocity," and "*andino*" that presented paradoxically either an overly positive view of health in the Andes, or a stereotypical model of the meaning of traditional practices and beliefs. Instead, research must synthesize a variety of perspectives, including a focus on the political-economic context of ill health in the Andes, a recognition of intracultural diversity within the Andean region, and the need to understand the complex interplay of local and global factors that contribute to this diversity. The research presented here is pointedly contextualized to reflect the understanding that current economic, political, and cultural conditions frame and structure what is observed, recorded, and analyzed.

Finally, during the many conversations about the current state of Andean medical anthropology from which this book emerged, there was also much interest and much discussion about the future directions of Andean research. While there is, of course, much more research that can and ought to be done on all of the themes addressed in this volume, our informal discussions are also pointed to areas where we still know so little, but which seem to affect the lives of Andean people so much. These topics include transnational migration and HIV/AIDS, the spread of infectious diseases including multidrug-resistant TB, the affects of state or non-state sponsored terrorism on health and well being, the health and social impacts of increasing environmental degradation including the use of pesticides and toxic chemicals, the health and nutritional considerations of increasing participation in global agricultural and horticultural markets, the increased and largely unregulated marketing of a wide variety of health products and treatments and the impacts of structural adjustment and privatization on health and health care delivery. These topics represent some of the most pressing concerns for health and well-being in the Andes and, not coincidentally, they highlight the positioning of the Andes within an increasingly global and "modernizing" world.

Notes

1 Joseph Bastien and John Donahue, *Health in the Andes*, American Anthropological Association Special Publication No. 12, 1981.
2 Jim Kim, *et al.*, "Sickness amidst recovery: public debt and private suffering in Peru." In *Dying for Growth: Global Inequality and the Health of the Poor*, Jim Kim, Joyce Millen, Alec Irwin, and John Gershman (eds), Common Courage Press, 2000.

3 Bastien and Donahue, *Health in the Andes*, pp. 1–7.
4 Bastien and Donahue, *Health in the Andes*.
5 Sherry Ortner, "Theory in anthropology since the sixties," *Comparative Studies of Society and History*, 1984, 26: 126–66.
6 John Murra, "Andean societies," *Annual Review of Anthropology*, 1984, 13: 119–41.
7 Joseph Bastien, *Mountain of the Condor: Metaphor and Ritual in an Andean Ayllu*, West, 1978.
8 Joseph W. Bastien, "Qollahuaya-Andean body concepts: a topographical-hydraulic model of physiology," *American Anthropologist*, 1985, 87(3): 595–611.
9 Hans C. Buechler, "Aymara curing practices in the context of a family history." In *Health in the Andes*, Joseph Bastien and John Donahue (eds), American Anthropological Association Special Publication No. 12, 1981, p. 39.
10 See William W. Stein, "The folk illness: entity or nonentity? An essay on Vicos disease ideology." In *Health in the Andes*, Joseph Bastien and John M. Donahue (eds), American Anthropological Association Special Publication No. 12, 1981, pp. 50–67.
11 Bastien and Donahue, *Health in the Andes*, p. 50.
12 Libbet Crandon-Malamud, "Why susto?," *Ethnology*, 1983*b*, 22: 153–67.
13 Libbet Crandon, "Grass, roots, herbs, promoters and preventions: a re-evaluation of contemporary international health care planning. The Bolivian case," *Social Science Medicine*, 1983*a*, 17: 153.
14 See Frank Salomon, "Andean ethnology in the 1970s: a retrospective," *Latin American Research Review*, 1982, 17: 75–128.
15 Salomon, "Andean Ethnology in the 1970s."
16 Irwin Press, "The urban *curandero*," *American Anthropologist*, 1971, 73(3): 753.
17 Steve Stern, *Resistance, Rebellion and Consciousness in the Andean Peasant World*, University of Wisconsin Press, 1987; J. Collins, *Unseasonal Migrations: The Effects of Rural Labor Scarcity in Peru*, Princeton University Press, 1991; B. Orlove, *Alpacas, Sheep and Men*, Academic Press, 1977; C. McClintock, "Why peasants rebel: the case of Peru's *Sendero Luminoso*," *World Politics*, 1984, 27(1): 48–84; Mary J. Weismantel, *Food, Gender and Poverty in the Ecuadorian Andes*, University of Pennsylvania, 1988; Catherine Allen, *The Hold Life Has: Coca and Cultural Identity in an Andean Community*, Smithsonian University Press, 1988.
18 W. Roseberry, *Coffee and Capitalism in the Venezuelan Andes*, University of Texas Press, 1983; Jose Maria Caballero, "Agriculture and the peasantry under industrialization pressures: lessons from the Peruvian experience," *Latin American Research Review*, 1984, 19(2): 3–41.
19 M. Cueto, "Andean biology in Peru: scientific styles on the periphery," *ISIS*, 1989, 80: 640–58.
20 Nancy Scheper-Hughes and Margaret M. Lock, "The mindful body: a prolegomenon to future work in medical anthropology," *Medical Anthropology Quarterly*, 1987, 1: 6–41.
21 Ruthbeth Finerman, "Experience and expectation: conflict and change in traditional family health care among the Quichua of Saraguro," *Social Science and Medicine*, 1983, 17(17): 1291–8; Ruthbeth Finerman, "The burden of responsibility: duty, depression and *Nervios* in Andean Ecuador." In *Gender, Health and Illness: The Case of Nerves*, Donna Davis and Setha Low (eds), Hemisphere, 1989, pp. 49–66; Michel Tousignant, "Sadness, depression and social reciprocity in highland Ecuador," *Social Science and Medicine*, 1989, 28(9): 899–904.
22 Libbet Crandon-Malamud, *From the Fat of Our Souls: Social Change, Political Process, and Medical Pluralism in Bolivia*, University of California Press, 1991.
23 Christine Greenway, *Summoning the Soul: Self and Cosmos in Quechua Healing Rites*, PhD Dissertation. University of Washington, 1987.
24 Joseph W. Bastien, "Exchange between Andean and Western medicine," *Social Science and Medicine*, 1982, 16: 799.
25 Tousignant, "Sadness, Depression, and Social Reciprocity."

26 Finerman, "The Burden of Responsibility."
27 Kathryn S. Oths, "*Debilidad*: a biocultural assessment of an embodied Andean illness," *Medical Anthropology Quarterly*, 1999, 13(3): 286–315.
28 Thomas L. Leatherman, "A biocultural perspective on health and household economy in Southern Peru," *Medical Anthropology Quarterly*, 1996, 10(4): 76–95.
29 Charles J. Erasmus, "Culture, structure and process: the occurrence and disappearance of reciprocal farm labor," *Southwestern Journal of Anthropology*, 1956, 12: 444–69; Paul F. Brown, "Population growth and the disappearance of reciprocal labor in a Highland Peruvian community," *Research in Economic Anthropology*, 1987, 8: 201–24; C. E. Aramburu and A. Ponce Alegre, *Familia y Trabajo en el Peru Rural*, Instituto Andino de Estudios in Poblacion y Desarrollo, 1983.
30 Kathryn Oths, *Medical Treatment Choice and Health Outcomes in the Northern Peruvian Andes*, PhD Dissertation. Case Western Reserve University, 1991.
31 Anne Larme, "Work, reproduction and health in two Andean communities," Working paper No. 5, from *Production, Storage and Exchange in a Terraced Environment on the Eastern Andean Escarpment*, Bruce Winterhalder (series ed.), University of North Carolina, 1993; B. Stoner, *Health Care Delivery and Health Resource Utilization in a Highland Andean Community of Southern Peru*, PhD Dissertation. Indiana University, 1989.
32 Jose Suárez-Torres and Dolores López-Paredes, "Development, environment and health in crisis: the case of Ecuador," *Latin American Perspectives*, 1997, Issue 95, 24(3): 83–103.
33 Bastien and Donahue, *Health in the Andes*, p. 1.
34 Kathryn S. Oths, "Assessing variation in health status in the Andes: a biocultural model," *Social Science and Medicine*, 1998, 47(8): 1017–30.
35 Laurie J. Price, "In the shadow of biomedicine: self medication in two Ecuadorian pharmacies," *Social Science and Medicine*, 1989, 28(9): 905–15.
36 Ann Miles, "Science, nature and tradition: the mass-marketing of natural medicines in urban Ecuador," *Medical Anthropology Quarterly*, 1998, 12(2): 206–25.
37 See Allen, *The Hold Life Has*.
38 See Finerman, "The burden of responsibility."
39 Salomon, "Andean Ethnology in the 1970s"; O. Starn, "Rethinking the politics of anthropology: the case of the Andes," *Current Anthropology*, 1994, 35(1): 13–38.
40 R. B. Thomas, T. L. Leatherman, J. W. Carey, and J. D. Haas, "Consequences and responses to illness among small scale farmers: a research design." In *Capacity for Work in the Tropics*, K. J. Collins and D. F. Roberts (eds), Cambridge University Press, 1988, pp. 249–76; A. Goodman, R. B. Thomas, A. Swedlund, and G. J. Armelagos, "Biocultural perspectives on stress in prehistoric, historical and contemporary population research," *Yearbook of Physical Anthropology*, 1988, 31: 169–202.
41 S. Morsy, "Political economy in medical anthropology." In *Medical Anthropology: Contemporary Theory and Method*, T. Johnson and C. Sargent (eds), Praeger, 1990, pp. 26–36; Merrill Singer, "The limitations of medical ecology: the concept of adaptation in the context of social stratification and social transformation," *Medical Anthropology*, 1989, 10: 223–34.

References

Allen, Catherine, *The Hold Life Has: Coca and Cultural Identity in an Andean Community*, Smithsonian University Press, 1988.
Aramburu, C. E. and A. Ponce Alegre, *Familia y Trabajo en el Peru Rural*, Instituto Andino de Estudios in Poblacion y Desarrollo, 1983.
Bastien, Joseph, *Mountain of the Condor: Metaphor and Ritual in an Andean Ayllu*, West, 1978.

Bastien, Joseph W., "Exchange between Andean and Western medicine," *Social Science and Medicine*, 1982, 16: 795–803.

——, "Qollahuaya-Andean body concepts: a topographical-hydraulic model of physiology," *American Anthropologist*, 1985, 87(3): 595–611.

Bastien, Joseph and John Donahue, *Health in the Andes*, American Anthropological Association Special Publication No. 12, 1981.

Brown, Paul F., "Population growth and the disappearance of reciprocal labor in a Highland Peruvian community," *Research in Economic Anthropology*, 1987, 8: 201–24.

Buechler, Hans C., "Aymara curing practices in the context of a family history." In *Health in the Andes*, Joseph Bastien and John M Donahue (eds), American Anthropological Association Special Publication No. 12, 1981, pp. 38–48.

Caballero, Jose Maria, "Agriculture and the peasantry under industrialization pressures: lessons from the Peruvian experience," *Latin American Research Review*, 1984, 19(2): 3–41.

Collins, J., *Unseasonal Migrations: The Effects of Rural Labor Scarcity in Peru*, Princeton University Press, 1991.

Crandon, Libbet, "Grass, roots, herbs, promoters and preventions: a re-evaluation of contemporary international health care planning. The Bolivian case," *Social Science Medicine*, 1983a, 17: 1281–9.

——, "Why susto?," *Ethnology*, 1983b, 22: 153–67.

Crandon-Malamud, Libbet, *From the Fat of Our Souls: Social Change, Political Process, and Medical Pluralism in Bolivia*, University of California Press, 1991.

Cueto, M., "Andean biology in Peru: scientific styles on the periphery," *ISIS*, 1989, 80: 640–58.

Erasmus, Charles J., "Culture, structure and process: the occurrence and disappearance of reciprocal farm labor," *Southwestern Journal of Anthropology*, 1956, 12: 444–69.

Finerman, Ruthbeth, "Experience and expectation: conflict and change in traditional family health care among the Quichua of Saraguro," *Social Science and Medicine*, 1983, 17: 1291–8.

——, "The burden of responsibility: duty, depression and *nervios* in Andean Ecuador." In *Gender, Health and Illness: The Case of Nerves*, Donna Davis and Setha Low (eds), Hemisphere, 1989, pp. 49–66.

Goodman, A., R. B. Thomas, A. Swedlund, and G. J. Armelagos, "Biocultural perspectives on stress in prehistoric, historical and contemporary population research," *Yearbook of Physical Anthropology*, 1988, 31, pp. 169–202.

Greenway, Christine, *Summoning the Soul: Self and Cosmos in Quechua Healing Rites*, PhD Dissertation. University of Washington, 1987.

Kim, Jim *et al.*, "Sickness amidst recovery: public debt and private suffering in Peru." In *Dying for Growth: Global Inequality and the Health of the Poor*, Jim Kim, Joyce Millen, Alec Irwin, and John Gershman (eds), Common Courage Press, 2000.

Larme, Anne, *Work, Reproduction and Health in Two Andean Communities*, Working paper No. 5, from *Production, Storage and Exchange in a Terraced Environment on the Eastern Andean Escarpment*, Bruce Winterhalder (series ed.), University of North Carolina, 1993.

Leatherman, T. L., "A biocultural perspective on health and household economy in Southern Peru," *Medical Anthropology Quarterly*, 1996, 10(4): 76–95.

McClintock, C., "Why peasants rebel: the case of Peru's *Sendero Luminoso*," *World Politics*, 1984, 27(1): 48–84.

Miles, Ann, "Science, nature and tradition: the mass-marketing of natural medicines in urban Ecuador," *Medical Anthropology Quarterly*, 1998, 12(2): 206–25.

Morsy, S., "Political economy in medical anthropology." In *Medical Anthropology: Contemporary Theory and Method*, T. Johnson and C. Sargent (eds), Praeger, 1990, pp. 26–36.

Murra, John, "Andean societies," *Annual Review of Anthropology*, 1984, 13: 119–41.

Orlove, B., *Alpacas, Sheep and Men*, Academic Press, 1977.

Ortner, Sherry, "Theory in anthropology since the sixties," *Comparative Studies of Society and History*, 1984, 26: 126–66.

Oths, Kathryn. S., *Medical Treatment Choice and Health Outcomes in the Northern Peruvian Andes*, PhD Dissertation. Case Western Reserve University, 1991.

——, "Assessing variation in health status in the Andes: a biocultural model," *Social Science and Medicine*, 1998, 47(8): 1017–30.

——, "*Debilidad:* a biocultural assessment of an embodied Andean illness," *Medical Anthropology Quarterly*, 1999, 13(3): 286–315.

Press, Irwin, "The urban *curandero,*" *American Anthropologist*, 1971, 73(3): 741–56.

Price, Laurie J., "In the shadow of biomedicine: self medication in two Ecuadorian pharmacies," *Social Science and Medicine*, 1989, 28(9): 905–15.

Roseberry, W., *Coffee and Capitalism in the Venezuelan Andes*, University of Texas Press, 1983.

Salomon, F., "Andean ethnology in the 1970s: a retrospective," *LARR*, 1982, 17(2): 77–128.

Scheper-Hughes, Nancy and Margaret M. Lock, "The mindful body: a prolegomenon to future work in medical anthropology," *Medical Anthropology Quarterly*, 1987, 1: 6–41.

Singer, M., "The limitations of medical ecology: the concept of adaptation in the context of social stratification and social transformation," *Medical Anthropology*, 1989, 10: 223–34.

Starn, O., "Rethinking the politics of anthropology: the case of the Andes," *Current Anthropology*, 1994, 35(1): 13–38.

Stein, William W., "The folk illness: entity or nonentity? an essay on Vicos disease ideology." In *Health in the Andes*, Joseph Bastien and John M. Donahue (eds), American Anthropological Association Special Publication No. 12, 1981, pp. 50–67.

Stern, Steve, *Resistance, Rebellion and Consciousness in the Andean Peasant World*, University of Wisconsin Press, 1987.

Stoner, B., *Health Care Delivery and Health Resource Utilization in a Highland Andean Community of Southern Peru*, PhD Dissertation. Indiana University, 1989.

Suárez-Torres, Jose and Dolores López-Paredes, "Development, environment and health in crisis: the case of Ecuador," *Latin American Perspectives*, 1997, Issue 95, 24(3): 83–103.

Thomas, R. B., T. L. Leatherman, J. W. Carey, and J. D. Haas, "Consequences and responses to illness among small scale farmers: a research design." In *Capacity for Work in the Tropics*, K. J. Collins and D. F. Roberts (eds), Cambridge University Press, 1988, pp. 249–76.

Tousignant, Michel, "Sadness, depression and social reciprocity in Highland Ecuador," *Social Science and Medicine*, 1989, 28(9): 899–904.

Weismantel, Mary J., *Food, Gender and Poverty in the Ecuadorian Andes*, University of Pennsylvania, 1988.

Chapter 2

Ethnography and the person

Reflections on Libbet Crandon's fieldwork in Bolivia

Joan D. Koss-Chioino

To reach Libbet's "field," I crossed Lake Titicaca from Peru to Bolivia in a miniature nineteenth-century cruise ship and debarked on a windy, yellowed moonscape, barely relieved by a few scattered dwellings. After a few hours, the train I boarded at the Bolivian port began to descend into a huge basin, a narrow, upside down wedding cake formation. I caught occasional glimpses of a large urban settlement increasing in density as we descended. The rolling view of ancient emptiness gradually transformed into a modern, chaotic agglomeration of people and dwellings. This was my first impression of Bolivia as a place of stark contrasts and endless brushes with the specter of death. My fortuitous meeting with that specter during the next few days, having suffered a severe case of salmonellosis and a military coup that closed all medical facilities, served to indelibly inscribe the specter-image on my memory. For my survival I am indebted to both a highly trained medical doctor and a wise woman who dispensed traditional remedies.

Why does an ethnographer choose a particular tribe, culture, or region to spend considerable time, energy, professional, and personal concern for what can become the better part of a lifetime? What thoughts, self-doubts, memories, and reflections shape the products of that work? Despite numerous personal reflections on fieldwork by anthropologists over the last several decades, few seem to approach a satisfactory answer to these questions despite long exegesis on their feelings and experiences while in the field. Is this because it is still not considered fully legitimate in academia (or anthropology) for ethnographers to publically reflect on their personal motives and actions? Or is it due to the current negative reaction by many anthropologists to the excesses of post-modern writing style? Or, as Pratt claims, is it only formal ethnography that earns professional capital and is considered authoritative, while personal narratives are "deemed self indulgent, trivial or heretical ... ?"[1]

Libbet Crandon-Malamud was in good company when she interwove aspects of her field persona with the narratives of the lives of the people of Kachitu, whom she refers to as a "cast of characters."[2] Fathers of modern ethnography, such as Firth and Malinowski, can hardly be described as practitioners of scientific detachment. Libbet's persistent presence as a "character" among others in the town, with intimate comments on the roles she often did not choose but felt compelled to play, not only clothes the scenes of the town and particular people with the personal authority of the ethnographer in interaction with the towns-people, but effaces the classic line between subjective and objective perspectives in ethnographic work in favor of a complex interplay of personae. As a result, a vivid ethnography emerges from Libbet's perspectives on herself as a "multifac-eted entity" participating in a fluid and changing social system. And her writing style parallels her central thesis, that, given medical pluralism, resort to medicine is much more than a therapeutic enterprise.[3] It can be, and is manipulated by its users to access secondary resources – social, economic, and political. Thus Libbet, like the townspeople she studied, became adept at manipulating second-ary resources and changing identities, all in the service of collecting her data.

While she was alive, for reasons that I cannot account for, I did not feel I could address questions about her fieldwork to Libbet, despite (or perhaps because of) the high level of enthusiasm and optimism she displayed when talking about "her village" in the *altiplano* of Bolivia. Even though the people she described verbally and in writing came to life as familiar friends or fictive family members, I could not ask her why she chose those people or that particular place over other peoples and places, or how she was affected by her experiences. Given my lack of foreknowledge of the future, I now address my inquiry to her book, *From the Fat of Our Souls*, which she left as her major intellectual legacy.[4]

This chapter discusses answers the book provided, augmented by my memories of Libbet over more than two decades of friendship and by a visit with her at the time she left the town of "Kachitu" and was living in La Paz. However, it also raises important questions. I cannot claim to know (deeply) why Libbet picked her particular field site and what she felt or gained from her experiences there, apart from what she herself tells us, but this exercise into her comments, reflec-tions, and behavior while in the field, enhanced by my reflective turn and memories, intends to raise issues about the Andean region as a site for the study of medical anthropology in general, and medical pluralism in particular. It also touches on the topic of ethnographers as personae, both during their work in the field and out of it, reflected by and contextualized by the field they choose. In a final section, I consider some implications of the ethnographic enterprise focused on ethical considerations and the search for cultural validity.

Choosing a field

Kachitu had a history of anthropological and missionary intrusion when Libbet selected it for study. She notes her consultation with, and debts to Judith-Maria and Hans Buechler, Bertha and William Carter, Phil Blair and Nathan Robison, a missionary who enhanced the town's life with a health clinic. (All had many years of experience working in Bolivia and they pointed to the area of the altiplano she ultimately chose.) Thus guided she decided on the town in which William Carter lived and studied in the early 1950s, which stands on the windy, cold and desolate altiplano some five miles from Lake Titicaca, 100 miles from La Paz and 13,000 feet above sea level. Libbet reports her fears and trepidations as she journeys toward the town in a bus with her small daughter, having been informed by physicians in La Paz that the move was dangerous to her daughter's health and perhaps held other dangers. My guess is that her enthusiasm mounted rather than declined in the face of warnings from highly prejudiced, upper class Bolivians about the "bad" Indians and the physical dangers and rejection she might face. Libbet was a person who loved challenges and the more so if they interfered with her favorite ideas (over which she could become wildly enthusiastic). She admits, however, to also being apprehensive (her words: "terrified and exhilarated"),[5] in part because both she and her daughter had contracted typhoid and paratyphoid during their initial five months in La Paz.

It is easy to envision Libbet proceeding, seemingly undaunted, into the potentially very difficult but not altogether unknown locale that met her requirement of possessing plural medical systems. She was a person who promptly adjusted to whatever constraints she met on her way to the larger goal, which existed for her as a shining ideal. So, although we get glimpses of many privations and physical discomforts that life in the town yielded up – particularly around lack of food – she dismisses them with short phrases such as "I consider myself lucky to have been sick only twice in Kachitu"[6] or, walking to a nearby Aymara settlement: "I figured there was a good possibility of freezing to death before reaching the haven of Seferino Qaruru's home, ..."[7] We immediately learn in the chapter on fieldwork, that she shares with her participants the struggle to get, prepare, and keep a supply of food. She has to slaughter, dry, and hang meat in order for her and her daughter to have adequate meals. Because she has access to meat from La Paz she reports to have rather quickly become part of the ongoing and complex system of exchange with townspeople, in which she cooks food to reciprocate participants' goodwill and information. Later in the book (and frequently) she acknowledges her status in the town as an outsider, *gringa* and anthropologist who had "possible" access to US AID funds. And even before that comment, she reports that she was successful in getting answers to "annoying" questions because she was a single woman with a child, and the townspeople came to be concerned about their welfare. However, she also remarks on the general fear of townspeople that she will exploit them, through profit gained by taking their stories and knowledge back to America.

These are all very different views of her role as ethnographer from the perspective of the townspeople, and there is ample commentary in the book that she cultivated all of them during her field stay, in direct proportion to what seemed to work with particular individuals, families, or institutions. It occurs to the reader that she led a chameleon-like social life in Kachitu, constantly trying to negotiate the appropriate role relationship that would predispose her participants to the task of providing information. Since her main thesis deals with manipulating social resources and ethnic identity (albeit through the vehicle of seeking health care) it seems as if she herself was ensnared by that very same process. In fact, she comments that an attempt to do a network analysis revealed that no one had "any best friends" and few even relied much on their families. Instead, most Kachitunos were "lonely" in an unpredictable world and had to "look inside themselves for strength."[8] Moreover, "there is little consensus on appropriate behavior." At first, the references to loneliness and suspicion of outsiders might seem a reflection of an ethnographer's typical dilemma in needing to be accepted by the people chosen for study, with the ethnographer perennially feeling like an outsider. However, this state of being and feeling is frequently mentioned by ethnographers in other accounts of Andean life which lends it some validity (see also Chapter 8).

Although Libbet cogently traces this state of social unpredictability through the political and economic history of the region, in that the older social categories were no longer viable, she seems also to be describing her own problematic social situation in the town as a person no one can classify. In societies with more stable social systems (no longer very common) the ethnographer often finds a role slot, a niche into which he or she "fits." He or she usually does this by being adopted into a family, clan, or other social unit, and thus acquires a reference point from which to gauge social distance and intimacy, as well as plot social regulations and mores. (See Chapter 13 by Glass-Coffin, who describes two stages in her relationship with her main informant, and how they were influenced at different times by the ethnographer's change in social status – from poor student to professor – in the world foreign to that of the Peruvian town.)

We can raise further questions: Given this kind of local world, to what extent was Libbet's perception of the fluidity and mobility of the Kachitu social system (in relation to ethnic identity in particular) a result of her own experiences as an outsider? Or, were her experiences and the many quandaries she so honestly describes shaped by the lack of anchoring of Kachitu social class (or of ethnic positions) which led to her central thesis? In addition, was Libbet especially attracted to this kind of local world, given her own lack of adjustment (her active rebellion, in my opinion) to the relatively rigid, traditional class system that was part of her childhood background in New England? Answers to these questions become more difficult when we encounter, in Chapter 3, the four metaphors or themes on which much of the material in the book is ultimately based.

Choosing themes

Libbet lays out four metaphors "that consistently appear in discussions about medical etiology and diagnosis" in Kachitu (and appear to be widespread in the Andean region, as noted in the Preface and repeated in several chapters).[9] These are: insatiable hunger; the vulnerability of subordination; victimization; and exploitation.[10] Her major thesis is stated after describing these themes: "In Kachitu, (illness) etiology is a metaphor for history and the use of Kachitu's metaphors in medical dialogue is an attempt to change history." In this section, I explore these themes, not for the sake of understanding their historical emergence or their importance in social processes related to medical pluralism, but in relation to Libbet as ethnographer and person.

Regarding insatiable hunger, I reflect on Libbet's own persistent hunger for particular foods, often at odd times. I remember one midnight, in a neighborhood where the Taco Bell closed at 10 o'clock. We had to go to extreme ends to reach other parts of that city to find an all-night Taco Bell or her hunger could not be assuaged! It was not that she ate a lot – quite the opposite – but she had strong cravings at times, and not only for food. When she was in Bolivia I remember wondering how she satisfied them. In her book she mentions that she carried soy sauce to her informants' houses to mask the flavor of the foods she was offered until she began to like them. The point here is that she deeply identified, I believe, with the hunger of the Kachituños, both *Mestizo* and Aymara, seeing it as much more than hunger for food (also the situation for many townspeople), but as a metaphor for all things – land, goods, power – that each ethnic group had been progressively denied at various times in the course of the twentieth century. Medicine is called into the metaphoric mix through a belief in "*El Tio*," a kind of fallen angel whose unsatiable hunger is credited with causing all kinds of misfortune. Supernatural beings depend on human beings to satisfy their hungers and will protect health or cause illness according to supernatural–human interactions. Libbet tells us that, "... *khan achachi* chooses its victims indiscriminately. He demands to be fed, and inflicts illness or death upon those who refuse such payment."[11] These beings are neither all-giving or always reliable; their actions are often unpredictable. Moreover, they attack many who lack enough food and resources to sustain themselves.

The hunger theme is closely related to the theme of exploitation. It is telling, that even though Libbet fed her neighbors and came to know some of them in quasi-familial ways, they still reacted with disbelief to her professed motives. The fear of exploitation that threads Katchitu life is a local reverberation of national Bolivian economic policies and politics. This serves to highlight a common dilemma of ethnographers because, most frequently, they study "down," that is, they study those social groups who are marginal, poor and lower in status. This is particularly the case in the Andean region where anthropologists, as comparatively well-to-do professional persons with light skin, generally enter into the worlds of indigenous or other marginal persons; they, therefore, can be identified with the oppressive elites of the society. Anthropologists' wealth includes certain types of knowledge as well as goods and first aid treatments. Libbet recounts frequent occasions when she offered first aid in Kachitu or escorted an ailing person to the clinic. One vividly described incident is the time Vicente comes to her house "very sick." She first feeds him the sausages he asks for, then takes him to the hospital when he discovers his son has left for the capital and cannot accompany him. However, she warns him that she "... will not pay the bill." Despite her admonition, when he receives the bill, he hands it to her, "explaining that I (she) will pay it."[12] When she reminds him of their agreement, he pulls out a "fat wad of fifty-peso bills."

The incident with Vicente is accompanied by her comment that the medical staff is amused by Vicente's behavior because "... so many people in town have handed me bills to the point of exasperation ... ." This incident comes full circle in its power to evoke an image of the extent to which some of Libbet's participants were highly vulnerable and in their vulnerability sought to exploit the ethnographer. Vicente dies of a medically unknown cause after the doctor states that his problem is anemia! Earlier, Vicente accounted for his illness with the diagnosis of *limpu* (an Aymara illness) made by a *yatiri* (healer). Libbet does not comment on the roles of each of the medical practitioners in this case, beyond her insistence that persons such as Vicente adopt Aymara illnesses for social rather than medical reasons. She is obviously loathe to judge the merits of one medical system over another (there is no attempt to study medical efficacy in any case, but only "social" efficacy). She also does not comment on the common situation, that in cases like that of Vicente (and perhaps also like that of Gonzalo, whom she accompanies to a psychiatric hospital in La Paz to receive treatment with a poor outcome), that even in affluent societies, those who are socially and economically impoverished are frequently medically underserved. With regard to Gonzalo, she laments her ethnocentric attitudes that led her to expect a cure from mental health care services in the city. Moreover, she seems to view these attitudes as signifying her own vulnerability.

This raises the important issue of how the medical anthropologist is viewed by participants in the field. Rasmussen describes this as a dilemma: an "anomalous position, caught between the ethnographic and the medical spaces of professional practice."[13] Libbet mentions dispensing first aid and being viewed in contradictory terms because she was not a medical professional, but was engaged in persistently seeking local knowledge of health care. The Tuareg do not distinguish between medical study and medical practice, yet there were cogent reasons why Rasmussen did not (or could not) enter into a healer apprenticeship – even though she reports that many of her participants expected her to do so. A good illustration of this problem is found in Libbet's account of the situation of Bartolo's accident with an unexploded firecracker. Libbet supplies a pain killer to Bartolo, which the doctor refused to give to the boy during and after surgical treatment. She confesses to feeling anxious that she was doing the "right thing" when the doctor insists that she take responsibility for any negative reactions that might occur.

It is not clear how Kachituños thought about Libbet, whether as healer or student of medicine, because she does not address this issue. We do get a sense that she was aware of the contradictions of her social position and of the ambivalence she herself experienced around her own identity when she facilitated or made medical choices on behalf of townspeople. Although in passing she mentions that she too had to make her own medical choices while living in the town, she does not inform the reader about how and why she made them. She comments that she was ill in Kachitu and that the townspeople cured her but she also acknowledges her Bolivian medical friends as having seen her "through several illnesses."[14] One thing seems clear; she would not allow herself to be victimized, either by illness or lack of cooperation or acceptance on the part of the townspeople.

Choosing a writing style

As discussed by Clifford and Marcus,[15] the ethnographer's most important task is his written report of the data he collects during fieldwork. The style in which the report is presented is directly related to the goals and outcomes of the study but also has much to say about the ethnographer's viewpoint and position *vis-à-vis* the people he or she observed and interviewed. There are several revealing aspects of the style Libbet employed. Glass-Coffin[16] describes and contrasts two writing styles: experiential approaches that are "realist" tales in which the "ethnographer is simply an educated scribe and faithful recorder of 'what is,'" and "experience-driven accounts" in which experience is not "'objective' but overtly constructed and intentional."[17] Perhaps there is really only a "realist" writing style, and never a "realist" report; ethnographic truth being perennially at contest.[18] In most experience-driven accounts ("impressionist" according to Van Maanan), the invocation of experience engages the reader in what will emerge or develop in the dynamics of ongoing lives. However, as noted (in another way) above, this puts a strain on anthropology's image as a social science with comparative and scientific aims, because a particular anthropologist-informant dialogue lacks the authority of portraying the community's way of life. It seems that Libbet was able to diagonally traverse these two styles quite successfully by recounting many of her own experiences as an actor on the many-peopled stage of town life. She used both types of approaches in *From the Fat of Our Souls*, in the sense that she also sought to develop an interpretive and historical frame for the experience of the actors (although not for herself within the context of town life). She was successfully able to tack between her own and others' experience and her interpretations of the social, historical and economic dimensions of both local and national life.

Cultural validity at issue: implications for the study of medical pluralism

Libbet does not describe her own views on the various medical choices available in Kachitu except for interstitial comments in the descriptions of the townspeople's experiences and her role in them. She makes it quite clear that the medical doctors have their own personal–social agendas (as well as ethnic identifications) that can influence their approaches to treating the townspeople. In his review of *From the Fat of Our Souls*, Kleinman,[19] while praising the book reports that he is shocked by the appendixes that describe and list the results of Libbet's survey of disease/illness terms. Here Libbet radically departs from the interpretive/experiential style of her report by offering a simple scheme categorizing the terms according to whether they implied that the illness was "natural," "magical," or "psychological," and listing the ethnic/class status of the interviewees. She states that she wished to show "the range of agreement among and between members" of the different social groupings.[20] Given this disjuncture from the rest of the book, could the survey have reflected her own confusion about how to represent and valorize these medical alternatives? Apparently not wishing to deal directly with the issue of medical efficacy (although her expressions of doubt are legion throughout the book) it is as if her own background, as the daughter of a physician to whom she dedicates the book, breaks through. Her doubts and ambivalence about the biomedical approach to illness may have gained the upper hand at this point in her work, and so she adds a very different type of technique and style of reporting – a survey – actually a lapse into positivism in contrast to the interpretative mode. She then "proves" what she reports as unexpected, that knowledge of nosology, causes and cures of illness is highly shared by all social divisions of the town's population. However, it appears that this knowledge is manipulated differently in these different social sectors. The final chapter, in which relativism in diagnosis is described (i.e. "Diagnosis is molded by individual perception and advice"[21]) in relation to ways in which sufferers negotiate identity and shift membership, maps the framework of these manipulations.

The most important statement for the discussion at hand is, "Medicine is a domain critical to our sense of selves, infused with enormous power and riddled with different paths that access material and nonmaterial wealth."[22] For me this is a Guernica-like statement of a battlefield that she herself traversed. Where did she fit herself (regarding the question of medical choice), both within that Bolivian town and her own cultural context? Since she is marginal to the town's social system, can we assume that Libbet felt that her own medical choices did not affect the central argument of the book? She does not mention her own use of medical care for social or any other reasons related to her own identity in the town or other social setting. Some other ethnographers who study healers and medical systems are explicit about how they personally utilized either biomedical or indigenous treatment when they fell ill in the field.[23] One might speculate that Libbet wanted to avoid the issue since she does not describe her own or her daughter's illnesses in the field or what actions she took. I speculate that at first she was uncertain about how to explicate medical pluralism in Kachitu, because she was unsure how to respond personally to any of these medical alternatives. Her case narratives are about how Kachituño sufferers talked about medical choices, ideologies and strategies, except where she comments on the failures of biomedical treatment in particular cases (from her own perspective). Indigenous treatment by a *yatiri* (an Aymara healer) in which her own financial stability was predicted is viewed as successful when she is notified (at a later time) that she has a summer job. None of the treatment alternatives in Gonzalo's case (emotional disorder?) are reported to have been successful. Mixed reviews of outcomes of resort to various medical alternatives may reflect reality, but they also reinforce Libbet's principal conclusion that a cure is only one of many goals or outcomes of medical choice. Coexisting, conflicting medical ideologies address diverse aspects of the biological and social etiologies of illness.

Ethical dilemmas in the study of medical pluralism

Given Libbet's social resource argument, as well as other approaches to medical pluralism in the Andean region (and perhaps elsewhere), the ethnographer studying medical pluralism faces a significant dilemma should he/she fall ill. In a socially pluralistic setting, choice of a medical alternative holds the same implications for the ethnographer that it does for anyone else; it addresses social standing and identity. As described above, Libbet worked hard to become a social chameleon in order to involve herself with individuals in all three of the major social divisions in the town. She worked to keep her acquired social identity in Kachitu fairly balanced among all three sectors. In the Andes (as described by Libbet for Bolivia) it appears that a focus on (and identification with) one social sector (i.e. indigenous, *vecino* or Methodist, as in Kachitu) would have obscured the dynamics of plural medical ideologies and choices in a town-wide context. Her election of a medical choice for her own illness would have made an obvious (and fairly powerful) social statement (viewed from her own theoretical perspective). On reflection, I think that this was the reason that she did not allow herself to become vulnerable to illness; she did not allow herself to focus on the possibility of illness, how she became ill or what she did about it (given the two incidents she mentions in passing and the occurrence of hepatitis in La Paz when she left the field). This lacuna strongly contrasts with her openness about how she responded and behaved in the extreme situations she labels as "embarrassing," such as being forced to feed participants when they would not talk with her, or her description of the time she and her dog disrupted a funeral service.

Thus, Libbet faced the moral dilemma shared by all researchers into issues of health and illness. In a cultural context of medical pluralism, she herself was unable to negotiate medical choice and so fell back on the type of choice she had brought with her to the field, but perhaps actually disdained. Given the way she managed her medical self presentation in the town she could only resort to biomedical care outside of it. She left the village when she or her daughter became ill and sought the type of biomedical care into which she had been socialized. When she describes the hopeless case of Gonzalo she says that, "When Gonzalo's condition deteriorated to the extent it did... I felt that what happened to him affected me and I fell prey to my own ethnocentricity."[24] She then emphasizes that psychiatric care in La Paz did not provide a solution for Gonzalo, and his family got him released. (He disappeared from the town some two months later.) Her distress over the fact that she had made psychiatric care in the metropolis available to him – with a worsening effect – is evident.

Issues around health and illness inevitably devolve around issues of self and identity as Libbet made so clear. The ethnographer has these same issues, and thus has a very difficult time being who he or she is, when also deeply and passionately related to study participants in a new milieu, and wanting and needing (for the fieldwork) to be involved with social and personal diversity. But there are times, when in the field, that the ethnographer has pressing need to be who he or she is; at those times, the study of medical pluralism can become an impossible

task when one's primary identity takes over. Fieldwork is a form of experimenta-
tion and critique, with the anthropologist and her culture as the subject "living
rather than paying lip service to a pluralistic ethos, attempting to move beyond
received opinions which ... condemn human beings to isolation from one another
in the name of essential difference."[25] As I have tried to illustrate in this chapter,
these attempts are difficult at best and sometimes impossible.

Notes

1 Pratt, M. L., "Fieldwork in common places." In *Writing Culture: The Poetics and
Politics of Ethnography*, J. Clifford and G. E. Marcus (eds), University of California
Press, 1986, p. 31.
2 Pratt, "Fieldwork in common places."
3 Kleinman, Arthur, *Writing at the Margin: Discourse Between Anthropology and
Medicine*, University of California Press, 1995.
4 Crandon-Malamud, Libbet, *From the Fat of Our Souls: Social Change, Political
Process and Medical Pluralism in Bolivia*, University of California Press, 1991.
5 Crandon-Malamud, *From the Fat of Our Souls*, p. 15.
6 Crandon-Malamud, *From the Fat of Our Souls*, p. 42.
7 Crandon-Malamud, *From the Fat of Our Souls*, p. 2.
8 Crandon-Malamud, *From the Fat of Our Souls*, p. 44.
9 Crandon-Malamud, *From the Fat of Our Souls*, p. 45.
10 Crandon-Malamud, *From the Fat of Our Souls*, pp. 45–7.
11 Crandon-Malamud, *From the Fat of Our Souls*, p. 1.
12 Crandon-Malamud, *From the Fat of Our Souls*, p. 149.
13 Rasmussen, S., "Parallel and divergent landscapes: cultural encounters in the ethnographic space of Tuareg medicine," *Medical Anthropology Quarterly*, 2000, 14(2):
242–70.
14 Crandon-Malamud, *From the Fat of Our Souls*, p. xv.
15 Clifford, J. and Marcus, G. E., *Writing Culture: The Poetics and Politics of
Ethnography*, University of California Press, 1986.
16 Glass-Coffin, Bonnie, "Portraying experience in ethnography: situated knowledge or
Castaneda's revenge," *Anthropology UCLA*, 1993, pp. 105–25.
17 Glass-Coffin, "Portraying experience," p. 107.
18 Van Maanen, J., *Tales of the Field: On Writing Ethnography*, University of Chicago
Press, 1988.
19 Kleinman, *Writing at the Margin*.
20 Crandon-Malamud, *From the Fat of Our Souls*, p. 211.
21 Crandon-Malamud, *From the Fat of Our Souls*, p. 203.
22 Crandon-Malamud, *From the Fat of Our Souls*, p. 205.
23 Glass-Coffin, Bonnie, *The Gift of Life: Female Healing and Experience in Northern
Peru*, University of New Mexico Press, 1998; Price, L., *Nepali Shaman*, Undine Press,
1980.
24 Crandon-Malamud, *From the Fat of Our Souls*, p. 200.
25 Jackson, Michael, *At Home in the World*, Duke University Press, 1995, p. ix.

References

Clifford, J. and Marcus, G. E., *Writing Culture: The Poetics and Politics of Ethnography*,
University of California Press, 1986.

Crandon-Malamud, Libbet, *From the Fat of Our Souls: Social Change, Political Process and Medical Pluralism in Bolivia*, University of California Press, 1991.

Glass-Coffin, Bonnie, "Portraying experience in ethnography: situated knowledge or Castaneda's revenge," *Anthropology UCLA*, 1993, pp. 105–25.

——, *The Gift of Life: Female Healing and Experience in Northern Peru*, University of New Mexico Press, 1998.

Jackson, Michael, *At Home in the World*, Duke University Press, 1995.

Kleinman, Arthur, *Writing at the Margin: Discourse Between Anthropology and Medicine*, University of California Press, 1995.

Pratt, M. L., "Fieldwork in common places." In *Writing Culture: The Poetics and Politics of Ethnography*, J. Clifford and G. E. Marcus (eds), University of California Press, 1986.

Price, L., *Nepali Shaman*, California: Undine Press, 1980.

Rasmussen, S., "Parallel and divergent landscapes: cultural encounters in the ethnographic space of Tuareg medicine," *Medical Anthropology Quarterly*, 2000, 14(2): 242–70.

Van Maanen, J., *Tales of the Field: On Writing Ethnography*, University of Chicago Press, 1988.

Chapter 3

Changing times and changing symptoms

The effects of modernization on *mestizo* medicine in rural Bolivia (the case of two *mestizo* sisters)

Libbet Crandon

Downward mobility and the reconstruction of medical beliefs

Under a specific but not unusual set of circumstances in a rural highland Bolivian town, the effects of "modernization" from 1952 to 1978 led to an increased use of indigenous medicine by members of those very classes and that same ethnic group that have, throughout the twentieth century, vocally aspired to modernization, westernization, and Victorian notions of progress. This use of indigenous medicine was possible because the processes influencing those social facts that pertain to illness and disease – such as illness perception and expression, the sick role, diagnosis, and therapy – are not always scientific and objective, but more often political, social, and economic.

A case of two *mestizo* sisters may be too limited to carry the argument that certain rural Bolivian *mestizos* enduring social, political, and economic pressures are abandoning Western or cosmopolitan for Aymara medical values, although data suggest that this is so. However, the case raises the possibility and demonstrates the logic underlying such a move and the process by which the shift can be made.

Consideration of this possibility is important because it does not coincide with the main assumptions behind the notion of "modernization" and development (e.g. Bryant 1969; Logan 1973; Navarro 1977; Read 1968; Unschuld 1979) and, therefore, raises new questions about the nature of medical pluralism. First, the case is an incident of rejection of cosmopolitan medicine in favor of indigenous medicine by members of the local, non-indigenous population, *mestizos*. I argue elsewhere that *mestizos* as a class are thoroughly knowledgeable in indigenous medicine – which reveals their reliance on it in spite of vociferous denials to the contrary – and the consequential pattern of multiple resource use (Crandon 1986). The case of two sisters, however, demonstrates a rejection of cosmopolitan medicine in favor of traditional medicine, by patient and healer alike, and for

Reprinted with permission from Gordon & Breach Publishers. This paper was originally published in *Medical Anthropology*, 1989, 10(4): 255–64.

fundamentally different reasons that are defined by their sociopolitical and economic contexts. Second, the sisters' reliance on indigenous medicine employed a transition in ethnic and class alignment that was not only downwardly mobile, but also involved negative political implications. The case is most satisfactorily understood in the context of an ethnically plural environment (*mestizo* and Aymara) defined by peripherally situated underdevelopment (Amin 1974; Cockcroft *et al.* 1972; Frank 1969). The ethnic boundary has traditionally been defined by class relations which in recent years are rapidly and radically changing. In this environment, cosmopolitan medicine cannot accommodate, cosmopolitan and psychological needs of many patients (Woods and Greaves 1973), particularly the downwardly mobile, the "victims" of "modernization" (e.g. Hughes and Hunter 1970). While indigenous medicine is employed because, among other reasons, it explains the inefficiency of cosmopolitan medicine (Janzen 1978; Landy 1974; Rubel 1964), it realigns the patient within the sociopolitical domain in order to do so. Such realignment makes the patient's future medical strategies more effective because it makes viable medical strategies more accessible. However, within the context, the choice of one medical system over another is an inherently political negotiation between the two groups whose ethnic differentiation, which has traditionally justified the domination of the *mestizo* over the Aymara in racial terms, masks class relations (Warren 1978).

This conceptual consideration of increasing reliance on Aymara medical resources by the downwardly mobile *mestizo* class, is not consistent with our understanding of resurgences of indigenous medical systems as part of nationalistic movements, like the revival of Unani, Ayurvedic, or Chinese medicines (e.g. Crozier 1968, 1970; Gould 1965; Leslie 1972, 1976). And it is not compatible with the position of the World Health Organization, which urges the incorporation of indigenous medicine into the delivery of Western primary health care. The case of these two sisters suggests that one dimension that affects the use of medical resources is the patient's understanding of his or her position within the sociopolitical order. Such understanding structures perception, options, and choice. This analytic approach permits a shift in the perception and use of decision-making models by anthropologists in their studies of patient choice of medical resources. This shift broadens decision-making models, previously limited to complex priority structures (e.g. Cosminsky and Scrimshaw 1980; Woods 1977), to include the social reconstruction of the meaning of illness events (e.g. Frake 1961; Low 1985; Sontag 1978; Turner 1963). In the case of the two sisters, the various interpretations of their illnesses as reconstructed by neighbors, kin, their mother, and most particularly themselves, was informed by the historical and political context of the town in which they lived.

Collecting the data

The case is based on research data collected between 1976 and 1978[1] in a small *mestizo*[2] and Aymara[3] village on the Bolivian altiplano. When participant observation, extensive interviews, and innumerable long discussions over *cerveza* brought the case of the two sisters to light, a specific set of questions about the case was asked of every individual in town who knew anything about it. Some questions were designed to elicit enough information to determine the exact nature of the diseases or illnesses the sisters suffered from, and to identify them in cosmopolitan terms. This attempt was unsuccessful. The present analysis pertains to the responses the illnesses elicited, how they were perceived, and what choices were made within historical context.

My two key informants were the one remaining sister and her mother. Others were relatives and *compadrazco*,[4] or fictive kin ties. Only the first sister was treated in a medical institution, which could not (or would not?) locate the sister's records. Consequently there are no written records of the illnesses; all the data derive from personal interviews. The informants' views were also retrospective, which may bias the value of the data. These limitations were somewhat compensated for by my insistence that my informants tell me their versions over and over again. Through this technique, I attempted to deconstruct myth and reconstruct history, by separating event and social relations from informants' personal analysis. Both facts and interruptions were significant, but were subject to different types of anthropological analysis. However, the technique tried my informants' patience. They often concluded that, since I asked the same questions so many times, I was lacking in certain fundamentals and perhaps shared something with the two sisters in whom I seemed so interested.

The first sister: Gladys

The two sisters, both members of the rural poor *mestizo* class, and here pseudo-named Gladys and Marisol Braojos, were affected by what one might call mental or psychosomatic disorders as they reached adulthood in the 1970s. Gladys became ill in 1971 at the age of 24. Her mother and sister believed that her illness developed after she voluntarily and effectively took cold baths to prevent menstruation. Besides Gladys's own statement to her mother and sister that she found it a bother, there is no further explanation for her wish to terminate her menstrual periods. Both her mother and sister felt she had never been open about it: "eramuy cerrada." Many people in town, however, associated Gladys's illness with an illicit love affair and subsequent forced wedding to a man who was already married to someone else. For two to four years, depending on the informant, Gladys suffered debilitating headaches and acted in a bizarre fashion, alternating between two states of mind. Sometimes she attempted to strip and sing and dance naked among whatever company was present; at other times she experienced profound depression and isolated herself. Eventually, she refused to eat or get out of bed. Her widowed mother, acting on the advice of her *mestizo* friends and relations, sought Western medical help and sent Gladys to a psychiatric hospital in La Paz, the cost of which was covered by national health insurance because Gladys had briefly taught school. After six months of hospitalization, these psychiatric resources remained ineffective. Sra. De Braojos then turned to what was for here more radical and desperate means, Aymara Indian shamans or *yatiris*. The *yatiris* consistently told Sra. De Braojos that Gladys would die within three days, which, in fact, she did. Her death occurred in the spring of 1974 from "congestion cerebral" according to the town death records.

The second sister: Marisol

In 1976, Marisol also became ill. She was 26. She described her experience to me on several occasions and consistently maintained her symptoms were profound weakness, a headache in which merely touching the head was painful, vomiting, inability to eat, a swollen white tongue, bleeding gums, and protruding teeth. Her mother immediately referred her to a *yatiri* (unavailable for interview). He diagnosed her as suffering because *El Tio*,[5] an Aymara transformation of the devil (Taussig 1979) was consuming her blood and soul in return for wealth the family had recently accumulated. Initial treatment was affected by the mother's questionable legitimacy in requesting this *yatiri's* help. He was her social inferior, a laborer employed by her latest husband; and she had recently offended him, rendering him more inclined to wreak vengeance rather than help her. A debate ensued in which the mother publicly acceded social inferiority to the *yatiri* who subsequently treated Marisol. She recovered within two weeks.

Sociopolitical identification and medical orientation

Gladys and Marisol were two of the six *mestizos* (three men, three women) in their village who suffered debilitating mental disorders as they reached adulthood in the 1970s, four of whom died. This amounted to 18 percent of the young adult *mestizo* population, a figure that has no known precedence in either the local Aymara or earlier local *mestizo* population as far as anyone can remember or local records indicate.[6] I have argued elsewhere that this wave of mental disorders among a specific population is a response to radical social change, as these six young men and women came from families who did not adapt easily to that change (Crandon 1983).

Here I wish to argue that during the eight-year period of increased mental illness, *mestizo* perceptions of these illness events, the expression of these disorders, and the curative resources mobilized against them shifted from Western ones to Aymara ones for sociopolitical reasons. This shift in perception, expression, and action, can be understood within the historical context of the village that explains the sociopolitics involved: since 1952, the social order in the village has been transformed from a colonially based to a class-based agricultural society. While *mestizos* have always perceived themselves as differing from Indians in terms of ethnicity and race and continue to do so, this social transformation has rendered class a far more appropriate and accurate concept with which to understand the relationship between these groups. In the post-revolutionary environment, the rigid boundaries between the two groups can no longer be maintained as some Aymara, no longer limited by law to peonage in the hacienda system, gain access to wealth and some *mestizos*, no longer protected from peonage by law, sink further and further into poverty.

Presently, the *mestizo* population in this rural village is poor and has no significant political representation in the capital, La Paz[7] from which most resources beyond subsistence emanate to the altiplano. The contemporary socioeconomic and political status of these people is a direct product of the modernization process stimulated by the MNR[8] revolution of 1952, the subsequent land reform of 1953, and the shifts in national economic and political interests from the altiplano to the lowlands, particularly to Santa Cruz.

Before 1952, the local *mestizo* class was quite powerful. For over four hundred years, this class in the countryside served the interests of the national elites in a national economy that was dominated by altiplano-based agriculture and tin. The rural *mestizo* class managed Aymara Indian labor on haciendas, collected taxes from Aymara communities, and acted as culture broker between the Aymara and the elites whom both *mestizo* and Indians served. After the revolution, land reform broke down the hacienda system. The value of mining deteriorated and the national economy shifted its focus to agribusiness in the lowlands. This process of modernization has turned parts of the altiplano into rural backwaters, inhibited capital investment there, and eliminated any interest in agricultural development, which is now centered in the valleys and lowlands. It has ignored any potential market growth, has not provided an industrial sector in La Paz with which to draw the altiplano population off the land and into urban poverty, and has simultaneously cut off access to economic and political resources for the rural poor altiplano *mestizo*. The land reform took away any large withholdings from the local *mestizos* (Klein 1982; Kelly and Klein 1981). Those who were able to leave the rural areas sought opportunities in the city, but many were not sufficiently educated, courageous, well connected, or simply at liberty to go, and remained in the village. Those who remained found themselves in the 1970s to be members of a class now relegated to a position of economic and political impotence.

Under these circumstances, the old *mestizo* status as culture broker between the Aymara and the elites has lost its significance. The land reform and the elimination of the hacienda system stimulated the growth of local peasant markets, and drastically reduced Indian dependence on the *mestizo* class. These changes also destroyed the economic base of the rural *mestizo*, specifically the extraction of Indian resources and labor (Carter 1964; Dandler 1969; Heath 1969; Malloy 1970). This in turn destroyed the foundation of their cultural identity, which one could define as a sense of generic and cultural superiority to the Aymara. This notion has justified *mestizo* economic and political superordination and control of the Indian population. The destruction of *mestizo* economic and political control over the local Aymara in the 1950s eliminated a *mestizo* sense of community in the village since many left the village for the city and those who remained competed with each other for increasingly scarce resources. They no longer felt they had access to elites or were connected to larger national processes. By the 1970s, their sociopolitical position in relation to the elites and to the national order approximated the exploitative relationship by Aymara had previously suffered under them; they saw the wealthy urban classes and the government in much the same manner as the Indians had once seen the rural *mestizos*.

During the 1950s, 1960s, and 1970s, those *mestizos* who had grown up under the pre-1952 social order and still remained in town struggled unsuccessfully for strategies of economic survival and to negotiate a new form of cultural identity based on their cultural heritage. The children who were born to these *mestizos* just after the revolution inherited the values of the old social order. When they reached adulthood, they faced a social environment in which such values played no role and in which they had to forge new lives and chart new strategies for which they were completely unprepared.

Comparative histories of Gladys and Marisol

Gladys and Marisol were two of six children (four girls, two boys)[9] born to the prestigious Don Ricardo Braojos Mendoza, landowner, *tienda* or shopkeeper, judge, *corregidor*,[10] town president, and center of the local social life. The land reform took away most of Don Ricardo's land. The revolutionary government gave all local political and administrative positions to the Aymara and prohibited any *mestizo* from assuming these offices and positions for well over ten years. Though the prohibition has been lifted, the *mestizos* in this village have never been able to regain their control of these offices. Economic and political changes isolated Don Ricardo from family and fictive kin ties as members of his social group moved to the city and assumed new lives, goals, and social strategies; these changes destroyed his social network. He then had to personally fulfill his own labor needs, till his own subsistence plot, and do his own house repairs. In 1954, he fell off the roof he was thatching and died in his late thirties. He left his twenty-six-year-old widow, Sra. De Braojos, with six children, without family to support her or provide aid, and with nothing but a small subsistence plot and a *tienda* to survive on. Like the other *mestizos* who remained on the altiplano after the revolution, Don Ricardo's widow had the glory of history but little of substance to pass on to her children, who were born members of a once-powerful social class, the present nature of which appeared as dubious as its past power had been absolute. Her best strategy lay in remarriage for herself, and in early marriage for her daughters, not with local boys, who were also poor, but with more promising outsiders who might take their new families to La Paz. As there were (and are) no acceptable opportunities in the city for young rural *mestizo* girls, the only possibility was (and is) a rural teacher's education.

One of the byproducts of Bolivian modernization has been the division of primary and secondary education into urban and rural spheres. A license in rural education does not permit practice in the city; and an urban education license takes several years longer and is much more expensive than the rural one. Hence the Braojos daughters, like most of the rural *mestizo* women, were sent to earn a rural education degree and then to some rural post that suited the political needs of the ministerial machinery in La Paz. Poor rural school teachers who have no social connections with the Ministry of Education often received posts in remote areas that were "undesirable," that is, culturally and linguistically different from the familiar altiplano.

After graduation, Gladys was assigned to a school several days' travel from home, among a Quechua-speaking population in a geographical location that was strange to her and to the Aymara of her section of the altiplano. They often construe these valleys in exotic and potentially dangerous terms; they differ from the altiplano culturally, linguistically, ecologically, and politically. Gladys's experience at this school, which began a year after the onset of her illness, exacerbated her condition. She ran away from her post on several occasions. In addition, she met a young *mestizo* there, whom she agreed to marry, and with whom she briefly lived until she left him because he had another lover during one of her frequent visits to her home on the altiplano. It was apparently significant to her that her fiancé's lover was black. The miniscule black population in Bolivia has rendered its members exotic to the altiplano population (many of whom have never seen a black before), and subject to extraordinary mythification. She accused her fiancé of being the devil. When his father came to visit Gladys on the altiplano to plead with her and her mother on his son's behalf, she accused the father of being the devil as well, threw things at him, and reverted to disrobing and dancing. She then spent six months in a psychiatric institute in La Paz, her expenses covered by insurance provided by the state to all state employees and to Gladys as a school teacher. As Gladys made no progress there, her mother was advised to take her home. Gladys refused to leave the house, eventually to get out of bed or eat, and died a year later. The town archives list the cause of death as "congestion cerebral."

Marisol was luckier. She traveled at the tender age of sixteen with a Peace Corps volunteer to Plattsville, New York. She and her mother assumed that a romantic relationship was involved. He was some twenty years her senior, had been assigned to her village, recognized her bleak future there, and took her to the United States to improve her education and thereby enable her to work in La Paz, "perhaps in a travel agency," he thought. After a year, she returned to her Bolivian village and for ten years has waited for mail and romance from the North American. In her own mind, she left New York as a strategy to manipulate the North American to feel the loneliness of her absence, recognize his love for her (and hers for him), and follow her back to Bolivia, or bring her back to New York. To the North American's mind she returned when her visa had run out and the educational purpose of the trip was completed.

After Gladys's death and before Marisol's return from New York, their mother married a *mestizo* miner, Edgar Benevides, whom she met as he frequently passed through the town on his way to the mine. Under the reform regulations of COMIBOL, which nationalized all major mining operations in Bolivia in 1952, his mine qualified as a "small mine" and permitted him private ownership of it. Benevides' mine is located outside an Aymara Indian community three-days travel from town. Its operation was dependent upon less than two dozen Aymara miners and a managerial staff of one young trusted *cholo*[11] male, all of whom live in the community in which the mine sits. The ethnic difference between owner-ship and labor and the lack of managerial staff placed the burden of supervision of the operation on Benevides himself who, now married, frequently transferred that responsibility to his new wife. Upon Marisol's return from the United States, he further transferred that responsibility to her, hoping to structure her daily activ-ity and take her mind off her unrequited love. As a result, Marisol frequented the mining community and met the young *cholo* who assisted Benevides. Somewhat reluctantly, and with her mother and stepfather's heavy encouragement, she accepted his invitation for marriage.

A week before the wedding Marisol fell ill. The onset of her weakness was relatively rapid, and she states she was barely able to sit up. We will never know definitely what kind of illness this was, but the dramatic symptoms, their sym-bolic interpretation, and the course of treatment provide significant data about the perception of the illness and how that perception related to social relations defined in this place and time by Aymara rather than *mestizo* values.

Marisol's mother chose to take no responsibility for her daughter's health care and felt that the fiancé should take over in prospect of his upcoming marital role. He sought the help of a *yatiri*, who attended to Marisol for four days. During that time an Aymara woman intimated to Sra. De Braojos that the *yatiri* was killing, not curing, her daughter. When Sra. De Braojos confronted the *yatiri* with this accusation, the *yatiri* admitted it. He argued that Sra. De Brajos had falsely accused his son of stealing from the mine. Indeed, on her visits to the mine to assist her new stepfather, Marisol noted that materials were missing. On this advice, Sra. De Braojos had concluded that these materials were stolen, and that a certain employee she thought to be suspicious, had stolen them. She did not realize that he was the *yatiri*'s son. The *yatiri* now sought revenge through the power of his supernatural status. Only after repeated obsequious displays acknowledging the *yatiri*'s superior powers by the entire mining community of Aymara and *mestizos* alike and a public and humiliating display of Sra. De Braojos' desperate pleading, did the *yatiri* agree to stop his curse and effect a cure.

Marisol and her mother agreed with the *yatiri*'s diagnosis of Marisol's illness, an illness which he had been exacerbating with his supernatural powers: *El Tio* was consuming her in exchange for the plenitude of ore in the mine, an exchange consummated when Marisol entered the mine in her supervisory missions for her stepfather. This construction of the role of gender in exchange between miners and *El Tio* substantiates the literature of many anthropologists and authors on Bolivian mining communities who have mentioned that women are prohibited in Aymara folklore from entering the mines (Nash 1978; Oblitas 1963). Apparently the ore in the mine did "disappear" upon Marisol's recovery; her stepfather closed the mine shortly thereafter.[12]

The shift from a Western to an Aymara orientation

Three aspects of Marisol's illness event demonstrate a resistance to or shift from Western values and Western medical beliefs. First, the *yatiri's* use of power through her illness effected both immediate and total compliance on the part of the gathered community and the longer term reinforcement of faith in and respect for the *yatiri's* office. This occurred in an era when one might suspect the *yatiri's* authority would be questioned because of increasing modernization, and the adoption of Western, "upper class," and commercial activities and resources that presumably accompany actual and aspired upward mobility in a class-based society.

Second, the *yatiri* was also revenged, since Marisol paid with her illness, and almost with her life, for their mother's accusation of the *yatiri's* son as a thief. He demonstrated to at least two *mestizo* women that he, as an Aymara, can demand justice on his own terms and through his own arts; he does not need to resort to *mestizo* officials, such as *corregidors* and judges. Here at the mine the *mestizo* will not exploit the Indian, even if the *mestizo* is the wife of the mine's owner.

Third, the curative strategies the mother employed to cure her daughter are very different from those she used when Gladys was sick. She did not take Marisol to the city for Western medical treatment. Indeed, she did not generate any aid herself at all, but asked the fiancé to assume responsibility. Clearly she did not abandon her concern for her daughter's welfare because she did interfere with the treatment when she suspected the *yatiri* was harming her daughter. Having been unsuccessful before, however, perhaps Sra. De Braojos feared she might be unsuccessful again, particularly in a cultural environment in which she is an outsider. In fact, there was no longer a cultural environment to which she could comfortably belong.

A comparison between Marisol's and Gladys's illness events, and between the experiences that led up to them, further accents the shift from a Western to an Aymara orientation. On the one hand, Marisol's travels and experience before her illness contrasted sharply with those of Gladys. From her home, Gladys traveled first to earn her teacher's certificate at an institute not far from home on the altiplano. But she became severely ill in the lowlands, the medical otherworld beyond the Andean passes where *apachitas* or protective offerings, left along the trail gave testimony to the evil and hungry supernatural beings that haunt the bridges between the security of home and the luscious fruits and magical dangers of the lowlands. She then turned to a psychiatric institute, a center of Western values in Bolivia, but was not relieved of her burden there.

She finally returned home and languished for a year until passing away. Gladys sought relief in several domains, in the magical optimism of an imagined world, in the promise of modern Western medicine, and in the security of her own backyard, and found nothing. Marisol, in contrast, traveled much farther away, to a place whose environs and people and illnesses and magic are entirely unknown. Whatever the villager's suspicions of potential evil in the United States might have been, the trip's effect upon Marisol was to vividly impress upon her the poverty and powerlessness of her home village and its *mestizos*. Denied access to United States society, she had to return to her village and to a powerless and poor, rural *mestizo* status. She then receded into the Aymara world of the mine, not because she sought it but because her mother had finally remarried the owner of a mine who exploited labor from that world.

Upon her illness, Marisol and her mother accepted a *yatiri* as curer more immediately than they had done during Gladys's illness at least in part because the *yatiri*'s abilities to unleash her from the claws of *El Tio* have become much more evident to her. Here she succumbed to those metaphors that she and her ethnic/class group have recently interpreted, in the post-evolutionary era of modernization, as not pertaining to themselves, and now use as a mechanism that establishes the boundary between her ethnic class/group and the Aymara. These metaphors as mechanisms, which say that *El Tio* and the *yatiri* are effective among the Aymara but not among those *mestizos* who "know better," are politically significant. They structure the relationship between the two groups hierarchically and asymmetrically. Marisol's strategy reversed that relationship. Furthermore, her strategy turned out to be highly successful for, unlike, Gladys, Marisol was cured.

Factors behind the shift

Juxtaposed with this contrast between the two illness events, however, is a striking similarity: neither Gladys nor Marisol wanted to take their mother's advice and marry. At school, when she effectively prevented her menstruation, Gladys's stopped her ability to procreate. It appears as well that she went to school only reluctantly. Gladys was in a position in which the values her mother and her social class taught her were no longer positive, adaptive, or viable. As a member of an impotent group in a revolutionary social order that made no room for that group, Gladys had to make decisions that no one had made before. Had she married and had children, she would have had no way of knowing who or what her children would be or what opportunities they would have. As a possible strategy, she lived with a man in the lowlands, a custom prohibited by the pre-revolutionary values of the *mestizo* class, but practiced commonly by the Aymara (e.g. Bolton and Mayer 1977, especially Carter in that volume). This strategy failed. Gladys's response to her fiancé's relationship with another woman who was black shows her acute consciousness about class, ethnicity, and racial relations. That is, the social order to which Gladys belonged was impotent in a universe that had become, for her class, chaotic and uncontrollable, and for which one could not prepare. The strain of her inability to make order of and control events in that universe as they pertained to herself and her future may be interpreted as having resulted in her illness and death.

Marisol was faced with the same set of values, the heritage of a dead social order, and a chaotic universe in which there was no niche for her. Her trip to the

United States, however, might have solved the problem of Marisol's social position and ethnic identity had the volunteer invited her there with the intentions she and her mother so mistakenly imputed to him. Though Marisol was active upon her return and willing to marry ten years later, a marriage to a *mestizo* would have been a social step down from the dreams she had harbored for ten years. Knowing that marriage was the only solution to her social predicament, she went through with a wedding that ultimately ended in divorce (and was never consummated) and which was marked by her near death at the hands of a symbol of Indian exploitation and oppression. However, she did try this solution, and she did recover from her illness.

The process by which other *mestizos* in Marisol's and Gladys's village are also increasingly acknowledging the inherent value of Aymara medical beliefs, and the extent to which this shift is related to the economic and political effects of the last thirty years of modernization on the altiplano, is evident in the opinion of the Braojo's *mestizo* neighbors about the etiology and treatment of Gladys's illness. Specifically, some *mestizos* expressed their opinions about what Gladys died from in a Western scientific and amoral mode. They said, for example, that she died of epilepsy or some disorder of the nerves. In this way these *mestizos* also expressed something about how they want to be identified, namely as falling within the modern stream, the Western oriented. These particular *mestizos* were distantly related to the Braojos family, had developed new and successful economic strategies in the village, and were relatively well off – they ate regularly. Other *mestizos* took a Western but Hispanic folk and highly moral view of Gladys's illness. These *mestizos* claimed that Gladys had died because she had to compete with her widowed mother for lovers, or because her mother's boyfriend had slept with her, or because her mother had forced a relationship upon her because she had had illicit sexual relations. These *mestizos* were closely related to the Braojos family, still tried to maintain pre-1952 economic strategies and cultural identities, and were consequently desperately poor. Still other *mestizo* neighbors took a typically Aymara and uncritical view of Gladys's illness. They held she had died because she suffered attacks in the head caused by *achachillas* and other Aymara spirits that indiscriminately search out victims upon which to prey. These *mestizos* were distantly related to the Braojos family, and had developed economic strategies that involved egalitarian relations with the Aymara and reciprocal exchanges between their *mestizo* and Aymara households. Like the Aymara they were poor, but were relatively secure since they had some source of income.

The nuances of these various responses reflect the changes in cultural identity each respondent had chosen, which in turn relates closely to the respondents' economic and social situations. Those who were relatively more secure economically, and successful in negotiating a politically and economically viable ethnic identity, were able to maintain sufficient distance from the post-1952 losses suffered by the village *mestizo* class; they look upon Gladys's misfortune without criticism. But those who were not able to weather this sociocultural upheaval smoothly suffer some insult to their own cultural identity from the tragedies and failures of their fellow *mestizos*. Furthermore, the more closely related that *mestizos* are to others who suffer from the changes brought on by the events of 1952, the greater the impact upon their own cultural identity, and the more difficult it is to negotiate a new one. "How can we succeed as an ethnic group," they seem to be saying, "if our own family is unable to do so?"

Most significantly, however, the mode in which the *mestizo* neighbors discussed Gladys's illness (whether they chose Western scientific medical, Hispanic-folk, or Aymara categories), expressed each maestro's conception of him or herself and his or her relationship to Gladys. In a similar fashion, Marisol's acquiescence to an Aymara medical universe, and her mother's rejection of the Western scientific one, parallel their relationship to Bolivian society at large as well as the process of modernization that has affected their lives over the previous twenty-five years.

Choices

We must conclude that these people hold medical views for social reasons. Furthermore, these views are not an after-the-fact product of socioeconomic and political realities; they are not mere metaphor (Sontag 1978). They are mechanisms by which people both make sense out of these realities, as well as facilitate strategies within them. Western psychiatric care makes no sense to a disenfranchised group who perceive themselves to have been betrayed by the type of people represented by that care, or who will never achieve entry into the world which that care represents. When modernization and development do not permit a social group effective participation in these processes, Western medical values may be inappropriate and even ineffective for that group. And traditional medicine may be a veritable locus of power.

Notes

1 This paper is based on one and a half years of fieldwork in 1977 and 1978 which was funded by a fellowship from the Organization of American States. Research was undertaken in the fictitiously named village of Kachitu (Crankshaw 1980) on the Bolivian altiplano. That name was taken from earlier work done in the same village by Williams Carter 1963.
2 *Mestizo* refers to that population of individuals in Latin America presumably of both Spanish and Indian extraction. The concept, however, is cultural. *Mestizos* are individuals who have identified themselves in opposition to Indian populations, who have tried to emulate the elite, and who have served the interests of the elite in both rural and urban sectors. Members of neither group, they are despised by both.
3 The Aymara Indian population is linguistically distinct from the Quechua, and is concentrated in the lake region of Bolivia.
4 Fictive kin ties, or *compadrazco* ties, between *mestizos* and Aymara, which the *mestizos* had used to extract Indian resources, lost the political advantage they had held for the *mestizo* as the Aymara developed independence from local *mestizo* control. Furthermore, when many *mestizos* moved to the city of La Paz and entered the grown commercial sector, they wished to ignore any responsibility they might have had with

their now "country cousins." The remaining *mestizo* class in the village lost its political power and sense of unity and became withdrawn into isolation and conflict. See Crankshaw (1980).

5 *El Tio* is not simply the Christian devil, but rather a transformation of Christian ideology through the worldview of the Aymara and Quechua under colonial domination and then post-colonial oppression. *El Tio* is particularly associated with the mines. The definitive analyses of this figure are in Nash (1978) and Taussig (1979).

6 Actual causes of death are not known for all six. Gladys probably died of starvation.

7 Sucre is the nominal capital of Bolivia, but La Paz is its effective capital. As the cocaine trade flourishes, Santa Cruz increasingly serves as the "real" capital.

8 The Movimiento Nacional Revolucionario, or National Revolutionary Movement, was responsible in 1952 for the only major "revolution" in Bolivian history. It effectively, though not entirely, destroyed the old hacienda system in the rural sector and instituted a land reform. While this revolution did not alter Indian–Hispanic relations, it did alter Indian–*mestizo* relations.

9 One son, over twenty, was completing high school and doing occasional odd jobs in La Paz to gain some income, and aspiring to move to La Paz when I left in 1978. One daughter was also over twenty, had married and moved to La Paz with her husband to find work. The remaining two children were twelve and six years old.

10 A *corregidor* is a prestigious town official who solves disputes and carries out other important village functions.

11 The term *cholo* refers to those Amman and Quechua Indians who are no longer agriculturally subsistence-based but are primarily involved in commercial transactions and, therefore, operate within a cash economy. They buy rather than make their clothes, speak Spanish as well as Aymara or Quechua, and very likely bring their children up to *visidos*, that is, people who wear Western dress, and hence *mestizos*.

12 For an interesting perspective on the image of the devil and its relationships to development and modernization among Bolivian miners as well as among Colombian plantation workers, the reader is referred again to Taussig (1979).

References

Amin, S., *Accumulation on a World Scale: A Critique of the Theory of Underdevelopment*, New York: Monthly Review Press, 1974, vols 1 and 2.

Bolton, R. and E. Mayer (eds), *Andean Kinship and Marriage*, Washington, DC: American Anthropological Association, 1977.

Bryant, J., *Health and the Developing World*. Ithaca: Cornell University Press, 1969.

Carter, W., *The Ambiguity of Reform: Man and the Land in Highland Bolivia*, Columbia University, 1977*a*.

——, *Aymara Communities and the Bolivian Agrarian Reform*, University of Florida Monographs, Social Sciences No. 24, Gainesville: University of Florida Press, 1964.

——, "Trial marriage in the Andes?" In *Andean Kinship and Marriage*, R. Bolton and E. Mayer (eds), Washington DC: American Anthropological Association, 1977*b*.

Cosminsky, S. and M. Scrimshaw, "Medical pluralism on a Guatemalan plantation," *Social Science and Medicine*, 1980, 14B, 267–78.

Cockcroft, J. D., A. G. Frank, and D. L. Johnson, *Dependence and Underdevelopment*, Garden City: Anchor, 1972.

Crankshaw, L., *Changing Faces of the Achachillas: Medical Systems and Cultural Identity in a Highland Bolivian Village*, PhD Dissertation, University of Massachusetts, Amherst, 1980.

Crandon, L., "Between Shamans, doctors and demons: illness, curing and cultural identity midst culture change." In *Third World Medicine and Social Change: A Reader in Medical Sociology*, J. H. Morgan (ed.), Cambridge: Cambridge University Press, 1983.

——, "Medical dialogue and the political economy of medical pluralism: a case from rural highland Bolivia," *American Ethnologist*, 1986, 13(3): 463–76.

Crozier, R., *Traditional Medicine in Modern China*, Cambridge: Harvard University Press, 1968.

——, "Medicine, modernization and culture crisis in China and India," *Comparative Studies in Sociology and History*, 1970, 12(3): 275–91.

Dandler, H. J., *El Sindicalismo Campesino en Bolivia*, Instituto Indigenisita Interamericano, Serie Antropologí a Social, Mexico, 1969, No. 11.

Frake, C. O., "The diagnosis of disease among subanun of Mindanao," *American Anthropologist*, 1961, 63(1): 113–32.

Frank, A. G., *Capitalism and Underdevelopment in Latin America*, New York: Monthly Review Press, 1969.

Gould, H. A., "Modern medicine and folk cognition in rural India," *Human Organization*, 1965, 24: 201–8.

Heath, D. B., "Bolivia: peasant syndicates among the Aymara of the Yungas: a view from the grass roots." In *Latin American Peasant Movements*, H. Landsbereger (ed.), Ithaca: Cornell University Press, 1969.

Hughes, C. C and J. M. Hunter, "Disease and development in Africa," *Social Science and Medicine*, 1970, 3: 443.

Janzen, J. M., *The Quest for Therapy in Lower Zaire*, Berkeley: University of California Press, 1978.

Kelly, J. and H. Klein, *Revolution and the Rebirth of Inequality*, Berkeley: University of California Press, 1981.

Klein, H., *Bolivia: The Revolution of a Multi-Ethnic Society*, New York: Oxford University Press, 1982.

Landy, D., "Role adaptation: traditional curers under the impact of Western medicine," *American Ethnologist*, 1974, 1: 103–7.

Leslie, C., "The professionalization of ayurvedic and unani medicine." In *Medical Men and Their Work: A Sociological Reader*, E. Friedson and J. Lorber (eds), Hawthorne, NY: Aldine de Gruyter, 1972.

—— (ed.), *Asian Medical Systems: A Comparative Study*, Berkeley: University of California Press, 1976.

Logan, M., "Humoral medicine in Guatemala and peasant acceptance of modern medicine," *Human Organization*, 1973, 32(4): 385–95.

Low, S., *Culture, Politics and Medicine in Costa Rica*, Bedford Hills, New York: Redgrave Press, 1985.

Malloy, J. M., *Bolivia: The Uncompleted Revolution*, Pittsburgh: University of Pittsburgh Press, 1970.

Nash, J., *We Eat the Mines and the Mines Eat Us*, New York: Columbia University Press, 1978.

Navarro, V., *Medicine Under Capitalism*, New York: Prodist, 1977.

Oblitas, P., *Cultura Callawaya*, La Paz: Talleres Graficos Bolivianos, 1963.

Read, M., *Culture, Health and Disease: Social and Cultural Influences on Health Programs in Developing Countries*, Philadelphia: Tavistock, 1968.

Rubel, A., "The epidemiology of a folk illness: susto in Hispanic America," *Ethnology*, 1964, 3: 268–83.

Sontag, S., *Illness as Metaphor*, New York: Farrar, Sraus and Giraux, 1978.

Taussig, M., *The Devil and Commodity Fetishism*, Chapel Hill: University of North Carolina Press, 1979.

Turner, V., *Lunda Medicine and the Treatment of Disease*, Occasional Papers of the Rhodesia Livingston Museum, 1963, No. 15.

Unschuld, P., "Comparative Systems of Health Care," *Social Science and Medicine*, 1979, 13A: 523–7.

Warren, K., *Symbolism of Subordination*, Austin: University of Texas Press, 1978.

Woods, C., "Alternative curing strategies in a changing medical situation," *Medical Anthropology*, 1977, 3: 25–54.

Woods, C. M. and T. Greaves, *The Process of Medical Change in a Highland Guatemalan Town*, Los Angeles: Latin American Center, University of California Press, 1973.

Chapter 4

Contributions to a critical analysis of medical pluralism

An examination of the work of Libbet Crandon-Malamud

Hans A. Baer

Since the emergence of medical anthropology as a distinct subdiscipline, many of its practitioners have grappled with the phenomenon of medical pluralism. In contrast to simple preindustrial societies, which tend to have a more-or-less coherent medical system, state societies manifest the coexistence of an array of medical systems, or a pattern of medical pluralism. Although I have had an interest in the political economy of health,[1] critical medical anthropology[2] and medical pluralism[3] for some time prior to my first meeting with Libbet, I had not been aware that she had functioned as one of the precursors of critical medical anthropology, or of her seminal work on medical pluralism. In her characteristic generosity, she gave me a copy of what became her most renowned work – *From the Fat of Our Souls: Social Change, Political Process, and Medical Pluralism in Bolivia*, published by the University of California Press. As I read her book and various essays that she had published prior to its release, I came to realize that Libbet had revolutionized the study of medical pluralism – an accomplishment that unfortunately has been overlooked in the literature on this phenomenon, although it continues to intrigue medical anthropologists.

It is my contention that Libbet's essays, and particularly her book on medical pluralism in the Bolivian *altiplano*, constitute significant contributions to the development of a critical anthropology of medical pluralism. In keeping with the effort of critical medical anthropology to make macro–micro linkages, she examines the connections between the Bolivian political economy – a peripheral nation within the capitalist world system – and the efforts of people in local communities to cope with the health consequences of exploitative practices by drawing upon a variety of medical systems. Within the Bolivian context, she views ethnicity as a product of class conflict, exploitation, resistance, and medicine.

Early anthropological perspectives on medical pluralism

Regardless of their degree of complexity, all medical systems are based upon the dyadic core consisting of a healer and a patient. In complex societies, the medical system – the ensemble of medical beliefs, practices, and social structures – consists of the totality of medical subsystems that coexist in a cooperative or competitive relationship with one another. Much of the early research on medical pluralism focused on the creation of typologies that recognize the existence of this phenomenon in complex societies. Based upon their geographic and cultural settings, Dunn[4] delineated three types of medical systems: (1) local medical systems, (2) regional medical systems, and (3) the cosmopolitan medical system. Local medical systems are "folk" or "indigenous" medical systems of small-scale foraging, horticultural or pastoral societies, or peasant communities in state societies. Regional medical systems are systems distributed over a relatively large area. Examples of regional medical systems include Ayurvedic medicine and Unani medicine in South Asia and traditional Chinese medicine. Cosmopolitan medicine refers to the global medical system or what commonly has been called "scientific medicine," "modern medicine," or "Western medicine." Complex societies generally contain all three of these medical systems. India, for example, has numerous local medical systems associated with its many ethnic groups. In addition to biomedicine, modern Japan has a variety of East Asian medical systems.[5]

Chrisman and Kleinman[6] developed a widely used model that recognized three overlapping sectors in health care systems. The popular sector consists of health care conducted by sick persons themselves, their families, social networks, and communities. Kleinman, who has conducted research in Taiwan, estimates that 70–90 percent of the treatment episodes on that island occur in the popular sector. The folk sector encompasses healers of various sorts who function informally and often on a quasi-legal or sometimes, given local laws, an illegal basis. Examples include herbalists, bonesetters, midwives, mediums, and magicians. The professional sector encompasses the practitioners and bureaucracies of both biomedicine and professionalized heterodox medical systems, such as Ayurvedic and Unani medicine in South Asia and herbal medicine and acupuncture in China. Whereas medical sociologists have tended to focus their attention on the professional sector of health care, medical anthropologists have also given much attention to the folk and popular sectors.

Despite the various classificatory schemes devised by anthropologists recognizing the diversity of medical systems in complex societies, as Brodwin observes, "Before long, however, the study of medical pluralism had reached a theoretical impasse ... Attempts to categorize plural medical systems often produced rigid functionalist typologies or broke down in a welter of incomparable terms."[7] Medical anthropologists turned to concerns such as the political economy of health, biomedical hegemony, alternative medical systems in Western societies, reproduction, the mindful body, and the social dynamics of clinical encounters.

Despite the validity of Brodwin's comments on the shortcomings of much of the research on medical pluralism, not all scholars interested in new theoretical concerns dropped their interest in medical pluralism. Indeed, various anthropologists interested in the political economy of health exhibited an interest in how power relations shaped plural medical systems. As subsequent sections of this essay indicate, Libbet became one of several "critical medical anthropologists" who began to explore processes of competition, co-option, collaboration, and even cooperation that exist within plural medical systems.

Critical medical anthropology understands health issues within the context of encompassing political and economic forces that pattern human relationships, shape social behaviors, condition collective experiences, re-order local ecologies, and situate cultural meanings, including forces of institutional, national, and global scale. The emergence of critical medical anthropology reflects both the turn toward political-economic approaches in anthropology in general as well as an effort to engage and extend the political economy of health approach.[8] Critical medical anthropology seeks to understand who ultimately controls biomedicine and what are the implications of such control. While certain professionalized medical systems, such as homeopathy, Ayurveda, and Chinese medicine, function in many parts of the world, biomedicine constitutes the *world medical system* par excellence. Biomedicine became the preeminent medical system in the world not simply because of its curative efficacy, but as a result of the expansion of the "capitalist world economy."[9] An analysis of the power relations affecting biomedicine addresses questions like: (1) Who has power over the agencies of biomedicine? (2) How and in what forms is this power delegated? (3) How is this power expressed in social relations of the various groups and actors that comprise the health care system? (4) What are the economic, sociopolitical, and ideological ends and consequences of the configuring power relations of biomedicine? and (5) What are the principal contradictions of biomedicine and associated arenas of struggle and resistance that affect the character and functioning of the medical system and people's experience in it?

Critical medical anthropology recognizes that patterns of medical pluralism tend to reflect hierarchical relations in the larger society. Patterns of hierarchy may be based upon class, caste, racial, ethnic, religious, and gender distinctions.[10] Medical pluralism flourishes in all class-divided societies and tends to mirror the wider sphere of class and social relationships. It is perhaps more accurate to say that national medical systems in the modern or postmodern world tend to be "plural" rather than "pluralistic," in that biomedicine enjoys a dominant status over heterodox and ethnomedical practices. In reality, plural medical systems may be described as "dominative" in that one medical system generally enjoys a pre-eminent status *vis-à-vis* other medical systems. The existence of dominative medical systems in complex societies predates capitalism. As Charles Leslie, an anthropologist who has conducted extensive research on South Asian medical systems, observes,

> All the civilizations with *great tradition* medical systems developed a range of practitioners from learned professional physicians to individuals who had limited or no formal training and who practiced a simplified version of the great tradition medicine. Other healers coexisted with these practitioners, their arts falling into special categories such as bone setters, surgeons, midwives, and shamans.[11]

Those physicians who practiced great tradition medicine invariably tended to regard medical practitioners of a humbler social status as either insufficiently trained, incompetent, or out-right charlatans or quacks.

While within the context of a dominative medical system one system attempts to exert, with the support of social elites, dominance over other medical systems, people are quite capable of "dual use" of distinct medical systems. Based upon her research among the Manus in the Admiralty Islands of Melanesia, Lola Romanucci-Ross[12] identifies a "hierarchy of resort" in which many people utilize self-administered folk remedies or consult folk healers before visiting a biomedical clinic or hospital for their ailments. Conversely, while this sequence is the most prevalent one, more-acculturated Manus often rely upon biomedicine initially or first after home remedies; if these two fail, they may finally resort to folk healers.

Medical pluralism in the modern world is characterized by a pattern in which biomedicine exerts dominance over alternative medical systems. With European expansion, allopathic medicine or what eventually became biomedicine came to supercede in prestige and influence even professionalized traditional medical systems. Third World societies are characterized by a broad spectrum of humoral and ritual curing systems. Some of these are associated with literate traditions and have schools, professional associations, and hospitals. Although the upper and middle classes resort to traditional medicine as a backup for the shortcomings of biomedicine and for divination, advice and luck, it constitutes the principal form of health care available to the masses. As Frankenberg observes, "The societies in which medical pluralism flourishes are invariably class divided."[13] India, the most populated country second only to China, is an outstanding example of a complex society exhibiting a dominative medical system. Leslie[14] delineates five levels in the Indian dominative medical system: (1) biomedicine, which relies upon physicians with MD and PhD degrees from prestigious institutions; (2) "indigenous medical systems," which have within their ranks practitioners who have obtained degrees from Ayurvedic, Unani, and Siddha medical colleges; (3) homeopathy, whose physicians have completed correspondence courses; (4) religious scholars or learned priests with unusual healing abilities; and (5) local folk healers, bone-setters, and midwives. Leslie succinctly summarizes the contradictory role that traditional medical systems play in South Asia and elsewhere,

> [Traditional] physicians ... are sometimes painfully aware that cosmopolitan medicine [or biomedicine] dominates the Indian medical system, yet a substantial market exists for commercial Ayurvedic products and for consultations with practitioners. The structural reasons that medical pluralism is a prominent feature of health care throughout the world are that biomedicine, like Ayurveda and every other therapeutic system, fails to help many patients.[15]

The American dominative medical system consists of several levels that tend to reflect class, racial/ethnic, and gender relations in the larger society.[16] In rank order of prestige, these include (1) biomedicine; (2) osteopathic medicine as a parallel medical system focusing on primary care; (3) professionalized heterodox medical systems (namely, chiropractic, naturopathy, and acupuncture); (4) partially professionalized or lay heterodox medical systems (e.g. homeopathy, herbalism, reflexology, massage therapy, and Rolfing); (5) Anglo-American religious healing systems (e.g. Spiritualism, Seventh Day Adventism, Christian Science, Unity, and Pentecostalism); and (6) folk medical systems (e.g. Southern Applachian herbal medicine; African-American folk medicine; Latino folk medical systems such as *curanderismo, espiritismo, and santeria*, and Native American healing systems). As a result of the financial backing of initially, corporate-sponsored foundations, and later the federal government for its research activities and educational institutions, biomedicine asserted scientific superiority and clearly established hegemony over alternative medical systems.

Nevertheless, biomedicine's dominance over rival medical systems has never been absolute. The state, which primarily serves the interests of the corporate class in advanced capitalist societies, must periodically make concessions to subordinate social groups in the interests of maintaining social order and economic productivity. As a result, certain heterodox practitioners, with the backing of clients and particularly influential patrons, were able to obtain legitimation in the form of full practice rights (e.g. osteopathic physicians, who may prescribe drugs and perform the same medical procedures as biomedical physicians) or limited rights (e.g. chiropractors, naturopaths, and acupuncturists). Lower social classes, racial and ethnic minorities, and women who have often utilized alternative medicine as a forum for challenging not only biomedical dominance but also, to a degree, the hegemony of the corporate class in the United States as well as other advanced capitalist societies.

The setting of Libbet's fieldwork in the Bolivian altiplano

Libbet examined power relations embedded in the Bolivian dominative medical system in a rural town on the altiplano. She conducted fieldwork in Kachitu between 1976 and 1978. Libbet referred to the town as "Kachitu" because William Carter adopted this pseudonym for the town when he wrote his master's thesis at Columbia University about the same community. Her daughter, Anna, lived with Libbet over the course of the fieldwork as well as a five-month stay in La Paz. My description of Kachitu refers to Libbet's ethnographic present – namely the period of her fieldwork there.

Kachitu is the center or *municipio* for canton consisting of some 16,000 Aymara Indians dispersed over thirty-six *communidades*. It is situated at about a 13,000 feet elevation and lies several miles from Lake Titicaca. The town proper has a population of about 1,000 people consisting of three ethnoreligious groups: (1) Aymara *campesinos*, (2) the Methodist Aymara or *Evangelicos*, and (3) Catholic *mestizos*. Both *mestizos* and Methodist Aymara claim to reject Aymara medicine. The *mestizos* constitute about one-third of the town's population. Prior to the revolution of 1952 and subsequent land reform, the *mestizos* supervised the Aymara for the national elites who generally resided in La Paz and other cities. Since the revolution, the *mestizos* have been seeking to avoid poverty in a shrinking economy. The *mestizos* are a socially fragmented ethnic category, which includes teachers, small shopkeepers, as well as poor people who work as occasional agricultural laborers.

About another third of Kachitu consists of Aymara *campesinos* or land-based peasants. Prior to 1952, they lived in Indian communities that were heavily taxed or on *haciendas*. Some Aymara were miners and performed personal services. Many *campesinos* migrated to Kachitu from the *haciendas* upon acquiring land through fictive ties with *mestizos*. Following the revolution and land reform, others moved to town and claimed land on the outskirts that had been confiscated from the *mestizos*. A few Aymara are active in the *campesino* movement which attempts to confront the state.

The Methodist Aymara constitute the final third of Kachitu's population. They are the converts or descendants of converts to the Methodist church which established a mission in the early 1930s. The Methodist Aymara were in Methodist mission schools and became entrepreneurs who took over local administrative and political offices when the revolutionary government threw the rural *mestizos* out. They presently function as the economic and political backbone of Kachitu.

While the 1952 revolution made many promises, in essence, it benefitted a few, impoverished others, confused ethnic identity, and contributed to class distinctions. Libbet described ethnic dynamics, at the time of her fieldwork, in the following terms:

> By the late 1970s, as social divisions multiplied, the content, meaning, and significance of mestizoness, Aymara Indianness, Catholicism, and membership in the Methodist church were being culturally redefined within an environment of political and economic instability and radically changing social relations. The resulting confusion left Kachitu, and throughout the altiplano, resources are scarcer than they have ever been in Bolivian history. Inflation in 1985 reached the highest known inflation rate in recorded history of the world outside of a war economy, with the exception of the Weimar Republic, until Argentina and Nicaragua threatened to surpass it: 25,000 percent in 1982.[17]

The literary style of and themes in Libbet's work on medical pluralism

Based upon fieldwork in 1978, Libbet wrote six essays in the form of book chapters or articles that were published between 1983 and 1991. *From the Fat of Our Souls* incorporates some of the material and arguments that Libbet presented in these essays touching upon medical pluralism in Kachitu. In contrast to her earlier articles and book chapters, Libbet provides readers with a much more holistic, dynamic, literary, and critical analysis of medical pluralism on the Bolivian altiplano in her book. As anyone who has written a book knows, this format of writing allows the author to explore the subtlety and nuances of his or her topic of interest more than an article or book chapter can permit.

Libbet forewarns readers that she is going to engage in a partially interpretive account filled with "thick description" of the Geertzian genre by noting in her preface that her book focuses on "opinions, rumors, gossip, and strategies concerning illness and health care, among and between Bolivian Aymara and *mestizos*, Catholic and Methodists, in Kachitu."[18] Like many other Latin Americanists, such as Rasnake[19] who examine relations between the Quechua-speakers and *vecinos* (*mestizos*) in the Bolivian town of Yura, she tends to conflate class and ethnicity and implicitly draws upon van den Berghe and Primov's concept of "ethno-class."[20] At any rate, by "wallowing in the data," ethnographers like Libbet have been able to discern the subtle nuances of social life in local communities that demonstrate how ethnicity can serve as a strategy for obtaining scarce resources, including medical ones.

Both Lynn Morgan[21] in her book review and Arthur Kleinman[22] refer to Libbet's book as an example of the "new ethnography." In keeping with the depiction of the new ethnography – a reflexive and literary endeavor which produces a text that entails a dialogic relationship between the ethnographer and his or her subjects, Libbet introduces readers to the cast of characters in her ethnography – one consisting of eight professionals (four of whom are physicians), thirty *mestizos*, seventeen Aymara, and thirteen Methodist Aymara. As Gruenbaum observes, "Crandon-Malamud's poignant and self-reflective descriptions make fascinating reading, infused as they are with the humorous and embarrassing moments which are usually reserved for private telling – the anecdotes anthropologists use for comic relief in lectures or conversations around hor-d'oeuvres."[23] Unlike Geertz and other symbolic anthropologists, however, she specifies that her book is "not about medical symbols or healing per se,"[24] but rather about the historical context of medical ideologies and how they define ethnic identity. Indeed, Libbet tends to see a conflation of ethnicity with social class. She maintains that "Aymara-ness," "mestizo-ness," and even Methodist religious identity constitute "masks for social class."[25]

At any rate, in the remainder of this section, I discuss three themes in Libbet's six essays and book on medical pluralism in Kachitu. These are: (1) culture-bound syndromes that affect both Aymara and *Mestizos*; (2) the impact of modernization on health care in Kachitu; and (3) the utilization of multiple medical systems in the community.

Culture-bound syndromes

In "Why *Susto*,"[26] Libbet examines *susto* – a culture-bound syndrome common to much of Latin America and among Mexican Americans – that has vexed numerous medical anthropologists.[27] Much of the research on *susto* recognizes that it emanates from stressful social conditions, an inability to carry out role expectations, and even the stigma of Indian ethnic identity. While recognizing some merit to theories that posit an organic basis for *susto* ("fright"), she argues that her fieldwork in Kachitu suggests that the "study of *susto's* diagnosis as a social process may significantly affect the study of its cause."[28] Libbet reports that, historically, *susto* is the "second highest cause of death of infants under age one for the village as a whole, and it occurs among all three cultural groups."[29] Conversely, she discovered that "the incidents of *susto* that occurred within the village during the time between 1970 and 1978 in adults over thirteen (an arbitrary cut-off date; the youngest case was about twenty) occurred primarily among male and female *mestizos*).[30] Libbet delineates five domains of medical resources utilized by Kachitu residents depending upon the diagnosis: Aymara home care, shamanistic or *yatiri* care, *mestizo* folk home care, biomedical clinical care, and hospital care in La Paz. The *mestizo* adults were treated for *susto* by *yatiris*. Libbet asserts the *susto* refers to a "variety of pathological disorders that differ in children and infants, and adults."[31] She contends a diagnosis of *susto* says more about the victim than it does about the actual pathology.

> *Susto* illness indicates that the illness lies within the supernatural domain, and hence within the world of the *curandero*, shaman, *yatiri*, and home care, and not the world of physicians, drugs, money exchange, clinics, and hospitals ... *Susto* says that the victim, be it child or adult, is spiritually vulnerable, susceptible to personal deprivation, and will be given familial care to provide the support for personal strength and rehabilitation, not the larger community's support.[32]

In Kachitu, *susto* is associated with infants and children (who invariably find themselves vulnerable in rural areas in Third World countries) and adults exhibiting "affinity with Indianness and its opposition to cosmopolitanness."[33] As we have already seen, many *mestizo* adults in Kachitu experienced downward mobility in the aftermath of the revolution of 1952. Susto appears not only to have an ethnic flavor but also a class in that, according to Libbet, "wealthier populations in Latin America ... do not suffer as much."[34] Ironically, when nearly twenty years ago I asked a medical anthropologist who is renowned for his expertise on Latin American conceptions of health and illness whether *susto* might not have a class-basis, he replied: "Don't be so narrow, Hans!" In retrospect, I feel that Libbet vindicated my hunch by demonstrating how poor and marginalized peoples are more susceptible to it than are those who are relatively affluent and integrated into their communities. Indeed, in a recent overview of various studies that have been done on *susto*, including Libbet's work, Mysyk concludes that "*susto* victims are primarily poor peasants and landless laborers, the working poor, and the downwardly-mobile."[35]

In "Medical Dialogue and the Political Economy of Medical Pluralism: A Case from Rural Highland Bolivia,"[36] Libbet examines two fatal Indian illnesses – namely *karisiri* and *limpu* – as manifestations of a medical dialogue that expresses the political and economic realities and the symbolism of ethnic relations in the Bolivian *altiplano*. According to a myth found among both the Aymara and the Quechua, the soul of a deceased Jesuit priest called *karisiri* steals fat from Indians' kidneys so that the bishop can make holy oil. A later version of the myth depicts the *karisiri* selling that fat as oil to North Americans who use it to generate electricity. A third version of the myth – one adhered to by both Indians and *mestizos* – views *karisiri* as the practice in which certain village *mestizos* sell the fat to pharmacies in La Paz or to factories that make perfumed luxury soaps for European and North American markets. Libbet views the *karisiri* myth as an example of medicine as metaphor for social relations and that the changes in its interpretation as reflections of changes in "political economy, in ethnic affiliation with the economy, and in the effects of that political economy on the very content of ethnic identity."[37] Libbet also interprets *limpu* – a condition caused by witnessing an Indian stillbirth – in a similar vein:

> [The] aetiology of *limpu* is a statement of Indian identity that ... differentiates Indian oppression from non-Indian or *mestizo* oppression and points to their unequal access to resources. *Mestizos* never cause *limpu* – because they do not live like or are not Indians – nor get it – because they never Indian myths.[38]

As these two examples illustrate, medical dialogue serves as an idiom by which a person defines his or her ethnic identity within the larger context of the Bolivian society – one which is characterized by frequent economic crises, unstable governments, and military coups. This larger context serves to maintain and even elaborate upon patterns of medical pluralism. As we have seen in her earlier essays, *mestizos* who find themselves downwardly mobile within the constantly shifting Bolivian political economy may in essence gain access to greater health care by turning to Indian indigenous medicine – an irony that flies in the face of "both modernization theory and standard medical anthropological wisdom."[39]

Impact of modernization on health care on Kachitu

In "Grass Roots, Herbs, Promoter and Preventions: A Re-Evaluation of Contemporary International Health Care Planning. The Bolivian Case," Libbet[40] provides insights into the interface between the two major components of the Bolivian dominative medical system – namely biomedicine and Aymara indigenous medicine. She does so in the course of evaluating a United States Agency for International Development Pilot Health Project which was implemented in the Montero district of Bolivia in 1975 but was terminated in 1980 purportedly due to a political coup. The pilot project called for the creation of community health committees and the position of a community-elected health promoter whose activities were to be supervised by an auxiliary nurse, an emphasis on preventive medicine, and the promotion of indigenous medicine. Despite the best of intentions, Libbet argues that the pilot project ultimately failed and inadvertently contributed to the deterioration of rural health because USAID failed to take into account the Bolivian national elite's hierarchical conception of community – one that was drastically in conflict with the relatively egalitarian notions of community to which Aymara adhered.

Indeed, Bolivia consists of many different types of communities which reflect class and racial/ethnic relations in the larger society. The elite class adheres to a Hispanic colonial tradition, despite the fact that its members are not entirely of Hispanic descent, monopolizes economic resources and political power, and is "the group which directly articulates with the world system."[41] Europeans and Asians have formed immigrant communities, particularly in the lowland areas. Libbet reports that *mestizos* constitute 25 percent of the total Bolivian population and historically have served as an intermediary class between the elites and the Indians. *Cholos* are Indians who function within the modern market economy. Libbet reports that the Aymara and Quechua, who make up 65 percent of the population, reside on ex-*haciendas* and in free Indian communities or *comunidades*, *Indian–mestizo* villages on the *altiplano*, and ethnically heterogenous mining communities.

Libbet maintains that the aims of the health project were most successfully achieved in the ethnically homogeneous and isolated Indian communities in the Montero district. In other communities, however, the national elite's definition of community relations – one based upon notions of *compadrazgo* and *personalismo* – permits health care programs to be manipulated by prestigious local peasant elites, by ambitious national elites, and unwittingly by USAID itself. Indeed, the vast majority of USAID funds supported the higher administrative levels of the Bolivian biomedical bureaucracy. Local rural elites tended to dominate committees as a means of serving their own interests and articulating with the national elite. Villagers were reluctant to hold offices on the health committees because they fear that their actions may be held against them once a new regime assumes power – a distinct possibility in a country which had nine different governments between 1978 and 1982. Although the project's health promoter was expected to become familiar with indigenous medicine, in contrast to rurally-based physicians and nurses, it was "relegated to the least prestigious rung in the medical hierarchy, thus increasing the gap between indigenous medicine and scientific medicine, and again creating the opposite of what project planners envisioned."[42]

In "Changing Times and Changing Symptoms: The Effects of Modernization on *Mestizo* Medicine in Rural Bolivia (The Case of Two *Mestizo* Sisters),"[43] Libbet examines a case of two *mestizo* sisters – Gladys and Marisol – who abandoned biomedicine for Aymara medicine. The two sisters began to suffer from psychosomatic disorders as they reached adulthood in the 1970s. They were both adversely affected by the political-economic changes that resulted in downward social mobility of much of the *mestizo* population of Katichu. In order to improve her socioeconomic status, Gladys underwent training as a school teacher and received an assignment in a remote Aymara community – an experience that she found very stressful. Following the devastation of rejection by her fiancé, she spent six months in a psychiatric institute in La Paz. Gladys's mother decided to take her home after her condition failed to improve. Unfortunately, Gladys refused to leave the house, eventually to get out of bed or eat, and died a year later.

At the age of sixteen, Marisol became romantically involved with a Peace Corps volunteer some twenty years older than her. He convinced her to move to the United States, ostensibly so that she could further her education. Following a year in the United States, Marisol returned home and hoped that her North American boyfriend would follow her back to Bolivia, or take her back to New York City. Her family attempted to pressure her into marrying a young *cholo*. Unfortunately, Marisol became sick a week before the wedding. With encouragement from Marisol's mother, her fiancé took her to a *yatiri* who successfully treated her condition. In contrast to Gladys who only underwent biomedical treatment, her younger sister's health improved after turning to Aymara medicine. In conclusion, Libbet asserts that "Marisol's acquiescence to an Aymara medical universe, and her mother's rejection of the Western scientific one, parallel their relationship to Bolivian society at large as well as the process of modernization that has affected their lives over the previous twenty-five years."[44] Again, we see how redefining one's ethnic identity provides certain residents of Kachitu with medical resources.

The utilization of multiple medical systems in Kachitu

In "Between Shamans, Doctors and Demons: Illness, Curing and Cultural Identity Midst Culture Change," Libbet proposes that "[s]imultaneous use of several medical traditions permits a dialogue about cultural identity to take place without directly addressing cultural identity itself, which is often too sensitive a topic to be addressed directly."[45] In order to examine her thesis, she presents a case study of Gonzalo, a twenty-two-year-old *mestizo* male who insisted that he had contracted an Aymara form of insanity caused by the loss of one of his three souls (the *alma*, the *ajayu*, and *animu*) to a demon. The first soul remains in the body of a Hispanic until death. The second soul can be stolen or eaten by malevolent spirits, resulting in irrational thinking, serious illness, and death. The third soul can be lost by both children and adults and results in a very serious, often fatal, illness.

At any rate, although two Aymara shamans or *yatiris* attended to him, neither one of them completed their cures. Gonzalo's illness had been preceded recently by four other cases in which the victims, all of whom died, had exhibited a similar socioeconomic background, age, type of illness, and absence of shamanistic cure. His family, as well as the families of the other victims, were the "cream of the prominent members of the local rural *mestizo* population who served in the countryside the interests of the Bolivian elites, by managing the local Aymara

Indian population."[46] In the wake of the MNR (*Movimiento Nacionalista Revolucionaria* or Nationalist Revolutionary Movement) revolution of 1952 and the subsequent land reform of 1953 which provided the Aymara with arms, sufferage, land, and the right to a minimum wage, many *mestizos*, including the families of Gonzalo and the other four victims, lost their privileged status. Don Magno, Gonzalo's father, died of alcoholism, and Hermana, Gonzalo's mother, became a drunken beggar. Gonzalo tried to make a living as a cook in Santa Cruz, a provincial city, but experienced discrimination because of his dark skin, thus prompting him to return home. Unfortunately, he soon found himself thrust into a marginal status there because he lacked a viable livelihood and had no immediate family who could provide for him. Unfortunately, unlike various other downwardly mobile *mestizos*, Gonzalo was unable to translate his effort to assume an aspect of Aymara cultural identity into social support from the Aymara community. The two shamans whom he consulted ultimately did not treat him because they did not perceive him as part of their world. Conversely, other *mestizos* succeeded in mobilizing assistance from Aymara villagers in their efforts to use medicine as a "particularly effective medium through which to negotiate cultural identity."[47] They took on new identities in terms of social mannerisms, views of disease, and dress. At any rate, Libbet concludes that the two *yatiris* refused to complete their cures of Gonzalo because he no longer occupied a "rightful position" as an Indian within the redefined social structure of Kachitu. As Libbet observes, "there is no place"[48] for a *mestizo* who inherited the ideology of a dying social system order and is blocked in all his attempts to fit into a new one. Thus, Gonzalo's fate was to exist on the periphery of Kachitu as a marginalized *mestizo* like others who are viewed as "filthy," "drunk," and "lazy."

From the Fat of Our Souls[49] constitutes the culmination of Libbet's examination of the utilization of multiple medical systems in Kachitu. In contrast to most ethnographers who describe the setting of their fieldwork in the introduction of their monographs, Libbet begins her text with a narrative that examines how Dr Sabas (a biomedical physician), Reverend Angel (a Catholic-born *mestizo* Methodist minister), and several Aymara responded to the symptoms presented by Seferino, a Methodist Aymara peasant. Dr Sabas initially diagnosed Serfino's condition as pneumonia, then tuberculosis, and eventually admitted to being unable to detect any disease, other than anemia, for which he prescribed intensive treatment in the local hospital. As a last resort, Serfino somewhat skeptically acts upon the belief of various Aymara acquaintances that the *khan achaci* – a "phantom" who feeds on meat and alcohol and other gifts it demands of its victims – is the source of his sickness. Rather than attempting to appease the *khan achachi*, Serfino dynamited its altar with the hope that this act would eradicate his ritual obligations – a strategy that apparently worked since he recovered from his illness. Despite Serfino's concession to Aymara medical belief, Reverend Angel continued to visit and pray for his parishioner. Cases like that of Serfino prompted Sabas to promote changes in hospital policy that paved the way for greater interaction and collaboration between *yatiris* and biomedical personnel and also induced Angel to incorporate more and more Aymara belief into Methodist doctrine. Libbet's introductory case study sets the stage for a more detailed examination of the ways in which Kachitu villagers employ medical discourse in establishing their ethnic identity and obtaining the material resources necessary to making life in an underdeveloped country bearable.

The first four chapters of the book set the stage for Libbet's critical-interpretive analysis of medical pluralism in Kachitu. In addition to discussing her research methodology, she examines four themes that permeate the dialogue about medical etiology and diagnosis in Kachitu: pervasive hunger, subordination, victimization, and exploitation. Libbet situates these four themes within the context of the Bolivian political economy. The first one – that of race – differentiates the purportedly white elites from *mestizos* and Indians as a means to justify unequal access to the political process; the second one entails the economic system that exploits Indian labor; the third one consists of *caudillo* political structures that suppress dissent on the part of rural *mestizos* and Indians; and the fourth one is the conflict that exists between *mestizos* and Indians.[50]

Libbet discusses the evolution of a series of "entrenched institutions" and how each of them shaped ethnic/class relations in Bolivia. These include colonialism, the hacienda system, tin production, and the complex of "new caudillos and dictators" following the Revolution of 1952. In responding to pressures from Washington, the Nationalist Revolutionary Movement adopted a state capitalist stance and shifted its strategy for economic development to the lowlands in terms of agriculture and oil production. In the process, the *altiplano* became the periphery of the Bolivian economy. Libbet maintains that Kachitu is an "ecological zone" that became economically dependent on three other regions, namely (1) the Lake Titicaca basin with its teeming supply of fish, many of which in turn carry tapeworms; (2) the upland puna with its pasture lands and small tin mining operations; and (3) the remote eastern slopes and valleys with their rich agricultural lands.

The remaining eight chapters of the book examine the intricate ways that residents of Kachitu utilize the local plural medical system for purposes of establishing their sense of cultural identity and obtaining the few resources available to them. As Libbet argues, Kachitunos utilize medical dialogue and curative strategies in order to "make alliances, disassociate themselves from others, exchange resources, and try to forge new identities that will open opportunities and improve their lives under conditions of extreme and seemingly unrelenting national economic contraction, regional peripheralization, and local marginalization."[51] Contrary to the wishes of biomedical practitioners and indigenous healers, decisions concerning illness etiology and diagnosis tend to be made primarily by patients themselves, their families, and other interested parties. Biomedical physicians who practice in Kachitu must abandon many of their preconceptions and adapt themselves to the local medical belief systems if they expect to establish rapport with their patients. The three medical ideologies in Kachitu function as options that address different types of ailments. As Libbet observes, "All things being equal, if one has tuberculosis, one goes to the physician in the Methodist clinic; if one suffers from *khan achachi*, one goes to the *yatiri*; if one has a stomach upset, one resorts to *medicinas caseras*."[52] As anthropologists have found to be the case worldwide, Kachitunos, regardless of their social standing, tend to be pragmatists rather than therapeutic purists when it comes to seeking medical treatment. Libbet argues that they employ medical dialogue as a mechanism of empowerment in the face of external hegemonic forces, including that of biomedicine. Unfortunately, this medical dialogue has served as a rather limited form of empowerment and in reality more as a coping mechanism within the larger context of the Bolivian political economy.

Indeed, health services in Bolivia underwent a serious decline during the 1980s. According to Morales, "The infant mortality rate was now the highest in all of Latin America, given the national average of more than 200 per 1,000 live births in 1985 and as many as 650 per 1,000 in some rural areas, compared to 150 per 1,000 in 1975: 50 percent of children between one and six years of age were malnourished; and 60 percent of school-aged children suffered from goiter and 45 percent from anemia as a result of iodine and iron deficiencies, respectively."[53] Cuts in government spending contributed to a lack of potable water in 65 percent of urban households. Elsewhere, Klein reports, "[L]ife expectancy at birth over the past three decades has only risen some five years, or from the mid-forties to fifty years of age. But this is still some twenty years from that of the more advanced Latin American societies."[54]

In large part, much of Bolivia's health problems and other socioeconomic problems emanate from a national social structure, in which "the wealthiest 5 percent control 39 percent of the national income and the poorest 20 percent, only 2 percent,"[55] and its peripheral status within the capitalist world system. Bolivia, along with Haiti, constitutes one of the poorest countries in the Western hemisphere. According to Klein, despite heavy state investments in health care and education, the "continuing poor performance of the economy has meant that the indices of health and welfare remain among the lowest in the Americas."[56] The ruined Bolivian economy has either forced many Bolivian peasants to revert to barter as the only means of economic exchange or to turn to coca production for the international cocaine market. Indeed, Bolivian peasants account for approximately one-third of the world's drug production.

Libbet's research on medical pluralism as part of a larger effort to understand power relations in dominative medical systems

Libbet's research on medical pluralism in Kachitu became part and parcel of the interest in power relations that became increasingly popular, particularly among critical medical anthropologists, in the late 1980s and 1990s. While within the context of complex societies, one medical system tends to exert, with the support of strategic social elites, dominance over other medical systems. People are quite capable of "dual use" of distinct medical systems. Just as Romanucci-Ross[57] found this to be the case among the Manus in the Admiralty Islands of Melanesia, Libbet observed the same pattern among Kachitunos in the Bolivian *altiplano*. More recently, Brodwin[58] describes how the villagers of Jeanty in Haiti negotiate between different healers and competing therapeutic systems – namely bio-medicine, Catholicism, *vodun*, and Pentecostalism. Libbet's research on such negotiations in Kachitu conforms to Stoner's assertion that "[p]luralism can now be examined as a multiplicity of healing techniques, rather than of medical systems."[59]

As Libbet's research indicates to be the case in Kachitu, biomedicine's dominance over rival medical systems or ideologies has never been absolute. Subaltern groups, including lower social classes, racial and ethnic minorities, and women, have often utilized and continue to utilize alternative medical systems as a forum for challenging not only biomedical dominance but also, to a degree, the hegemony of ruling groups throughout the world. As undoubtedly Libbet herself would readily admit, medical pluralism in Kachitu constitutes one of many microcosms of the Bolivian dominative medical system – a national system that includes a diversity of biomedical practitioners (such as physicians, nurses, and vaccinators), herbalists, midwives, and indigenous healers.[60] Libbet's research in a remote Andean village constitutes both a seminal work in critical medical anthropology in that it attempts to make global–local linkages and a pioneering effort in a "processual and practice-based approach to medical pluralism."[61]

Notes

1 Hans A. Baer, "On the political economy of health," *Medical Anthropology Newsletter*, 1982, 14(1): 1–2, 13–17.
2 Hans A. Baer, Merrill Singer, and John Johnsen (eds), *Towards a Critical Medical Anthropology*. Special Issue of *Social Science and Medicine*, 1986, 23(2); Merrill Singer, Hans A. Baer, and Ellen Lazarus (eds), *Critical Medical Anthropology: Theory and Research*. Special issue of *Social Science and Medicine*, 1990, 30(2); Merrill Singer and Hans A. Baer, *Critical Medical Anthropology*, Baywood Press, 1995; Hans A. Baer, Merrill Singer, and Ida Susser, *Medical Anthropology and the World System: A Critical Perspective*, Bergin & Garvey, 1997.
3 Hans A. Baer, "Prophets and advisors in black spiritual churches: therapy, palliative, or opiate?," *Culture, Medicine, and Psychiatry*, 1981, 5: 145–70; Hans A. Baer, "The organizational rejuvenation of osteopathy: a reflection of the decline of professional dominance in medicine," *Social Science and Medicine*, 1981, 15A: 701–12; Hans A. Baer, "The American dominative medical system as a reflection of social relations in the larger society," *Social Science and Medicine*, 1989, 28(11): 1103–12.
4 Fredrick Dunn, "Traditional Asian medicine and cosmopolitan medicine in adaptive systems." In *Asian Medical Systems: A Comparative Study*, Charles Leslie (ed.), University of California Press, 1976, pp. 133–58.
5 Margaret Lock, *East Asian Medicine in Urban Japan*, University of California Press, 1980.
6 Noel J. Chrisman and Arthur Kleinman, "Popular health care, social networks, and cultural meanings: the orientation of medical anthropology." In *Handbook of Health, Health Care, and Health Professions*, David Mechanic (ed.), Free Press, 1983, pp. 569–90.

7   Paul Brodwin, *Medicine and Morality in Haiti: The Contest for Healing Power*, Cambridge University Press, 1996.
8   Baer and Singer, *Critical Medical Anthropology*; Soheir Morsy, "Political economy in medical anthropology." In *Medical Anthropology: Contemporary Theory and Method*, Carolyn F. Sargent and Thomas M. Johnson (eds), Praeger, 1996, pp. 21–40; Baer, Singer, and Susser, *Medical Anthropology and the World System*.
9   Immanuel Wallerstein, *The Capitalist World System*, Cambridge University Press, 1979; Ray H. Elling, "The capitalist world-system and international health," *International Journal of Health Services*, 1981, 11: 21–51.
10 Baer, "The American dominative medical system as a reflection of social relations in the larger society," 1989, pp. 1103–12.
11 Charles Leslie, "The modernization of Asian medical systems." In *Rethinking Modernization*, John Poggie, Jr. and Robert N. Lynch (eds), Greenwood Press, 1974, p. 74.
12 Lola Romanucci-Ross, "The hierarchy of resort in curative practices: the admirality islands." In *Culture, Disease, and Healing: Studies in Medical Anthropology*, David Landy (ed.), Macmillan, 1977, 1989, pp. 481–7.
13 Ronald Frankenberg, "Allopathic medicine, profession, and capitalist ideology in India," *Social Science and Medicine*, 1981, 15A: 198.
14 Charles Leslie, "Medical pluralism and legitimation in the Indian and Chinese medical systems." In *Culture, Disease, and Healing: Studies in Medical Anthropology*, David Landy (ed.), Macmillan, 1977, pp. 511–17.
15 Charles Leslie and Allan Young, "Introduction." In *Paths to Asian Medical Knowledge*, Charles Leslie and Allan Young (eds), University of California Press, 1992, p. 2.
16 Baer, "The American dominative medical system as a reflection of social relations in the larger society," pp. 1103–12.
17 Libbet Crandon-Malamud, *From the Fat of Our Souls: Social Change, Political Process, and Medical Pluralism in Bolivia*, University of California Press, 1991, pp. 19–20.
18 Crandon-Malamud, *From the Fat of Our Souls*, p. ix.
19 Roger Neil Rasnake, *Domination and Cultural Resistance: Authority and Power among an Andean People*, Duke University Press, 1988.
20 Pierre van den Berghe and George Primov, *Inequality in the Peruvian Andes: Class and Ethnicity in Cuzco*, Columbia University Press, 1977.
21 Lynn M. Morgan, Review of *From the Fat of Our Souls*, *Medical Anthropology Quarterly*, 1992, 6: 75–7.
22 Arthur Kleinman, *Writing in the Margin: Discourse Between Anthropology and Medicine*, University of California Press, 1995, pp. 193–201.
23 Ellen Gruenbaum, "Positioning medical anthropology's audience," *Reviews in Anthropology*, 1994, 23: 261–2.
24 Crandon-Malamud, *From the Fat of Our Souls*, p. ix.
25 Crandon-Malamud, *From the Fat of Our Souls*, p. x.
26 Libbet Crandon-Malamud, "Why *susto*," *Ethnology*, 1983, 22: 153–67.
27 Ralph Bolton, "*Susto*, hostility, and hypoglycemia," *Ethnology* 1981, 20: 261–76; Janice Klein, "*Susto*: the anthropological study of diseases of adaptation," *Social Science and Medicine*, 1978, 12: 23–8; Arthur J. Rubel, Carol W. O'Nell, and Rolando Collado-Ardon, *Susto, A Folk Illness*, University of California Press, 1984.
28 Crandon-Malamud, "Why *Susto*," p. 154.
29 Crandon-Malamud, "Why *Susto*," p. 156.
30 Crandon-Malamud, "Why *Susto*," p. 156.
31 Crandon-Malamud, "Why *Susto*," p. 161.
32 Crandon-Malamud, "Why *Susto*," p. 164.
33 Crandon-Malamud, "Why *Susto*," p. 165.

34 Crandon-Malamud, "Why *Susto*," p. 165.
35 Avis Mysyk, "*Susto:* an illness of the poor," *Dialectical Anthropology*, 1998, 23: 187–202.
36 Libbet Crandon-Malamud, "Medical dialogue and the political economy of medical pluralism: a case from rural highland Bolivia," *American Ethnology*, 1986, 13: 463–76. Libbet's essay "Phantoms and physicians: social change through medical pluralism" that appears in *The Anthropology of Medicine: From Culture to Method*, Lola Romanucci-Ross, Daniel E. Moerman, and Laurence R. Tancredi (eds), Bergin & Garvey Publishers, 1991, pp. 85–112, is an expanded version of this article and incorporates text from *From the Fat of Our Souls*.
37 Crandon-Malamud, "Medical dialogue," p. 464.
38 Crandon-Malamud, "Medical dialogue," p. 465.
39 Crandon-Malamud, "Medical dialogue," p. 472.
40 Libbet Crandon-Malamud, "Grass roots, herbs, promoters and preventions: a re-evaluation of contemporary health care planning. The Bolivian case," *Social Science and Medicine*, 1983, 17: 1281–9.
41 Crandon-Malamud, "Grass roots, herbs, promoters, and preventions," p. 1283.
42 Crandon-Malamud, "Grass roots, herbs, promoters, and preventions," p. 1286.
43 Libbet Crandon-Malamud, "Changing times and changing symptoms: the effects of modernization on mestizo medicine in rural Bolivia (the case of two sisters)," *Medical Anthropology*, 1989, 10: 255–64.
44 Crandon-Malamud, "Changing times," p. 262.
45 Crandon-Malamud, "Between shamans, doctors, and demons," p. 70.
46 Crandon-Malamud, "Between shamans, doctors, and demons," p. 73.
47 Crandon-Malamud, "Between shamans, doctors, and demons," p. 75.
48 Crandon-Malamud, "Between shamans, doctors, and demons," p. 78.
49 Libbet Crandon-Malamud, *From the Fat of Our Souls: Social Changes, Political Process, and Medical Pluralism in Bolivia*, University of California Press, 1991.
50 Crandon-Malamud, *From the Fat of Our Souls*, pp. 46–47.
51 Crandon-Malamud, *From the Fat of Our Souls*, pp. 138.
52 Crandon-Malamud, *From the Fat of Our Souls*, pp. 202–3.
53 Waltraud Queiser Morales, *Bolivia: Land of Struggle*, Westview Press, 1992, p. 135.
54 Herbert S. Klein, *Bolivia: The Evolution of a Multi-Ethnic Society*, Oxford University Press, 1992, p. 280.
55 Morales, *Bolivia*, p. 203.
56 Klein, *Bolivia*, p. 279.
57 Romanucci-Ross, "The hierarchy of resort in curative practices," pp. 481–7.
58 Brodwin, *Medicine and Morality in Haiti*.
59 Brad Stoner, "Understanding medical systems: traditional, modern, and syncretic health care alternatives in medically pluralistic societies," *Medical Anthropology Quarterly*, 1986, 17(2): 47.
60 Joseph W. Bastien, *Drum and Stethoscope: Integrating Ethnomedicine and Biomedicine in Bolivia*, University of Utah Press, 1992.
61 Brodwin, *Medicine and Morality in Haiti*, p. 201.

References

Baer, Hans A., "Prophets and advisors in black spiritual churches: therapy, palliative, or opiate," *Culture, Medicine, and Psychiatry*, 1981, 5: 145–70.
——, "The organization rejuvenation of osteopathy: a reflection of the decline of professional dominance in medicine," *Social Science and Medicine*, 1981, 15a: 701–12.

——, "On the political economy of health," *Medical Anthropology Newsletter*, 1986, 14: 1–2, 13–17.

——, "The American dominative medical system as a reflection of social relations in the larger society," *Social Science and Medicine*, 1989, 28: 1103–12.

——, Merrill Singer, and Ida Susser, *Medical Anthropology and the World System: A Critical Perspective*, Bergin & Garvey, 1997.

Bastien, Jospeh W., *Drum and Stethoscope: Integrating Ethnomedicine and Biomedicine in Bolivia*, University of Utah Press, 1992.

Bolton, Ralph, "*Susto*, hostility, and hypoglycemia," *Ethnology*, 1981, 20: 261–76.

Brodwin, Paul, *Medicine and Morality in Haiti: The Contest for Healing Power*, Cambridge University Press, 1996.

Chrisman, Noel J. and Arthur Kleinman, "Popular health care, social networks, and cultural meanings: the orientation of medical anthropology." In *Handbook of Health, Health Care, and Health Professions*, David Mechanic (ed.), Free Press, 1983, pp. 569–90.

Crandon-Malamud, Libbet, "Between shamans, doctors and demons: illness, curing and cultural identity midst culture change." In *Third World Medicine and Social Change: A Reader in Social Science and Medicine*, John Morgan (ed.), University Press of America, 1983, pp. 69–79.

——, "Grass roots, herbs, promoters and preventions: a reevaluation of contemporary international health care planning. The Bolivian case," *Social Science and Medicine*, 1983, 17: 1281–9.

——, "Why *Susto*," *Ethnology*, 1983, 22: 153–67.

——, "Medical dialogue and the political economy of medical pluralism: a case from rural highland Bolivia," *American Ethnology*, 1986, 13: 463–76.

——, "Changing times and changing symptoms: the effects of modernization on *mestizo* medicine in rural Bolivia (The case of two sisters)," *Medical Anthropology*, 1989, 10: 255–64.

——, "Phantoms and physicians: social change through medical pluralism." In *The Anthropology of Medicine: From Culture to Method*, Lola Romanucci-Ross, Daniel E. Moerman, and Laurence R. Tancredi (eds), Bergin & Garvey Publishers, 1991, pp. 85–112.

——, *From the Fat of Our Souls: Social Change, Political Process, and Medical Pluralism in Bolivia*, University of California Press, 1991.

Dunn, Frederick, "Traditional Asian medicine and cosmopolitan medicine in adaptive systems." In *Asian Medical Systems: A Comparative Study*, Charles Leslie (ed.), University of California Press, 1976, pp. 133–58.

Elling, Ray H., "The capitalist world-system and international health," *International Journal of Health Services*, 1981, 11: 21–51.

Frankenberg, Ronald, "Allopathic medicine, profession, and capitalist ideology in India," *Social Science and Medicine*, 1981, 15A: 115–25.

Gruenbaum, Ellen, "Positioning medical anthropology's audience," *Reviews in Anthropology*, 1994, 23: 257–67.

Klein, Herbert S., *Bolivia: The Evolution of a Multi-Ethnic Society*, Oxford University Press, 1992.

Klein, Janice, "*Susto*: the anthropological study of diseases in adaptation," *Social Science and Medicine*, 1978, 12: 23–8.

Kleinman, Arthur, *Writing at the Margin: Discourse Between Anthropology and Medicine*, University of California Press, 1995.

Leslie, Charles, "The modernization of Asian medical systems." In *Rethinking Modernization*, John Poggie, Jr. and Robert N. Lynch (eds), Greenwood Press, 1974, pp. 69–107.

——, "Medical pluralism and legitimation in the Indian and Chinese medical systems." In *Culture, Disease, and Healing: Studies in Medical Anthropology*, David Landy (ed.), New York: Macmillan, 1977, pp. 511–17.

—— and Alan Young, "Introduction." In *Paths to Asian Medical Knowledge*, Charles Leslie and Alan Young (eds), University of California Press, 1992, pp. 1–18.

Lock, Margaret, *East Asian Medicine in Urban Japan*, University of California Press, 1980.

Morales, Waltraud Queiser, *Bolivia: Land of Struggle*, Westview Press, 1992.

Morgan, Lynn M., Review of *From the Fat of Our Souls, Medical Anthropology Quarterly*, 1992, 6: 75–7.

Morsy, Soheir, "Political economy in medical anthropology." In *Medical Anthropology: Contemporary Theory and Method*, Carolyn F. Sargent and Thomas M. Johnson (eds), Prager, 1996, pp. 21–40.

Mysyk, Avis, "*Susto*: an illness of the poor," *Dialectical Anthropology*, 1998, 23: 187–202.

Rasnake, Roger Neil, *Domination and Cultural Resistance: Authority and Power among an Andean People*, Duke University Press, 1988.

Romanucci-Ross, Lola, "The hierarchy of resort in curative practices: the admirality islands, Melanesia." In *Culture, Disease, and Healing: Studies in Medical Anthropology*, David Landy (ed.), Macmillan, 1977, pp. 481–7.

Rubel, Arthur J., Carl W. O'Nell, and Rolando Collado-Ardon, *Susto: A Folk Illness*, University of California Press, 1984.

Singer, Merrill and Hans A. Baer, *Critical Medical Anthropology*, Baywood Press, 1995.

Stoner, Brad, "Understanding medical systems: traditional, modern, and syncretic health care alternatives in medically pluralistic societies," *Medical Anthropology Quarterly* 1986, 17(2): 44–8.

Van den Berghe, Pierre and George Primov, *Inequality in the Peruvian Andes: Class and Ethnicity in Cuzco*, University of Missouri Press, 1977.

Wallerstein, Immanuel, *The Capitalist World-Economy*, Cambridge University Press, 1979.

Part II

Choices, changing times, and medical pluralism

Even isolated communities in the Andes appear to have offered some choice between medical practitioners. In the more distant communities that choice was likely to have been between midwives, bonesetters, herbalists, and diviners. Oths' and Greenway's chapters offer new types of analysis of what may be loosely termed "traditional healers." In contrast, it appears that diversification of healer types is accelerating in urban communities as exemplified in the chapter of Miles who views diversification of healer activity as the result of entrepreneurial activities. It is of interest that Oths focuses on the embodiment of distress in sufferers' skeletal structures parallel to the way in which Greenway's villagers talk about soul loss as an expression of powerlessness. The underlying theme of all three chapters is vulnerability in the face of economic crisis, that is, the increasing burdens of heavy labor in Oths' village; in Miles's urban community, the burden of an increasing orientation towards a capitalistic economy and the strain in social relationships; and in Greenway's study, the need to adapt to rapid changes in access to their markets and to disadvantageous political representation.

These chapters build on the central focus of Libbet Crandon-Malamud's work – that medical choice and the content of the medical encounter have both cause and ramifications much beyond health seeking/illness solving activities. Put as a question: What do these Andean people gain when they seek out a healer of one or another persuasion? In Greenway's case study they acquire an identity that inverts the existing power structure. In Oths' community they not only acquire a higher level of bodily comfort but also attain a confirmation of their goodness as workers in the face of the inequity of rewards in the system. And in Miles' urban community, her competing healers offer their clients potential access to higher social status commensurate with biomedical-like healing practices, and reassurance in the face of insecurity in a rapidly changing economy.

What roles beyond medical practice do healers enact in these communities? Libbet was perhaps the first to point out that healers negotiate ethnic and class identity on behalf of their clients which frequently led to actual change in social status as they acquired greater material and social resources. In Miles' case study, in a precarious and volatile economic situation, the healers acquire similar secondary resources. In Oths' community the bonesetters appear to reinforce their higher social status through essential healing practices. The coca diviner in Greenway's study plays an important role in influencing community decisions regarding social and economic change.

Chapter 5

Setting it straight in the Andes

Musculoskeletal distress and the role of
the *componedor*

Kathryn S. Oths

I found myself in the plaza of the market town nearest to Chugurpampa (Peru)
one brilliant, crisp-aired morning without the faintest idea how I would get my
baggage on up to the hamlet, that speck of fields and houses just barely visible
on the next mountain top to the east. Some folks from Chugurpampa happened
by and offered to have their donkey cargo my possessions. My already considerable elation became nearly uncontainable. It was all really going to happen!
The steady pace of the two-hour approach allowed me to drink in the spectacular, almost dizzying pitches, curves, and colors of the freshly plowed countryside. Peasants came out of their houses to stare and smile, as they had never
seen a white person *walking* in these parts. It felt like coming home.

It had earlier been my good fortune to assist with a vaccination drive in the
region, jointly carried out by the Ministerio de Salud and the GTZ, a German
aid agency. Of the twenty-seven communities we visited, I chose Chugurpampa
because it most closely matched the characteristics of Pichátaro, Mexico, the
site of James Young's and Linda Garro's seminal study of treatment choice, such
as having a variety of healers available and a health post within reasonable walking distance of the hamlet. Most importantly, though, the community welcomed
my stay and I was offered board with a prominent midwife and her family.

Introduction

A biocultural explanation and interpretation of the phenomenon of musculoskeletal distress requires a multi-layered analysis which includes the bodily
state, ecological conditions, cultural meaning, and impinging sociopolitical and
economic forces in regional and national arenas. In this account, I attempt to
expand upon the seminal body of work of Robert Anderson on "bonesetting" in
Mexico and Nepal by presenting an in-depth description of the etiology, frequency, and understandings of musculoskeletal disorders in the Andean highlands, the practice of the Andean *componedor*, and the need for their services in
highland agricultural communities.[1] This will be accomplished, following the
work of Libbet Crandon-Malamud, while setting the problem of musculoskeletal
disorders in the wider sociopolitical and cultural context of Andean peasant life.

Crandon-Malamud's work on the social structural elements of medical treatment choice in "Kachitu," Bolivia, caused a paradigm shift in thinking about therapy decision making processes.[2] She demonstrated the extent to which medical dialog may be used as a vehicle for communicating notions about one's social identity in a pluralistic society and, in effect, may mobilize needed secondary resources such as material goods, power, and social position. This chapter is intended to complement her work by presenting a case in which medical pluralism exists but ethnic and religious plurality do not.

Health in the northern Peruvian Andes is maintained by numerous strategies, beginning with a wide variety of home remedies such as herbal tea, over-the-counter medicinal water and pharmaceuticals, baths, enemas, smoke, poultices, rinsing, and guinea pig rubdowns, and often advancing to the engagement of healers who employ traditional and/or biomedical practices.[3] While healers in the pluralistic highland medical system are generally labeled according to their primary form of ministration – that is, as herbalist, soul caller, bonesetter, shaman, midwife, lay biomedical practitioner, doctor, etc. – in practice, they may freely mix and match the techniques for which they have acquired knowledge, facility, and a reputation.

The *componedor/a and huesero/a*, as those doing body work in the Andes are commonly known, are types of healers found throughout Latin America and the rest of the world. *Componedor* translates literally as "one who fixes or repairs," and refers to a healer who mobilizes joints and repositions or sets straight the minor movements or major dislocations of the vertebrae as well as other joints, muscles, and even organs whose improper position may cause pain, discomfort, dysfunction, and immobility.[4] They are alternately said to *componer* (compose, fix), *arreglar* (arrange, put in order), *juntar* (join, connect), or *acomodar* (arrange, adjust) the bones and muscles, and a treatment is commonly called a *compuesta*. The *componedor* is the rough equivalent of a lay physical therapist or chiropractor. The *huesero*, or bonesetter, the more skilled of the two practitioners, sets broken bones as well as performing the skeletal manipulation of the *componedor*. In other words, while all *hueseros* are *componedores*, not all *componedores* are *hueseros*. Besides the *componedor*, the midwife is a regular practitioner of the musculoskeletal healing arts, with shamans (*curanderos*), herbalists and others occasionally employing simple techniques of bodily manipulation as well. In the community I studied, broken bones were rare; thus, my account will focus on the work of those who do manipulative therapy. I refer to them as *componedores*, whether they be officially labeled as *huesero, componedor*, midwife, or other.

A review of the literature reveals that, in contrast to the Andes, in the Southwest and Mesoamerica there is a great deal of ambiguity in the use of terms for the two types of healers, with bonesetter the preferred translation in English. Sometimes the labels are used interchangeably.[5] At times the term *sobador* (similar to the *componedor*) in Mexico appears to refer to one who does only massage,[6] but usually includes those who adjust bones and/or set fractures;[7] in some instances, those labeled as a bonesetter (*huesero* or *arreglador de huesos*) do not set broken bones.[8] Shutler describes her Yaqui bonesetters simply as curers (*hitevim*),[9] Mull and Mull in Southern California call their massage-oriented healer a *curandero*, though acknowledging that he does not use the label,[10] and Paul does not give an emic name for the Mayan bonesetters he studied in Guatemala.[11] Young explicitly notes that curers who set bones in Pichátaro are referred to neither as *sobadores* nor *hueseros* despite the usage in other parts of Mexico.[12] Scott Anderson (1998) in his video documentary on Mexican healers, makes the point that the terms *huesero* and *curandero* describe a variety of healers of musculoskeletal disorders.[13] Only Redfield and Villa Rojas in Chan Kom make a clear distinction between bone-setters, or "bone tyers" (*kax baac*), and those who only treat dislocations and sprains (*chen zahi*),[14] but it is possible that the distinction has disappeared since their work there. The normative glossing of the various musculoskeletal therapists simply as "bonesetters" may have as much as anything to do with the poverty of the English language for describing the domain of bodily illness and its treatment.

Musculoskeletal pain, especially of the back and neck, has been ubiquitous in human history, though its location and degree vary by population and occupation.[15] Despite the claim by the father of modern chiropractic, D. D. Palmer, to have discovered the healing technique in 1895 when he aligned the spine of and restored hearing to an Iowa janitor, bodily manipulation to correct skeletal dysfunction is an ancient therapy. Evidence of its use is found, among other places, in early Greece and Peru, and in later Peru, India, and Europe;[16] in most countries it continues to thrive as a modality today.

Though widely used, the reason that "bonesetters" and their modern counterparts (chiropractic, rolfing, physical therapy, massage, polarity therapy) have escaped more than cursory attention by anthropologists might be the lack of exoticism or ritual aspect to their therapy. Harder to understand is why the renewed interest in the body and embodiment in social science has not quickened the interest of researchers in bodily therapy.[17] The *componedor* represents a superb example of a healer who orients to a sick person by means of what Csordas has called a somatic mode of attention, that is, a culturally elaborate way of attending to and with one's body in an intersubjective milieu,[18] the inter-subjectivity here facilitated by the healer laying hands on the patient. Hinojosa, following Csordas, has recognized the intuitive, pre-objective level at which Guatemalan "bonesetters" diagnose and treat bodily distress: "Through their bodies, bonesetters achieve a direct link with their patients' bodies and use this linkage to bring about change in the injured bodies."[19]

Chugurpampa and its people

I begin by highlighting the significant contrasts between Kachitu, where Crandon-Malamud worked in the Bolivian altiplano, and my own research site, Chugurpampa, a northern Peruvian high altitude hamlet located in the province of Otuzco, department of La Libertad.

In the town of Kachitu, the seat of a thirty-six community canton, three ethnic-religious groups vied for status and survival after the revolution of 1952 upended the social hierarchy. The social world of Kachitu was rapidly changing, along with the identities of its inhabitants. Both Spanish and Aymara were spoken. The dense settlement pattern typical of highland towns meant that families lived in close proximity to one another, and that everyone knew all the intimate details of, and discussed at length, every case of illness that occurred.[20] While Andean towns represent regional commercial centers with highly concentrated populations, and as a mode of social organization are in a distinct minority compared to outlying farming communities, virtually all anthropological studies of Andean communities have been conducted in such towns with the exception of the research I present here. The bias towards studying Andean towns can result in the over-generalization of findings, with little understanding of the diversity of cultural and social patterns that contribute to health in the Andes.[21]

The peasant community (*comunidad campesina*) of Chugurpampa is dispersed over 1,000 hectares spanning 3,000 feet in altitude and several mountain sides, with houses scattered among the fields. It is one of twenty-seven rural agricultural hamlets linked to the district capital and central market town of Julcan two hours distant. In contrast to Kachitu, Chugurpampa is much more homogeneous in population. No ethnic divisions persist; the indigenous locals, while speaking only Spanish, are called *campesinos* (peasant farmers), serranos (highlanders), or sometimes *gente humilde* (humble people), to distinguish them from *mestizos*, or *gente decente* (decent people), who are concentrated in Julcan. In Chugurpampa, land reform in the 1970s dismantled the existing *hacienda*, a *comunidad indigena* (later converted to an incorporated *comunidad campesina*) with communal land rights was formed, and all but one *mestizo* has since moved away.[22] While no cultural community ever stops changing, the sleepy hamlet of Chugurpampa was not undergoing any significant social or political upheaval at the time of my research. Social distinctions were minimal, as well. While some families were better off socioeconomically than others, people refused to comment openly about differences in wealth, and class distinctions did not obtain. The portion (10 percent) of the population who had recently converted to Evangelical Protestantism did not espouse ideological differences from the majority Catholics in terms of medical treatment.

Thus, Crandon-Malamud's statement that "what people say about their social world through the idiom of medicine are statements about political and economic realities" holds true for Chugurpampa, though these do not constitute "statements about ethnic relations."[23] As in Kachitu, exploitative socioeconomic conditions prevail in Chugurpampa. The social relations that oppress these rural peasant people, while all too real, for the most part remain nameless and faceless, or at least not visible in daily interaction. They have nothing to gain, then, by engaging in public discourse through treatment decisions to change social group affiliation, as there is only one viable local group.[24] Though people love to discuss their health and are endlessly curious about that of their neighbors, with population density low and homes dispersed among the fields, illness and healing largely remain private matters in a way nearly impossible for a town setting.

The principal crop in this rich agricultural zone is the potato, a part of which is sold in the Sunday market in the district capital, Julcan, to middlemen who in turn sell to coastal distributors. As anthropologists have long recognized, peasants are dependent upon the market, a steady source of cash income for their produce with which they then purchase desired and necessary consumer goods not available in their home communities.[25] Low profits over the years, due to trade policies designed to disadvantage the peasants *vis-à-vis* their buyers, have resulted in overproduction and subsequent erosion of the soil. The highlanders, caught up in a vicious cycle of usurious interest rates on government loans for essential fertilizers and insecticides and artificially deflated market prices to pacify coastal consumers, end up suffering physically and economically as a result. Andean peasants "break their backs" in the process of feeding the nation virtually for free. The present form of absentee economic exploitation barely constitutes an improvement over that of *hacienda* days, as older locals clearly articulate.

So accustomed, sierran people will bear a tremendous amount of musculoskeletal pain and illness, often derived directly from their work, yet continue to labor. I refer to their brand of stoicism as *aguantismo* (from a term they often employ, *aguantar*, to bear up, withstand). As one informant stated, "even though we might be hurting, we are working" (*aunque nos duela, estamos trabajando*). They might die of an illness if they do not attend to it, but they might sooner die of poverty and starvation if they do not tend to their fields and family. Bodily pain is seen as a natural and expected condition of life, with medical attention sought only in debilitating cases (Anderson noticed the same in Nepal[26]). Other commonly heard phrases are, "it just hurts normally today" (*me duele normal hoy*), and "it hurts in a natural way, nothing more" (*duele natural no mas*). Reliant upon their own production for subsistence, there is simply no other option but to endure.

Highlanders have a work ideology that rivals the Protestant work ethic in its intensity – though survival, not the virtue of pecuniary gain, is their primary motivation. Only an *haragán* (lazy person, loafer) stays home from work. It is seen as best to be up and about: "The pure air gives us more resistance. Getting up composes the body." Thus, when people do resort to healers such as the *componedor*, it is due to the serious nature of a musculoskeletal ailment, not to a form of malingering behavior (which can be the charge against patients of chiropractors in the United States). A healer often legitimizes the need to rest by insisting that to leave one's bed after a treatment will result in calamity – an attack of an *aire* (dangerous air) or spirit being, perhaps – because of one's weakened condition. The exploitative social relations that create their difficulties are not lost on the highlanders, by any means. The words of an elder Chugurpampino sum up the sierran condition: "We poor Christians![27] The same poverty that makes us ill obliges us to work hard."

The ability of Andeans to bear difficult circumstances does not negate another of their traits, being *acojedor*, or receptive to new opportunities and ideas, always ready to improve their situation if possible. The Chugurpampinos empirical bent allows for the rapid trial of and, if a benefit is clearly demonstrated, incorporation of a new technology or medicine. Hence, the fact that traditional *componedores* have endured in the face of the pressures of modernization attests to an inherent efficacy of their practice of bodily attention, an efficacy that may be psychosocial, economic and cultural as well as physical.

Sample and methods

Data for this research were collected between 1987 and 1989. In addition to a census and health survey of the entire community ($n = 902$) which included socioeconomic questions regarding land tenure, yearly potato production, consumption and sales, animal and home ownership, and political offices held, all somatic and psychological symptoms were recorded across ten visits to thirty-two (i.e. 19 percent of 166) randomly chosen households over a twenty-four week interval.

Standard field methodology for case illness collection typically consists of a one time rapid assessment of a household's health status and is built upon the epidemiologic model of short-term acute infectious disease. In this study, case illness collection entailed repeated visits to the same household to take into account the chronic and recurring nature of highland illness, especially musculoskeletal problems. It often took multiple visits to tease out the full illness picture for a family. With rapport established, people began to share more intimate or, on the other hand, seemingly unimportant problems. This method also avoided gathering information that exceeded the two week recall period. Rather than interviewing only those people from a particular healer's patient load, that is, using a clinical sample, I chose to visit people in their homes and record information on all treatments employed for all illness episodes.[28] Household members were interviewed regarding cause, severity, duration, and change in and recurrence of symptoms for each illness episode reported, as well as the consequences of illness on their daily activities.

Musculoskeletal distress

In Chugurpampa, the common perception of the ideal state of health interrelates the realities of bodily state, food, and work.[29] Health might be summarized as the freedom from debilitating pain, the maintenance of adequate body weight and a hearty appetite, and the desire and ability to work. Or, as Sigerist defined it years ago, health means an undisturbed rhythm.[30] To work hard and productively for the benefit of one's household, even if ultimately at the expense of one's health, is to prove oneself a worthy person,[31] and Andeans would prefer to do this in the absence of pain, if possible. Thus, expanding on Crandon-Malamud's notion of efficacy as more than simply symptom relief,[32] remedies are deemed efficacious if they stimulate appetite, renew strength and vigor, and especially, alleviate bodily aches and pains that might diminish or prohibit work in the fields, all with the ultimate aim of maintaining the spirit to work (*tener gusto de trabajar*).

One finds a pattern of illness in Chugurpampa characterized by a relatively low rate of infectious disease and high prevalence of chronic disorders, particularly of the musculoskeletal variety. Factors contributing positively to this rural Andean hamlet's illness pattern include adequate nutrition, ample resource base, pure water supply, appropriate fecal disposal, excellent immunization coverage, low population density, and community autonomy, while physical duress due to ecological and occupational conditions contributes negatively.[33] Though respiratory problems were the most common in Chugurpampa, accounting for 40 percent of all reported illness episodes, the vast majority of these were mild, short-lived episodes of head cold or flu. In contrast, the second most common category of ailments was musculoskeletal disorder (18 percent), which were often chronic in nature. While 29 percent of cases ameliorated within two weeks, 59 percent lasted more than six weeks. The majority (64 percent) of musculoskeletal aches, pains, and immobility are stress-related primarily due to physical exertion and overwork. This subcategory also includes degenerative problems such as rheumatism and chronically cold feet. Injuries from work, play, and falls due to the rough mountain terrain account for the remainder of musculoskeletal problems.

Musculoskeletal complaints figure saliently in the illness profiles of other highland agricultural communities as well. In a household survey of symptoms in a rural Nepalese agricultural village, Anderson found that 18 percent of adults currently suffered from back or neck problems. When physical examinations were performed on a clinical sample among the same population an even higher rate was found, with 44 percent having at least mild spinal pain or dysfunction and 11 percent with musculoskeletal problems in other areas. Carrying loads by tumpline was heavily implicated in the etiology of body pain there.[34] In Tlalpizahuac, Mexico, Medina recorded that 53 percent of illness complaints among school age children were of a musculoskeletal nature.[35] According to Larme, 18 percent of illness episodes in Cuyo Cuyo in southern Peru were musculoskeletal in origin.[36] Jurmain, Landy, Finerman, and Sorofman and Tripp-Reimer all report similar work-related physical complaints for agricultural and/or highland populations.[37] Thus, the pattern of a high incidence of bodily distress among peasants is not unique to Chugurpampa.

The degree to which a subject is detailed in the taxonomy of a language and the frequency with which it is discussed signal the importance that domain holds for a culture. Frake, in analyzing Subanun skin diseases, postulated, "The greater the number of distinct social contexts in which information about a particular phenomenon must be communicated, the greater the number of different levels of contrast into which that phenomenon is categorized."[38] The focus on the back and neck area in the sierra attests to a great concern with musculoskeletal function, to its prominence as a health problem, and to the significance such problems have for maintaining life and social relations. The uniqueness of pain perception to

Andeans in contrast to other Latin American indigenous people bears note. Fabrega and Silver found in Zinacantan, for instance, that although people referred to localized pain in one of four specific body parts (leg, arm, throat, stomach), pain was a "relatively general and undifferentiated construct that may be associated with a large subset of illness conditions."[39] While Chugurpampinos' view of the anatomy and functioning of the body and internal organs does not differ substantially from that of biomedicine (e.g. no "extra" organs exist such as the *latido* in Pichátaro and the *tipte* among the Maya),[40] the spatial division of the body into definable and understandable units is conceptually distinct from Western notions, especially concerning the head and trunk areas. I derived the composite sketches in Figures 5.1 and 5.2 from descriptions of actual symptoms by study participants and drawings by several key informants.

The upper region of the dorsal trunk is subdivided into two outer quadrants comprising the shoulders (*hombros*), an upper quadrant comprising the head and neck, and a middle quadrant which subsumes the lungs (*pulmones*) (see Figure 5.1). The nuca corresponds to the cervical area and upper trapezius muscles, while the pulmones below it refers to the midback area surrounding the upper thoracic vertebrae between the shoulder blades. Any pain falling into one of the quadrants will be described according to the general name for the area. For example, the hombros can be a general category which includes the shoulder blades (*paletillas*). As another example, the pulmones are conceived of as two sacs located inside the body at the center of the middle quadrant. However, any generalized pain in this section, including vertebral displacement, is referred to as pulmones.

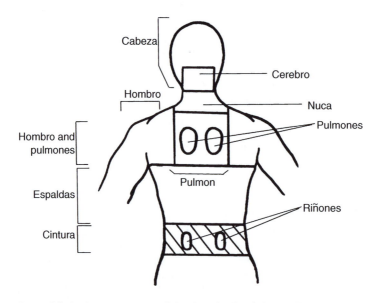

Figure 5.1 Andean taxonomy of the dorsal side of the trunk.

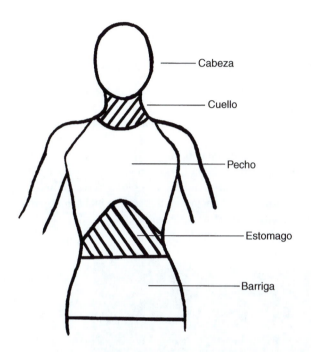

Cabeza

Cuello

Pecho

Estomago

Barriga

Figure 5.2 Andean taxonomy of the ventral side of the trunk.

The head is conceptually divided into two parts when categorizing pains and illnesses. The *cabeza* is the upper half of the head, including the temples and cerebrum, while the *cerebro* specifically refers to the lower back portion of the head, consisting of the cerebellum as well as the occipital and upper nuchal muscles.

The term "backache" (*dolor de espaldas, dolor de la columna*) is reserved primarily for pain and discomfort in the upper lumbar and lower thoracic regions, the middle section marked on Figure 5.1. *Dolor de cintura* (pain in the waist) in the sierra refers to any pain along the lower back, but not the front or sides of the body. This includes kidney pain and lower back pain of the muscles or spinal column, particularly in the upper sacral and lower lumbar regions. Therefore, *dolor de cintura* and *dolor de riñones* (kidney pain) can both be referents for the same problem.

The ventral side of the trunk is spatially divided into five vertically adjacent parts, the head (*cabeza*), throat (*cuello*), chest (*pecho*), stomach (*estomago*) and abdomen or gut (*barriga*). Pulmones are distinguished from the *pecho*, the latter being the site of respiratory congestion, coughing, and pain. The *pecho* can also be the site of musculoskeletal pain from injury to the upper ventral side of the trunk. Pain in the pulmones and *pecho* are seen to correspond to each other in some instances.[41] The uterus (*vientre*) is known to be located in the barriga, but is rarely glossed separately.

Lay persons and healers alike use the above elaborated taxonomy of the body in daily discourse as well as when describing illness and injury.

Causes and varieties of musculoskeletal distress

Four main causes of bodily distress can be identified in the northern Peruvian Andes based on self-report by the highlanders: (1) *injury*, from falls and lifting, (2) *aging*, as in the case of rheumatism, (3) *the elements*, and (4) *stress*, primarily from work tasks.

The elemental forces of nature are seen as dominating the state of one's health; thus, a tremendous preoccupation is found with preventing illness by limiting one's exposure to the sun, the damp or night air, cold water or rain, and also a sudden change in temperature which may either cause musculoskeletal pain directly or complicate already strained muscles and joints.

Plate 5.1 Young man harvesting potatoes.

As for work related stress, potato agriculture in Chugurpampa requires constant stooping, due in part to the use of the short handled hoe, and to the lifting, carrying and swinging of heavy loads and sharp tools. The most risky maneuver I witnessed and experienced was the positioning of a heavy load onto the back for transport. People tend to stoop and, with a lateral twist of the spine, swing the sack, object, or child around to the back from a resting position next to them, then thrust upwards to a standing position with the weight positioned across one or both shoulders.

During the harvest, old and young, men, women, and children alike, may typically fill, lift, and carry their weight in sacked potatoes at fifteen minute intervals throughout an eight to ten-hour work day, easily amounting to one ton

Plate 5.2 Woman carrying sack of potatoes uphill.

Plate 5.3 Men lifting sack of potatoes onto carrier's shoulder.

Plate 5.4 Family finishing the day's harvest.

of weight per day for the adults. Some will unload, weigh, and stack the sacks, bending over from the waist (instead of squatting) to dead lift a sack in a bear hug fashion. I queried highlanders why they use 150 pound potato bags instead of something more manageable and less back rending. Their response was that the Peruvian Department of Agriculture, ENCI (*Empresa National para la Comercialización de Insumos*), requires that standard size. The official bags must be purchased from ENCI at no small cost. The middlemen buyers, buying by the pound, deduct – previously three, then five, now ten – pounds from the weight of each full sack "for the sack." Thus, they reason, sales would be even less profitable if smaller sacks were used.

When I asked a porter loading an entire cargo truck with oversized (250 lb) bags how he managed to work so hard with such little apparent effort, he spoke

Plate 5.5 Porter carrying large sack of potatoes to cargo truck.

for highlanders in general with his philosophy: "One must master the weight. There are no limits to what the human being can do." Lamentably, the super-human effort needed for survival takes its toll on the body over time. In the long run, the result of such arduous labor, with little respite under harsh climatic con-ditions, is a high incidence of physical degenerative conditions. Sierrans simply wear their bodies out. One day in the cold rain, I came across a man of about thirty trotting barefoot along the precipitous muddy trail to market, his sandals draped across his digging pick in his left hand and a 150 pound sack of potatoes balanced on his back with his right. I could only wonder in what state he would find himself in thirty years.

Weaving by loom is also seen as deleterious to the back and hands over time. Many older women had gnarled, arthritic fingers from "weaving, then getting the hands wet." Carrying buckets of water from a spring for household use, stirring and lifting heavy cook pots on low set fires, food processing such as grinding grain on a mortar, washing clothes, and child transport on the back are other strenuous tasks women do in addition to agricultural labor. The strain of preg-nancy and childbirth also add up over a woman's lifetime (Oths 1999). Other men's labor which can cause strain includes house building and tree felling; sports injuries are not uncommon.

The activities outlined above help to explain the majority of musculoskeletal aches, pains and strains, injuries, and lacerations in my sample. The physical problems created by such work are then complicated by inclement weather. Foot travel with heavy loads at a slight back flexion over steep, rough terrain particu-larly stresses the back and legs, as well as the ankle, knee, and hip joints.[42]

Various types of bodily distress, some symptoms, some illnesses, are commonly reported by Andeans. Symptoms include muscle cramps (*calambres*), which occur in the feet, shins, knees, arms, and stomach. A pulled or stretched nerve (*nervio estirado*) can occur in the elbow, knee, thigh, foot, leg, and kidney (nerves are spoken of only in a mechanical, not emotional, sense.[43] Sharp pain (*punzada*) occurs in the upper body cavity, either in the ("mouth" of the) stomach, lungs, ("foot" of the) chest, or the middle back. Bones are described as trembling (*tem-blado*), contracted (*engarotado*), or hardened (*endurecido*), while joints (*gonces*) are said to be knotted (*nudoso*), especially when referring to arthritic damage. A blow to an area (*golpe, chancado*) often results from a fall, accident, or occa-sionally from violence. To speak of the entire body, terms are used such as shivers (*tirita*), pain, "as if you had been beaten" (*dolor, "como si le diera majas"*), asleep, "like a corpse" (*endormecido, "como un muerto"*), weakness (*descaecimiento, muy debil*), out of order (*descompuesta*), and suffocation (*sofocaciones*).

Several ailments of the joints are seen to require manipulation to correct. A bone may be twisted (*torcido*), impacted or slightly out of situ (*embagado*), moved (*movido, tronchado*), scraped (*rajado*), or "open" (*abierto*). The hips, mid-dle back, or the entire body can be open, meaning in need of a manual reduction, or *compuesta*. For instance, it is standard therapy for a women's pelvic area to be "closed" shortly after giving birth.

Organs that move out of their proper place are seen to need manual manipulation. These include conditions such as displaced or dropped abdominal or reproductive organs (*barriga bajada*), risen abdominal/reproductive organs (*barriga levada*), and risen stomach (*estomago subido*). Severe cramping or contraction from pooled or retained blood or fluids (*recogido*) is often reported for the stomach, uterus, head, or feet areas.

The *componedor* in action

The highland Peruvian *componedor* is seen as a healer of natural problems who possesses no supernatural powers.[44] Problems as commonplace as injuries and sprains are not likely candidates for being considered supernatural in origin. Highlanders understand that "getting up (out of bed) composes the body" and that one may cough "just enough to compose the chest"; the *componedor's* practice, then, is an extension of these everyday natural processes. Of *componedores* I heard none of the fear or complaints often leveled at healers of supernatural ailments. The *componedores* I knew were in no manner charismatic, though they were well-respected and admired for their prowess. In the highlands, the healing role is generally part-time, compared to the urban areas of Peru where a larger population may ensure a constant client load. (One coastal *componedor* I knew attended at a "clinic" site, the waiting room of which was always occupied.) Unlike in other parts of America,[45] those practicing body therapy in Northern Peru are somewhat more likely to be female then male.

When asked where they learned the techniques they utilize, *componedores* claimed to have received the gift from God (*Dios me enseñó*), as do many other healer types in Chugurpampa and "bonesetters" elsewhere.[46] I observed that healers tend to be the grandchildren of healers and may absorb knowledge and develop an interest in healing, probably unreflexively, when as young children they are asked to accompany and assist an aging relative on his or her house calls. Healing role recruitment serves to underscore the empirical nature of highland healing. Healers tend to be self-taught and to piece together a personal style largely from trial and error, though a continuation of the healing modality from generation to generation belies a lack of apprenticeship, or at least close observation, of others' practices. This manner of acquiring knowledge is a means of economic survival for those shut out from formal, "legitimate" avenues of learning because of their class, ethnicity, and poverty.

Styles of healing

In contrast to treatments in other parts of the world,[47] healing illness in Chugurpampa, while "a social activity serving social purposes,"[48] is not a matter requiring or encouraging public, nor even extended family, participation. In keeping with this, the *componedor's* healing techniques are not highly ritualized.

Thus, the degree to which therapeutic efficacy derives from a public display and manipulation of symbols is circumscribed with bodily therapy.

Regardless of the common aim among *componedores* of realigning the body's structural features, there is great variety in manipulative treatment styles used in Chugurpampa. During treatment, the fully clothed client may be positioned to lie face down or prone, sit, stand, or kneel on all fours while the healer kneads and presses the body to correct its alignment (see Figure 5.3(a), (b) and (d)). Some shake and roll the client in a blanket with the assistance of another person (see Figure 5.3(c)). The kneeling technique is one I have witnessed only in the Andes. The *componedor* encircles the client's trunk with his or her arms at the level of the misalignment, locks hands at the client's distal side, and gently pulls the trunk inward (Figure 5.3(b)). The movement is repeated after the healer palpates the spine again to locate another displaced vertebra.

The *compuesta* "closes," or pulls back together, bones which have been untowardly opened. Unlike with other treatment modalities, such as chiropractic, pops and cracks are not generally audible during treatment and are not an expected outcome of therapy.[49] Firm but gentle stretching, prodding, and pressure is applied smoothly and gradually to the affected body part, without sharp or quick jerks, twists, or pushes. Massage of the muscles often accompanies the adjustment.

While Paul reported that Mayan bonesetters use a sacred object, a special searching bone, to locate and treat the injury,[50] the hands alone are the tools of the Andean *componedor*. Before beginning the body composition, the *componedor* pronounces the articulations of the bones tactually, like a Braille text, to determine what bones are misaligned. Knowledge of irregularities in another's bone and muscle tissue is embodied in the healer and perceived through the hands intuitively by means of a somatic mode of attention.[51] This helps explain why *componedores* preferred to demonstrate their techniques to me rather than describe them.

After receiving manipulation, the affected area is dressed with a special salve (*ontura*, from *Sp. untar*), usually *chuncho* (a trade item from the jungle for rheumatism, muscle, and joint aches the contents of which are secretly prepared by specialists), then wrapped securely with a bandage or long flat cloth sash (*fajado*) to keep the joint or organ from shifting back out of place. At this stage the body is vulnerable (*tierno*). The person is instructed to remain inactive, preferably in bed under warm blankets, until the following morning. At the very least, one should avoid getting chilled or walking, especially up and down hills where one could easily slip or fall and wrench the body again, making it worse than before. One needs to avoid lifting for several days.

While *chuncho* is the preferred salve, Vasoline, Vaporub, and animal fat (of the bear, wildcat, hen, etc.) may also be used; arnica, cat's claw, eucalyptus, and Milk of Magnesia with *pisco* (anisette) are also recommended for bruises and muscle aches. In a symbolic sense, the preference for topical, or external, non-invasive treatments reflects the highlanders' resistance to intrusion and respects the inviolate, impenetrable, closed character of Andean family, person, and body. It is

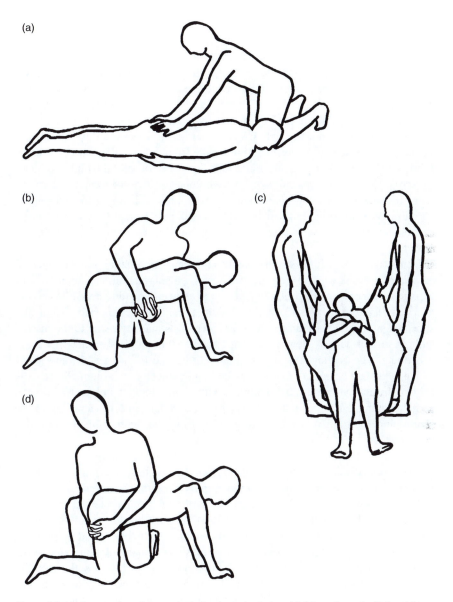

Figure 5.3 Various styles of musculoskeletal manipulation (a) Manual manipulation lying face down, (b) Back adjustment while kneeling, (c) Adjustment using blanket technique, and (d) Midwife manipulating mother's pelvis.

consistent with a cultural emphasis on privacy, a resistance to intrusion, manifested in the minimal physical contact between people.[52]

I witnessed many cases of treatment by a *componedor*; however, one stands out in my mind as near miraculous in terms of biomedical understanding of joint disorders. One morning, I was making the two hour journey on foot to the market town of Julcan with my assistant, Amable, and her fiancé, Julio, a strapping *campesino* in his late twenties. We were headed down a steep trail when Julio slipped and twisted his ankle. The sprain was serious, and his ankle immediately swelled to double its normal size. I was despairing how we would transport him, since, it being mid-trip, we were an hour away from either village. It occurred to Julio that we were about a quarter of a mile from the house of the highly reputed *huesero*, Don Artemio (pseudonym), so why not go there for treatment? To my mind, it seemed a foolish decision, since the detour would simply add distance to our ultimate destination, but Amable and I nonetheless helped Julio hobble along to Don Artemio's house. As luck would have it, he was home and willing to attend.

Don Artemio had Julio sit on a chair and began mobilizing, massaging, and palpating the ankle. Knowing my interest in manipulation, he attempted to explain his techniques carefully in addition to showing me (and even allowed me to try my hand at the ankle). Within a short time, the swelling had all but disappeared, mobility had returned, and the three of us made our way to the market without further delay. A few days later, I ran into Julio and asked how his ankle was doing. The healing was so complete that he had to pause and think about which ankle had been hurt. Curiously, this is an ailment that in biomedicine calls for lengthy and uncomfortable treatment with alternating hot and ice water baths and bandaging. Many a football player has been sidelined for weeks due to the same injury that Julio recovered from, within half an hour, with the aid of a *componedor*.[53]

Musculoskeletal problems in Chugurpampa were most often treated with home or patent remedies, but the traditional *componedor* was the preferred healer if one was needed, with biomedical practitioners only occasionally resorted to. In the case of pregnancy and childbirth, however, a midwife is the preferred specialist.

The midwife, usually a post-menopausal female, is contracted to deliver babies. This entails not only assisting at the point of birth, but providing pre- and postnatal care as well in the form of massages, skeletal manipulation, positioning of the baby (including external cephalic inversions), advice, and baths.[54] While manipulative therapy may or may not be given during pregnancy and delivery (one pregnant woman admitted she had not been going for her prenatal manipulations because "they were too addictive"), a *compuesta* after delivery is viewed as imperative. The mother is required to stay in bed for several days, preferably an entire month if possible, to stay warm, avoid harmful airs, and prevent damage to her tender internal organs. Getting up too soon may cause weakness in the abdomen (reproductive organs) later in life. One means of strengthening the mother at this time and insuring future health is to "compose" or pull back together her pelvic bones, stretched during childbirth. While the woman kneels on all fours on the bed, covered in blankets to avoid chilling, the midwife, kneeling at her side, encircles the woman's opposite hips and pulls toward her with steady force and a slight jerk. She repeats the procedure for the other side. While treatment is still gentle as with other *componedores*, this is one adjustment in which loud popping sounds typically occur. Shoulder and back alignment are also carried out. As with the other *componedores*, the midwife follows up with salve and binding, which may remain in place for days and even weeks. Another *compuesta* may follow within the week. Midwives in the study were occasionally called upon to treat minor non-pregnancy related sprains and dislocations as well.

The maintenance of community health

The *componedor* is of critical importance for maintaining health and production in Andean peasant communities. The therapy *componedores* provide is accessible, affordable, culturally appropriate, efficacious, and otherwise unavailable.

There were one *huesero* (male) and eight *componedores* (five women, three men) in and around Chugurpampa to whom persons in the study resorted, as well as five midwives (four women, one man); other *componedores* were identified who did not treat persons chosen for study. That there are as many *componedores* as any other type of healer in Chugurpampa attests to the high demand for their services occasioned by the high degree of orthopedic stress and injury in the Andes. Their services are cheap relative to other healers, possibly because no special instruments and minimal remedies are usually employed, and supernatural powers need not be contended with. *Campesinos* feel comfortable receiving care from a *componedor*, who does not make them undress, prescribes needed rest, and understands the humoral belief system and the contributions of exposure and work to musculoskeletal problems. The embodied experience *componedores* have with the same type of stresses and strains afflicting their clients, in essence their shared habitus[55] – experiences foreign to the coastal, upper class doctors who attend in the clinic – helps them understand and accumulate knowledge about the nature of the problems they work on.[56]

Efficacy can be defined as the perceived capacity of a practice to affect disease in a positive way.[57] Measuring efficacy is a formidable task, which most researchers have avoided.[58] For physicians and social scientists alike, utilizing scientific standards of evidence in the field to assess changes in a patient's condition is next to impossible,[59] even more so when the study is lengthy. Given these problems, one measure of the efficacy of a treatment might be the duration of symptom alleviation, or comfort, it affords, especially the case with long-term or recurring problems, which the majority of musculoskeletal problems are. That is, how well does a therapy manage a complaint when a cure is unlikely. Another valid measure of efficacy would be, following Crandon-Malamud, the ability of medical dialog to mobilize needed political, social, economic, or nutritional resources at the local level. In this scenario, medical efficacy as it is understood in biomedicine, is relegated to a secondary role in medical choice.[60] The latter interpretation, while an exceedingly important consideration, tends to be salient where there is ethnic plurality and medical treatment competition, which do not obtain in Chugurpampa. Social, economic, and nutritional resources, while mobilized, remain secondary to the goal of somatic relief from musculoskeletal problems that impede everyday survival activities.[61]

Thus, with the understanding that the goal of symptom relief is inseparable from the motivation to work, in this study a definition of efficacy is emphasized based on the self-reported perceptions of the ill person and family. Drawing principally on the research of Young, Gaines and Farmer, and on suggestions in the works of Kleinman and Finkler,[62] I constructed a four dimensional measure of treatment efficacy. The criteria are (1) relief of symptoms (degree and change of each), (2) overall improvement in health status (is condition better, worse, or same since last visit), (3) functional capacity (the ability to conduct work and other activities), and (4) meaning provided to the ill person by a treatment (especially in terms of diagnosis and explanations given).

Of the 116 illness cases in my study for which one or more healers were utilized, nearly 20 percent entailed resort to a *componedor* (no cases of prenatal or postnatal care by midwives figured in my sample). Astoundingly, based on responses to the above items that informants provided during my in-home interviews, the healers were rated as effective in all twenty-two cases of treatment. An example will help illustrate the significance of the finding: In addition to being a *huesero*, Don Artemio was an herbalist and the community's health promoter. While many in the community were skeptical of Don Artemio with regard to his health promoter practices and often rated his herbal remedies as ineffective, even his worst critics conceded he was a superb *componedor*. Village officials even complained publicly at a district level health meeting that he was in such demand by other communities that he was often unavailable when Chugurpampinos needed him (he was the healer in six of the twenty-two cases reported).

Thus, the *componedor*'s treatments are an effective means to manage aches and pains, that is, to alleviate them for a time, if not permanently. The chronicity of mild and moderate bodily complaints is occasioned not by the ineffectiveness of local palliatives, but by the constant assault made on the body by the highland environment and agricultural life. Anthropologist Robert Anderson, also a licensed chiropractor and MD, found Mexican sobadores to be safe (except for the potentially dangerous cervical adjustment), efficacious, and low cost as judged by biomedical standards.[63] Dennis Mull, MD, MPH (1983), from his observations of the same type healers, concurs in their talents and the benefits they provide to patients.[64] The 1997 Peruvian National Household Health Survey found that 63 percent of all Peruvians rated the *huesero* as therapeutically efficacious, much higher than any other traditional healer (e.g. herbalists 48 percent, shamans 5 percent).[65]

As Crandon-Malamud found in Kachitu, members of different ethnic groups did not distinguish themselves from each other by expressing different medical beliefs, but rather by perceiving themselves as holding different positions within the same medical universe.[66] In Peru, *mestizos* and *costeños* (both middle-class and elite coastal dwellers), as befitting their social station, denigrate supernatural illness beliefs such as *daño* or *susto* in public but in their time of doubt or need may adhere to the beliefs in private.[67] However, in the case of a musculoskeletal distress there is virtually no public debate over treatment. The instrumental cause is usually obvious (overwork in the fields, violation of humoral tenets, a fall, or injury) and viewed as natural rather than supernatural. This type of ailment is widely acknowledged throughout Peru to be well-treated by the *componedor* – as it stands, a therapist with virtually no competition from other healing modalities. As an example, the one mestiza in Chugurpampa (see Introduction) divided her time between a regional city and her *chacra* (cultivated fields) in the hamlet. She customarily sought the services of a *componedora* who lived near her chacra. It is possible to read her comportment either as an attempt to fit in by adopting highland medical practices or as seeking convenient medical attention when she strained her body working. Yet her identity was secure. She was well-liked, respected, and, following the order of things Andean, somewhat deferred to by other community members. Thus, there was no need or intention of aligning herself any differently than usual with the *gente humilde*. Whatever the preferred explanation, the reality is that she would have had no other recourse for her ailing lower back than to visit a *componedor*.

Skeletal manipulation is one area of traditional medical practice that appears to be accepted – or at least less maligned than other practices – by biomedically trained personnel, since *componedores* offer services not duplicated by the physician or health post. Correspondingly, the use of *componedores* is not stigmatized by *mestizos*, and thus resort to them is not a clear signal of ethnic identity as it might be with other healers such as shamans and herbalists, as Crandon-Malamud reported for Kachitu. While in the United States, the medical profession has been loathe to cede turf to other healing modalities in the treatment of orthopedic pain (witness the longstanding antagonism between the AMA and professional chiropractic[68]), the same tension is not apparent between doctors and healers in Peru. But biomedicine's notorious neglect of musculoskeletal problems[69] continues to leave the highlanders to their own devices in pursuing relief for what constitutes their largest category of illnesses after the common cold and flu. Thus, *componedores* provide an essential and valuable service for conditions not well addressed by biomedicine.

There were no broken bones suffered by persons in my sample nor by anyone else I accompanied Don Artemio to see during the entire course of my study. It was my observation, corroborated by Don Artemio and physicians, that people despite their strenuous work and frequent accidents, rarely break bones.[70] Thus, he was reduced to hypothetically demonstrating to me how he sets the occasional broken bone. He was, however, enduringly proud of an incident that had occurred some years before.

A *campesino* had presented to a physician at the Julcan health post with a severe fracture of the femur. The physician declined to help, and the patient became a client of Don Artemio. Don Artemio set the bone and it healed well.

Later, the same physician was astounded, upon doing an x-ray of the bone, to see that it had mended so cleanly. He showed the x-ray to Don Artemio, and praised him for his skill. Another health post doctor and the district health technician verified the story.

Though musculoskeletal problems are rarely of a gravely serious nature, the belief is that the longer a moved bone is left unattended, the more the bone hardens and is difficult to manipulate. Therefore, the *componedor's* services are sought relatively soon after an injury occurs. Don Artemio also functioned at fiestas and sports events as a sort of "team doctor" to attend quickly to any casualties that might arise. He once even ministered without pay to the wounds of a captured thief from another village.

Conclusion

In the rural hamlet of Chugurpampa, unlike in many larger towns of the Andes, there are no socially distinct groups between which people shift affiliation and renegotiate identities, and thus medical treatment choice does not provide a basis for expressing social or cultural difference. This is not to deny that families, or individuals within families, have their preferences for traditional or biomedical therapies, and that these preferences may be expressed to promote a more modern image for oneself or one's family, but only that these preferences do not variably assign, or attempt to assign, people to different social groups. At any rate, healing rituals tend to be private matters that are kept from the watchful eyes of others, a feat more easily accomplished in a dispersed rural settlement than in a densely settled town. It is my contention that, even where ethnic pluralism does exist in the Andes, it is unlikely that a decision to seek the services of a *componedor* is used to express identity, since for musculoskeletal care there are no competing healing options. The Peruvian national survey cited above, though random, was conducted by telephone and was thus heavily biased toward the urban middle and upper classes. Despite this, bonesetters were rated as highly efficacious.

The above conclusion, rather than challenging the findings of Libbet Crandon-Malamud, can serve to bolster her thesis. Peru is a constantly changing country with a political and social order that can be described as unstable at best. It will be instructive to continue to observe the treatment choice behaviors of rural highland peasants over time and place, to see if changes in land use patterns, community membership, and migration to urban areas that increase the social and ethnic diversity of communities also produces a corresponding use of medical decisions to achieve new ends, such as the procurement of the secondary resources of prestige, power, mobility, and material goods. On the weight of Crandon-Malamud's compelling evidence, I have no doubt it will. My intensive research was of a rural hamlet; a careful study of socio-ethnic relations *vis-à-vis* medical dialog in the district towns – where *mestizos* and *campesinos* share social space – is clearly called for.

As for the representativeness of the data presented on musculoskeletal ailments and their healers, I can only speak for the highland Peruvians with whom I worked. However, I believe these findings may be applicable to other rural third world contexts wherever life is characterized by strenuous agricultural work, limited resources, and a relatively low incidence of infectious disease.

Componedores provide an unparalleled contribution to health care in the rural Andes. The high demand for their services corresponds with the high frequency of musculoskeletal complaints found among highland peasants, a result of the onerous burden of physical labor and injuries they endure in their position of lowest rank in an exploitative political–economic system. National policies have never favored the advancement of Peru's native peoples. Until the social, political, and economic conditions change to become more favorable for the sierran agriculturalist – even if only to provide a fair price for goods produced – the physical burden of existence will not be eased, the conditions described above can be expected to remain chronic, and the need for *componedores* will endure.

Acknowledgments

I wish to sincerely thank Bill Dressler, Bob Anderson, Servando Hinojosa, and the editors of this volume for helpful critique and commentary on earlier drafts of this chapter. Deborah Hughes and Thavone Phengphan worked wonders with the graphics. Also, this work could not have been accomplished without the hospitality of the people of Chugurpampa, who, with humor and wisdom, put up with my endless questions and shared all they knew.

Notes

1 My experience with manipulative healing is both personal and professional as well as cross-cultural. Since my youth, I have worked for pay as a massage therapist on numerous occasions in the United States and Peru and regularly performed minor chiropractic procedures on friends and family (my skills being acquired by accretion through apprenticeship, observation, trial and error, reading, etc.). I have also been treated for structural misalignments and pain (brought on primarily by a history of participation in contact sports and other nonsense) by numerous lay and professional therapists, including friends, an osteopath, a chiropractor, many *componedores* and *hueseros*, a few physical therapists and two rolfers. I have observed countless treatments of others by the same therapists. Additionally, my research for my master's degree was based on observation in a chiropractic clinic in Cleveland, Ohio, from which I published two papers. The very real benefits I have received and witnessed from musculoskeletal care, and that I believe I have provided to others on occasion, motivate me to disseminate the knowledge I have accumulated on a long overlooked health problem and its efficacious, low technology treatment.

2 Libbet Crandon-Malamud, *From the Fat of Our Souls: Social Change, Political Process, and Medical Pluralism in Bolivia*, University of California Press, 1991.

3 Kathryn S. Oths, "Some symbolic dimensions of Andean materia medica," *Central Issues in Anthropology*, 1992, 10: 76–85; *Medical Treatment Choice and Health Outcomes*

in the Northern Peruvian Andes, PhD Dissertation, Case Western Reserve University, Cleveland, 1991.

4 Mobilization refers to rhythmic circumscribed movements of a joint to restore range of motion (see Robert Anderson, "The treatment of musculoskeletal disorders by a Mexican bonesetter (sobador)," *Social Science and Medicine*, 1987, 24: 43–6, p. 44 for a detailed explanation).

5 Anderson, "The treatment of musculoskeletal disorders."

6 Margarita A. Kay, "Health and illness in a Mexican-American barrio." In *Ethnic Medicine in the Southwest*, Edward H. Spicer (ed.), University of Arizona Press, 1977, pp. 99–166.

7 Anderson, "The treatment of musculoskeletal disorders."

8 Brad R. Huber and Robert Anderson, "Bonesetters and curers in a Mexican community: conceptual models, status and gender," *Medical Anthropology*, 1996, 17: 23–38; Anderson, "The treatment of musculoskeletal disorders."

9 Mary E. Shutler, "Disease and curing in a Yaqui community." In *Ethnic Medicine in the Southwest*, Edward H. Spicer (ed.), University of Arizona Press, 1977, pp. 169–237, 204.

10 J. Dennis Mull and Dorothy S. Mull, "A visit with a *curandero* (cross-cultural medicine)," *Western Journal of Medicine*, 1983, 139: 730–36.

11 Benjamin D. Paul, "The Maya bonesetter as sacred specialist," *Ethnology*, 1976, 15: 77–81; *Secular and sacred bonesetters in Mesoamerica*, Paper presented at the 97th annual meetings of the American Anthropological Association, Philadelphia, 6 December 1998.

12 James C. Young, *Medical Treatment Choice in a Mexican Village*, Rutgers University Press, 1981, p. 109, 202.

13 Scott T. Anderson, *Bonesetters and* Curanderos *from Tzintzuntzan*, Video presented at the Annual Meeting of the Society for Applied Anthropology, San Juan, Puerto Rico, 22 April 1998.

14 Robert Redfield and Alfonso Villa Rojas, *Chan Kom: A Maya Village*, University of Chicago Press, 1934.

15 Robert Anderson, *The Antiquity and Ubiquity of Back Pain*, Paper presented at the annual meeting of the Southwestern Anthropological Association, Long Beach, CA, 13 April 1990.

16 Robert Anderson, "On doctors and bonesetters in the 16th and 17th centuries," *Chiropractic History*, 1983, 3: 11–15; Diane R. Karp, *Ars Medica: Art, Medicine, and the Human Condition*, University of Pennsylvania Press, 1984, plates 25*a*, 29; Helen Lambert, Of Bonesetters and Barber-surgeons: Traditions of Therapeutic Practice and the Spread of Allopathic Medicine in Rajasthan. In *Folk, Faith and Feudalism: Rajasthan Studies*, N. K. Singhi and Rajendra Joshi (eds), Rawat Publications, 1995, pp. 92–111; Henry E. Sigerist, *Civilization and Disease*, Cornell University Press, 1944, plate 43; H. Valdizan and A. Maldonado, *La Medicina Popular Peruana*, vol. 1, Imprenta Torres Aguilar, 1922.

17 Thomas Csordas (ed.), *Embodiment and Experience: The Existential Ground of Culture and Self*, Cambridge University Press, 1994; Elaine Scarry, *The Body in Pain*, Oxford University Press, 1985; Nancy Scheper-Hughes and Margaret Lock, "The mindful body: a prolegomenon to future work in medical anthropology," *Medical Anthropology Quarterly*, 1987, 1: 6–41.

18 Thomas Csordas, "Somatic modes of attention," *Cultural Anthropology*, 1993, 8: 135–56.

19 Servando Z. Hinojosa, *The Nature of Huesero Work: Maya Men and Body Knowledge*, Paper presented at the annual meeting of the American Ethnological Society, Portland, OR, 27 March 1999.

20 Libbet Crandon-Malamud, "Phantoms and physicians: social change through medical pluralism." In *The Anthropology of Medicine: From Culture to Method*, 2nd edn, Lola Romanucci-Ross, Daniel E. Moerman, and Laurence R. Tancredi (eds), Bergin and Garvey, 1991, p. 88.

21 Kathryn S. Oths, "Assessing variation in health status in the Andes: a biocultural model," *Social Science and Medicine*, 1999, 47: 1017–30.
22 That is, there are no *mestizos* apart from the temporarily assigned school teachers, who spend as little time as possible in the community, have neither land nor family there, and are not considered integrated into hamlet life in any meaningful sense. This does not keep a small group of the long removed *mestizos* from returning to a community meeting every few years to demand land and threaten legal action if they aren't granted it. Locals politely but steadfastly reject these claims, stating one must work the land to maintain rights to it.
23 Crandon-Malamud, "Phantoms and physicians," p. 86.
24 Kathryn S. Oths, "*Debilidad*: a biocultural assessment of an embodied Andean illness," *Medical Anthropology Quarterly*, 1999, 13: 286–315, 306.
25 Alfred L. Kroeber, *Anthropology*, Harcourt Brace and Company, 1948, p. 284; Robert Redfield, *The Primitive World and its Transformations*, Cornell University Press, 1953, p. 31.
26 Robert Anderson, "An orthopedic ethnography in rural Nepal," *Medical Anthropology*, 1984, 8: 46–59.
27 The term Christian is equated with "civilized person" in Peru.
28 Also see Anderson, "The treatment of musculoskeletal disorders: investigating back pain: the implications of two village studies in South Asia." In *Dimensions of Social Life*, Paul Hocking (ed.), Mouton de Gruyter, 1984, pp. 385–96.
29 Oths, "Medical treatment choice and health outcomes."
30 Henry E. Sigerist, "The special position of the sick." Reprinted in *Culture, Disease and Healing: Studies in Medical Anthropology*, David Landy (ed.), Macmillan, 1977 (orig. 1960) pp. 388–94.
31 Oths, "*Debilidad*."
32 Crandon-Malamud, *From the Fat of Our Souls*.
33 Oths, "Assessing variation in health status."
34 Anderson, "An orthopedic ethnography."
35 Aída Heras Medina, "Plantas medicinales de Tlalpizahuac, Estado de Mexico," *Tlahui-Medic*, 1997, 4: 1–5.
36 Anne Larme, *Work, Reproduction and Health in Two Andean Communities*, Working Paper No. 5. Production, Storage and Exchange Project. Department of Anthropology, University of North Carolina, Chapel Hill, NC, 1993.
37 Robert D. Jurmain, "Stress and the etiology of osteoarthritis," *American Journal of Physical Anthropology*, 1975, 46: 353–66; David Landy "Medical anthropology: a critical appraisal." In *Advances in Medical Social Science*, vol. 1, Julio Ruffini (ed.), Gordon and Breach Science Publishers, 1983 p. 185–314; Ruthbeth Finerman, *Health Care Decisions in an Andean Indian Community: Getting the Best of Both Worlds*, PhD Dissertation, University of California, Los Angeles, 1985; Bernard Sorofman and Toni Tripp-Reimer, *Health Care Choices in an Iowa Old Order Amish Community*, Paper presented at the American Anthropological Association Meetings, Washington DC, December, 1989.
38 Charles O. Frake, "The diagnosis of disease among the Subanun of Mindanao," *American Anthropologist*, 1961, 63: 113–32, 124.
39 Horacio Fabrega Jr. and Daniel B. Silver, *Illness and Shamanistic Curing in Zinacantan: An Ethnomedical Analysis*, Stanford University Press, 1973, p. 307.
40 Young, "Medical treatment choice," p. 50; Brigitte Jordan, *Birth in Four Cultures*, 4th edn, Waveland Press, 1978, p. 26.
41 It is of note that in Japanese *shiatsu* (chi meridian) theory, the location of the pressure points for the lungs are precisely in the location that highlanders indicate the *pulmones* are located, which corroborates to some extent their view of the location of the lungs and the musculoskeletal pains associated with them. Refer to Shizuto Masunaga and Wataru Ohashi, *Zen Shiatsu*, Japan Publications, 1977, p. 23.

42 Foot travel is the primary means of transportation. Transport of cargo by *burro* is preferred, but only 56 percent of households have one. Even when a *burro* is used or borrowed, highlanders will often walk beside it with their own load.

43 Oths, *"Debilidad."*

44 Also see Richard N. Adams and Arthur J. Rubel, "Sickness and social relations." In *Handbook of Middle American Indians*, Manning Nash (ed.), University of Texas Press, 1967, 6: 333–56; Hinojosa, *The Nature of Huesero Work*; and, Huber and Anderson, "Bonesetters and curers in a Mexican community," but cf. Mayan healers documented by Paul, "The Maya bonesetter," and Fabrega and Silver, *Illness and Shamanistic Curing.*

45 Hinojosa, *"The Nature of Huesero Work,"* Huber and Anderson, "Bonesetters and curers in a Mexican community."

46 Huber and Anderson, "Bonesetters and curers in a Mexican community," Paul, "The Maya bonesetter," Young, *Medical Treatment Choice.*

47 John M. Janzen, "The comparative study of medical systems as changing social systems," *Social Science and Medicine*, 1978, 12B: 121–7; Arthur Kleinman, *Patients and Healers in the Context of Culture*, University of California Press, 1980.

48 Kleinman, *Patients and Healers*, p. 373.

49 Kathryn S. Oths, "Communication in a chiropractic clinic: how a D.C. treats his patients," *Culture, Medicine and Psychiatry*, 1994, 18: 83–113; Allan Young, "Order, analogy, and efficacy in Ethiopian medical divination," *Culture, Medicine and Psychiatry*, 1977, 1: 183–99.

50 Paul, "The Maya bonesetter."

51 Csordas, *"Embodiment and experience,"* Hinojosa, *The Nature of Huesero Work.*

52 Kathryn S. Oths, "Some symbolic dimensions of Andean *materia medica*," *Central Issues in Anthropology*, 1992, 10: 76–85.

53 I am apparently not the only researcher impressed by ankle cures. Three others supply case studies of sprained ankles being treated by "bonesetter"-types (Paul, *Secular and Sacred Bonesetters*; Huber and Anderson, "Bonesetters and curers in a Mexican community," and Clarence McMahon, *The Sacred Nature of Maya Bonesetting: Ritual Validation in an Empirical Practice*, [M.A. thesis, Texas A&M University, 1993]), with excellent photos of the maneuver provided by McMahon.

54 Also see Kay, "Health and illness in a Mexican–American barrio"; Shutler, *"Disease and curing in a Yaqui community"*; and, Jordan, *Birth in Four Cultures.*

55 Pierre Bourdieu, *Outline of a Theory of Practice*, Cambridge University Press, 1977.

56 Also see Csordas, *Embodiment and Experience*, p. 147.

57 Allan Young, "The relevance of traditional medicine to modern primary health care," *Social Science and Medicine*, 1983, 17: 1205–11, 1208.

58 For a review, see John P. Gilbert, Richard J. Light, and Frederick Moteller, "Assessing social innovations: an empirical base for policy." In *Evaluation and Experiment: Some Critical Issues in Assessing Social Programs*, Carl A. Bennett and Arthur A. Lumsdaine (eds), Academic Press, 1975 pp. 39–193; and, Robert Anderson, "Research methods in trouble," *Medical Anthropology*, 1991, 13: 1–17.

59 Anderson, "The treatment of musculoskeletal disorders"; "The efficacy of ethnomedicine."

60 Crandon-Malamud, *From the Fat of Our Souls*, p. 205.

61 Oths, *"Debilidad."*

62 Young, "The relevance of traditional medicine"; "Order, analogy, and efficacy"; Atwood D. Gaines and Paul Farmer, "Visible saints: social cynosures and dysphoria in the Mediterranean tradition," *Culture, Medicine, and Psychiatry*, 1983, 10: 295–330; Arthur Kleinman and L. H. Sung, "Why do indigenous practitioners successfully heal?," *Social Science and Medicine*, 1979, 13: 7–26; Kleinman, "Patients and healers"; Kaja Finkler, "Spiritualist healers in Mexico: successes and failures of alternative therapeutics," Bergin and Garvey, 1982.

63 Anderson, "The treatment of musculoskeletal disorders."

64 Mull and Mull, "A visit with a *curandero*."
65 Felix Murillo Alfaro, *Demand de Atención en Servicios de Salud, 1997*, Peruvian National Institute of Statistics and Information (INEI), 1998.
66 Crandon-Malamud, *From the Fat of Our Souls*, p. 151.
67 For corroboration see Donald Joralemon and Douglas Sharon, *Sorcery and Shamanism: Curanderos and Clients in Northern Peru*, University of Utah Press, 1993.
68 Robert Anderson, "Medicine, chiropractic and caste," *Anthropological Quarterly*, 1981, 54: 157–65; Walter I. Wardwell, "Chiropractors: evolution to acceptance." In *Other Healers: Unorthodox Medicine in America*, N. Gevitz (ed.), Johns Hopkins University Press, 1988, p. 157–91.
69 Anderson, "Medicine, chiropractic and caste."
70 For biological reasons not covered by texts on highland pathology and physiology, bones that grow at high altitude seem to enjoy a greater than average tensile strength. For example, bones of cooked chickens are too hard to be chewed or cracked with the teeth.

References

Adams, Richard N. and Arthur J. Rubel, "Sickness and social relations." In *Handbook of Middle American Indians*, Manning Nash (ed.), University of Texas Press, 1967, 6, pp. 333–56.
Anderson, Robert, "The efficacy of ethnomedicine: research methods in trouble," *Medical Anthropology*, 1991, 13: 1–17.
——, *The antiquity and ubiquity of back pain*, Paper presented at the annual meeting of the Southwestern Anthropological Association, Long Beach, CA, 13 April 1990.
——, "The treatment of musculoskeletal disorders by a Mexican bonesetter (sobador)," *Social Science and Medicine*, 1987, 24: 43–6.
——, "An orthopedic ethnography in rural Nepal," *Medical Anthropology*, 1984, 8: 46–59.
——, "Investigating back pain: the implications of two village studies in South Asia." In *Dimensions of Social Life*, Paul Hocking (ed.), Mouton de Gruyter, 1984, pp. 385–96.
——, "On doctors and bonesetters in the 16th and 17th centuries," *Chiropractic History*, 1983, 3: 11–15.
——, "Medicine, chiropractic and caste," *Anthropological Quarterly*, 1981, 54: 157–65.
Anderson, Scott T., *Bonesetters and* Curanderos *from Tzintzuntzan*, Video presented at the Annual Meeting of the Society for Applied Anthropology, San Juan, Puerto Rico, 22 April 1998.
Berrin, Kathleen (ed.), *The Spirit of Ancient Peru: Treasures from the Museo Arqueológico Rafael Larco Herrera*, Thames and Hudson, 1997.
Bourdieu, Pierre, *Outline of a Theory of Practice*, Cambridge University Press, 1977.
Crandon-Malamud, Libbet, *From the Fat of Our Souls: Social Change, Political Process, and Medical Pluralism in Bolivia*, University of California Press, 1991.
——, "Phantoms and physicians: social change through medical pluralism." In *The Anthropology of Medicine: From Culture to Method*, 2nd edn, Lola Romanucci-Ross, Daniel E. Moerman, and Laurence R. Tancredi (eds), Bergin and Garvey, 1991.
Csordas, Thomas (ed.), *Embodiment and Experience: The Existential Ground of Culture and Self*, Cambridge University Press, 1994.
——, "Somatic modes of attention," *Cultural Anthropology*, 1993, 8: 135–56.
Fabrega, Horacio, Jr. and Daniel B. Silver, *Illness and Shamanistic Curing in Zinacantan: An Ethnomedical Analysis*, Stanford University Press, 1973.
Finerman, Ruthbeth, *Health Care Decisions in an Andean Indian Community: Getting the Best of Both Worlds*, PhD Dissertation, University of California, Los Angeles, 1985.

Finkler, Kaja, *Spiritualist Healers in Mexico: Successes and Failures of Alternative Therapeutics*, Bergin and Garvey, 1982.

Frake, Charles O., "The diagnosis of disease among the Subanun of Mindanao," *American Anthropologist*, 1961, 63: 113–32.

Gaines, Atwood D. and Paul Farmer, "Visible saints: social cynosures and dysphoria in the Mediterranean tradition," *Culture, Medicine, and Psychiatry*, 1983, 10: 295–330.

Gilbert, John P., Richard J. Light, and Frederick Moteller, "Assessing social innovations: an empirical base for policy." In *Evaluation and Experiment: Some Critical Issues in Assessing Social Programs*, Carl A. Bennett and Arthur A. Lumsdaine (ed.), Academic Press, 1975, pp. 39–193.

Hinojosa, Servando Z., *The Nature of Huesero Work: Maya Men and Body Knowledge*, Paper presented at the annual meeting of the American Ethnological Society, Portland, OR, 27 March 1999).

Huber, Brad R. and Robert Anderson, "Bonesetters and curers in a Mexican community: conceptual models, status and gender," *Medical Anthropology*, 1996, 17: 23–38.

Janzen, John M., "The comparative study of medical systems as changing social systems," *Social Science and Medicine*, 1978, 12B: 121–7.

Joralemon, Donald and Douglas Sharon, *Sorcery and Shamanism: Curanderos and Clients in Northern Peru*, University of Utah Press, 1993.

Jordan, Brigitte, *Birth in Four Cultures*, 4th edn, Waveland Press, 1978.

Jurmain, Robert D., "Stress and the etiology of osteoarthritis," *American Journal of Physical Anthropology*, 1975, 46: 353–66.

Karp, Diane R., *Ars Medica: Art, Medicine, and the Human Condition*, University of Pennsylvania Press, 1984.

Kay, Margarita A., "Health and illness in a Mexican–American barrio." In *Ethnic Medicine in the Southwest*, Edward H. Spicer (ed.), University of Arizona Press, 1977, pp. 99–166.

Kleinman, Arthur, *Patients and Healers in the Context of Culture*, University of California Press, 1980.

—— and L. H. Sung, "Why do indigenous practitioners successfully heal?," *Social Science and Medicine*, 1979, 13: 7–26.

Kroeber, Alfred L., *Anthropology*, Harcourt Brace and Company, 1948.

Lambert, Helen, "Of bonesetters and barber-surgeons: traditions of therapeutic practice and the spread of allopathic medicine in Rajasthan." In *Folk, Faith and Feudalism: Rajasthan Studies*, N. K. Singhi and Rajendra Joshi (eds), Rawat Publications, 1995, pp. 92–111.

Landy, David, "Medical anthropology: a critical appraisal." In *Advances in Medical Social Science*, vol. 1, J. Ruffing (ed.), Gordon and Breach Science Foundation, 1983, pp. 185–314.

Larme, Anne, *Work, Reproduction and Health in Two Andean Communities*, Working Paper No. 5. Production, Storage and Exchange Project, Department of Anthropology, University of North Carolina, Chapel Hill, NC, 1993.

McMahon, Clarence, *The Sacred Nature of Maya Bonesetting: Ritual Validation in an Empirical Practice*, M.A. thesis, Texas A&M University, 1993.

Masunaga, Shizuto and Wataru Ohashi, *Zen Shiatsu*, Japan Publications, 1977.

Medina, Aída Heras, "Plantas medicinales de Tlalpizahuac, Estado de Mexico," *Tlahui-Medic*, 1997, 4: 1–5.

Mull, J. Dennis and Dorothy S. Mull, "A visit with a *curandero* (cross-cultural medicine)," *Western Journal of Medicine*, 1983, 139: 730–6.

Murillo Alfaro, Felix, *Demand de Atención en Servicios de Salud, 1997*, Peruvian National Institute of Statistics and Information (INEI), 1998.

Oths, Kathryn S., "Debilidad: a biocultural assessment of an embodied Andean illness," *Medical Anthropology Quarterly*, 1999, 13: 286–315.

——, "Assessing variation in health status in the Andes: a biocultural model," *Social Science and Medicine*, 1999, 47: 1017–30.

——, "Communication in a chiropractic clinic: how a D.C. treats his patients," *Culture, Medicine and Psychiatry*, 1994, 18: 83–113.

——, "Some symbolic dimensions of Andean *materia medica*," *Central Issues in Anthropology*, 1992, 10: 76–85.

——, *Medical treatment choice and health outcomes in the northern Peruvian Andes*, PhD Dissertation, Case Western Reserve University, Cleveland, 1991.

Paul, Benjamin D., "The Maya bonesetter as sacred specialist," *Ethnology*, 1976, 15: 77–81.

——, *Secular and Sacred Bonesetters in Mesoamerica*, Paper presented at the 97th annual meetings of the American Anthropological Association, Philadelphia, 6 December 1998.

Redfield, Robert, *The Primitive World and its Transformations*, Cornell University Press, 1953.

—— and Alfonso Villa Rojas, *Chan Kom: A Maya Village*, University of Chicago Press, 1934.

Scarry, Elaine, *The Body in Pain*, Oxford University Press, 1985.

Scheper-Hughes, Nancy and Margaret Lock, "The mindful body: a prolegomenon to future work in medical anthropology," *Medical Anthropology Quarterly*, 1987, 1: 6–41.

Shutler, Mary E., "Disease and curing in a Yaqui community." In *Ethnic Medicine in the Southwest*, Edward H. Spicer (ed.), University of Arizona Press, 1977, pp. 169–237.

Sigerist, Henry E., "The special position of the sick." Reprinted in *Culture, Disease and Healing: Studies in Medical Anthropology*, David Landy (ed.), Macmillan, 1977 (orig. 1960) pp. 388–94.

——, *Civilization and Disease*, Cornell University Press, 1944.

Sorofman, Bernard and Toni Tripp-Reimer, *Health Care Choices in an Iowa Old Order Amish Community*, Paper presented at the American Anthropological Association Meetings, Washington, DC, 15–19 November 1989.

Valdizan, H. and A. Maldonado, *La Medicina Popular Peruana*, 1, Imprenta Torres Aguilar, 1922.

Wardwell, Walter I., "Chiropractors: evolution to acceptance." In *Other Healers: Unorthodox Medicine in America*, N. Gevitz (ed.), Johns Hopkins University Press, 1988, pp. 157–91.

Young, Allan, "The relevance of traditional medicine to modern primary health care," *Social Science and Medicine*, 1983, 17: 1205–11, 1208.

——, "Order, analogy, and efficacy in Ethiopian medical divination," *Culture, Medicine and Psychiatry*, 1977, 1: 183–99.

Young, James C., *Medical Treatment Choice in a Mexican Village*, Rutgers University Press, 1981.

Chapter 6

Healing soul loss
The negotiation of identity in Peru

Christine Greenway

It took nearly a week to travel from Cusco to Mollomarca the first time. This was due to the fact that the former hacienda owner's sister's small pick-up truck broke down and it took us days to get parts. We were also impeded by the fact that a waterfall had washed out part of the small dirt road from Paucartambo to Mollomarca. The effect of the arduous travel was to make my first impressions of Mollomarca colored by a sense of remoteness and isolation. The small village appeared to cling to the sides of an improbably vertical landscape on the steep slopes of a dramatic river canyon. Far below curved the milky, glacier-fed stream that flowed from snow-covered Ausungate. I later wrote in a letter about my first impressions, "I am recognizing patterns *as* patterns, where before I saw either barren landscape, random behavior, or groups of strangers. I first noticed this in my changing perception of the landscape that in the beginning looked like the most barren, dry, unused, and unusable land I had ever seen. Now I can tell that the slightly different shaded areas are fields placed at the most improbable angles on the steepest hillside imaginable … I can now spot grazing areas, paths, and people seated, working, walking." The brilliant colors of peoples' brightly woven clothing, the aroma of eucalyptus fires, the scurrying run of people doing chores, herding animals, going to their fields were all part of the initial blur before I started seeing beyond the dramatic landscape and the shy, formal, quiet strangers into the patterns of the lives of godchildren, friends, neighbors, healers who shared their world with me.

Introduction

I encountered Libbet Crandon-Malamud's work in Andean medical anthropology after I first conducted fieldwork beginning in the 1980s in the southern Peruvian Andes.[1] I had already written an analysis of soul loss and ritual healing when I read Libbet's "Why *Susto*?" article and other pieces.[2] Her work on social change, political process, and medical pluralism in Bolivia illuminated how individual notions of personhood and cultural identity are negotiated through medicine. I reframed my perspective on Andean concepts of fright, soul loss, and symbolic healing and began to understand their meaning in a broader sense, as a result of her compelling theoretical arguments about the ways in which social identity and power

are negotiated through the treatment of illness. Here I reconsider the content of healers' talk during symbolic healing ceremonies for soul loss.[3] I am indebted to
Libbet's insistence that we must recognize that medical and political ideologies and
practices in the Andean context are linked; an individual's activities in one arena
may serve as metaphors for one's position in the other. Libbet's work challenged
scholars of the Andes to consider the political, economic, and social context of illness diagnosis. Illness and treatment in her view were metaphors for complex,
historically shaped power inequities between ethnic and class groups.[4] They also
provided strategies for maneuvering one's social position, power, and access to
resources.

The narratives by healers during healing ceremonies convey Quechua (*runa*)
notions of the coexistence of present and past, physical and spiritual, alive and
dead, well and sick, *runa* and non*runa*. In an analysis of illness stories told by sufferers in Ecuador, Price argues that such stories often "transcend their topical
focus" – that is, the illness – and express more general models of family and
social hierarchy.[5] The narratives I discuss here are similar – at times it seems as if
families and healers talk about everything *except* the illness, or the specific complaints, or even the specific patient with whom they are working. As I returned to
my notes and tapes and on later visits to Mollomarca (asking myself "what would
Libbet say about this?"), I realized that during cures and interviews about health
I had recorded countless stories about topics that I initially assumed were unre-
lated to illness. I had dutifully made note of them – but I did not fully interpret
them in my original analysis. I had returned, doggedly, to Quintin, Paukar, Maria,
Mariano, Felix, and other healers with lists of questions about what caused illness,
what was used to treat it, what particular symptoms meant, and so forth because
they rarely talked about these issues during treatment. I pursued, with determina-
tion what I thought were the most important things to know in order to represent
the Quechua view of illness and well being and the practices associated with prevention and cure. They answered my questions. But, I would have to admit, that
they rarely spontaneously talked about illness and healing in some of the ways
that I asked them to. Instead, they talked about trucks, loans, police checkpoints,
Incas, gold, devils, and community gossip with each other and during healing.

In this chapter, I focus on what healers discuss when they investigate the source
of illness, diagnose, explain their treatment, and educate patients about the course
of treatment. The conjunction of these narrative topics with the Quechua understanding of individual vulnerability, suffering, and treatment merits further investigation. After all, the people the healers are relating these stories to are people
who are sick or who are caring for suffering family members. Evidently, such talk
is expected and appropriate. It comforts and heals. Talk of landlords, devils, and
buried gold is used to make sense of illness; and talk of illness, as Crandon-
Malamud reminded us, is itself a metaphor for ethnic, social, and economic status.

The majority of the narratives I focus on here, are by Quintin, one of the most
widely sought after healers in the community of Mollomarca. However, other healers also brought up many similar themes. After listening countless times to the

stories that he narrated during divinations and sacrificial offerings, it became clear that they offered not only evidence of his personal supernatural power, but they included elements that drew upon both indigenous and *mestizo* symbols of power to provide legitimacy for Quintin's claims of knowledge. He told stories that established his authority in a variety of ways – those tales demonstrated divine election, Incaic heritage, supernatural power, successful healing outcomes, and moral superiority over others, including non*runa* or *mistis* (Quechua term for *mestizos*, upper class, or outsiders).[6] Such legitimacy allowed him to challenge his patients and their families to question the presumed superior power of *mestizos* and whites.

Research setting

Mollomarca is located in the south central Peruvian Andes 120 km east of Cusco, Peru in the district of Paucartambo. It is a small, remote, Quechua hamlet of sixty-seven households (approximately 250 people) scattered on the steep slopes of a river canyon at an altitude of 3,020–4,200 m.[7] Like other primarily subsistence-based, rural Andean communities in Peru, Mollomarca has been increasingly drawn into the national political and economic scene with the dissolution of the hacienda system during the agrarian reform period in the late 1960s and early 1970s. Mollomarquinos have little or no access to biomedical care. Although in July and August 2000 a small medical post was completed and visiting rural health workers were occasionally present, it is more typical for people to rely on traditional healers and remedies. It is possible to walk 28 km to Paucartambo where there is a medical post, but during the period of this study medical supplies and personnel were rarely available and people were infrequently motivated to make the trek. In 2000, the situation was much the same; people could not afford to use the medical post and many told of being treated rudely by staff. People were also doubtful about the knowledge and ability of non*runa* health care practitioners to treat ailments caused by ancestor spirits, evil winds, or other similar causes.

For health care, Mollomarquinos rely on shared knowledge of medicinal plants and on ten or more people in the community and neighboring villages who have specialized knowledge to cure illness, to divine the future, to pay the earth, to repel misfortune, or to retaliate for the evil acts of others. These healers have their supernatural powers revealed to them in various ways and each has different talents for diagnosing and healing that include coca divination, pulsing, candle reading, feeding the earth, and preparing herbal remedies.[8]

Runa believe that at birth everyone is linked with a star that determines one's character and potential destiny. People make offerings to this star and to the earth spirits over the course of their lifetime in order to positively influence this destiny. A few individuals are further selected through a process of divine election to be healers or intermediaries with the spiritual realm. Proof of this election can take place by means of dreams, recognition of descent from an Inca ruler, illness, or being struck by lightning. A healer is thus related to the ancestors and deities differently than ordinary people are, and derives the ability to heal by manipulating, calling, and serving these forces. The most powerful healers (*altomisayoqs*) have the ability to communicate with the earth spirits both through divination and oracular messages and discover what sacrificial offerings they demand; by making such sacrifices of coca and other items they are able to maintain harmony and equilibrium in the world and in terms of people's health, family life, and livelihoods.[9]

However, many people in Mollomarca doubted the existence of such healers: the world would not be in such a desperate state they reasoned, with its proliferation of natural disasters, murders, and poverty-stricken Indians if *altomisayoqs* could still hear the demands of the earth. Some diviners argued that they do have the knowledge and skill to make good and proper offerings and to fathom the will of the earth spirits. But many people simply ignore or find too costly their obligations to mountain spirits, stars, and ancestral beings or are harmed by devils as they come in contact with non*runa*.

How Quintin became a healer

Quintin consistently told the story of how he became a healer whenever a patient or family member consulted him. The story clarifies his source of supernatural power. His divine election alone, however, did not give him sufficient power to heal animals or people of illness, accidents, or misfortunes. Although healers are selected or designated from birth, a proof of election is required, and Quintin is no exception. Most of the healers in the community claimed to have been struck by lightning, had a dream or a vision, received a gift from the earth, or experienced near death. Many claimed some combination of these kinds of personal experiences.

Quintin was caught by a "bad lightning": like a wind, it struck him with a great blast of noise, whirling his poncho over his head. He called the spirit who attacked him Juaniquillo, who (like the archetypical *hacendado* (estate owner of Spanish descent) depicted on old calendars that still hung on the crumbling hacienda walls) wore a cape, sat astride a white horse, and possessed many animals, abundant food, and lots of money. The encounter left Quintin gravely ill; while near death he was treated by another healer who made sacrificial offerings to appease the spirit who had sickened Quintin. Yet Quintin could not be fully "separated" from his sickness, so he had to serve the spirit who "grabbed" him. The only way he was able to recover was to "accept his paper" from Juaniquillo and to start reading coca and making offerings for others. Paukar, a coca diviner from a nearby community stated that Quintin's alliance with Juanaquillo is a connection to *mestizos*; as a result many people viewed Quintin as potentially dangerous and allied with the spiritual "left" or evil side. He was often blamed by other curers for using sorcery against people. His claims to connections with this *mestizo* spiritual guardian was regarded ambivalently and some people would not go to Quintin as a result.

Another female healer described her election taking place in a gruesome dream encounter with Christ – he threatened to kill her with a large knife if she did not heed the call to be a coca diviner. He proved his intent to provide her with healing power by killing her abusive husband with a rapid, fatal illness and thus saving her life. Interestingly, both of these cases offer examples of selection by supernatural entities associated with *mestizos*, Christ and "Little Juan." In contrast, three additional practitioners, Felix, Justina, and Paukar tell more traditional stories about being struck by lightning or encountering unusual objects (stones, Inca artifacts, or other oddities), becoming ill, hovering near death, and being revived with the help of a healer. They were then motivated to learn to cure themselves or were apprenticed to the one who had saved them. Healers are often perceived of in an ambivalent way, as having the power to both help or harm. They are also viewed as mediators between the world of the community and the world of the spirits. It is not surprising that they would embody conflicting identities – human/spirit, *mestizo/runa*, good/evil, alive/dead, and so forth.

During divinations and healing rites, in addition to making references to the sources of their supernatural power, healers discuss other people who they have healed, misfortunes they have altered, and their familiarity with appropriate rituals and medicines to cure. Often the other clients and their problems are remarkably similar to the person who asked for help. These stories demonstrate the healers' abilities and past successes in similar circumstances and contrast with other healers who perform the rituals improperly. Obviously, such tales are meant to inspire confidence in those who consult with the healer. They also tell patients of the deaths, grievous harm, bad luck, and ruptured families that result when their instructions are not followed.

Political, economic, and ethnic discourse in healing narratives

Because healers act as intermediaries with the supernatural realm, they must claim supernatural authority. So it is not unusual that they would detail personal experiences and successes to demonstrate the source of their knowledge and power. However, many other more mundane kinds of stories were told during healing. Sometimes Quintin recounted community events, analyzed the causes of particular problems, and told jokes. The stories told in consultations with people were also interspersed with comments about life's inequities, reasons for people's failures, and the difficulties of making decisions. Quintin offered advice about the importance of thinking before acting and guided people's future decision making. He reminded his clients that people are out to do harm to others and that problems of illness or misfortune are a result of disharmony in the community and people's evil intentions and interference in each other's lives. Almost all of these stories served to admonish, instruct, and remind people of their reciprocal obligations to deities, relatives, and community members. The dangers of greed, envy, and selfishness are illustrated with dramatic, tragic stories of people who have been jailed, eaten by the earth, or fatally afflicted. The moral of many of the stories was that only by maintaining traditional patterns of reciprocal exchanges and obligations could health, prosperity, and well-being be attained. Healers' narratives thus demonstrate, sanction, and critique appropriate modes of behavior for Mollomarquinos. In this sense, the role of healers in resisting change and assimilation into the *mestizo* world differs from the strategies and negotiations of people in the town

Crandon studied; Mollomarquinos are less occupied with upward social mobility in terms of changing ethnic identity. For example, Quintin stated often, "I am an example to younger men. I tell them that they shouldn't work with money from the bank. 'Are you women?' I ask. What are you – working with loaned money? You are not like me a man." He is preoccupied with the dangers of indebtedness to outsiders. Yet there does exist a tension between the views of many people of his generation and the younger Mollomarquinos who desire greater wealth, educational opportunities, and an easier life. Perhaps, the reason he and so many of the healers use the context of the soul calling ceremony to underscore the potential dangers of leaving Mollomarca and allying with non*runa* is that such occasions provide a highly charged, spiritual context in which to work through such social tensions and negotiations about identity and community cohesion.

Quintin and other healers also told stories about the Incas, devils, buried gold treasure and *mestizos*. Such topics moved the discourse beyond healing and provided him with further moral grounding and authority in a broader social context. The claims of authority implicit in these narratives also provide a critique of regional, political, economic, and ethnic power relations that impact the lives of Mollomarquinos. Some of the most interesting stories that reflect a tension about ethnic identity, economic change, and political power have to do with stories about involvement with non*runa*. These stories provide an implicit analysis and critique of the asymmetrical power relationships that exist between Mollomarquinos and the former *hacendado*, local political officials, and other *mestizos*, and non*runa* they encounter. The following topics recurred in the discourse of many healing ceremonies: the *hacienda* era, trucks, judges, doctors, lawyers, Incas, gold, buried treasure, and airplanes. The following provides some examples of the ways in which these themes represented a deeper concern with the negotiation of *runa* identity in the face of economic and political oppression.

During the time of the *hacienda*

Quintin often referred to events that occurred during the time the *hacienda* was intact and Mollomarquinos provided labor in exchange for land use rights. In one example, a man lingered close to death for days because of fright sickness contracted while he was pasturing sheep for the *hacendado*. Quintin performed a sacrificial cure to recover the man's departed soul. The *hacendado* objected to that type of treatment and came to the man's house insistent on giving him an injection. Quintin barred the door. He refused to allow the shot for fear that it would interfere with his treatment:

> I told him 'No. You can't do anything, *viracocha* (lord), because it is already done. I have done the cure (*lloqesqa*).' 'If this man dies, I will take you to jail,' said the Señor. But later he couldn't take me to jail because nine days later that man was cured. He was healthy, really healthy. I went with him to the Señor and I said to him, 'Here I am – the man you wanted to put in jail.' After seeing the man healthy, the Señor told me, 'Very good, son.' He paid me cigarettes and one pound of sugar and I left happy. So it is, I go anywhere.

I have a license. I work with the authorities. I can go to the police station, the judge, anywhere.

In reality, it would be very unlikely for Quintin to enter a police station or other such location voluntarily. He did not speak Spanish, did not leave Mollomarca, and had very little dealings with outsiders.

In another narrative Quintin recounts being called upon to heal thirty of the *hacendado's* horses that were dying of an illness caused by the *hacienda's* resident devil. Quintin cured all of the horses with a burnt offering and reported that he earned the *hacendado's* respect. "The Señor has always esteemed me and asked for me. He always brings me bread. As much as I want. If anyone offended me or hit me, the Señor would go to the judge or do anything for me, his son. I am loved by them (*mistis*), they don't abuse me."

In spite of his claim of affiliation with the estate owner, he also reported making preventative offerings for people before they undertook their rotation of servitude on the *hacienda* to keep them from being eaten by devils or from suffering premature aging and withering that would occur when they were "grabbed" by the earth there. Many tales detailed the kinds of illnesses one could still contract through association with the *hacienda* lands or the shared labor that the former *hacienda* owner continued to solicit through the 1980s after the *hacienda* had been dismantled.

Numerous versions of these stories review for Quintin's listeners the dangerous imbalance of relationships between Mollomarquinos and the estate owner who continued on reduced land holdings to exploit Mollomarquinos' labor. The accounts he offers to his patients underscore the differences between *runa* and non*runa*. Like the fickle ancestor and earth spirits, the devils associated with the *hacienda* are still capable of grabbing and eating a person's heart, soul, and fat causing them to waste away and die. Interestingly, Quintin reports that defiance of the *hacendado's* orders resulted in a cure for the patient and respect by the *hacendado* for *runa* ways. The former owner stated, however, that he viewed Quintin's practices as backward and superstitious. He complained that people begged him constantly for medicine and received the best treatment from him and his family. This conflict of interpretations serves to highlight the challenge Quintin's glorification of his defiance and his superior knowledge poses for the negotiation of power between *runa* and *misti*. Both parties in this event had very different interpretations of its meaning and the relative status of the individuals involved. Quintin remains firm in his conviction, however, that his skills as a healer are superior to any that *mistis* might have.

Trucks

Quintin's stories about the *hacienda* have been supplemented with other stories since the reallocation of *hacienda* power and land after the agrarian reform period. Now, other kinds of people, such as *mestizo* truck owners, are the subjects of his narratives. One story was about a man who owned eight trucks, which would have made him enormously and improbably wealthy (and perhaps in Quintin's estimation more comparable to my American wealth and status because it was clearly out of the bounds of village experience). He was having marital problems and asked Quintin to help him get his wife to forsake an incestuous relationship with a godson and return to him. Quintin agreed to accompany him on the way to the jungle to find his wife. Along the way to perform this service, the truck broke down. Quintin diagnosed bewitchment by people envious of the man's success and status. Quintin performed two divinations and sacrifices at the site of the breakdown – one for the truck and one for the man. The truck restarted, the couple reconciled, and Quintin and his helpers were reportedly paid huge amounts of money, food, and alcohol.

Stories about cures of trucks were common in Quintin's repertoire and people who ignored his advice to make sacrificial offerings to mountain spirits often had disasters involving trucks. Trucks are high status objects keenly desired by many Mollomarquinos; they represent the ability to gain access to regional markets and a cash economy.[10] Yet, Quintin's stories warn of the dire consequences of greed and of focusing one's economic activities outside of the network of community reciprocity. His tales warn of the seductive and destructive power of technology and change. Many of his examples discourage young people from leaving to find outside work. He told of people who ignored his advice and the calamities that befell them: one teenaged boy died in a truck accident and another young woman suffered from attacks of nerves whenever she was in town trying to work as a domestic laborer. Individuals who did try to leave the community were often diagnosed by their families as suffering from fright sickness and soul loss. They had to be cured with soul calling rituals and many young people ended up returning to Mollomarca and settling there permanently.

Judges, doctors, and lawyers

Stories of curing the relatives of judges, lawyers, police, political officials, and doctor's patients were frequently told by Quintin and a few other healers. One example involved Quintin's cure of a political official's sister who had been possessed by a devil. This official queried Quintin about what was needed for the cure and dutifully wrote the instructions and list of ingredients down. The official purchased all of the required medicines (*hampi*) and hired Quintin to complete a burnt sacrificial offering. Ultimately, the woman was healed and went on to marry and raise a family. Paukar, another healer, told stories of *mestizos* who wanted to become doctors and lawyers but who were attempting to do so without proper sacrificial offerings to the earth and *apus* (mountain spirits). He said that if such people came to him for help, the *apus* would help them become professionals quickly and successfully. But, if they did not make such sacrifices, they would not succeed. Even trained doctors, he pointed out, who did not pay the spirits would die themselves without the help of the *apus* and people like him who knew what payments were demanded by such beings.

These types of stories differ from Quintin and Paukar's other claims of supernatural power. In spite of economic poverty and political powerlessness in *mestizo* terms, such narratives establish a moral authority that renders non*runa* powerless, vulnerable to devil possession, and dependent on the greater knowledge of *runa* diviners. The wealth, bureaucratic paperwork, and political positions of whites and *mestizos* mean nothing in the world of Quintin and Paukar's narratives. Quintin is capable of healing the animals and relatives of powerful people because of his Incaic heritage, links to mountain spirits, and divine election to be an intermediary with the spirits. Although Quintin asserted that when he was younger he could only cure animals and children, he has now accumulated more power. "Look *comadre,*" he said, "now that I am old I can call the souls of adults. For this reason I am not afraid to go to the judge, or the military post, or any other place. I feel so sure of myself that I can put myself in front of them and perform the duties of my office." He referred to himself as having "titles," "papers," and "documents" – legitimizing his spiritual authority and power with the symbols of legal, bureaucratic power. These are papers, he claims, that all will recognize and that no one can invalidate or take from him – they are supernatural and invulnerable to earthly destruction. "Look how long I've lived. Now I'm old and everything I do is something legal." Quintin also referred to his star and the knowledge that it gave him as "being able to see and know like in a book." Yet, merging these metaphors with more traditional Andean symbols, he also reminds listeners that there is a lion behind him who will gobble up the souls of people who threaten him or disbelieve his authority. And if he does not obey the supernatural laws, he fears a devil-like dog will bite him in his dreams to prevent him from performing evil.

I conducted these interviews and observed Quintin in 1983–5, 1986, and 1987. It is interesting to note that with the dissolution of the *hacienda* and the establishment of Mollomarca as an officially recognized *communidad campesino*, the villagers were required to establish an elected governing body and to record all community decisions and activities in a Book of Acts that had to be stamped annually as legal by a judge in the provincial capital of Paucartambo. I have had the opportunity to see and record all of the Books of Acts since their inception in 1974 through July 2000; some of the things that are recorded include the documentation of deaths caused by fright and soul loss as well as consensus decisions about community priorities regarding building a road, buying a truck, constructing a medical post, planting trees, among other issues. It may be that much of Quintin's discourse about papers and legal authority, although stated with reference to *mistis* in Paucartambo, in fact provide a medium for public discussion of the new form of conflict resolution and governance that Mollomarquinos are working out in the wake of such dramatic social change. Certainly, individuals are claiming power in Mollomarca who would not have been able to compete with older men like Quintin in the past. Some of those competing for new status are semi-literate, have increasing facility in Spanish, and are eager for more experiences and economic ties outside of the community boundaries. These traits and other changes have continued to escalate in the late 1990s.

Quintin asserts constantly that he has mastered coca reading, has valid supernatural authority and great success in curing illnesses. But in his stories he also informs patients and families that his authority is such that he could call upon police or judges to punish those who harass him or question his authority. Implicit in his challenge, is that these younger upstarts do not have the same ability to rally such upper class allies. In addition to drawing upon the coercive power of the state in his narratives, he takes on doctors and biomedicine in statements such as the following addressed to me, made during a soul calling:

> I am not a witch. I am a *sanitario*. I cure people from evil. We heal ourselves with offerings to the earth to protect ourselves for the bad intentions of others. It is that way among us *runa*. But among your people or *mistis*, you give injections. An injection can't cure witchcraft. It can cure pneumonia or stomach ache. But these devil things cannot be cured by injection. So we read coca. And we pay the earth and then we call the spirits and this is how we heal ourselves.

Although he asserts that health care workers, lawyers, judges, and police respect him, his commentary also provides critiques of these same people, for they are unable to do what he does. They cannot cure themselves or their families. Further, they are incapable of maintaining a harmonious balance with the earth spirits or their *communeros*. They must rely on him for guidance and skill. He demonstrates in his narrative constructions of himself and of healing that the *mestizo* legal, economic, and political structure is not morally grounded; it does not have the same spiritual authority to right wrongs or to maintain well being that Quintin and other *runa* have. The healer's narratives reveal a unique relationship with the supernatural that non*runa*, even official ones, do not have.

Incas, gold, buried treasure, airplanes

In spite of their apparent wealth, these non*runa* also cannot, in Quintin, Maria, and Paukar's stories, obtain access to gold without dying or suffering devil possession. Quintin, on the other hand, because of his connection as a *runa* to an Inca, who he says was once the original owner of Mollomarca and all the neighboring communities all the way to Mt Ausungate, has legitimate rights to buried gold. According to one of Quintin's versions of historical events, the Spaniards left the region after "our Incas" paid them gold and silver. Some of the animals that carried the treasure died on the journey while they accompanied the fleeing Spaniards. Today it is possible for people to find where the animals with their loads were buried. Quintin explained that people (such as *gringo* (foreigners) and *mestizo* miners recently in the area) who search for and take the buried gold do so in vain: they die gruesome deaths. One of these *gringo* miners reported to me of boulders rolling down on the camp at night – a story also reported by Mollomarquinos. Quintin, however, because of his relationship to the mountain spirits is able to find and take the buried treasure without suffering the ill effects of devil possession. He simply has chosen not to go and get the gold because he is too busy working in his fields earning his livelihood in a proper way. He does not have the desire or greed necessary to motivate him to upset the *apus*.

Another story offers commentary on foreigners who are also seen as morally inferior to *runa* and ignorant to the proper order of the cosmos and the demands of reciprocity.

> There is a peak near Mt Ausungate. In this peak there grows a cross of gold and silver. All the foreigners want to get it out. Only foreigners. Peruvians, no – they are not interested. When the foreigners try to get the cross, it bewitches them and throws them and their airplane into the lake. The foreigners are still there in the lake. Still living. Under the water. They don't eat. They don't speak. They are in shock. It happened because they wanted the gold and tried to take it without paying the earth.

He embellishes such stories with information about the Incas, admonitions against borrowing money, examples of people who have died when seeing Inca gold, and the value of relying on oneself, one's *compadres*, and offerings to earth spirits to make a living. The life that Quintin has, a balanced relationship with the earth, potatoes for his family and good relations with neighbors is better, in his estimation, than the fate of those greedy for gold and money from the bank. Establishing a debtor relationship with a bank is as dangerous in his view as taking the gold from the veins of the earth – one must traffic with the devil in order to do so.

Conclusion

After I became familiar with Libbet Crandon-Malamud's attention to the broad socio-political context in which illness diagnosis and healing occur, I was compelled to ask why Quintin, Maria, Paukar, Justina, and others spend so much time on these topics in the presence of people who are suffering and who have consulted them for a cure for physical and spiritual ailments. Crandon-Malamud analyzes the diagnostic process as one of negotiation for social status and access to secondary resources. In a pluralistic system, the choice of practitioner reveals the strategies that the patient and family are using to position themselves in a newly emerging social context in which they are negotiating new identities.[11] In the community discussed here, it is significant that the practitioners themselves are critiquing the power dynamics involved in the relationships between *runa*, *mestizos*, whites (*hacienda* owner, upper class Peruvians), and foreigners even though Mollomarca is a relatively homogeneous community. The patient and family derive a context within which to situate themselves during the illness for which help is being sought. But they are also led to evaluate the circumstances that contributed to their current situation and their potential future state of being. Healers clearly provide information that justifies their own power and authority to heal – but the stories they tell reveal far more than simply the chronological tale of their own professional development. Healers do include stories of their own divine selection, apprenticeships, past cures, and failures. But the stories also convey critiques of the power relations between Quechua villagers and *mestizos*, discussions of the impact of Inca/Spanish actions, and the economic realities of the community. If asked, healers will discuss the causes of illness, symptoms,

medicines, and curing rituals. But if these are discussed they are typically embedded in stories of devils, Incas, *hacendados*, bank loans, trips to market, and broken-
down trucks. The stories that are told convey moral lessons about appropriate *runa*
behavior and the negative consequences of ignoring the prescriptions of diviners.

Quechua healers in the Peruvian Andes relate narratives during healing ceremonies that situate the healers in specific networks of power, class, and ethnic
relations. Their authority to heal is linked to the construction of legitimacy in
social and cosmological contexts that juxtapose *mestizo* and Quechua symbols.
Medical anthropologists have long looked at the actions of healers during treatment in terms of their effect on the resolution of patients' ailments. The efficacy
of traditional healers, the ways healers are elected or take on their specialized
roles, and the manner in which they attain and demonstrate specialized knowledge have been described extensively for a variety of cultural contexts. Some
works have also focused on the ways that healers develop narratives in the course
of treatment that influence patient compliance and so on. In the context in which
I observed healers talking to patients and families they attempt to inspire patient
confidence – as they tell of past successes in similar kinds of cases and this focus
may affect treatment outcome and their payment. But they also let themselves off
the hook – in case of failure – by telling stories of patients who did not follow
instructions, or sought help too late, or consulted other healers whose actions
nullified those presently being taken.

Clearly, in order to be consulted in times of crisis, healers must be perceived
by people as having special skills and knowledge and the narratives of Quechua
healers provide supporting evidence. Healer's narratives not only establish one's
power to heal, but contain a critique of the inequities in class and ethnic relations
in Peru and thus have important social and political implications. By establishing
their authority in the context of such a critique, healers assert moral superiority
over dominant elites. Healing thus becomes an act of political resistance and a
way of asserting ethnic identity and difference and may influence the actions of
patients in contexts of suffering beyond the physical discomfort of the patient.

Mollomarca, as a former *hacienda*, provides an example of a community of farmers with a long relationship with a landowning class that appropriated their labor.
The asymmetrical relationship of power established during the era of the *hacienda*
and the continuing difficulties Mollomarquinos have in participating in a cash economy provide the context from which discourses about devils, sick *mestizos*, and
buried gold emerge. Such narratives foster "awareness of social differentiation" that
separate distinct ways of life and create boundaries between the two groups.[12]

Healers manipulate the symbolic world of their patients by conveying that they
have a unique, supernaturally-based power and authority – a power gained by
constructing legitimacy with both indigenous and mestizo symbols – and in doing
so they challenge the existing class and ethnic structure, for their narratives
undermine the authority of non*runa*. To reinforce their authority they retell
elements of their personal life histories, collective myths, and history. Quintin's
apparent ability to cure all people – even family members of *hacendados*,
police, judges – are evidence that he has a superior moral authority grounding in

supernatural power and historical links to the Incas. This provides him with abilities to overcome the evils of devils in a way that the economically and politically dominant elite and the newly emerging leaders of the community cannot. All the stories he tells demonstrate his ability to counter the negative effects of the inequities of power. The fact that he tells stories with outcomes that contradict expectation urges his audience to a collective reconstruction of *runa* moral superiority.

His critique extends beyond how people get sick and how they can be treated. He identifies the source of people's problems in the realm of bank loans, migration from the community, participation in wage labor, and so forth. He inverts and challenges the accepted value placed on material possessions and social hierarchies. He argues that he is better off, more powerful and lives a more harmonious life by not searching for buried gold, not getting a bank loan, and not having paper documents. He can feed his family, is not indebted except through reciprocal labor (*ayni*) arrangements, and has powerful spiritual certification. Such a critique has political implications beyond Quintin's own personal economic choices and offers more than entertainment during long healing ceremonies. In 1987, the community as a whole decided not to pursue a loan from the government for agricultural development or the purchase of a community truck. Change is not always desired from some Mollomarquinos' perspective. Nor is individuality, which intrudes on the reciprocal relationships between kin, community members, ancestors, and earth spirits. Certainly, there are intergenerational disagreements about issues central to cultural change.

There is a link between changes in the community after the dissolution of the *hacienda* and the increase in the numbers of soul calling rituals that emphasize the need to transform children and teenagers into *runa*, appropriately behaving, cultural beings. Anxieties about the community's well-being in the face of wider political, economic, and social pressures may be reflected in these practices and in the topics that emerge in the soul calling ceremonies. Many significant changes occurred during the 1980s and into the 1990s that significantly affect Mollomarquinos' perceptions of self and community identity. The decision to cure themselves by calling souls reasserts *runa* identity. It is not surprising that many of the behavioral changes disliked by many in the community become a focus of discussion in ceremonies which aim to reestablish *runa* identity: moving away, learning Spanish, altering *ayni* relationships, adopting new foods, altering economic ties and obligations would be perceived by family members as symptoms of a disruption of balance between a person's body and spirit that would require the intervention of a spiritual healer who could correct those imbalances. The commentary provided by healers in the soul calling ceremonies may demonstrate Mollomarquinos' resistance to submersion in a wider national identity or concern over a lack of control over what is encountered in the market, school, and wage labor situations. The diagnosis of illness and the content of the healing ceremony reaffirm and strengthen the cultural construction of a Quechua person who is grounded in particular relationships to the family, community, and spiritual realm.

The stories healers share late at night in the darkened, hushed homes of their clients are important metaphors of *runa* vulnerability and recovery on many levels. Quintin establishes authority in creating a stark contrast between morally bankrupt politico-legal officials and himself. He incorporates a critique of technological and economic changes and community relations; only Quintin's burnt offerings can make trucks work, devils disappear, and people well. His stories address broader issues of Mollomarquinos' vulnerability and pushes for a reconfiguring of Mollomarquinos' images of themselves and their society in a way that impels action and decision making, and sustains *runa* identity.

It is important, if we are to understand how illness and healing both convey and alter conceptions of identity in complex and shifting social landscapes, to explore fully how bodies, suffering, and treatments are integrated into other aspects of cultural reality. Libbet Crandon-Malamud provided a model for the inclusion of a variety of such cultural features into the concerns of medical anthropologists. Her contribution was useful in reflecting on healers' narratives even in a setting such as Mollomarca that was far less pluralistic in terms of ethnic groups and medical choices than her field site. Following her lead, I found in the gossip and story telling of late night healing sessions, a deeper discourse about power, identity, vulnerability, and resistance.

Notes

1 The first period of field research was conducted in 1983–84 for 15 months supported by a Fulbright award and a University of Washington Graduate School Fellowship. Subsequent fieldwork was conducted in 1986, 1987, 1997 and 2000. A return research period in 1997 was supported by a Holy Cross College Faculty award.
2 Libbet Crandon-Malamud, "Why Susto," *Ethnology*, 1983, 22(2): 153–67.
3 For a description of a soul calling ceremony, see Christine Greenway, "Objectified Selves: An Analysis of Medicines in Andean Sacrificial Healing," Medical Anthropology Quarterly, Vol. 12, No. 2, 1998, pp. 147–167. An analysis of fright sickness and soul loss in terms of Quechua constructions of personhood and ethnicity can be found in Greenway, Christine, "Hungry Earth and Vengeful Stars: Soul Loss and Identity in the Peruvian Andes," *Social Science and Medicine*, vol. 47, no. 8, 1998, pp. 993–1004.
4 Libbet Crandon-Malamud, *From the Fat of Our Souls: Social Change, Political Process, and Medical Pluralism in Bolivia*, University of California Press, 1991.
5 Laurie Price, "Ecuadorian illness stories: cultural knowledge in natural discourse." In *Cultural Models in Language and Thought*, Dorothy Holland and Naomi Quinn (eds), Cambridge University Press, 1987, pp. 314–42.
6 For discussions of these themes, see Billie Jean Isbell, *To Defend Ourselves: Ecology and Ritual in an Andean Village*, Waveland Press, 1985; Catherine J. Allen, *The Hold Life Has*, Smithsonian Institution Press, 1988.
7 The population of Mollomarca in 2000 was nearly doubled and the numbers of households had increased to eighty. Discussions with Mollomarquinos pointed to decrease in infant mortality rates due to vaccination programs for infants and teenage girls. A new school had to be built to accommodate more children; young parents had more living children than their parents had in the early 1980s, and community officials were concerned about lack of sufficient available land to divide up among all of the new households.
8 See F. Aguilo. *Enfermedad y salud segun la concepcion aymara-quechua*, (Qori Llama, 1982); B. Stoner, *Health Care Delivery and health resource utilization in a highland Andean community of Southern Peru.* (Dept. of Anthropology, Ph. D. Dissertation, Indiana University, 1989); Joseph Bastien, "A Shamanistic Curing ritual of the Bolivian Aymara," *Journal of Latin American Lore*, 1989, Vol. 15, pp. 73–94; J. Carey,

Distribution of culture-bound illnesses in the Southern Peruvian Andes, Medical Anthropological Quarterly, 1983,Vol. 7, pp. 281–300; Anne Larme, *Work, Reproduction and Health in two Andean Communities*, Working Paper No. 5, (Chapel Hill, N.C., 1993); D. Montalvo de Maldonado, *La Medicina Tradicional en el Peru*, (Lima, 1989) for examples of Andean ethnomedical categories and/or healing practices.

9 For a discussion and classification of types of healers, see Juan Nunez del Prado Bejar, El Mundo Sobrenatural de la Comunidad de Qotabamba, Allpanchis Phuturinqa, vol. 2, 1970, pp. 57–120.

10 In fact, the Fujimori government gave Mollomarquinos a loan for a truck in the 1990s; when I visited in 1997 and again in 2000, the truck had been sitting without tires, and not working for a number of years. Another truck was purchased by the community in the mid-1990s and one young man learned how to drive it. Tragically, it careened off of a curve leaving Mollomarca. The accident killed two young men, leaving behind their widows and eight young children. When I visited in 2000, there were no immediate plans to replace the truck.

11 Libbet Crandon-Malamud, *From the Fat of Their Souls*, p. 150.

12 Mary Crain, "Poetics and politics in the Ecuadorian Andes: women's narratives of death and devil possession," *American Ethnologist*, 1991, 18(1): 76.

References

Aguilo, F., *Enfermedad y salud segun la concepcion aymara-quechua*, Qori Llama, 1982.

Allen, Catherine J., *The Hold Life Has*, Smithsonian Institution Press, 1988.

Bastien, Joseph, "A Shamanistic curing ritual of the Bolivian aymara," *Journal of Latin American Lore*, 1989, 15: 73–94.

Carey, J., "Distribution of culture-bound illnesses in the Southern Peruvian Andes," *Medical Anthropological Quarterly*, 1983, 7: 281–300.

Crandon-Malamud, Libbet, "Why Susto," *Ethnology*, 1983, 22: 153–67.

——, *From the Fat of Our Souls: Social Change, Political Process, and Medical Pluralism in Bolivia*, University of California Press, 1991.

Crain, Mary, "Poetics and politics in the Ecuadorian Andes: women's narratives of death and devil possession," *American Ethnologist*, 1991, 18(1): 67–89.

Greenway, Christine, "Objectified selves: an analysis of medicines in Andean sacrificial healing." *Medical Anthropological Quarterly*, 1998, 12(2): 147–67.

——, "Hungry earth and vengeful stars: soul loss and identity in the Peruvian Andes." *Social Science and Medicine*, 1998, 47(8): 993–1004.

Isbell, Billie Jean, *To Defend Ourselves: Ecology and Ritual in an Andean Village*, Waveland Press, 1985.

Larme, Anne, *Work, Reproduction and Health in two Andean Communities*, Working Paper No. 5 (Chapel Hill, N.C., 1993).

Montalvo de Maldonado, D., *La Medicina Tradicional en el Peru*, Lima, 1989.

Juan Nuñez del Prado Bejar, "El Mundo Sobrenatural de la Comunidad de Qotabamba," *Allpanchis Phuturinqa*, 1970, 2: 57–120.

Price, Laurie, "Ecuadorian illness stories: cutural knowledge in natural discourse." In *Cultural Models in Language and Thought*, Dorothy Holland and Naomi Quinn (eds), Cambridge University Press, 1987, pp. 314–42.

Stoner, B., *Health Care Delivery and Health Resource Utilization in a Highland Andean Community of Southern Peru*. (Dept. of Anthropology, PhD Dissertation, Indiana University, 1989.)

Chapter 7

Healers as entrepreneurs

Constructing an image of legitimized potency in urban Ecuador

Ann Miles

After spending months in Guayaquil's hot, sticky, and bawdy squatter settlements, my first impression of Cuenca in 1988 was one of exquisite relief. The air was clear and redolent of eucalyptus, the weather was cool but sunny and I felt completely safe on the city's crowded cobblestone streets. The pace of life in Cuenca was considerably slower than what I had experienced in Guayaquil which suited me just fine. I came to Cuenca on the invitation of some scholars to continue the work I had been doing in Guayaquil on rural to urban migration, and to begin research on transnational migration of Cuencaños to the United States. Since then I have returned to Cuenca four times and have explored a variety of topics including research into the symbolic dimensions of the meanings of medical systems and medical commodities. Over the years Cuenca has changed considerably; I am surprised at how expansive the city has become in population, physical size, and identity. Whereas once the city's spatial boundaries seemed fairly defined from the surrounding countryside, those borders now seem impossible to discern as the population grows and suburban bumps up against rural. Even more importantly, the "borderlessness" of Cuencan culture is more obvious today as a host of global processes, such as transnational migration and mass media, make their mark on the physical and social landscape of the city.

In 1999, Ecuador faced a host of economic problems comparable only to those experienced during the Great Depression. Cuenca, the third largest city in the country, located in the southern highlands, was bankrupt, as was almost every other municipality. By May of that year there was so little money circulating that the local economy was deemed in a depression. Orphanages and children's homes which are at least partially supported by the local government were reduced to scouring the food stalls at the markets and asking for hand-outs from vendors. In the midst of the crisis, however, the police force in Cuenca found the resources to conduct a series of highly publicized raids on the practices of a number of "unscrupulous *brujos*" (witches) in town. Most of these *brujos* had been "denounced" by citizens who claimed that they had been charged exorbitant fees to be "cured" of a variety of health related conditions. Graphic television coverage showed a *brujo* being bodily removed from his licensed "Nature Store" where outdated medicines (both pharmaceutical and natural) had been confiscated.

A photograph in the daily paper *El Mercurio* artfully displayed some of the confiscated materials which included a statue of a seated Bhudda, two cellular phones, several bottles of perfumed water and some pharmaceuticals. Most of the *brujos*, it had been reported, claimed a measure of professional training that could not be validated. The arrested men were publically accused of defrauding the "most gullible" of Cuenca's citizens.

However, these "natural *curanderos*"[1] as the newspaper once dubbed them, are just the most obvious manifestation of what is a larger and usually more hidden phenomenon. Across the city, in middle class neighborhoods with paved streets and landscaped yards, and poorer ones, where roads are pitted and scarred and houses only partially completed, *curanderos* not all that dissimilar from those arrested, are actively at work. Most work more privately than do the men in the "Nature Stores" downtown and, in fact, word of mouth is the only way to find their homes, indistinguishable as they are from their neighbors. Most know that because they are selling commodities such as herbal remedies, pharmaceuticals or self-fashioned medicines without a license that they are working at the margins of state legitimacy. They are in the awkward position of hoping that word-of-mouth brings them business but not notoriety. In this chapter, I explore the notion that urban *curanderos* are true entrepreneurs who seek innovation in order to attract clientele but who must also try to minimize the risks, both financial and personal, of doing business.

Despite the fact that they are popularly known by the traditional title "*curanderos*" (healers), many urban healers today, especially those working out of their private homes, practice a type of healing that is distinctly modern. Borrowing from traditional medicine of this region and others and incorporating aspects of modern medicine, today's urban *curandero* is the symbolic embodiment of the eclecticism of the modern age. Seated behind desks in their *consultorios* (consultation rooms) where there may also be a shrine to the Virgin Mary and a display case of North American perfumes and pharmaceuticals, these healers employ varied diagnostic and curative techniques that range from the overtly biomedical to the purely spiritual. It is the *curandero's* ability to incorporate divergent symbols into a coherent practice that gives potency to the healing encounter. Situated as they are in a modernizing world, they employ the diverse symbols of power manifest in their increasingly cosmopolitan world.

However, the healing encounter should not be simply seen as a moment when the traditional world is "translated" into a modern idiom or mediated into some comprehensible hybrid. Rather, urban *curanderos* in Cuenca, like others reported elsewhere, use pluralistic techniques and methods in an effort to distinguish themselves and their art in an increasingly competitive marketplace.[2,3] Their cultivated aura of mystery, if not mysticism, and their idiosyncratic mimicry of practices and ideas from multiple medical systems becomes a means of controlling healing knowledge, personal image, and, ultimately, access to resources.[4,5]

In 1971 Irwin Press wrote a very insightful article on urban *curanderismo* in Bogota, Colombia.[6] Published long before anthropology's overt concern for heterodoxy and the ways in which social actors manipulate rather than enact cultural models, Press' article discusses the range of possibilities open to urban curanderos and suggests that further study might consider the notion of an "urban curanderismo complex which in variety and quality of overall services offered, appears to accommodate particularly urban needs."[7] This complex, he suggests may include examination of such variables as curing style, payment methods, impersonality of the healing encounter and increased use of mechanical, rather than only supernatural, methods of healing. However, Press is quick to note that the "complex" he identifies should not be seen as a description of what *is*, but rather as a "model for the elicitation and analysis of data."[8] Rejecting work that simply typologizes healing modalities, he calls for studies that "report on the range of curer types and their relative importance in the healing complex they serve."[9]

In this chapter, I focus on the practices of two urban *curanderos* in Cuenca, a middle-aged man and a younger woman, as a means of understanding the recent configurations of *curanderismo* in Cuenca and how these are reflective of larger cultural responses to social and political upheaval and uncertainty. I show how these two healers incorporate symbols and practices from diverse medical traditions in an effort to draw attention to, validate and "sell" their practices in a very competitive marketplace. In particular, they combine elements from medical traditions like witchcraft and modern medicine and in doing so are creating dynamic and idiosyncratic practices that they then have exclusive access to and control over. I position these healers as entrepreneurs who assess the marketplace of medicine and who know that to be successful one must offer a "product" that is worth paying for, yet be able to present that product with an aura of authenticity and legitimacy or risk ultimate ruin. In other words, I argue that to be successful *curanderos* in Cuenca in the 1990s must walk a fine line to create an image of themselves as both potent and legitimate. In the following sections, I will position urban curanderos in the wider health system and describe possibilities for how this image of "legitimized potency" is constructed.

In a broad sense, one intent of this chapter is to highlight the theoretical usefulness of one of the most central themes in Libbet Crandon-Malamud's work, that is, the argument that medical knowledge, medical ideologies, and medical choices are used by individuals to position themselves in relation to the acquisition of resources. In the final section of her book, *From the Fat of Our Souls* which is, perhaps ironically, titled "Applicability, or so What?"[10] Libbet Crandon-Malamud argues that her findings in Kachitu are not an exclusively Bolivian phenomenon and that medicine everywhere is used as a primary resource, one from which people then derive secondary resources. Medical choices in pluralistic settings, she argues, can transform social relationships and lead to "real" changes in access to resources and power. I highlight the therapies and styles of two urban *curanderos* here as a means of demonstrating how they are creating distinctive medical practices which, in a very competitive medical marketplace, allows them to construct an image of legitimized potency, an image that appears to be selling rather well. In particular, I will show how these two urban healers have taken *curanderismo* which was once associated with universal knowledge – more or less available to all (or obtainable from a specialist at a nominal fee) – and transformed it into something that is most effectively practiced by trained professionals.[11] This transformative process is based on innovations which, in fact, rely upon the careful mimesis of other healing traditions, most of them deemed more potent than traditional *curanderismo* and, therefore, more profitable.

Taussig has recently argued that people engage in mimesis, or imitation, in part to capture the inherent "qualities" from that which is imitated. In particular, Taussig claims that in the process of imitation the "copy takes power from the original."[12] However, mimesis should not be understood as a process whereby something is completely transformed, but rather it is "a play to become – but not become – the other."[13] In other words, imitation is not an attempt to become that which it copies, rather it is done only to garner some of its symbolic potency which is then transformed into something quite different. Furthermore, according to Taussig, in imitation, it is the idea of, or *memory*, of the original (not the original itself) that is copied, allowing for localized interpretations to emerge that resemble, reflect, and evoke the original but, in fact, do not (and do not desire to) replicate it. It is the memories of other healing traditions and the ways they are utilized by urban *curanderos* that is of most interest here.

The economic and social landscape

As Press pointed out more than twenty-five years ago, "curer related services reflect the nature of the particular milieu they serve."[14] Central to the discussion that follows is the notion that medical systems are dynamic and fluid and that they not only reflect, they also respond to changing, locally salient, social, economic, and political realities.[15] Therefore, the popularity and form that any healing system takes at any given historical moment is neither haphazard nor pre-ordained but rather reflects localized understandings and controversies about how the social world is constituted, and how and where power and influence are manifest. With this in mind, I turn to a brief description of the localized contexts of Cuenca, an urban setting that is experiencing both locally produced social upheaval and a national level economic crisis.

I have been conducting ethnographic research in Cuenca, a city now of about 275,000 in the southern Ecuadorian Andes, for more than ten years. Over the years, and despite many changes in my research agendas, I have closely followed the lives of a number of rural to urban migrant families. In general, with each returning visit I saw that the quality of their lives had marginally improved, that is, however, until my most recent visits in 1997 and 1999. In fact, in 1997 for the first time I found my friends and acquaintances doing worse than they had been doing just two years previously. Some had moved to shoddier housing in that period of time, others had stopped buying new clothes and consumer goods and all had started to cut back on meals, dropping the rice dish from lunch, or skipping meat and poultry altogether. By 1999, many families were struggling simply to put food on the table.

What I saw reflected in the homes and kitchens of these families was representative of a general decline in the state of the Ecuadorian economy, especially as it affected the lives of the poor. The psychological effects of the crisis were particularly devastating after the hope that was generated by small economic gains in the early 1980s. Since then, however, national level structural adjustment policies combined with a virtual collapse of the banking system and wholesale government corruption have crippled the Ecuadorian economy.[16] Contributing to the overall sense of insecurity was the political crisis ignited by deposed President Abdala Bucaram, known as "el Loco" (the crazy one) who in 1996 reduced (and some claim eliminated) all national level support for the southern highlands. When he fled the country two years into his presidency, he left it virtually bankrupt. Elsewhere, I have written about the serene and ordered nature of life in Cuenca,[17] a perspective that, ten years later, no longer seems all that accurate. Cuenca, long associated with traditionalism and old world manners, has truly entered the modern world and the interplay between national level politico-economic problems and the global financial crisis makes daily life a struggle for many Cuencanos.

In 1999, the insecurities felt by the poor were palpable with little relief in sight. Confidence in the government was so low that national coffers were literally empty, a visible sign of the inability of the state to regulate banks, collect taxes from its citizenry, and, even more ominously, of the inevitable depletion of the nation's most important source of foreign revenue, petroleum.[18] The poorer classes resent the assistance that the government has given to save failing banks, believing that, yet again, the government functions first and foremost for the benefit of the wealthy. Because of the financial crisis, public services have become increasingly ineffectual sparking riots and demonstrations that closed roads, schools, and health clinics and all but shut down the Ecuadorian economy for nearly two months. Bank accounts in dollars were frozen at the same time that there was unprecedented devaluation of the *sucre*. By May of 1999, rampant inflation seemed to be under control only to be replaced by what local economists called a depression. The production and consumption of consumer goods had slowed considerably in the first half of 1999 because, quite literally, "the people have no money."[19] The government's plans for economic reform primarily involve the privatization of public services, an approach which many fear will put an increased burden on the poor. In fact, one of the first "reforms" that was implemented was the assessment of client fees for public hospital out-patient consultations which were once free. It is, in short, a time of real economic and social distress for all Ecuadorians and all predictions are that things will only get worse before they get better.

Today, many families in the Cuenca region make ends meet only with the help of remittances sent by loved ones (usually male) in the United States.[20] Emigration, primarily to the United States, has been occurring from this region for the past two decades, with rates of exodus increasing sharply in the past two years. While this transnational migration does provide some economic relief for some families, it is also a contributor to the stresses and anxieties of the family members left behind. Concern for the migrants' safety as they make the increasingly arduous journey, the loss of family unity, inability to pay back debts quickly, family disputes over remittances and who controls them, and nasty run-ins with neighbors whose sons are sending more (or less) money are just a few of the preoccupations that the family members of migrants report. In almost all cases transnational migration is, at best, a mixed blessing.

In a situation of increasing scarcity, social upheaval, poverty, and insecurity such as I have just described for Ecuador, individuals often feel a lack of control over their life conditions. The best laid plans, from saving money in the bank to sending a loved one illegally to New York (via Panama) can be laid to waste by circumstances that are completely out of the individual's control. It should come as no surprise under these conditions that health concerns have magnified[21] or that people are seeking answers to health and social problems from non-institutional sources. Salomon, for example, discusses how popular interest in, and the political importance of shamans increased in northern Ecuador during the colonial period under very different but equally compelling conditions of social distress.[22] When popular expectations of how lives ought to unfold are over-turned and misfortune seems impossible to shake, and when the institutions of power are rendered impotent, health and well-being suffer. Relief is sought from practitioners who minister specifically to the fundamental concerns and insecurities of the sufferer.

It is precisely at this juncture that the modern *curandero(a)* practices his/her craft. Modern urban *curanderos* not only provide credible explanations for the illnesses and misfortunes facing the poor but the fact that they work on the margins of state authority may actually afford them greater legitimacy in these times. As the modern Ecuadorian government continues to fail its citizenry, the *curandero*, who under discourses of modernity was once marginalized as backward, now stands today as a symbol of the potential of counter-state rhetoric. They not only cross international borders both literally and figuratively in search of superior techniques and medicines (circumventing state regulations), they openly position themselves as morally superior primarily because they are outside the orbit of state control. *Curanderos* are aware that they risk public censure and even jail every day that they practice but they continue to do so, they argue, not for material gain but simply to help others. In other words, they defy the state for the good of the community. Implicitly, of course, they must have their clients' collusion in their illegality, making them partners in this largely unspoken, counter-state critique. As I argue in the following sections, this collusion (as well as a healthy practice) is more easily won if the *curandero* is careful to construct an image that does not fly in the face of locally understood perceptions of what constitutes a "legitimate" healer.

Health and healing in the Ecuadorian Andes

Cuenca has a medically pluralistic environment where differing medical systems and traditions exist alongside one another and often inter-mingle. These systems include (among others) "traditional" options such as *curanderismo* (healing) and "modern" medicine – most potently represented by biomedicine, but including alternative therapies as well. However, despite the fact that patients will often utilize multiple systems in an illness episode or "trajectory"[23] – depending on the stage of the illness, the success or failure of other healing options, or the perceived cost and convenience of any particular option – these medical systems are not equally legitimate. As elsewhere, in recent decades biomedicine has emerged as the "dominative"[24] system, associated with Cuenca's elite classes and representing the power and influence of science and technology (read modernity) over traditionalism. However, traditional medicine is not without its unique justifications, appeals and potencies. In the following discussion, I will elaborate on the different healing options in Cuenca with special concern for describing the ways in which they have been commonly practiced in the region and their perceived sources of both legitimacy and/or potency. Later, I will discuss how particular aspects of these systems have been selectively incorporated by each of the two urban *curanderos*.

In Ecuador, traditional healing, as it is usually described, incorporates a notion of spiritual intervention. It is represented by a cadre of specialists including *curanderos* (curers), *brujos* (witches) and, especially in the northern Andes and in the Amazon, shamans.[25,26] In traditional medicine, illness is believed to be caused by intentional (through sorcery) or unintentional (through accidental encounters) spiritual intrusion resulting in soul loss and/or bodily imbalance.[27] Illnesses such as *susto* (fright), *mal ojo* (evil eye) and *mal aire* (evil wind) are among those commonly treated by traditional healers.

However, in contrast to more indigenous areas of the Andes,[28,29,30] in this exclusively Spanish speaking, "mestizoised" region, traditional healing is practiced primarily by female *curanderas* (not shamans) and it does not involve elaborate diagnostic and curative rituals or altered states of consciousness. Hallucinogens such as mescaline or ayahuasca are not employed. The typical urban *curandera* of this region is an older woman who diagnoses simply by a visual examination of the afflicted, accompanied perhaps by a verbal description of the symptoms and the course of the illness. While some *curanderas* will on occasion use a few diagnostic techniques such as examination of an egg for persistent cases of illness, for the most part the *curandera* relies heavily on the self report of the afflicted. In other words, the patient reports to the *curandera* what she believes she (or, quite commonly, her child) suffers from and the treatment, which differs little according to the illness, follows from that.

Similarly, the healing rituals of *curanderismo* in the city of Cuenca tend to be less elaborate than those reported elsewhere.[31,32] There are no elaborately fashioned individual altars or *mesas, despachos* or other offerings employed. In general, *curanderas* conduct ritual cleansings primarily involving commonly available herbs which are rubbed over the body (a process known as the *limpieza*) and flower water and/or alcohol which are spewed from the mouth (*soplado*). These cleansings are always accompanied by ritualized prayer. Most mothers in Cuenca have the basic knowledge of *curanderismo* and they will often perform a cleansing at home if the case seems mild and uncomplicated. Most often, a *curandera* is consulted only after home treatments have failed. However, it is important to note that *curanderas* are thought to be more effective than mothers at healing primarily because of their personalities, not because they have specialized knowledge unavailable to the average person. Typically a good *curandera* is an older woman who has a "strong" personality and is able to "absorb" negative spirits without becoming ill herself. This strong personality is interpreted as a gift from God and therefore even though her practices are scorned by the church, she is popularly seen as doing God's work. Although patients are expected to pay *curanderas* a nominal amount if they wish the "cure" to be effective, most *curanderas* earn very little from their work and they are popularly thought to enter into healing because of altruism and a desire to "help people" and not personal enrichment or greed.

On the other hand, those who practice healing techniques that deviate significantly from the standard local repertoire of *limpieza, soplado*, and prayer are associated with the largely indigenous regions of the country such as quichua speaking communities in the neighboring province of Cañar or groups in the Amazon. Shamans of the north or the Amazon are generally considered to be much more powerful than local *curanderas* but they are also significantly more likely to be suspected of practicing damaging witchcraft. In fact, in Cuenca, powerful healers whose knowledge is more specialized and is, therefore, less commonly understood are at risk for earning the appellation of *brujo* (witch) instead of *curandera* (healer).[33]

Whereas the *curandera* has universal knowledge[34] and she is thought to receive special healing powers from God, a *brujo* has specialized knowledge and attains potency from the devil. The word *brujo* in Cuenca is usually a pejorative one and witches are associated with inter-personal remoteness, uncontrolled power, a propensity for doing evil, and as reported elsewhere, they are linked to the "other."[35,36]

While most rural communities in Ecuador have at least one *curandera* practicing fairly openly, as Quiroga, who works on the northern coast of Ecuador states, "Wherever one goes, the great *brujos* are elsewhere"[37] Quiroga also notes that on the coast *curanderas* are local women who are like everyone else, "poor and afflicted with the same problems as their patients," while *brujo(a)s* are associated with secret knowledge and are viewed as outsiders even within their own communities. This is generally true in Cuenca as well, with the caveat that, potentially, there is a fine line between a healer and a witch. Healers, especially younger ones and men who cultivate an image of mystery, of exotic knowledge and remote power, put themselves at risk for accusations of sorcery. Yet, this may not be entirely bad for business. In my conversations with Cuencanos, I noted an increasing consolidation of what Salomon calls the "Old World, New World" difference in the interpretation of witchcraft, where the power of the witch is simultaneously considered evil and "abhorrent" but, at the same time, there is an acknowledgment that the degree of power a witch can access really is enviable.[38] Hence, while *curanderas* may have a degree of legitimacy that has been conferred by God, *brujos* are more readily associated with unlimited, but possibly useful, potency. All the same however, healers attempt to avoid the designation of *brujo* since it is often associated primarily with greed and avarice. Hence, the newspaper headlines detailing the raids described earlier pointedly identified the arrested individuals as *brujos*.

Modern medicine in Cuenca consists of biomedicine and, increasingly, "alternative" therapies. Biomedicine can be found in the rudimentary and increasingly dilapidated public clinics and hospitals, in private physician's offices and in glossy and technologically advanced tertiary care hospitals.[39] Because Cuenca is the home to two medical schools, there is, in fact, a documented surplus of physicians in the city and biomedicine is the officially sanctioned "legitimate" medical system, an idea that even the poorest segments of the population largely accept. Biomedicine's legitimacy stems from the perceived efficacy of pharmaceuticals but also its symbolic association with science, technology, and modern social power.[40] Yet, biomedicine has not managed to eclipse other systems completely, in part because of its very associations with institutionalized power. Doctors are often perceived by the poor as being remote and unsympathetic, or, alternately, of seeking to exploit the sick and poor for profit. Additionally, a further threat to biomedical hegemony can be found in current social conditions. As clinics and public hospitals continue to deteriorate and remain chronically under-supplied, the perception that the biomedicine is failing Cuencanos grows. As I have documented elsewhere, the use of multiple therapies, including alternative medicine seemingly continues to increase.[41] Despite this, I think it is safe to say, however, that physicians are much like *brujos* in that even though their motivations are often suspect, their knowledge is appealing on multiple levels.

The growing alternative medicine[42] community in Cuenca includes practitioners of homeopathy, acupuncture, and most prominently, commercial "natural" medicine. The latter option is the most easily accessible to poor Cuencanos through the numerous natural medicine stores scattered throughout the city center. These stores market commercially processed and packaged vitamins, herbal supplements, and tonics among other products. Natural medicine, I have argued, has real appeal to poor Cuencanos, in part because of its potent amalgamation of scientific and natural symbols and discourses.

The example of commercial natural medicine is the most obvious reminder, however, that despite the frequent use of discourses of altruism and service, healing systems are commercial enterprises too, ones that manipulate locally meaningful symbols of power and efficacy to further their success. Ultimately, control over the knowledge associated with any healing system provides both real (monetary) and symbolic power to the practitioner.[43,44] In the following discussion

I will explore the ways in which the modern urban *curanderos* in Cuenca have altered the traditional *curandera* healing repertoire in such a way that the knowledge they possess is no longer considered common-place and universal. In fact, the eclecticism of their techniques and the idiosyncratic nature of their practices assures that they are perceived as providing a very specialized service. Similar to a practice noted in rural China by Farquhar,[45] urban *curanderos* in Cuenca are independent entrepreneurs who are attempting to carve out a profitable practice in a medically pluralistic and competitive marketplace by expanding the boundaries of their practice and ultimately redefining local *curanderismo*.

Similar to other healers in the Andes,[46] these new urban healers have re-fashioned traditional medicine and transformed it into a profitable commodity whose appeal lies at least in part in its eclecticism, its aura of specialization, and the charismatic appeal of the healer. Because some aspects of their healing repertoire are illegal in Ecuador – especially the dispensing of tonics and pharmaceuticals – *curanderos* in Cuenca keep a very low public profile. Unable to advertise their practice or hang a sign to attract customers as doctors, nutritionists, and homoeopaths do, they must rely on reputation to build and maintain a client base. Reputation is partially constructed from perceived success in healing, which is, of course, linked to the healers' abilities to meet the client's needs and expectations.

While the two urban healers highlighted here are quite different in significant ways, they do share a common tendency to add to, alter, and/or mystify the practices of "traditional" local *curanderismo*, creating an image of efficacy that far exceeds that which is generally associated with traditional local *curanderismo*. Combining different traditions is essential to the construction of a professional image of potency since traditional *curanderismo* holds only very limited commercial potential. Quite simply, *curanderismo* while it is "of the people" and is accorded God-given legitimacy, in its traditional form it really should not cost too much money. However, the reverse is true of biomedicine, shamanism, and witchcraft. All of these medical options are based on specialized knowledge and are linked to a more powerful "other." It is understood that accessing this specialized knowledge will cost the patient significantly more.

In the medical marketplace of Cuenca, where physicians abound and alternative practitioners of all kinds are cropping up daily, where pharmaceuticals and commercial natural medicines can be purchased in single units over the counter, and where even the casual tourist can stumble upon a market healer, carving out a successful medical practice takes some ingenuity. In the following section, I will document just how two healers have managed to do this by harnessing the perceived potency of "others" through mimicry and imitation of their practices, while simultaneously cloaking themselves in an aura of the familiar and legitimate.

The two healers

Nora's practice is less well established than Don Pedro's and she is also much more willing to discuss herself and her practice. Nora is thirty-nine years old and portrays herself as being a woman of the world. She works with the poor, claims to have gone to school with the middle and upper classes and is very well read on local history, folklore, and politics. Nora seemed to enjoy talking to me about the politics of medicine, including the inability of biomedicine to address the concerns of the "whole" person. Don Pedro on the other hand, at age fifty-four, is older and more conservative in demeanor. Whereas Nora is open to discussion, Don Pedro, while soft-spoken, pleasant, and very likable, is often inscrutable. Both healers work out of their homes and practice exclusively on the traditionally potent healing days, Tuesday and Friday.

Nora, who is from a small town two hours from Cuenca now lives in a house located in a new neighborhood on the outskirts of town. Like many of the new neighborhoods of Cuenca, a number of the newest homes belong to migrants to the United States. The house itself lies behind a high concrete wall with a metal gate that shuts tightly when she is not receiving clients. The courtyard is strewn with children's toys. Nora has only been practicing in Cuenca for about five years and believes that her client base is still growing. She claims that she established her practice in Cuenca after spending nearly ten years as an apprentice to a shaman named "Victor" in Huancabamba, Peru. She welcomed my visits as a sign of her increasing reputation and enjoyed our conversations at the same time that she was cautious about how I had found her and who I might tell about her. Nora knows she is working on the margins and is aware that selling some products, especially pharmaceuticals, from her home is illegal.

Nora's *consultorio* has two rooms. The outer room most prominently displays a shrine to the Virgin of Bronce, a locally popular saint of healing. Candles are lit around the two foot high icon that is surrounded by flowers – both real and plastic. Bundles of healing herbs, such as are used in "traditional" *curanderismo* and can be purchased in the peasant market, lie at the side of the shrine. On the opposite wall are two glass display cases. In one she has a selection of perfumes, soaps, and other beauty products, many of them foreign brands, and in the other are pharmaceuticals, vitamins, and packaged natural medicines. Nora's primary claim to specialized knowledge comes from her apprenticeship in Peru where she learned about herbal remedies and also about how to effectively use pharmaceuticals and conduct ritual cleansings, which she refers to as her "Peruvian" *soplado*. However, she does not employ *mesas* in her healing, an essential element, of Peruvian *curanderismo* according to Joralemon and Sharon.

Nora discusses her work discursively moving easily between discourses of "science" (as she perceives it) and spirituality when discussing her healing philosophy. For example, she claims that Peruvian herbal medicine, which takes years to master, has scientific proofs of efficacy, but admitted that there is nothing "scientific" about working only on Tuesdays and Fridays. She does so only because that is what people in Cuenca expect of *curanderas*. Most of the illnesses that she sees she attributes to an underlying "organic" causes such as poor nutrition, "energy imbalances," "infection," or "stress." However, she believes that ritual therapies like the *limpieza* are important for the mental and spiritual health of her clientele. She told me that while she believes in the possibility of supernatural intrusions and soul loss, what is more important is that her clients believe in them. Nora is very aware of recent discussions in medicine about the mind/body connection in relation to healing, and in addition to providing spiritual comfort, she claims the *soplado* is at least partially effective because it is a type of "aromatherapy." She is capable of achieving the altered states of consciousness practiced by many Peruvian shamans, but does not practice this in Ecuador.

In keeping with her eclectic approach, most of the illnesses that she diagnoses are difficult to place exclusively in either the organic or supernatural domain. Indeed, one of the most common diagnoses of both Nora and Don Pedro is a generalized condition called *debilidad*, or weakness. Both healers noted the increasing frequency of cases of *debilidad* among their clients which Nora explained was a direct result of the stresses placed on people because of the economic crisis. *Debilidad* has a diverse symptomology including most commonly fatigue, anxiety, weight loss, and insomnia. It is caused by disturbing life conditions which may be coupled with the intrusion of bad spirits. Evil spirits are thought to be lurking everywhere and those who have been physically weakened by life's struggles and worries (death of a loved one, loss of a job, too much work, migration of a husband or son, etc.) are more vulnerable to illness-causing spiritual intrusions.[47] Therefore, the *curandero's* job is to remove the malignant spirits if necessary and to restore physical strength and vitality. Treating *debilidad* can call for both organic and supernatural measures. While *debilidad* sounds very much like *daño* as it is described in the literature on Peru[48,49] it differs in that it does not always involve spiritual intrusion and, if it does, it may have been caused purely accidentally.

Don Pedro is a bespeckled man in his fifties who has been practicing from the same home in Cuenca for about ten years. He is well known in town but, in contrast to Nora, does not seem to enjoy speaking about himself or his practice. He was always cordial to me, but never particularly forthcoming. Don Pedro is scrupulously careful about seeing all who come to his very busy practice taking short lunch breaks and making sure that his first clients of the afternoon are the people turned away in the morning. His clients appeared to span a range of social positions in Cuenca from rural poor to working class urban. While Nora saw my visits as an opportunity to talk about healing and perhaps expand her reputation (and therefore improve her business), Don Pedro really had very little to gain from our association and perhaps something to lose. On a daily basis he has more than enough clients, and, as I will describe later, his distribution of medicines is significantly more suspect than Nora's.

Don Pedro, a life-long Cuencano, has a house in one of the oldest streets in Cuenca which is easily accessible from most areas of the city as well as many outlying towns. Similar to Nora he meets with patients in a private *consultorio* off the main courtyard. The courtyard itself however is noteworthy for the monkeys and parrots (reportedly from the *oriente* – or tropical lowlands) that live in large cages under a tree. The monkeys in particular are a real source of interest and amusement to the gathered clientele. These exotic creatures no doubt contribute to the persistent rumor that Don Pedro has received specialized training from powerful and mystical shamans of the Ecuadorian Amazon. Next to his *consultorio* is a small room resembling a chapel with a candle festooned altar, a statue of the Virgin Mary and benches for client use.

Don Pedro's understanding of disease etiologies are less well articulated and eclectic than are Nora's and he believes much more intensely in the supernatural origins of illness. While he recognizes the role that "infection" plays in the lives of his clients, especially young children, he believes that the vast majority of cases he sees are due to the intervention of malignant spirits – usually accidental encounters (as in most *debilidad*) but sometimes through sorcery. Sorcery illnesses are usually caused by one person's envy of another and they are usually more complex and difficult to heal than accidental intrusions. In these cases, Don Pedro must work against the witchcraft perpetrated by someone else, pitting his specialized knowledge against that of an unknown *brujo*.

A practice transformed

As I described earlier, traditionally, a *curandera's* reputation in this region is based not so much on her healing repertoire but on her perceived personal characteristic. Because the "technology" and knowledge of *curanderismo* is available to all, the best healers are thought to be effective not for what they know but for personal qualities such as their willingness to cure and the strength of their characters. It is, in fact, this strength that gives them the ability to confront and draw out the spirits that are lingering in others. Most people are just a little bit afraid of the best traditional *curanderas*, not because they believe that they will do them harm but simply because they are often *brava* (fierce), a surface manifestation of their inner strength of character. Maintaining a gruff demeanor, which supposedly belies real altruism, is a marker of true effectiveness among the most successful *curanderas* in Cuenca.

In the urban contexts, the more "traditional" *curanderas* such as those who work at the markets and some who work from their homes are much like spiritualist healers in Mexico,[50] or the urban *curanderos* in Bogota that Press describes; they do not interact with their clients to any significant degree and very little personal information is exchanged during the healing encounter (Press 1971). In fact, very few words ever pass between the *curandera* and her client. Furthermore, most traditional *curanderas*, even those who work from their homes, provide patients with little privacy. Usually there is a line of clients waiting to see the healer with cleansings performed in the open in a rather brisk and impersonal manner.

Both Nora and Don Pedro conduct themselves and organize their spaces in very different ways from traditional *curanderos*. For example, in conversations I had with clients as we waited in line to be seen, both Nora and Don Pedro were described as *amable* (nice, kind) or *muy buena* (a reference to both personality and effectiveness). In fact, both healers greet each patient warmly with a smile and a handshake or kiss, even clients like myself, whom they had not attended previously. Each patient is led to a private inner office where diagnosis and/or a treatment regime is explored and the patient may also be taken to another room where, behind closed doors, a ritual cleansing, or in Nora's case an herbal bath or a *soplado* are administered.

Nora and Don Pedro resemble doctors as they sit behind their desks in Western clothing where telephones, ink blotters, numerous pens and pencils and, in Nora's case, a prescription pad are strewn. Don Pedro even has what looks like a framed diploma behind his desk while Nora has a drug company poster on hers (see also Joraleman and Sharon 1989). The practice of meeting with clients in a private inner office is meant to evoke the practices of allopathic physicians in the area, but it also serves to increase their reputation for having specialized knowledge. Because each client meets privately with the healer, no one really knows what has occurred with another patient and therefore cannot be sure of the full extent of the healers repertoire or skills.

It is at the point of diagnosis that the practices of Nora and Don Pedro deviate significantly from one another. Both healers discuss symptomology with their patients privately but what happens behind those closed doors is quite different. In keeping with his emphasis on the supernatural origins of illness, Don Pedro's diagnostic techniques are particularly mystical. On his desk is a clock radio (an older model with the plates that fall down revealing the minute and hour) which is sometimes covered with a small carpet and other times with a piece of card-board. The patient places her hands on the clock radio and answers a few simple questions such as: "How long have you felt anxious? Where do you live? How many children do you have?," while Don Pedro takes notes. Then, abruptly, he may stop the questioning and announce his diagnosis. He told me that he "sees" the problem through the radio and is also able at that time to assess the personal characteristics of the individual, important information for the ultimate prescription of a remedy.

Nora's diagnostic techniques borrow less from the overtly mystical and, given her organic orientation to illness, they rely more heavily on quasi-scientific ideas currently popular in the local alternative medical community concerning energy and energy loss. Nora generally spends more time talking with her clients about their lives, illnesses, and problems than does Don Pedro and she also conducts some physical tests. In particular, she may assess the energy of an individual through examination of pressure points on the wrist, the base of the neck and temples. Nora explains that illness is often linked to an imbalance of the individual's vital energies (both mental and physical) which can be restored through ritual cleansings, diet, and the use of both biomedical and natural medications.

Although Don Pedro delves more into mystical terrain and Nora uses what she considers to be "scientific" knowledge as a means of diagnosis, the commonality between them is that they both mystify *curanderismo* and place authoritative knowledge about it squarely in their own hands.[51] The clients of Don Pedro with whom I spoke believe that he has learned his healing techniques from long study among shamans of the Amazon. "Why else the monkeys and parrots?" one woman concluded. Remember that Amazonian healers are popularly viewed with a mixture of admiration (for their healing potential) and fear (for their potentially dangerous abilities). No one really understood what occurred when they placed their hands on the clock radio, but there were no doubts among his clients that Don Pedro has special training and abilities. Don Pedro himself only smiled cryptically at me when I asked him if the rumors about his training were true.

Nora, on the other hand, openly admits to, and in fact is quite talkative about her specialized training abroad among Peruvian shamans. She made a point of telling me that Peruvian healers are far more "powerful" and "knowledgeable" than any in Ecuador, rendering her apprenticeship with them doubly valuable. Interestingly, since very little is known about Peruvian *curanderismo* in Cuenca, Nora really is quite free to construct her own image of what it entails. That image selectively incorporates elements that "sell" in Cuenca and omits those that probably would not. For example, she describes a facility with prescribing medicines both herbal and pharmaceutical, and has improved upon the local *soplado* by incorporating potent "Peruvian" herbs. Instead of a Peruvian *mesa* she displays the locally salient Virgin of Bronce and while she does not heal through altered states of consciousness she knows of those who do in Peru and can help the patient locate someone there if their case warrants it.

Both healers rely to some degree on ritual cleansings, especially for children and very poor clients, but they each have also added significantly to the traditional repertoire of curative technologies. In most adult (and therefore more complicated) cases, Don Pedro requires at least two visits. The first visit is when he makes his diagnosis and it is free. Then, the patient is told to return on the following Tuesday or Friday when Don Pedro delivers the remedy. His remedies usually include bottled formulas (in some cases in recycled pharmaceutical containers) that he has specially prepared for the client. He would not reveal to me what was in the bottles except to say that they were "effective medicines." Directions for use of the products usually involves dissolving either seven or twenty-one drops of the liquids in water, three times a day. Additionally, Don Pedro may provide a talisman or a good luck piece to ward off malignant spirits and strengthen the patient. He occasionally supplements his prescriptions, especially for chronic sufferers, with suggestions about pharmaceuticals or patent medicines. However, he sees these medicines generally as palliative solutions that may alleviate symptoms while his own formulations are curative.

Whereas Don Pedro literally controls the production and knowledge of the medicinal products he sells, Nora is more likely to use packaged pharmaceuticals, natural medicines (herbal supplements and vitamins) and give out recipes for foods and poultices that patients can try out at home. In keeping with her own self described image as a student of healing in its broadest sense, Nora considers herself an expert in a number of different medical approaches and she combines therapies in ways that she thinks will be particularly effective for an individual client. This may include some or all of the following; a recommendation about a dietary change or herbal preparation or the addition of commercially prepared vitamin supplements or tonics to the diet, a series of baths and *soplados* or herbal cleansings, and/or the prescription of a commercial herbal remedy or pharmaceutical.

Both Don Pedro and Nora charge considerably more for their services than do traditional *curanderas* in the region whose average cost per *limpieza* is about $1 US. While it is impossible to quote a price for either healer since prices vary considerably according to what is prescribed and performed and who the client is, the clients of both healers reported that they pay a good deal more for their services than they would for a "*curandera* of the market." Both Nora and Don Pedro surely make a considerable amount of their profit from the medicines they sell – which in Don Pedro's case can be quite expensive reaching up to $10 or $15 per preparation. Yet, they do not charge so much as to risk being "denounced" by a patient. This of course is a delicate tightrope that the healer must walk. The pricing of medicines and treatments should be high enough to imply that it is a specialized service, yet not so high as to provoke speculation as to the healer's true motivations. Popular conceptions are that *curanderos* should be in the business of healing because they want to help, not because they wish to make a lot of money.

Creating an image of legitimized potency

In his discussion of healers and witches (*curanderas and brujos*) in Esmeraldas, Quiroga notes that both types of healers are deeply suspicious of, and avoid all associations with, allopathic medicine. Biomedicine, he argues, is seen as a threat to traditional healing and traditional healing is thought to better preserve its domain by limiting contact with biomedical influences. In Cuenca however, a very different dynamic is emerging. Urban *curanderos* here are purposely imitating particular aspects of biomedicine, as well as combining *curanderismo* and *brujeria* in an effort to harness the symbolic potency of that which is imitated.

Yet, as stated above, this process of mimesis is not a veiled attempt to "become" the other – in this case a medical doctor, shaman, or witch. The first would be impossible and undesirable given the surplus of doctors and the social distancing associated with physicians in Cuenca, and the symbolic identification with shamans and witches would ultimately be counter-productive given local perceptions of the altruism that "healers" should display. Besides, it is the very ability of the urban *curandero* to move between the scientific and the spiritual, the known and the unknown, us and them, that makes him/her so appealing. An encounter with Nora or Don Pedro reminds the patient just enough of a consultation with a *curandera* (an emminently legitimate practitioner), to seem comfortably familiar, at the same time that their biomedical and mystical practices suggest the potential for greater efficacy than the patient has come to expect from a traditional *curandera*.

Of course, one of the most powerful symbolic tools that Don Pedro employs is the dispensing of medicaments that he himself produces. Elsewhere in the anthropological literature it has been shown that medicines are potent symbolic vehicles that communicate varied social messages. Arguing that the world-wide popularity of medicines is not justified by their effectiveness, van der Geest and Whyte have proposed that medicines are like fetishes that can have multiple and complex meanings.[52] Furthermore, because medicines are meant to heal, those who control their production and distribution garner a measure of social power. According to these authors, pharmaceuticals, in particular, carry powerful associations with science and technology, and consequently, those who control their distribution are symbolically associated with the power of advanced technology. By selling his own medicines Don Pedro accomplishes something of a symbolic double play. First, he gains authority over the healing process since his medicines can only be acquired through him. They literally cannot be obtained through any other source. Then, he links himself to the potent qualities of both biomedicine and witchcraft since his medicines look like pharmaceuticals (and even sometimes smell like them) but, they are to be used in seemingly magical ways (such as his common prescription to take seven or twenty-one drops at a time for seven or twenty-one days at a time).

Nora has taken a different approach and has chosen to associate herself with a powerful and foreign "other." All of her clients know she has worked in Peru and this is universally interpreted as a very good thing. Even before the current economic crisis, educated Ecuadorians would joke about the national "inferiority complex" and explain that both goods (and knowledge) produced elsewhere are always more highly valued than national or local ones. In fact, by associating herself with Peruvian shamans whose work is so little understood or known in Cuenca, she is able to construct a practice that links potency and legitimacy to the very same source. Peruvian shamans, she tells everyone, are versed in the judicious use of biomedicine, they understand natural medicine and they are adept at spiritual cleansings. Of course, there is no one locally who has more experience with Peruvian *curanderismo* to refute the image of broad competency and potency that she has constructed.

Finally, by incorporating *debilidad* as a fundamental diagnosis both healers have given themselves the flexibility to respond to their clients' individualized needs and expectations. The diagnosis of *debilidad* always includes an organic and a social dimension such as a lack of appetite brought on by social stress, which can be treated with natural or pharmaceutical preparations. However, a diagnosis of *debilidad* also gives the healer the option of finding that spiritual intrusions exist, and if they do, the possibility of determining whether they are accidental or the result of intentional sorcery. In such cases the *limpieza, soplado* of other treatment might be prescribed. In a large cosmopolitan setting like Cuenca where clients may come from a variety of age groups, classes, and regional backgrounds, such diagnostic flexibility allows the healer to provide treatments that are tailored to the client's individual expectations and preferences.

Concluding thoughts

Ecuador's economy is in such a state of disarray that even those who are optimistic about the country's future believe that they have only seen the beginning of the hardships that are yet to come. As more large companies fail and small businesses go under, the country shows increasing signs of entering what may be an extended depression. As the economy has deteriorated, many Ecuadorians have responded by fleeing the country and looking for economic opportunity elsewhere. Others are making do as best as they can in Ecuador. Most feel anxious and express little hope for the immediate future. Life in Ecuador, as in Bolivia of the 1980s described by Libbett Crandon-Malamud, is fragile.

Curanderos, and especially those like Nora and Don Pedro, may be better positioned than most to weather (if not profit from) the economic and social crises facing the country. These two healers are both acutely aware of the social and personal struggles of their clients and they both admit that while their patients have less money today, they in fact have more clients than they had even a few years ago. Economic insecurity and the distresses of everyday life have combined with a generalized distrust of the official institutions of power to create a social climate in which the urban *curandero* can flourish.

The entrepreneurial success of Nora and Don Pedro is based on a calculated mastery of what might sell in this crowded urban medical marketplace. Their therapeutic choices and the ways in which they manipulate symbols of power and efficacy has meant that they have created a practice that is both desirable and clearly worth paying more for. They have managed to do this in part because they have cleverly juxtaposed *curanderismo* with other medical specialities. They have also positioned themselves as firmly outside the authority of the state whose overall mismanagement is perceived as instrumental in creating the deteriorating social conditions. Unlike the state, *curanderos* work *for* the poor, sometimes taking personal risks in the process.

It will no doubt be interesting to watch the paths of these *curanderos* in the upcoming years as Ecuador struggles out of its economic woes. It is too early to predict whether their success is only linked to hard times and a generalized distrust of state sponsored medicine or whether, in fact, they will have long term appeal. If they do, then we must also wonder what impact they will have on the roles of the more traditional *curanderas*. Will the older women who have few claims to special skills or knowledge be literally pushed out of the marketplace by these more eclectic practitioners, or will there be room, as there seems to be now, for multiple types of *curanderismo?* What is not really in question, however, is whether *curanderismo* of some form or another will persist. Medical alternatives are essential, Libbet Crandon-Malamud told us, not because they promote technological competition but because they create possibilities both for healers and patients to negotiate political issues, express identity, create social meaning, and garner access to resources.

Notes

1 I use the term *curandero* to refer to male healers, the term *curandera(s)* when I am specifically discussing female healer(s) and the term *curanderos* to refer to male healers (plural) or male and female healers as a group (plural). Similar to other reports, in Cuenca the more specialized healers tend to be male; however, Nora, who I highlight here is an exception.

2 Alex Kroeger, *La Medicina tradicional de los andes y al alto amazonas*, Abya-yala, 1989, pp. 489–505.

3 Donald Joralemon and Douglas Sharon, *Sorcery and Shamanism: Curanderos and Clients in Northern Peru*, Utah University Press, 1989.

4 Libbet Crandon-Malamud, *From The Fat of Our Souls: Social Change, Political Process and Medical Pluralism in Bolivia*, University of California Press, 1991.

5 Michael Taussig, *Shamanism, Colonialism and the Wild Man: A Study of Terror and Healing*, University of Chicago, 1987.

6 Irwin Press, "The Urban Curandero," *American Anthropologist*, 1971, 73: 741–56.

7 Press, "The Urban Curandero," 73: 753.

8 Press, "The Urban Curandero," 73: 753.

9 Press, "The Urban Curandero," 73: 753.

10 Crandon-Malamud, *From The Fat of Our Souls*, p. 209.

11 Hans C. Buechler and Judith-Maria Buechler, *The World of Sofia Velasquez* Columbia University Press, 1996.

12 Michael Taussig, *Mimesis and Alterity: A Particular History of the Senses*, Routledge, 1993, p. 39.

13 Taussig, *Mimesis*, p. 39.

14 Press, "The Urban Curandero," 743.

15 Joralemon and Sharon, *Sorcery and Shamanism*, Introduction.

16 For a longer view see, Wendy Weiss, "Debt and devaluation: the burden on Ecuador's popular class," *Latin American Perspectives*, 1997, 24: 9–33.

17 Ann Miles, "The urban Chola and the transmission of class and gender ideologies in Cuenca, Ecuador." In *Balancing Acts: Women and The Process of Social Change*, P. Lyons Johnson (ed.), Westview Press, 1997, pp. 120–39.

18 Throughout the 1980s and most of the 1990s oil was the most important source of foreign revenue for Ecuador and they were receiving as much as $35–50 a barrel from crude. By 1999 production of crude was significantly reduced as were the prices obtained for it, and Ecuador was once again a "Banana Republic" with bananas topping the list of exports (*El Mercurio*, 24 May 1999).

19 "Ecuador estaría entrando en depresión económico," *El Mercurio*, May 1999, 26, p. 14.

20 Ann Miles, "The high cost of leaving: illegal emigration from cuenca Ecuador and family separation." In *Women and the Process of Economic Change*, A. Miles and H. C. Buechler (eds), American Anthropological Association, 1997, pp. 55–74.

21 Jose Suárez-Torres and Dolores López-Paredes, "Development, environment and health in crisis," *Latin American Perspectives*, 1997, 24: 83–103.

22 Frank Salomon, "Shamanism and politics in late-colonial Ecuador," *American Ethnologist*, 1983, 10: 413–28.

23 Kaja Finkler, *Physicians at Work, Patients in Pain*, Westview Press, 1991.

24 Hans Baer, "The American dominative medical system as a reflection of social relations in the wider society," *Social Science and Medicine*, 1989, 28: 1103–12.

25 There are also other specialists such as *parteras*, traditional birth attendants who may or may not also be *curanderas* and bone-setters, who usually are not. However, it should be noted that making distinctions as I have done here between different types of healers may suggest to the reader that there is a static healer identity and one is of a certain ilk and not another. The reality is of course much more complex as healers manipulate their identities and labels are used to both construct and reconstruct, legitimize and delegitimize healers.

26 See also Diego Quiroga, *Saints, Virgins and the Devil: Witchcraft, Magic and Healing in the North Coast of Ecuador*, PhD Dissertation, University of Illinois, 1994.

27 Carmen Bernard, "The many deaths of Manuel: illness and fate in the Andes," *History and Anthropology*, 1985, 2: 145–52.

28 See, Catherine Allen, *The Hold Life Has: Coca and Cultural Identity in an Andean Community*, Smithsonian Press, 1988.

29 See, Christine Greenway, "Objectified selves: an analysis of medicines in Andean sacrifical healing," *Medical Anthropology Quarterly*, 1998, 12: 147–67.

30 See, Joseph Bastien, *Mountain of the Condor: Metaphor and Ritual in an Andean Ayllu*, Waveland Press, 1978.

31 Greenway, "Objectified selves," 147–67.

32 Bonnie Glass-Coffin, *The Gift of Life*, University of New Mexico, 1998.

33 Rogers (1997) notes the fluidity of this term. If one "believes" in the healer he/she is a shaman, if one does not believe in him, he is a witch.

34 Buechler and Buechler, *The World of Sofia Velasquez*, p. 133.

35 Quiroga, *Saints, Virgins*, p. 87.

36 Taussig, *Shamanism*.

37 Quiroga, *Saints, Virgins*, p. 151.

38 Salomon, *Shamanism and Politics*, p. 425.

39 The latest addition to clinic services in Cuenca is the gleaming, and by Cuencan standards high-rise "Mount Sinai Hospital." One of my informants, a rural to urban migrant informed me that the name "Mount Sinai" originated from an Amazonian Indian group.

40 See, Sjaak van der Geest and Susan Reynolds Whyte, "The charm of medicines: metaphors and metonyms," *Medical Anthropology Quarterly*, 1989, 3: 345–67.

41 Ann Miles, Science, "Nature and tradition: the mass-marketing of natural medicines in urban Ecuador," *Medical Anthropology Quarterly*, 1998, 12: 206–25.

42 I am not completely satisfied with the term "alternative" therapies here since its western associations imply that biomedicine is the "standard," and everything else a deviation from that. That said, I do use the term "alternative" medicine to describe those therapies that cannot be termed "traditional" but which deviate substantially from biomedicine.

43 van der Geest and Whyte, "The charm of medicines."

44 Bridgette Jordan, *Birth in Four Cultures: A Cross-Cultural Investigation of Childbirth in Yucatan, Holland, Sweden and the United States*, 4th edn, Waveland Press, 1993.

45 Judith Farquhar, "Market magic: getting rich and getting personal in medicine after Mao," *American Ethnologist*, 1994, 23: 239–57.

46 Donald Joralmon, "The selling of the Shaman and the problem of informant legitimacy," *Journal of Anthropological Research*, 1990, 46: 105–18.

47 Oths, discussing *debilidad* in highland Peru notes that it is an illness of cumulative stress which may include productive (too much work etc.), reproductive and "other" factors such as the supernatural. Intriguingly, she also notes that *debilidad* in men is more often found among those who have done better economically, but who are

finding it increasingly difficult to keep up (Oths 1999). This latter point is worth exploring further in the urban contexts of Cuenca.
48 Bonnie Glass-Coffin, "Discourse, daño and healing in north coastal Peru." In *Anthropological Approaches to the Study of Ethnomedicine*, M. Nichter (ed.), Gordon and Breach, 1992, pp. 33–56.
49 Joralemon and Sharon, *Sorcery and Shamanism*.
50 Kaja Finkler, "Sacred healing and biomedicine compared," *Medical Anthropology Quarterly*, 1994, 8: 178–96.
51 Jordan, *Birth in Four Cultures*.
52 van der Geest and Whyte, "The charm of medicines."

References

Allen, Catherine, *The Hold Life Has: Coca and Cultural Identity in an Andean Community*, Smithsonian Press, 1988.
Baer, Hans, "The American dominative medical system as a reflection of social relations in the larger society," *Social Science and Medicine*, 1989, 28: 1103–12.
Bastien, Joseph, *Mountain of the Condor: Metaphor and Ritual in an Andean Ayllu*, Waveland Press, 1978.
Bernard, Carmen, "The many deaths of Manuel: illness and fate in the Andes," *History and Anthropology*, 1985, 2: 145–52.
Hans C. Beuchler and Judith-Maria Beuchler, *The World of Sofía Velasquez*, Columbia University Press, 1996.
Crandon-Malamud, Libbet, "Medical dialogue and the political economy of medical pluralism: a case from rural highland Bolivia," *American Ethnologist*, 1986, 13: 463–76.
——, *From The Fat of Our Souls: Social Change, Political Process, and Medical Pluralism in Bolivia*, University of California Press, 1991.
El Mercurio, *Ecuador estaría entrando en depresión económico* (May 1999), 26, p. 14.
Farquhar, Judith, "Market magic: getting rich and getting personal in medicine after Mao," *American Ethnologist*, 1994, 23: 239–57.
Finkler, *Physicians at Work, Patients in Pain*, Westview Press, 1991.
——, Kaja, "Sacred healing and biomedicine compared," *Medical Anthropology Quarterly*, 8: 178–96.
Glass-Coffin, Bonnie, "Discourse, daño and healing in north coastal Peru." In *Anthropological Approaches to the History of Ethnomedicine*, M. Nichter (ed.), Gordon and Breach, 1992, pp. 33–56.
——, *The Gift of Life*, University of New Mexico Press, 1998.
Greenway, Christine, "Objectified selves: an analysis of medicines in Andean sacrificial healing," *Medical Anthropology Quarterly*, 1998, 12: 147–67.
Joralemon, Donald, "The selling of the Shaman and the problem of informant legitimacy," *Journal of Anthropological Research*, 1990, 46: 105–18.
—— and Douglas Sharon, *Sorcery and Shamanism: Curanderas and Clients in Northern Peru*, Utah University Press, 1989.
Jordan, Brigette, *Birth in Four Cultures: A Cross Cultural Investigation of Childbirth in Yucatan, Holland, Sweden and the United States*, 4th edn, Waveland Press, 1993.
Kroeger, Alex, "La Medicina tradicional de los Andes y al alto Amazonas del Ecuador." In *Antropológia del Ecuador*, Segundo E. Moreno Yánez (ed.), Abya-Yala, 1989, 489–505.

Miles, Ann, "Pride and prejudice: the urban Chola and the transmission of class and gender ideologies in Cuenca, Ecuador," In *Balancing Acts: Women and the Process of Social Change*, P. Lyons Johnson (ed.), Westview Press, 1992, pp. 120–39.

——, "The high cost of leaving," In *Women and the Process of Economic Change: Andean Perspectives*, A. Miles and H. C. Buechler (eds), American Anthropological Association, 1997, pp. 55–74.

——, "Science, nature and tradition: the mass-marketing of herbal medicines in urban Ecuador," *Medical Anthropology Quarterly*, 1998, 12: 206–25.

Oths, Kathryn, "*Debilidad*: A biocultural assessment of an embodied Andean illness," *Medical Anthropology Quarterly*, 1999, 13: 286–315.

Press, Irwin, "The urban curandero," *American Anthropologist*, 1971, 73: 741–56.

Quiroga, Diego, *Saints, Virgins and the Devil: Witchcraft, Magic and Healing in the Northern Coast of Ecuador*, PhD Dissertation, University of Illinois, 1994.

Rogers, Mark, *"I Believe a Little Bit," Multiple Knowledge and the Politics of Medical Decisions in Ecuador* Paper presented at the XX Meetings of the American Anthropological Association, 1997.

Salomon, Frank, "Shamanism and politics in late-colonial Ecuador," *American Ethnologist*, 1983, 10: 413–28.

Suárez-Torres, Jose and Dolores López-Paredes, "Development, environment and health in crisis," *Latin American Perspectives*, 1997, 24: 83–103.

Taussig, Michael, *Shamanism, Colonialism and the Wild Man: A Study in Terror and Healing*, University of Chicago Press, 1987.

——, *Mimesis and Alterity: A Particular History of the Senses*, Routledge, 1993.

van der Geest, Sjaak and Susan Reynolds Whyte, "The charm of medicines: metaphors and metonyms," *Medical Anthropology Quarterly*, 1989, 3: 345–67.

Weiss, Wendy, "Debt and devaluation: the burden on Ecuador's popular class," *Latin American Perspectives*, 1997, 24: 9–33.

Part III

Andean bodies: metaphors and medicine

Andeans have a legacy comprised of the properties and images associated with their bodies and bodily connections to other people in their community, to the land they till and depend upon, and to a well-defined, ever present spiritual realm. The body is seen as vulnerable in all of these domains. The idioms that express these notions about the body, such as "sucking fat from one's soul," or being eaten by the earth which can obliterate the soul, are closely related to the sociopolitical environment of exploitation of the poor, and extreme contrasts in power relationships and access to resources.

In McKee's chapter, we learn how children acquire perceptions of vulnerability that link these notions about the body to widespread sources of distress such as hunger, harshness of the natural environment and unpredictability of social support in the community and family environment. The theme of hunger is further elaborated by Graham who explores reasons for food choices and looks at what satisfies hunger across social and physical domains. In a somewhat different fashion, Bastien explores all of the ramifications of an endemic disease and indigenous etiological notions compared to biomedical explanations. At the forefront of indigenous etiology are the pervasive Andean metaphors of "blood and fat sucking" that have implicit meanings connecting them to local, social, and political sources of oppression.

For several decades, medical anthropologists have tended to dichotomize medical systems into an opposition between Western biomedicine and traditional healing systems. It seems that Andean peoples are actually encountering more public health and medical practitioners, if only through the ubiquitous non-governmental and foreign health agencies. To what degree this will affect their medical notions is a topic that needs study. The three chapters in this section, taken together, elucidate a process that might assist the prediction of negotiation and potential conflict that can occur when two types of medical systems meet within a local world. McKee shows us how beliefs become integrated within medical worldviews of Ecuadorian villagers; Graham describes larger social processes by which indigenous views about the diet and the body change as a result of migration; and Bastien provides a view of the consequences of the intersection between traditional medical and biomedical beliefs in the presence of a widespread parasitic disease.

Chapter 8

Ethnomedicine and enculturation in the Andes of Ecuador

Lauris A. McKee

A one-and-a-half hour dirt road to Patate departs from the Ambato-to-Baños highway. It descends the mountainside (in sharp curves that are ice-slick when it rains) to the ferociously rapid Patate River. High above, stands the village, built around a *parque* (central plaza). There, red bottle-brush trees and white trumpet-shaped flowers of floripondio perfume the air and mix with the odors emanating from pigsties in *huertas* (gardens) and donkey-droppings in the streets. Most village houses are two-storied constructions of cane and wattle, sharing at least one wall with a neighboring house.

When I think of Patate, I remember clouds hanging on the slopes of the volcano, Tungurahua. The white-capped volcano, starred skies, and fragrance of eucalyptus from wood cook-fires seduce the senses, but cannot hide the other realities, of poverty, subsistence insecurity, and the danger of earthquake and landslide where mountains loom above the village on three sides. The church bells begin ringing at 5 o'clock in the morning. They sound like a black-smith's hammer hitting an anvil.

On a cold morning in a mountain village in Ecuador, a child awakes complaining of diffuse pains in her body. In between yawns, she cries and wants to sleep again. She develops diarrhea, some fever and vomiting. Her worried mother seeks out a *curandera* (female folk-healer), who thoroughly rubs the child all over her body with an egg, newly laid that day. After breaking the egg into a glass of water, the *curandera* examines it closely. She calls the mother to witness that the yolk is liq-uefied and the egg appears to have been "beaten" before it was broken. This is evi-dence that the child is afflicted by *mal aire* (an evil spirit carried on cold puffs of air). Close questioning of the mother reveals that on the previous night, her husband had played cards in the local *cantina* until a late hour. The *curandera* asks if he used the protective device of smoking a cigarette upon entering the house. When the answer is negative, she announces that, surely, he brought *mal aire* with him when he came home. It has "hit" and "stuck to" (*pegado*) the body of his daughter.

Belief in *mal aire*, a potentially fatal sickness sent on the wind from the dead to the living, is deeply rooted in Andean thought and tradition,[1] and documented in contemporary texts concerned with folk medicine.[2] Though *mal aire* is said to attack humans of any age, *mestizos* in Ecuador's highland regions state that the young are particularly susceptible to its depredations. Children diagnosed with a supernatural illness, such as *mal aire*, are ritually cleansed (*limpiada*) by relatives or *curanderas* to rid them of the pathogenic agent's "filth."

In this essay, I argue that ethnotherapy for *mal aire* not only is a traditional means of curing, but is a vehicle for enculturation: for the inter-generational transmission of cultural beliefs that fosters intersubjectivity. The relationship I posit between curing and children's acquisition of cultural ways of seeing the world rests on the conviction that if significant others attribute specific meanings to a salient experience, this experience eventually will acquire a similar meaning for the child. This "informal instruction" establishes certain expectations in young minds. As they internalize the interpretations their social group gives to a phenomenon such as *mal aire*, young children gain access to basic cultural representations (schemas) that include cognitive models of illness and of well being.[3]

A brief disclaimer is necessary: informants, of course, do not think of ritual cleansing as an enculturative device. In their (emic) view, cleansing is a logical therapeutic response, given the ethnoetiology of an illness. Despite the growing influence of Western medicine, in all study sites, children who manifested the illness syndrome associated with *mal aire* were ritually cleansed prior to visiting a medical professional.

Although enculturation processes are operative to some degree in *all* social interactions, this discussion is limited to the information children can glean from a single folk-medical practice. I suggest that cultural models of human body – structure, and of the pathogen *mal aire*, are imparted to children during cleansing processes. I speculate that because the perceptions and interpretations embedded in these cultural models are shared by their intersubjective group, they prepare children for social life in their communities.

The features of these models (to be discussed below) are taken from the informants' explanations and from the mothers' conversations with *curanderas*. This discourse is available to young ears, and is, I argue, a significant informational source influencing the children's perception of *mal aire*, and how and why it makes them sick. Discourse informs these perceptions, and the experience of cleansing confirms them. Through ritual cleansing, the spirit is reified, *made concrete*, in the nonverbal actions of the curer. The *curandera's* stereotypic operations represent the presence of "something else" (the spirit) to her young patients. When children repetitively experience or witness cleansings, the cognitive model they internalize will eventually become a source of analogy that is available to aid in understanding other life events.

Schemas and models

I make use of cognitive theory in my argument linking enculturation to ethno-medical procedures, which requires a brief discussion of cognitive models and schemas: mental structures that some theorists propose as central to human thought processes. The term, schema, has a number of connotations for psychologists and anthropologists, but discussion of the multiplicity of these approaches is beyond the scope of this essay.[4] I focus, instead, on a particular class of schemas, that encode basic cultural values and thus, are intrinsic elements of a community's world view. These are *foundational schemas*.

In theorist Bradd Shore's formulation, a foundational schema is a very general, highly abstract mental model. It has profound significance in structuring cultural thought and action, though group members usually do not consciously articulate its premises. Foundational schemas are derived from a group's historical experience and the information they contain undergirds the group's most basic values, ideals, fears, and concepts of social and cosmic order.

A foundational schema is mobile, for the knowledge it encodes provides the bases for analogy. Through analogical reasoning, as well as through metaphor, metonym, and simile cultural knowledge can be transferred from one cognitive domain to another.[5]

Shore's analyses are especially useful for anthropological studies of cultural world views, for he includes *meaning* as a significant component of schemas and models. The concepts "schema" and "model" have overlapping features though a model may be more restricted in focus and content. Models, generally, are constituents of schemas, which, therefore, are structurally more complex.

It is my aim to add another dimension to these studies, namely, the role of cultural models in the process of enculturation. I propose that the models incorporated in traditional ethnotherapies offer anthropologists a means to explore relationships between children's early experiences and the internalization of world view. Traditional folk therapies regularize certain illness experiences and discourse endows them with conventional meanings. Through repetitive exposure to these experiences, children's representations of a folk illness are developed within a context featuring tacit adult agreement as to its cause and its cure. Close studies of ethnotherapies, will open interesting possibilities for anthropologists who study enculturation.

Family and "others"

I suggest that in the Ecuadorian research sites discussed here, the cognitive model for the spirit, *mal aire*, pertains to a foundational schema that links *otherness* with opportunism. Cultural perceptions of "otherness," in these Ecuadorian contexts, do not necessarily connote ethnic or cultural alterity. Rather, *otherness* refers to any person (or being) outside the intimate consanguineal family and network of fictive kin (godparents).

One notes that in social discourse, the family is depicted as the only social group a person really can rely on. Cultural expectations of kindred solidarity are evident in the tone of local gossip (ranging from disapproval to outrage) when kin engage in nasty disputes, for example, over land inheritances. Similar norms more loosely govern expectations of intra-community relations, but there is little surprise when *opportunism* rather than altruism underlies a person's motives for interaction.

This expectation applies even to children. Eleven parental pairs, out of a stratified sample of twelve whom I interviewed in 1976, stated that they forbade their children to play with anyone except their siblings or cousins. "Other" children, they said, entered their houses in order to steal things, or to pick up items of gossip for the entertainment of their own families. All twelve couples asserted that their children learned bad language and bad habits from other youngsters.

Traditional Andean thought envisions an animistic world. Supernatural beings and natural objects (such as mountains, large rocks, and trees) are invested with conscious life. Their motives, often hostile, resemble those of human beings, particularly in the realm of desire. The majority of Ecuadorians in the communities studied perceive both the social world and the natural landscape as posing potential dangers to themselves.[6] This perception is evidenced in ethnomedical practices.

During the early stages of cognitive development, Ecuadorian children may experience several ritual cleansings for *mal aire* and/or witness the cleansings of siblings and cousins. Cultural prescriptions for curing *mal aire* require three separate cleansings for each episode. These must occur on three different days (Tuesdays, Thursdays, or Fridays) and at specific propitious hours (6 o'clock in the morning or evening, or 12 o'clock, at noon or midnight).

This redundancy is significant. Repetition and rehearsal of patterned experiences figure in the emergence of children's earliest mental representations. These experiences coalesce as a cognitive model – in this case – of an illness, its cause and its cure. Such a model, as Shore suggests, is implicated in the formation of *foundational cognitive schemas.*[7]

If we consider the possibility that cleansing for *mal aire* contributes to the development of a particular foundational cognitive schema, then redundancy is a salient aspect of the practice. Although each cleansing varies (in personnel present, in the selected day or hour of its occurrence, or in the particular plants a curer selects), certain factors were universally present in all observed cleansings. These included: (1) an initial diagnosis performed by rubbing an item over the victim's skin, and interpreting the "signs" of spirit-caused pathology the item evidences; (2) removing the spirit by vigorously rubbing or beating the patient's skin with a selected object, never with the curer's bare hands; and (3) use of special, strongly scented attractants (e.g. odiferous plants, tobacco smoke, or cane alcohol) in order to "hold" the spirit and prevent its return to its victim's body.

Exposure to these repetitious, patterned operations increases the likelihood a child will form a conceptual representation of them that eventually is cognitively integrated (i.e. assimilated and accommodated) as a *schema*. The effect on schema formation of redundant exposures to a phenomenon has been analogized to the effect multiple exposures have on a photograph, "[I]mages pile up [in thought], one on top of the other, the common traits become clear and the differences become blurred."[8] One could envision a schema as a kind of cognitive palimpsest in that the information from successive cleansing experiences overwrites and elaborates preexisting representations.

My emphasis on the effect of structural repetitiveness that marks ritual cleansing shares some similarities with Bourdieu's notion of the *habitus*, defined as "[A] system of lasting transposable dispositions which functions as a matrix of perceptions, appreciations, and actions." Young children become cultural beings through "[P]ractical mastery of practical schemes, *which in no way implies symbolic mastery*" (my emphasis).[9] My argument, however, focuses on the symbolic transmission of cultural knowledge, and the origins of intersubjectivity. As such, it depends on the children's gradual acquisition of the meanings coded in a shared symbol system that also includes *nonverbal* symbolic actions.[10] This system obviously is useful, for despite access to practitioners of allopathic medicine, ethnomedical practices remain important as family resources in all study-sites.[11]

Research sites

The beliefs and therapeutic practices researched in Ecuador and discussed below are common to three Andean communities that are situated in inter-Andean valleys ranging in altitude from 7,300 to 8,500 feet. The data are drawn from thirty cleansings I observed over a two-year period of fieldwork from 1982 to 1984 and during the summer of 1994. Additionally, I conducted interviews with mothers and *curanderas* in each community concerning the etiologies of *mal aire*, its mild and severe forms, and the rationales supporting cleansing. Each of the communities is unique, but in all sites there are resident *curanderas* and all women interviewed had knowledge of *mal aire*, and the tenets of traditional ethnomedicine. The relative economic status of the women interviewed was determined based on family resources. Relative to average incomes and material possessions, the interviewees were either lower-class or middle-class. Urban Ecuadorians would classify most of our informants in each site as mestizas, and a few of them as índias.

Patate, in Tungurahua Province, is the capital of its Cantón (a provincial administrative unit).[12] Its population (of 1,577) lives in tile-roofed houses constructed of adobe and cane, or cinder block. Patate is surrounded by steep slopes marked by zig-zagging chaquiñans (foot roads). Irrigation canals descend from the highest hilltops and nourish lush green gardens in what otherwise would be a desert-like valley. Tangerine orchards, avocado trees, babaco, papaya, and tree tomatoes flourish inside the walled gardens behind houses and give the community its unique beauty.

The sale of grains (wheat, barley, and corn), fruits, tubers, and other produce is a significant source of income. Less remunerative but important to family welfare is the sale of poultry, eggs, or bread. Women prepare special foods for sale in the weekly market such as pork, roasted or fried, hominy (*mote*), tamales or *llapingachos* (cheese-filled potato pancakes). Locally crafted goods such as furniture, shoes, and clothing are sources of some family incomes. There are a few cantinas (bars), and more than 25 percent of families devote the front room of their house to a small shop where a few necessities (matches, candles, bread) or luxuries (candy, soft drinks, trago) are sold.

Both men and women are hired to work in the vineyards and small factories owned by local producers of *pisco* (a fruit-flavored liquor). Landless families work as share-croppers or seek seasonal wage work as agricultural laborers or fruit-pickers.

Tumbaviro a parroquia in Imbabura Province is a village of some 1,505 inhabitants who are mainly engaged in agriculture. There is a government-run health clinic, and the central plaza, planted in ceiba (kapok-producing) trees, is flanked by tile roofed adobe and cane houses, the parrochia's administrative offices, the church and a few house-front shops.

Food production is the primary source of income, and in a mountain environment, altitude determines the choice of crops. Corn is cultivated in fields above the village (the ruin of a scorpion-shaped precolumbian temple stands in one cornfield by the road), whereas sugarcane is the dominant cultivar at lower altitudes. Guava trees and vegetables grow in small gardens behind houses where pigs and chickens also may be kept. Following a pattern common in *mestizo* communities, farmers generally live in town and walk to their outlying fields.

The incomes of a few citizens are augmented on weekends when Ecuadorian tourists seeking to improve their health arrive by bus. They pay to bathe in a pool of hot mineral water piped in from the natural spring, Chachimbiro. Two small tourist inns provide visitors with housing and food.

The third community, Guaranda, is the capital of Bolívar Province. It is a large market town, (with a population of 15,730). There is a small university, a charming central square (*parque*), stores, many churches, a few hotels, and small industries. On market days, Guaranda is a bustling commercial center that attracts local producers selling their own grains and vegetables as well as professional vendors who travel to regional markets in both the highlands and the montaña, the lower Western slopes where the Andes rise from the Pacific Coastal plain.

In Guaranda markets, one finds (among other items) fresh fish, beef, pork, fruits and vegetables, prepared foods, medicinal plants, stalls full of useful tools, manufactured clothing, handmade pottery, poultry, guinea pigs (*cuyes*, which are an important prestige food), and commercially produced foodstuffs. A livestock market is held once a week at the city limits, where pigs, sheep, horses, mules, burros, and cows are sold. The data below are compiled from fieldwork carried out in all three communities.

Andean constructions of the body: vulnerability, homeostasis, and permeability

Health, as culturally perceived, depends on corporeal homeostasis, defined as an internal equilibrium that is achieved if body organs are arranged in their proper places, and if the relative proportions of the body's vital substances are in balance.[13]

Illness results when somatic equilibrium is disrupted. This can occur for a variety of reasons. For example, as depicted in ethnoanatomy, the skin is not the body's "sealed container," skin is porous and open to invasion by esoteric entities and ambient air.[14]

In the communities studied, women conceptualize the skin as a protective but permeable covering. The skin's porosity permits it to be penetrated by spirits, by hot or cold air, and by the "electrical" energy emitted by the eyes of some persons, who with a glance, can produce illness in others. (This is the "evil eye," in Ecuador, termed *el ojeado*.)

Body orifices are perceived as open channels that allow air to flow into the central core and the organs. But air intake may be passive or active. Just as nostrils and mouths suck in air, so the anus is perceived as having this capability. An excess of cold air "sucked in" (*chupado*) through orifices can concentrate internally. Women say that the anus of a bare-bottomed child seated on a cold floor can suck in sufficient cold to cause a certain type of diarrhea.

Excessive internal concentrations of cold or heat produce illness due to the body's internal thermatic lability. (The term *thermatic* refers to humoral concepts of hot and cold and their physiological effects.[15]) This concern for thermatic homeostasis is evidenced in dietary prescriptives. Diets (normatively) are governed by the cultural perception that foods and beverages possess intrinsic qualities of "hotness," or "coldness," or they are temperate (*templado*).

Generally, these qualities are neither objectively perceptible nor thermally measurable. Rather, they are perceived as the *internal* effects a comestible produces.[16] To maintain health and strength, the body's internal climate should be "*templado*" in a state of (metaphorical) thermatic equilibrium. However, the body's openess also allows the (measurable) temperature of ambient air to interact with internal thermatic states, and is taken into account when food is consumed.

In the cold of mountain mornings and nights, one should consume "hot" (*cálida*) foods, such as coffee to warm the body; but in the heat of the day, one requires cool foods (*comidas frescas*) or a meal that balances hot and cold comestibles. The principle of opposites governs consumption: the effects of too much cold food will cause internal imbalance, but can be mitigated or countered by ingesting hot foods or beverages, and vice versa.

With these concerns in mind, mothers often use protective tactics when they take infants into public spaces. Babies are swaddled and carried in shawls to cover their bodies, heads, and often, their faces as well. Swaddling for at least three months also is said to be necessary for the limbs to grow straight and strong.[17]

The cultural model of weakness

Informants cite normal growth and development as a factor predisposing a child to weakness or illness. They perceive any biological change as disruptive of internal equilibrium, and as such, potentially pathogenic. Infants and children are said to be weaker relative to adults due to their continual growth and corporeal changes. Because of their weakness, children are more susceptible to *mal aire* and other illnesses.

Each stage of development is perceived as altering the degree of physiological equilibrium attained in the preceding stage. Thus, when children begin to sit, crawl, walk, or talk, mothers expect them to get sick.[18] "Weakness" (*debilidad*) is also associated with the blood, which is conceptualized qualitatively as a continuum from weak to strong. Children's diet determines the strength of their blood, and corporeal fatness is an external, objective index of the blood's current status.[19] In these Andean communities, blood and fat are conceived as primary principles of vitality and energy.[20] Malnourished children are weak and are easy targets for *mal aire* attacks.

Although to Western ears "malnourishment" connotes simply a lack of sufficient food, the Andean folk concept, "weak blood" is more complex in its referents: there is, as Wachtel notes, "[A] relationship, even an equivalence between fat and blood."[21] Blood and fat are personal properties that can be stolen. This is evidenced in the belief that the Andean vampires (the *ñaqaq*, *pishtaco*, and *kharisiri*) extract the fat/blood of their victims in order to sell it to foreigners, or use it for their own consumption.[22] (The conflation of native demonic figures and foreign "others" is clearly indicated here.)

Curanderas diagnose children suffering from severe protein-calorie malnutrition as victims of *mal aire* that has penetrated to the blood. Folk healers consider them incurable. Given the indices of weakness noted above, clearly, children of the poorest families are most liable to illness from *mal aire*.

Andean humoral theory and the practices involved in dietary choices are highly complex[23] and I give them only a cursory mention here to emphasize the ethnomedical significance of internal equilibrium. It is a concept that governs behavior in the satisfaction of a basic biological need – the need for sustenance. The possible disruption of internal equilibrium is perceived as a major factor in body vulnerability.

The cultural construction of *mal aire*

The practices used to protect children from *mal aire* or to cure them of the illness it produces arise from cultural models of the body's susceptibilities described above. But, as Csordas and Kleinman state, "[W]hat counts as therapy depends first on what is defined as a problem."[24]

Mal aire is the spirit of a dead person or one of the Devil's demons. As a dead thing, it is "icy cold" and seeks out warm victims. As a weak, airy thing, its success depends on finding (weak) victims with little capacity to resist its efforts to penetrate their skin and consume their blood. *Mal aire* is indestructible and ubiquitous; it circulates freely in the environment, but surprisingly, it is said to avoid populated places.[25] Most often, it is encountered in remote and lonely mountain reaches, ravines, abandoned houses, on empty footpaths (*chaquiñans*), and in the dead of night, in a town's empty streets.[26] It avoids areas where people concentrate, and is less likely to attack children who are surrounded by family. Some or all of this information emerges in discourse: in the caretakers' accounts of the onset of illness, in the curer's questions, or in their explanations.

Mal aire as an illness syndrome manifests in a multiplicity of ways: as nervousness, sleeplessness, dermatological problems, fever, vomiting, facial paralysis, weight loss (wasting), or diffuse somatic pain. Once the spirit is "stuck" to human skin, it tenaciously and perniciously works through and past it until it reaches its victims' blood and fat, which it voraciously consumes. Once *mal aire* is in the child's blood, it is incurable[27] so it is important to begin the cleansing process promptly.

Informants insist that doctors cannot cure *mal aire* or other supernaturally caused illnesses. Their medicines only kill germs, not immortal spirits. If, after three cleansings to dispel the spirit, the illness persists, then caretakers view it as a kind of material damage the spirit caused prior to its removal. Doctors can treat these *material* sequelae so children are taken to the clinic.

Folk healers have the knowledge to cure *mal aire* because they are versed in its preferences, predilections, and dislikes. These determine their choice of paraphernalia for detaching it from a child's body. They know that *mal aire* is drawn to warmth. It locates victims by their emissions of body heat and perspiration. It is lured away from a child by the fragrance of certain wild plants, or the warmth and fragrance of tobacco smoke or burning herbs such as rosemary, or the odor of cane alcohol (*trago*).[28] It is repelled by foul-smelling herbs such as the pungent *ruda* (rue: *Ruta graveolens*) and leaves its victim's body to escape the odor. As an evil spirit, it fears the power of the Christian God and the Saints. For the latter reason, cleansings generally incorporate spoken or silent prayers, and *curanderas* make the sign of the cross on the child's body with herbal bouquets or (more rarely) with saints' pictures.

Children receive a direct, tactile "message" confirming the spirit as a being with desires and preferences. The objects used to rub, beat, or sweep the pathogenic spirit off their skin, reify it. It is a "thing" (sticking to the skin, that must be removed). All body surfaces receive treatment. But spirits are tenacious. Once detached, *mal aire*, immediately returns to its victim unless its attention is "captured" by a more attractive lure. *Curanderas* entice it with another body that shares its victims attractions (e.g. weakness, warmth and blood, as do guinea pigs and setting hens) or alternatively, with irresistible fragrances. *Mal aire* attaches to fragrant wild plants, and clings to them until they wither, dry, and lose their scents. If exposed to the fragrance and warmth of smoke, the spirit moves into it and is carried off into the air. Clearly, given the culture's construction of *mal aire*, the strategies used in ritual cleansings are technically and performatively rational.[29]

Consistency is an issue here, and in thirty cleansings, I observed regularities in the three main modes of concretizing the presence of the spirit "thing:"

1   using friction: vigorously rubbing or lightly beating the body with plants, an animal, or a sweat-soaked item of human clothing;

2   using smoke to partially cover or to envelop the body;

3   spitting alcohol (*trago*) on the skin, or rubbing flowers or cologne over the body.

Mode 1 was used in all thirty cleansings. In twenty-nine cleansings, modes 1 and 2 were combined. Eighteen cleansings combined modes 1 and 3.

In twenty-nine of thirty observed cleansings, curers used freshly cut wild plants (*montes*) such as *chilca* (*Baccharis polyantha*), the flowers or leafy branches of *guantug* or *floripondio* (*Datura sanguinea* or *Datura arborea*). Smoke from cigarette tobacco or herbal scented fires was used in twenty-nine cleansings. Only one *curandera* used roses and cologne. Pungent cane alcohol was used in eighteen of the cleansings. *Mal aire* also is attracted to human sweat, so the thermatically "hot" sweaty clothes of a "strong" (*fuerte*) person are said be used but I did not observe this practice.

Enculturation and cognition

The mental representations that very young Ecuadorian children form during the cleansing process most likely are concrete, rather than conceptual in nature. But as their symbolic capacities develop between age two and four, the redundant, nonverbal messages implicit in cleansings and other ethnomedical treatments lead toward formation of a body schema that is eminently cultural.

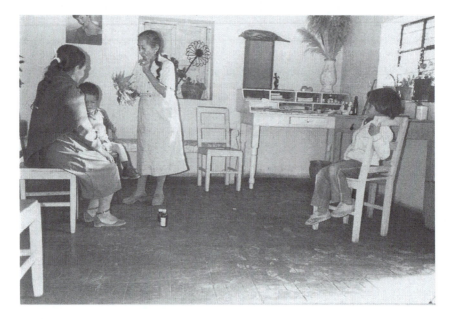

Plate 8.1 The curandera uses wild plants, tobacco, and alcohol to cure a child. His cousin is an attentive observer.

This schema is constructed such that it includes a sense of existential precariousness. "Embodiment," then, entails awareness of the certain vulnerabilities, and of mysterious beings that take advantage of these weaknesses. Thus, early in life, children learn to perceive themselves as at risk in a world that harbors entities with evil motives.

Ethnographers have noted similar concerns in other Andean sites. In the Peruvian community of Cuyo Cuyo, Larme found that people perceived "their bodies, health and well-being as in a constant state of threat from environmental forces both natural and supernatural."[30] Crandon-Malamud notes four themes that appear consistently in discussions of illness in the Bolivian community of Kachitu: insatiable hunger, vulnerability (fear of soul loss to mountain spirits), victimization, and exploitation.[31]

In the Ecuadorian sites, the concepts explaining the illness, *mal aire* – the motives of its agent, its progressive stages, and how it can lead to death – all are symbolically represented for young patients through the cleansing operations and their accompanying discourse. In this sense, this ethnomedical treatment can be viewed as a kind of initiation, in which the patient acquires some of the culture's esoteric knowledge.

Cleansings are framed as structurally liminal moments. The social ambience is emotionally charged by the child's suffering and the mother's feelings and concerns. The child is the sole focus of adult attention and the treatments she receives (such as the unusual stimulation of all areas of her body), radically vary in tone and content from quotidian routines of child care. Cleansings are temporally bounded (normatively restricted to certain days and hours), and are thought to be transformative (i.e. have the object of moving a child from illness to health).[32]

The child's visual, olfactory, tactile, and auditory senses are virtually barraged with information. Simultaneously, the child experiences proprioceptive (internally registered) sensations of discomfort caused by the illness itself. The hyperintensity of the sensory phenomena is phrased to form indelible memories, easily triggered because of the numerous perceptually cued routes to their retrieval. The illness is discursively constructed prior to initiating the cleansing, and provides the reasons for its operations.

This is not to say that children will automatically, or even, readily register this plethora of messages and their meanings. Transmissions are never perfect or complete. A child's personal fears, degree of malaise, temperament, level of curiosity, or outright misunderstanding all may filter or block message reception. Thus, to varying degrees, cultural models and the foundational schemas that incorporate them remain open to reinterpretations and thus, to potential cultural change.

Mal aire and world view

I suggest that *mal aire* serves as a metaphor for *otherness*. Cleansing activities symbolically establish the "reality" of a mysterious other, who wishes to steal one's life's blood. The opportunism that characterizes the spirit can be cognitively configured in either human or supernatural terms. In the Ecuadorian sites, it informs expectations when interactions take place between the self and the society. The schema encoding this information (as I suggest above), is a precipitate of early experiences whose fundamental features and symbolic referents are shared by the majority in these cultural groups.

A recurrent theme in family discourse is the victimization of well-meaning or foolishly trusting persons by devious locals or by strangers who despoiled them. Family members' personal disasters, especially their economic reverses, usually are attributed to the greed and cynical exploitation of *personas ajenas*: (outsiders to the intimate group of personal kindred and ritual kin). To be in the company of kin is the optimal type of social association, and the home is portrayed as an area of safety, especially for children.

I have argued that interactions in the Andean societies studied are influenced by a foundational schema that links opportunism to *otherness*. Any event that confirms these expectations is remembered, and increases their strength, whereas an outsider's disinterested helpfulness is regarded as an exception to the "rule."

Opportunism, and its active component, exploitation, models expectations of *personas ajenas* and Andean supernaturals outside the Christian pantheon. During five hundred years of colonial and post-colonial rule, autochthonous Andean spirits (e.g. the ancestral dead; the aquatic, chthonic, and celestial Gods and spirits), who once played both helpful and harmful roles in human lives, have been reinvented. Cultural models now inscribe them as just another class of exploiters: single-minded predators who rob people of their souls and consume their vital substances. In contemporary society, "They act for members of a community as shared and ready-made source domains for analogical schematization. They are the stuff on which the cultural imagination feeds."[33] In the discourse of Ecuador's urbanites, one frequently hears rural farmers and townspeople stereotyped as *cerrado* (closed). By this term, they imply that highland peasants are suspicious, mistrustful, and often overtly hostile to outsiders.

First, let me affirm that in personal relations with family members or compadres, non-urban highlanders are equally as open and warm as urbanites. Second, a defensive stance and suspicious regard often *does* characterize highlanders' contacts with outsiders, but with good reason. Over the course of five centuries of oppression, to be *cerrado* has been one of the few nonviolent, semi-effective forms of defending one's self and one's family against would-be exploiters. Suspicion appears eminently rational given a past and a present in which successive groups of "others" institutionalized discrimination of native populations and *mestizo* peasants, through legal and illegal means. These are convincing grounds for highlanders' to conclude that a stranger, most likely, is not a friend.

Notes

1 Poma de Ayala, Felipe Guaman, *La Nueva Cronica; y Buen Gobierno*, J. Murra, R. Adorno and J. Urioste (eds), Historia 16, 1987 [1613]; Foster, G. W., "Relationships

between Spanish and Spanish–American folk medicine," *Journal of American Folklore*, 1953, 16: 201–17, see pp. 203, 207; Paredes Borja, V. *Historia de la Medicina en el Ecuador*, Editorial Casa de la Cultura, 1963, pp. 136, 143; Estrella, E., *Medicina Aborígen*, Editorial Epoca, 1977.

2 Larme, A., "Environment, vulnerability and gender in Andean ethnomedicine," *Social Science and Medicine*, 1998, 47: 1005–15; Muñoz-Bernand, C. *Enfermedad, Daño e Ideología*, Abya Yala, 1986; Mauro, Cifuentes, M., Sola, J., Paredes, H., Bedoya, J., and Sanchez Parga, J., *Medicina Andina*, Centro de acción Popular, 1992; McKee, L., "Ethnomedical treatment of children's diarrheal illnesses in the highlands of Ecuador," *Social Science and Medicine*, 1987, 25(10): 1147–57; Greenway, C., "Objectified selves: an analysis of medicines in Andean sacrificial healing," *Medical Anthropology Quarterly*, 1988, 12(2): 147–67.

3 Nerlove and Snipper call attention to the interaction between internalized expectations for (certain) behaviors, and how the context in which they occur serves to maintain them. See Sara Nerlove and Ann Snipper, "Consequences of cultural opportunity." In *Handbook of Cross-Cultural Human Development*, Ruth Munroe, Robert Munroe, and Beatrice Whiting (eds), Garland STPM Press, 1981, pp. 423–74.

4 Jean Piaget formulated a theory of cognitive development that depicted schemas as simple or complex mental structures that model actions. "Actions" were construed as either internalized thought processes, or as overt motor behaviors. Schemas adapt by assimilating and accommodating novel information. Piaget, J., *The Construction of Reality in the Child* (translated by M. Cook), Ballantine Books, 1954. Piaget maintains that until the age of 18–24 months, children cannot cognitively represent the world, although they can imitate a model's actions. Recent research indicates that representational thought occurs earlier than his theory predicts. For a critical analysis of Piaget's theories, see Baldwin, A., *Theories of Child Development*, John Wiley and Sons, Inc. 1967, especially pp. 231–41.

5 See Shore, B., *Culture in Mind*, Oxford University Press, 1996 for a fascinating theoretical explication of schema mobility and analogy, and variations in types of cultural models. Foundational schemas are more global, more abstract and more general forms. Although many cultural models are not part of foundational schemas, those that are instantiate schemas; as "socially mediated forms of knowledge," they afford a sense of shared world view and "culturally typical practices" (ibid. 11, 53). I find Shore's conception of cultural models brilliant and far more useful to anthropologists. The notion of model-formation helps us understand how meaning is constructed and integrated in cultural thought. Models are more accessible to anthropological analyses than are schemas. Models reveal cognitive orientations and meanings that are significant for the collectivity. Foundational schemas are resistant to change, but models are more adaptable to changes in the social environment (Shore 1996: 45, ch. 5, especially 117–18). I agree with Shore that schema are mobile and that transfer across domains operates analogically (ibid. 343–72). Foundational schemas informing cultural worldviews are sources of analogy for other instituted models and can connect different domains of thought. The constellation of cognitive structures Shore offers differentiates among models and schemas in terms of their relative complexity and/or the breadth of the domains of thought and activity they represent within a cultural context (ibid. 45–69 and passim).

6 Allen's remarkable ethnographic account of Sonqo, a community in the Andes of Peru, is a nuanced and extensive revelation of the close relationship between people and the personified landscape. Allen, C. *The Hold Life Has*, Smithsonian Institution Press, 1988.

7 Shore, 1996, p. 44. Shore defines foundational schemas as "[V]ery general models which work across empirically heterogeneous domains of experience and underlie a community's world view." Despite their cognitive centrality, foundational schemas

generally are not explicitly, verbally formulated. They are tacit assumptions about the nature of certain things that exist in the world, and, in Shore's view, these schemas structure "a large number of apparently divergent cultural models."

8 Shapiro, S. A. and Gerke, E. D., 1928, discussed in L. S. Vigotsky, *Mind in Society*, M. Cole, V. John-Steiner, S. Scribner and E. Souberman (eds), Harvard University Press, 1978, p. 22.

9 Bourdieu, P., *Outline of a Theory of Practice*, Cambridge University Press, 1991 [1977], pp. 82, 83, 88 and passim.

10 Mead and Bateson's anthropological analyses included nonverbal aspects of culture. They examined differences in cultural styles of movement and in nonverbal norms of interaction between mothers and children. See Mead, M., *Growing Up in New Guinea*, Morrow Quill, 1962 [1930], Bateson, G. and Mead, M., *Bathing Babies in Three Cultures*, Film distributed by Penn State Audiovisual Services, 1954.

11 This consistency is evidenced in a series of Documentary videos on ethnomedicine and children that I made in 1984 with the valued assistance of Lcda. Silvia Argüello and a talented Ecuadorian staff. See Evil Wind, Evil Air, Birth and Belief in the Andes of Ecuador, and Diagnósticos.

12 Population data for all sites is taken from Ecuador's *IV Censo de Población y IV de Vivvienda: Resultados Definidos. Resumen Nacional*, Talleres Gráficas del INEC, 1990, pp. 15, 16, 23, 31.

13 McKee, 1987.

14 *Susto*, a wasting illness marked by disturbed sleep and nervous startling, is thought to be due to soul loss caused if a child is frightened or shocked. One consequence is that the body's internal arrangement of organs is disturbed. If her mother is present when the fright occurs, she quickly turns the child upside down and shakes her while reciting "shungo shungo" in order to re-situate her internal organs.

15 Bastien and Schaedel pose the possibility that the Qollahuayas, historically famous Bolivian folk-healers, empirically observed the physiological effects different plants had on the human body. The authors use the term *thermatic* to refer to Andean categories based on the "fresh," "warm," or "hot" qualities ascribed to these plants. Bastien, Joseph and Schaedel, R., "Cognitive patterns of continuity in Andean studies," in *Past and Present in the Americas: A Compendium of Recent Studies*, J. Lynch (ed.), Manchester University Press, 1984, pp. 139–42.

16 For historical information on humoral beliefs see Foster, G., "Hippocrates' Latin American legacy: "hot" and "cold" in contemporary folk medicine," *Coll. Anthropology*, 2: 3–19. Also see Foster, G. and Anderson, B., *Medical Anthropology*, Alfred A. Knopf, 1978, p. 59.

17 In the highlands, mothers say babies should be swaddled for at least three months from shoulders to feet, to ensure that their limbs grow straight and strong. Some mothers continue to swaddle infants six months to a year, but only from hips to feet. In his Royal Commentaries of the Incas and General History of Peru, Part I, University of Texas Press, 1996, p. 212, Garcilaso de la Vega describes similar swaddling customs and beliefs among the Incas.

18 In Guaranda, some mothers associate particular types of diarrhea with specific stages of children's development, such as cutting teeth, being made to sit alone too soon, beginning to crawl, etc. McKee, 1987 discusses the criteria mothers use to determine if a child's illness is serious or mild, and the corresponding treatment he/she should receive. Their diagnoses depend on traditional ethnomedical classifications of types of diarrhea.

19 See Oths for a discussion of another form of weakness that is a culturally significant illness for Peruvian women and their families. She views it as "a result of the embodiment of life's accumulated hardships." Oths, K., "*Debilidad*: a biocultural assessment of an embodied Andean illness," *Medical Anthropology Quarterly*, 1999, 13(3): 286–315.

20 Muñoz-Bernand, 1986.
21 Wachtel, N., *Gods and Vampires. Return to Chipaya* (translated by Carol Volk), University of Chicago Press, 1994, p. 72.
22 Muñoz-Bernand, Carmen, 1986, p. 57.
23 Other aspects of highland dietary regimens are described in Weismantal, M. J., *Food, Gender and Poverty in the Ecuadorian Andes*, University of Pennsylvania Press, 1988.
24 Csordas, T. and Kleinman, A., "The therapeutic process." In *Medical Anthropology. Contemporary Theory and Method*, T. M. Johnson and C. E. Sargent (eds), Praeger, 1990, p. 12.
25 Gow's work in a Peruvian lowland community revealed the belief that spirits avoid places where people concentrate because they find human urine repugnant. Gow, P., *Of Mixed Blood. Kinship and History in Peruvian Amazonia*, Clarendon Press, 1991, pp.190–1. I have not recorded this belief in Ecuador, but it is interesting that ten mothers in my sample reported that a small amount of the urine of an opposite sex child could be used as medicine for a sick infant. Also see Muñoz Bernand, 1986, p. 36.
26 Finerman examines the relationships between disease and the environment as perceived by the Saraguro peoples in southern Ecuador. Finerman, R., "Inside out: women's world view and family health in an Ecuadorian Indian community," *Social Science and Medicine*, 1987, 25(10): pp.1157–62.
27 McKee, 1984.
28 Among indigenous Amerindians, smoke was and is an important symbolic device for attracting supernatural attention, whether in religious rituals or in curing ceremonies. For an extensive survey of the uses of tobacco in the Americas, see Wilbert J., *Tobacco and Shamanism in South America*, Yale University Press, 1988. For a discussion of alcohol use in contacts with spirits, see McKee, 1987, pp. 1147–56.
29 Cf. Kleinman, Arthur, *Writing at the Margin. Discourse Between Anthropology and Medicine*, University of California Press, 1995, p. 213. Given the importance of scent in ritual cleansing, it is interesting that Inca rituals actively engaged the senses of touch, taste, sight, hearing, and smell and "It was considered necessary to involve all of the senses in order for the ceremony to be completely effective," Classen, C., *Inca Cosmology and the Human Body*, University of Utah Press, 1993, p. 79.
30 Larme, 1998.
31 Crandon-Malamud. L., *From The Fat of Our Souls*, University of California Press, 1991, p. 45.
32 Turner, V., *The Forest of Symbols*, Cornell University Press, 1967, p. 94 discusses van Gennep's theories on rites de *passage*, "as rites which accompany every change of place, state, social position and age" and which are "marked by three phases: separation, margin (or limen), and aggregation." For analyses of the Ecuadorian practice of postpartum seclusion as a rite of passage, see McKee, *Los Cuerpos Tiernos: Simbolismo y Magia en las Practicas Post-Parto en Ecuador, América Indígena* XLII (4), 1982, pp. 616–28, or McKee, "The dieta: postpartum seclusion in the Andes of Ecuador." In *Generations*, A. Cohn and L. Leach (eds), Pantheon Books, 1987, pp. 205–15.
33 Shore, 1996, p. 364.

References

Allen, Catherine, *The Hold Life Has, Coca and Cultural Identity in an Andean Community*, Smithsonian Institution Press, 1988.
Baldwin, Alfred, *Theories of Child Development*, John Wiley and Sons, Inc., 1967.
Bastien, Joseph and R. Schaedel, "Cognitive patterns of continuity in Andean studies." In *Past and Present in the Americas: A Compendium of Recent Studies*, J. Lynch (ed.), Manchester University Press, 1984.

Bateson, Gregory and Margaret Mead, *Bathing Babies in Three Cultures*, Film distributed by Penn State Audiovisual Services [1954].
Bourdieu, Pierre, *Outline of a Theory of Practice*, Cambridge University Press, 1997.
Cifuentes, Mauro, J. Sola, H. Paredes, J. Bedoya, and J. Sanchez-Parga, *Medicina Andina: Situaciones y Respuestas*, Centro Andino de Acción Popular, 1992.
Classen, Constance, *Inca Cosmology and the Human Body*, University of Utah Press, 1993.
Cole, Michael and Sylvia Scribner, *Culture and Thought*, John Wiley and Sons, Inc., 1974.
Crandon-Malamud, Libbet, *From The Fat of Our Souls*, University of California Press, 1991, p. 45.
Csordas, Thomas, and Arthur Kleinman, "The therapeutic process." In *Medical Anthropology, Contemporary Theory and Method*, T. M. Johnson and C. E. Sargent (eds), Praeger, 1990.
Estrella, Eduardo, *Médicina Aborígen*, Editorial Epoca, 1977.
Finerman, Ruthbeth, "Inside out: women's world view and family health in an Ecuadorian Indian community," *Social Science and Medicine*, 1987, 25(10): 1157–62.
Foster, George, "Relationships between Spanish and Spanish American folk medicine," *Journal of American Folklore*, 1953, 66: 201–17.
——, "Hippocrates' Latin American legacy: "hot" and "cold" in contemporary folk medicine." In *Colloquia in Anthropology*, vol. II, R. K. Wetherington (ed.) Southern Methodist University, 1978, pp. 3–19.
——and Barbara Anderson, *Medical Anthropology*, Alfred A. Knopf, 1978, p. 59.
IV Censo de Población y IV de Vivienda. Resultados Definidos. Resumen Nacional, Talleres Gráficas del Instituto Nacional de Estadística y Censos, 1990.
Garcilaso de la Vega, El Inca, *Royal Commentaries of the Incas and General History of Peru, Part I* (translated by H. Livermore), University of Texas Press, 1966 [1609].
Gow, Peter, *Of Mixed Blood. Kinship and History in Peruvian Amazonia*, Clarendon Press, 1991.
Greenway, Christine, "Objectified selves: an analysis of medicines in Andean sacrificial healing," *Medical Anthropology Quarterly*, 1998, 12(2): 147–67.
Harvard Health Letter, Harvard University Press, 2000, 25(3): 8.
Kleinman, Arthur, *Writing at the Margin. Discourse Between Anthropology and Medicine*, University of California Press, 1995.
Larme, Ann, "Environment, vulnerability and gender in Andean medicine," *Social Science and Medicine*, 1998, 47(8): 1005–15.
Mead, Margaret, *Growing up in New Guinea*, Morrow Quill, 1962 [1930].
McKee, Lauris, "Ethnomedical treatment of children's diarrheal illnesses in the highlands of Ecuador," *Social Science and Medicine*, 1987, 29(10): 1147–55.
McKee, L. (Video Series, Ethnomedicine y Niños, 1984): *Evil Wind, Evil Air* (distributed by Penn State Audiovisual Services), *Birth and Belief in the Andes of Ecuador* (distributed by the University of California-Berkeley), *Diagnósticos* (distributed by Latin American Video Archives).
——, "The dieta: post-partum seclusion in the Andes of Ecuador." In *Generations. A Universal Family Album*, Anna Cohn and Lucinda Leach (eds), Pantheon Books, 1987.
——, *Los Cuerpos Tiernos: Simbolismo y Magia en las Prácticas Post-Parto en Ecuador*, *América Indígena*, 1982, XLII(4): 615–28.

Muñoz-Bernand, Carmen, *Enfermedad, Daño e Ideologia*, Ediciones Abya Yala, 1986.

Nerlove, Sara and Ann Snipper, "Cognitive consequences of cultural opportunity." In *Handbook of Cross-Cultural Human Development*, Ruth Munroe, Robert Munroe, and Beatrice Whiting (eds), Garland Press, 1981, pp. 423–74.

Oths, Kathryn, *Debilidad*: a biocultural assessment of an embodied Andean illness, *Medical Anthropology Quarterly*, 1999, 13(3): 286–315.

Paredes, Borja, V. *Historia de la Medicina en el Ecuador*, Editorial Casa de la Cultura, 1963.

Piaget, Jean, *The Construction of Reality in the Child* (translated by Margaret Cook), Ballantine Books, 1954.

——and B. Inhelder, *The Psychology of the Child*, Basic Books, 1969.

Shore, Bradd, *Culture in Mind: Cognition, Culture and the Problems of Meaning*, Oxford University Press, 1996.

Poma de Ayala, Felipe Guaman, *Nueva Crónica y Buen Gobierno*, John V. Murra, Rolena Adorno, and Jorge Urioste (eds), Impresión TEMI,1987 [1607].

Turner, Victor, *The Forest of Symbols*, Cornell University Press, 1967.

Vigotsky, L. S., *Mind in Society. The Development of Higher Psychological Processes*, Michael Cole, Vera John-Steiner, Sylvia Scribner, and Ellen Souberman (eds), Harvard University Press, 1978.

Wachtel, Nathan, *Gods and Vampires. Return to Chipaya* (translated by Carol Volk), University of Chicago Press, 1994, p. 72.

Weismantal, M. J., *Food, Gender and Poverty in the Ecuadorian Andes*, University of Pennsylvania Press, 1988.

Wilbert, Johannes, *Tobacco and Shamanism in South America*, Yale University Press, 1988.

Chapter 9

Food, health, and identity in a rural Andean community

Margaret A. Graham

Plate 9.1 Agricultural terraces during the rainy season, District of Cuyo Cuyo, Peru.

First impressions of Cuyo Cuyo

My research colleagues and I left Juliaca early one cold July morning to make the long trip to Cuyo Cuyo. We spent hours crossing the treeless *altiplano*, slowly inching higher toward the pass where we would begin our descent onto the eastern slope. The relatively straight road of the *altiplano* was now a narrow single lane skirting the edge of steep mountainsides. After another few hours of slow driving, we made our final turn into the Cuyo Cuyo valley. It was a spectacular sight! The steep hillsides were covered with stone-faced terraces that looked like steps from our bird's-eye perspective. I could see the small town of Cuyo Cuyo and the surrounding peasant communities, several of which seemed to be clinging onto the steep valley walls in defiance of gravity. As we wound our way down the road to town, the effects of the previous year's mud-slide became more apparent. I could see where the hillsides had slipped down and covered houses and sections of the road. The Catholic church, located in the central plaza, had been badly affected and now stood as a roofless shell with rocky debris piled high against its partially standing walls. I felt subdued and a bit overwhelmed during those first few minutes in Cuyo Cuyo. Perhaps it was the destruction or the grey overcast of that late afternoon or the *calamina* (corrugated metal) roofs that made the town look like a hastily built fron-tier settlement. Whatever the reasons, the feelings passed rather quickly as we dealt with the business at hand – unloading the jeep, meeting the mayor, and cooking our meal. Although I associate greyness with my first impressions, I soon learned that village life was intensely vivid.

Introduction

The production of food is a central concern of farmers worldwide. In Ura Ayllu, a rural community in southern Peru, people spend a great deal of time working in their fields and talking about the social, natural, and supernatural forces that can affect the food they grow and will ultimately eat. Farming, however, is only one of the economic pursuits that occupy the thoughts and energies of people in the community. Since the 1970s, Ura Ayllinos have increased their participation in the market economy, primarily through gold mining. Every year, beginning in November, most adult men and teenage boys leave the community for several months to generate cash incomes in the placer gold mines of Madre de Dios Department, a week's journey by truck. Those who remain behind – women, children, the elderly, and a few men who have immediate responsibilities at home – are responsible for household and field maintenance. These dual economic pursuits – farming and mining – can create conflicts over how people spend their time and how they value the products of their labor.

One arena in which such conflicts erupt is that of food. Villagers today view their diet as "pluralistic" and recognize the increased use of commercial foods in recent decades, a phenomenon Pelto and Pelto describe as dietary delocalization.[1] Commercial foods that previously were purchased irregularly and in small quan-tities are now, according to a thirty-year-old male informant, "dancing in the kitchen" with local foods.

In this chapter, I explore the "dance" of local and commercial foods through an examination of the complex ways Ura Ayllinos think about and use them. In *From the Fat of Our Souls*, Crandon-Malamud argues that rural Bolivians in the com-munity of Kachitu express social identity in the ways they think and talk about medicine and illness.[2] She shows that Kachitunos selectively combine elements from different medical systems to express ethnic identity, wealth, and prestige within a changing socioeconomic context. In parallel fashion, I draw upon Crandon-Malamud's framework to examine how Ura Ayllinos use food to define themselves in regard to social identity, health, and wealth.

Dietary delocalization in the Andes

Recent dietary studies in the Andes have shown that rural subsistence producers rely on both locally produced and commercial foods purchased on the market.[3] In his analysis of stability and change in the Andes, Orlove summarizes the various factors that can lead to the increased use of commercial foods in the diet of rural communities.[4] For example, ecological factors that influence agricultural productivity and increased population pressure on those resources may result in an increased reliance on commercial foods to compensate for production shortfalls. The increased monetization of the economy that has drawn smallholders increasingly into the market economy and commercial networks and away from local production also can result in decreased agricultural productivity due to conflicting time and energy demands required by the cash economy. Such declines in traditional production can further reinforce participation in the market economy and can lead households to rely increasingly on cash to meet their biological and social needs. National food prices and food subsidy programs also affect what people can buy and sell and thus can greatly influence dietary patterns and ability to purchase commercial foods. For example, Orlove cites Appleby's analysis of marketing in Puno Department (the same department in which Ura Ayllu is located) that shows that rural households retained more of their own produce and bought fewer commerical food staples than they had in the past as prices for those market items rose.[5] This highlights the effect of price on food purchasing patterns as well as the non-linear process of dietary delocalization.

Dietary delocalization may also result from cultural factors such as the symbolic association of commercial foods with participation in the wider national monetized economy.[6] Under such conditions, people may prefer commercial foods because of the prestige value associated with them, a value that has little to do with their cost or nutritional value.[7] Weismantel's study of the symbolic aspects of food and diet in rural Ecuador shows that the shift from barley gruel to wheat bread in the early morning meal is a "contradictory and conflict-filled process" for the households experiencing it.[8] Her analysis shows that while wheat bread has been part of the diet for some time, it is its changing role in the diet specifically as a substitute for the symbolically important morning barley gruel that makes the shift so culturally significant and emotionally charged.[9]

Like Weismantel, I was struck by the people's contradictory attitudes about local and commercial foods. On the one hand, local foods are generally held in high esteem with much physical and emotional energies devoted to their successful cultivation. On the other hand, some local foods were also the object of denigration and shame. Likewise, commercial foods that were used in public, status-marking events like fiestas were, under different circumstances, markers of poverty and economic insecurity. By unraveling the multiple, and sometimes contradictory, meanings attached to local and commercial foods, I argue that Ura Ayllinos, like the Kachitunos, consciously use these foods to define different, conflicting, aspects of their identity which are considered important in this rural community undergoing economic change. I also critically examine the view that market goods of many types, including commercial food, carry a social "prestige" value that influences their increased consumption.

The community and methods

Ura Ayllu is one of three legally recognized peasant communities in the Cuyo Cuyo District, Province of Sandia, located on the eastern slope of the southern Peruvian Andes. The village lies in a steep valley in a Quechua-speaking region of the Department of Puno, north of Lake Titicaca. It is a nucleated village of some 168 households located on a dirt road that links the lower-lying fruit and coca producing areas of Sandia to the regional market town of Juliaca. Like the rest of the district, Ura Ayllu does not have electricity but does have a piped water system although its flow is unreliable. Public buildings and services are limited to an elementary school, community building, Catholic Church, and Seventh Day Adventist meeting hall. A number of family-run stores stock an assortment of imported foodstuffs (e.g. flour, rice, noodles, sugar, and bread), beer and soft drinks, and items used regularly by peasant households (matches, candles, batteries, soap, school supplies, kerosene, etc.).

Ura Ayllinos make their living through a combination of subsistence, petty commodity production, and wage labor. Each household cultivates corn, fava beans, and several species of native tubers, most importantly potato and oca (*Oxalis tuberosa*), in a number of small fields dispersed throughout the valley. Families also maintain small garden plots adjacent to their homes where garnish vegetables (kale, onions, carrots), herbs (for cooking and medicine), and a few potato plants are grown. Animals, such as sheep, chickens, and cattle are used primarily for the wool, eggs, and dung they produce. These meats are seldom consumed although suet (*cebo*), which is purchased, is added to most soups for flavor. Guinea pigs, an Andean domesticate, are raised in every household kitchen for food although their consumption is reserved primarily for ritual occasions.

Off-farm incomes are obtained through the mining of gold, the sale of coca leaf, and wage labor. Since the 1970s, gold mining has become the most important source of income, providing Cuyo Cuyeños seven times more income than from all other sources combined. Cash incomes from gold mining are used to buy food and essential material goods, such as agrochemicals, clothing, school supplies, radios, and cooking fuels, considered necessary for both biological and social reproduction. Migrants work alone on their own claim, form business associations with relatives, work as wage laborers, or utilize a combination of these types of labor relations. Migration to the gold fields is timed with the rainy season, taking men and adolescent boys out of the community after the planting has ended. Due to the distance of the mining sites, migrants do not return for several months, usually during the harvests in April. One of the consequences of this seasonal migration cycle is that agricultural responsibilities are falling increasingly on the women and children who remain in the community. Another consequence, according to Recharte, has been a decrease in the household production of food-stuffs and an increased reliance on commercial commodities, including food.[10] The widening of economic spheres that began in the second half of the nineteenth century has undermined peasant capacity for self-sufficiency in the subsistence sphere, although not irreversibly, as some miners invest their earnings in farmland and other agricultural inputs.[11]

Ura Ayllu is located about 2 kilometers downstream from the district capital, Cuyo Cuyo. The town is the political and commercial center of the district and houses government offices, the high school, the health post, and the police station. Villagers from the neighboring peasant communities can purchase food from several well-stocked stores in town or from individual vendors who resell produce and bread purchased from larger markets in Juliaca or Sandia and who can be found most days seated near the town's central plaza.

Historically, the town of Cuyo Cuyo was the center of local *Mestizo* residence and power in the district. *Misti* was the Quechua name given by Cuyo Cuyeños to local *mestizo* elites. *Mistis* described themselves as "white," as opposed to "Indian," and most were merchants, landowners, judges, or political representatives of the Peruvian state. *Misti* domination of the local population was at its strongest during the latter half of the nineteenth century and the first decades of the twentieth century.[12] Although differences in the economic status of *mistis* and *comuneros* (members of a legally recognized peasant community) are much less marked today, unequal social relations are maintained between the two groups. *Mistis* are said to represent the dominant culture and class; they are "white" Spanish speakers who have greater wealth and status as a result of their fuller participation in the national economy. In contrast, *comuneros* are described as Quechua speakers of Indian descent who adhere to indigenous values and dress, and earn their living through agriculture. In fact, this definition applies more to Ura Ayllu women than men, who have abandoned locally made clothing for factory-made apparel, increased their command of Spanish, and taken up seasonal migration to earn cash. Although today the boundaries between the groups are not rigid, Ura Ayllinos continue to make distinctions between themselves, *comuneros*, and *mistis*, and this distinction can be seen in the way people classify their food.

I collected the ethnographic data in this paper during informal and semi-structured interviews and participant observation over seventeen months (1985–7) of fieldwork in Ura Ayllu. The quantitative data on food consumption were collected during my dietary study of a random sample of fifteen households. I measured individual food intake by the food weighing method. Food weights were converted to nutritional values with food composition tables for Andean and Latin American foods. Dietary and interview data were collected with help from two trained, local assistants who were bilingual in Spanish and Quechua. To document seasonal dietary change, I collected consumption data on each of the households at three periods in a single agricultural cycle: pre-harvest, harvest, and post-harvest. Our lengthy presence (6–8 hours per day) in the households throughout the process of food preparation, cooking, and meal consumption permitted wide-ranging discussions about food as well as detailed observations of food-related behaviors that could be compared with people's statements about food and diet.

Patterns of food consumption in Ura Ayllu

Ura Ayllinos differentiate locally grown food from commercial food through a classification that reflects a longstanding ethnic and class division in the Andes: the native Indian versus the elite *Mestizo*. Local foods are referred to as *yana mikhuy* (dark or black food) while commercial foods are referred to as *misti* or *yuraq mikhuy* (*Mestizo* or white food). This cognitive separation of the two kinds of food has implications for how foods are used in the cuisine and the value of each to peasant households in Ura Ayllu.

As noted earlier, villagers acknowledge that the composition of their diet has changed in recent decades. Two or three decades ago, when middle-aged informants were children or adolescents, people were said to purchase *misti* foods irregularly and in small amounts. Today, in contrast, all households use *misti* foods frequently and in larger amounts. This dietary shift toward increased household consumption of commercial foods can be seen when data from a 1958 dietary survey[13] are compared to those of this study. Although the results of these two studies are reported differently, the findings do support verbal accounts that commercial foods have assumed a larger role in the Ura Ayllu diet in the last three decades.

A survey of food consumption in Peru was conducted by a team of researchers in the late 1950s.[14] Cuyo Cuyo was one of the study sites and forty-one families from the district participated in the July 1958 survey. Their results show that foods grown locally were the mainstay of the diet in 1958. Oca was consumed by 100 percent of the families, followed by, in descending order, *khaya* (freeze-dried oca) (97 percent), olluco (90 percent), potatoes (88 percent), kale (83 percent), dried broad beans (63 percent), and maize (58 percent).[15] The survey also shows that commerical foods played only a small role in the diet. At the time of that study, the only non-local food eaten by 25 percent or more of the families was brown sugar (*azucar rubia*). Forty-six percent of families consumed brown sugar (with average per person intake of 23 grams per day) and it was used then as it is today, to sweeten beverages like herbal teas and not in the preparation of sweets and desserts. One drawback of the Collazos study is that data were collected at a single point of time, during the post-harvest season when local food supplies are greatest.

Food consumption data from my 1985–6 dietary survey in Ura Ayllu are shown in Table 9.1. It shows caloric composition of the diet by season for the fifteen households included in my sample. Fresh tubers (e.g. potato, oca, olluco) contribute more than 60 percent of energy during the harvest season and drop to only about 20 percent during the pre-harvest months. In contrast, purchased grain products (e.g. pasta, rice, wheat flour) comprise about 15 percent of the diet during

Table 9.1 Composition of the Ura diet by season (percentage of
          kilocalories)

Food grouping	Season		
	Pre-harvest (% of Kcals)	Harvest (% of Kcals)	Post-harvest (% of Kcals)
Fresh tubers	22	63	46
Processed tubers	8	7	11
Local grains and legumes	14	3	13
Commercial grain products	39	16	17
Animal products	3	4	5
Other	12	7	9

the harvest and post-harvest months when local produce is abundant. The per-centage of calories coming from purchased grains increases to 39 percent during the pre-harvest months, the time of the year when household supplies of tubers are at their lowest point. At this time of the year, commercial grain products are the most important source of energy even when all local sources are combined. These data indicate that the *kinds* of food eaten by Ura Ayllu households do not appear to vary greatly over the course of the year but their relative contribution to total energy intake does. Commercial foods today appear to play a significant role in meeting household food needs during the pre-harvest season when supplies of local food are low or exhausted.

The value of local foods

The ways people think about and value their food influence the ways they are used and consumed. While commercial foods have become necessary to meet household food needs, people do not necessarily consider them as better than or equivalent to local foods. Ura Ayllinos consider oca and potatoes to be the foun-dation of their diet and essential to health. They take the production of these prod-ucts and the display of stored food as evidence of the well-being of a household. Containers of stored food and ears of corn hung from the beams of the house are obvious signs of the wealth of a family to any visitor. Women take pride in their ability to plan ahead and to make their food stretch, as far as possible, from one harvest to the next.

Local foods are valued for their flavor, health-promoting qualities, and what they "say" about a household's economic well-being. Native foods produced in Ura Ayllu through hard physical labor are highly valued by women, men, and children alike.[16] Tubers, grains, and legumes produced by households are consid-ered delicious in both their fresh and dried forms. Each of the many varieties of potatoes grown in the community is prized for its distinctive culinary (as well as agronomic) qualities such as appearance, color, texture, and flavor. The dryness and flavor of potatoes is considered a delicious complement to the moist sweetness of

Plate 9.2 Two Cuyo Cuyo women cutting potatoes for soup.

fresh oca, with which they are often eaten. Freshly harvested corn and broad beans are considered a seasonal treat as they are quickly dried to inhibit rotting. Overall, the delicate flavors, aromas, and textures of local foods are savored and remarked upon during mealtimes.

In addition to their gustatory value, local foods are also important in the context of health. In Ura Ayllu, Andean ethnomedical concepts dominate people's views of health and illness prevention. Food is considered central to health primarily through its role in maintaining one's strength or *fuerza*.[17] Weakness or *debilidad* is thought to make one vulnerable to the precarious agents – both natural and supernatural – that can cause illness. According to Larme's analysis of health in this community, a healthy person must have a physically healthy body and a strong *animu* or life force.[18] Loss of bodily fluids (e.g. blood, semen, tears) and fat weakens a person's life force, making a person weak and sickly.[19] Food and drink of the proper intrinsic qualities (hot–cold; wet–dry) and eaten at the proper time of day are thought to maintain strength and health. Hot fluids such as soups and teas also help to replace vital body fluids.

Heavy physical labor (*llank'ay*) like that in agriculture also is considered crucial to good health, because sweating cleanses the body of impurities. Local foods, especially dehydrated potatoes and oca, are seen as necessary for giving a person the strength needed for strenuous physical labor. Likewise, Ura Ayllinos believe that *mistis*, government workers, students, and anthropologists do not need to eat these foods – or to eat much food at all – because they do not perform "real" work like the villagers do.

Two periods when Ura Ayllinos invoke the *yana-misti* food classification system to guide their health behaviors are for women, immediately after a birth or miscarriage and, for men, on their return from mining in Maldonado. The post-partum period is a time when *misti mikhuy* is prohibited. Childbirth and miscarriages are perceived as threats to women's health due to the loss of blood and other bodily fluids. It is thought that women are vulnerable to illnesses that may enter their body in their weakened state. Rest, avoidance of activities that expose a woman to "heat" or "cold," and dietary restrictions are the behaviors prescribed for the postpartum rest period. It ideally lasts a month but in fact may be followed for only a few days or weeks depending on a woman's work demands and the household's supply of proper foods. During this period, women consume only *yana mikhuy* and avoid *misti mikhuy* which is thought to impede the healing process and make women susceptible to postpartum reproductive complications. Special care is taken to prepare a soup that properly balances the liquid (wet) and dry components to yield a soup of smooth consistency. Soups made with *ch'uño*, *khaya*, meat or fat, and fresh tubers are cooked by the new mother or by another family member (e.g. husband or daughter) for her personal consumption. Oca and *khaya* are an especially important component in this postpartum soup because oca is thought to be a galactagogue, a substance that increases the production of breastmilk.

Another period when *yana* foods are encouraged for health reasons is when men return to the community after their gold mining season. Returning gold miners are thought to be in a weakened and vulnerable state of health as a result of eating an improperly balanced diet while performing a different *kind* of strenuous work, in a very different climate and setting. One of the reasons men become weak and get sick in Maldonado is because they are not eating local foods that maintain one's strength to fight off other disease-causing organisms. Their diet while mining consists mostly of *misti* foods meals and consists of large portions of rice and very few tubers. On work days, *misti* foods purchased at stores in the region are eaten at the mining campsite. Sundays are reserved usually for rest, recreation, and restocking their supplies of food from the local market town. Although many men take some of the local foods with them, the supplies are small and do not last for very long. Upon their return to the community, men are thought to need to eat large quantities of local foods to restore their greatly diminished health. Their return coincides with the harvest season ensuring a good supply of the local foods to counteract the weakening effect of months of rice consumption. The influx of cash from mining also allowed women to prepare *misti* meals, called *segundos*, that replicated their mining diet and included large portions of rice. Although wives prepared these meals only occasionally and because they thought their husbands had become accustomed to eating this kind of food, men later confessed to me that they were tired of rice and preferred to eat local foods until they returned to Maldonado.

Although local food is generally valued by all, freeze-dried potato and oca – *ch'uño* and *khaya* – are foods that have a more contested meaning among Ura Ayllinos. *Ch'uño* and *khaya* are stigmatized by urban Peruvians as foods suitable only for poor peasants who have little choice or are indiscriminant about what they eat. Some Ura Ayllinos, particularly men, are aware of the negative connotations associated with these foods at the national level and, as a result, view the consumption of *ch'uño* and *khaya* as a public admission of poverty and low social status. From their perspective, the fact that people in nearby communities have nicknamed Cuyo Cuyeños as "*khaya* eaters" [loose translation of the Quechua word *khayawalakichis*, "those who wallow in *khaya*"] is considered an insult and a source of embarrassment.

Khaya and *ch'uño* do not elicit negative images of poverty or low social status among all Ura Ayllinos however. I rarely heard these kinds of disparaging remarks from women who appear to value the foods they themselves grow, process, and cook. It is, of course, the consumption of precisely these foods that is thought to restore a woman's healthful balance after childbirth. Although men also think *yana mikhuy* is good for their health, they are more likely to express contradictory opinions about them. During my fieldwork, it was clear that men's expressed opinions were sometimes influenced by my presence as an outsider. For example, a husband denigrated and intercepted a bowl of thick, dark *ch'uño* soup before it could reach me, the "*gringa*" guest. His comments indicated that he was less embarrassed by his wife preparing it for the family than by her offering it to someone like me who, by virtue of heritage and social standing, was assumed to disdain "Indian" food as a matter of course.

The value of commercial food

Ura Ayllinos buy a variety of commercial foodstuffs with their gold and cash income – rice, noodles, sugar, bread, wheat flour, cooking oil, condiments, and animal fat. Most of these items are available in local stores although people prefer to buy flour, sugar, and rice in bulk quantities directly from wholesale vendors in Juliaca, rather than from local merchants who charge higher prices. The returning gold miners purchase bulk supplies of rice, pasta, and sugar to bring home at the end of the mining season; their return with quantities of commercial foods thus marks their success in mining and the ability of husbands to meet their families needs. Many of these foods are included in public and ceremonial meals and are considered signs of economic well-being and success in off-farm pursuits.

Commerical foods have been incorporated into Ura Ayllu peasant cuisine. A handful or two of rice or noodles may be added to soup to provide variety for the texture and flavor of the soup and to thicken the broth. Soup made of locally grown foods may be considered more visually appealing and flavorful when a packet of Aji-no-moto (a brand of mild chili powder with MSG) is used. A hot beverage of herbal tea or coffee is considered unpalatable without a heaping tablespoon or two of sugar added to it.

Although *misti* foods and condiments have an important role in the diet, they are not the subject of the lengthy, detailed discussions that mark conversations about potatoes and oca, for example. *Misti* foods are thought to add some variety to the diet but little is said about their taste or other culinary attributes. Furthermore, as stated above, *misti* foods are not thought to have health-promoting or restorative qualities that local foods have. The weakened and sickly health status of the gold miners is, in part, attributed to a diet comprised of *misti* foods. Sugar, while an indispensible ingredient in tea, is also thought to nourish intestinal parasites. *Misti* foods are seen by villagers as appropriate for those people who do not engage in agriculture and, as a result, do not work hard. Villagers state that the hard physical labor associated with farming requires local foods that give a person strength and stamina. While they may see *misti* food as a sign of economic status, they express ambivalence toward it as well. Commercial food may convey prestige when people have a choice and are not dependent on it, as illustrated in the case study below.

Food as a sign of economic well-being

Ura Ayllinos see themselves as primarily as *comuneros* who farm their own lands and who supplement that income with cash obtained through off-farm labor. "Wealth" is defined emically as a combination of land and money. According to the villagers' repeated comments, those with only land, and those with only cash, are less "well off" than those households who have access to both land and money. Local landless people are almost all descendants of people who came to the valley as sharecroppers, laborers on road construction projects, or workers at the local, now defunct, *hacienda*. Ura Ayllu smallholders need cash for their households, community-based obligations, and agriculture. Surplus money is used to sponsor *fiestas* and other activities that afford personal prestige such as house construction.

Cash also buys food. As indicated above, commercial grain products become increasingly important to the Ura Ayllu as the supply of fresh produce diminishes. One of these products, wheat flour, deserves closer examination because of the multiple and contradictory meanings attached to it in the community. Flour is used in the village in two ways – to make bread and to thicken soup. Bread may be made locally or purchased from local vendors in Cuyo Cuyo who either bake it themselves or who resell "city bread" made in Juliaca. Fry bread (Qu., *toq'tochis*), cooked in oil in a frying pan, is prepared infrequently by households as cooking oil is expensive and used sparingly in local cuisine. Flour is considered a desirable food when made into bread, a process that requires a significant expenditure of time and cooking fuels. Most households in Ura Ayllu, however, do not have access to the fuel resources needed to bake bread on a regular basis; thus they purchase the bread they consume. Thus, bread is considered a "luxury" food since its consumption requires cash or other resources like fuel that are out of reach for most households on a daily basis.

During the rainy season, household supplies of both local food and cash are diminishing or completely exhausted. At this time of year, flour becomes important for those households who must stretch their food supplies as much as possible. In these cases, flour is not made into bread but is cooked with water to make a filling and bland porridge, or *mazamorra*, to which small amounts of vegetables, collards, or herbs may be added.

During the pre-harvest season phase of my dietary survey, I found that heavy reliance on flour for soup was strongly stigmatizing. Eufracina and her husband Jorge (both pseudonyms) were 40 years old and had seven children ranging in age from newborn to eighteen years. Eufracina's parents had moved to the district as workers for the road project in the 1940s. As a young girl, Eufracina worked for and was raised by the owner of the local *hacienda*. She married Jorge when she was quite young, but unlike the typical Ura Ayllu bride, she did not inherit land to bring into the marriage. All the couple's landholdings come from Jorge's family who is from Ura Ayllu. Jorge supplements his agricultural work by selling his labor, when possible, in gold mining. He does not own a claim to land but works as a wage laborer for others. Because his income is irregular and scanty, he decided against gold mining for the 1986–7 season. Rather, he remained in the area and made short trips down valley to work in the harvests of corn and coca. The older children also contribute to the household economy and food supply through their agropastoral work for other households in the region. Eufracina remains full time in the community where she devotes her time to agriculture and household maintenance. This family has few material possessions and falls at the lower end of the socioeconomic scale. Eufracina spoke frequently and emotionally about the difficulty of raising a large family on insufficient landholdings and erratic cash incomes and struggling to make ends meet.

At the time of their pre-harvest consumption measurement at the beginning of November, the family was feeling their lack of local food acutely. As shown in Table 9.2, a dramatic change in the composition of their diet, expressed as percent of energy (kilocalories), occurs at this time of year. During the harvest and post-harvest seasons, most of the energy consumed by this household comes from local foods such as fresh tubers and local grains and legumes. Once the supply of local foods, especially tubers, is diminished, commercial grain products contribute more than 50 percent of the kilocalories consumed by the household at this time of the year.

A comparison of the ingredients used in Eufracina's morning soups, Table 9.3, shows an important shift in the proportions of local and commercial ingredients (relative to the others). Comparing the soups made during the harvest and pre-harvest survey rounds, the first soup fed five people and it was a typical, potato-vegetable soup with a light to moderate thickening of the broth with flour. In contrast, the pre-harvest soup was a flour gruel, with few vegetable ingredients, that fed eight people. The small amount of potato, yielding an average 28.5 g (about 1 ounce) per person, was used to provide a morsel of flavor and to break up the monotonous pasty porridge. In this case, the two basic elements of the

Table 9.2 Caloric composition of Eufracina's household diet by
season (percentage of kilocalories)

Food grouping	Season		
	Harvest (% of Kcals)	Post-harvest (% of Kcals)	Pre-harvest (% of Kcals)
Fresh tubers	87.5	69.7	17.3
Processed tubers	0	0	0
Commercial grains	5.2	0	51.0
Local grains/legumes	0	22.7	23.0
Animal products	1.2	1.95	2.3
Other	6.1	4.7	6.3

Table 9.3 Ingredients for Eufracina's morning soups by season

Season	Ingredients
Harvest	potato (791 g), flour (130 g), kale, suet, salt, onion, oregano, water
Post-harvest	olluco, fava bean, chard, oregano, green onion, suet, salt, water
Pre-harvest	flour (356 g), potato (228 g), suet, salt, water

soup were juxtaposed – the thickener or *allpi* (Qu.) became the main ingredient while the vegetables became the "extras" that gave the porridge a little texture and flavor.

This change from tubers to commercial grains, mostly flour used to make a thick porridge, was not experienced by Eufracina as a simple substitution of one kind of food for another. The household's dependence on flour for the bulk of the diet was a source of anxiety for Eufracina who stated that morning that the family had already gone through one 100-pound bag of flour and had begun their second. With the new harvest still months away in March, Eufracina remarked: "It's only November … and if I'm this way now, what will I be like in January when the real hunger comes?" In this case, Eufracina was measuring the passage of time until the next harvest in bags of flour.

The social unacceptability of the wheat-based porridge was demonstrated in two ways. The first occurred a few days earlier when I came to Eufracina's home with a young Ura Ayllu woman assistant to conduct the final round of the dietary survey. My arrival with an Ura Ayllu assistant was met with unspoken resistance, and Eufracina refused to participate without explanation. Unaware of the full extent of this household's food situation at this point, I returned a few days later to find out what had happened with a different assistant (from Cuyo Cuyo) who had accompanied me previously. Eufracina explained that she could not allow the local woman to see what they were eating for fear that she would gossip with her family and others in the community. She went on to say that while she was embarrassed to have us observe her current situation, she had deemed us trustworthy since she had no evidence that we had talked about her after our previous visits. Eufracina gave me her permission to continue my study, which I did with the Cuyo Cuyo assistant a few days later.

The stigma attached to the flour porridge was again demonstrated during the final measurement round during the midday meal. When I returned at midday, Eufracina was busy cooking potato soup and a pot of steamed potatoes (*wayk'u*), dishes that were typical of what she would prepare for her family at other times of the year when her supplies of local food were plentiful. She explained that this food was for her neighbor, a *compadre*, who was helping the family that day with a home construction project. As the soup and tubers cooked, Eufracina began to prepare another pot of soup for her and the children. Like the morning's meal, this was a flour-based porridge with a small amount of potato. While her husband and neighbor ate their soup and steamed potatoes outside the kitchen in the patio, the rest of the family ate the porridge inside the kitchen, away from the gaze of the neighbor. When I expressed mild surprise at the sight of potatoes, Eufracina stated that she always hid away a small supply of tubers so that she would be able to fulfill her social obligation of provisioning food and coca in exchange for a *compadre*'s labor. It was clear that giving her *compadre* the flour porridge would have been absolutely unacceptable.

Eufracina's case illustrates several important points. One, wheat flour has contradictory meanings in this community. While flour made into bread may be considered an acceptable, even prestigious, food, flour used as a main ingredient for soup is clearly unacceptable, a fact that was noted and frequently commented on by other families who claimed they never resorted to using flour in this way. Eufracina's situation shows that too great a dependence on commercial foods, especially flour to make a bland, pasty gruel with few if any additional ingredients, is evidence of poverty and a family's inability to provide for itself. This shift from thickening agent to main ingredient violates local culinary practices and conveys a message of extreme economic insecurity and shame.

Second, while economic stratification is recognized within the community, households may not be aware of the full extent of deprivation experienced by their neighbors. Eufracina's preparation of an acceptable meal for her *compadre*, while expected, may also have concealed their food deprivation, thus preventing a loss of economic and social status within the community. A household does not publicly demonstrate dependence on flour, given the stigma attached to it, and parents may sacrifice their most desirable food to meet their social obligations.

And finally, a household's ability to activate reciprocal labor exchanges with other households in the community requires appropriate kinds of food prepared in appropriate ways. Eufracina, despite her family's desperate situation, managed her food supply with this requirement in mind. When these small stores of potatoes are exhausted, so too is her household's ability to draw upon their social network to meet their social reproductive needs. While Eufracina's household members can continue to participate in reciprocal exchanges in the role as the provider of labor, they will be unable to call upon others to work for them when they are no longer able to provide the proper food to feed the workers.

Conclusions

I believe the variable and conflicting attitudes expressed by Ura Ayllinos about local and commercial foods are related to changing economic conditions in the community. Ura Ayllinos use the language of ethnicity and class to classify their food. By distinguishing locally produced *yana* food from *misti* food purchased in the market, cultural and economic distinctions between *comuneros* and *Mestizos* are reinforced. While this polarized classification scheme accentuates the differences between the groups, it also masks the flexibility of the social and economic borders between the groups and the ways in which villagers selectively use food to define themselves socially. A closer examination of the meanings and uses of foods within each category reveals much more complexity.

In Ura Ayllu today, both kinds of food are used as markers of economic well-being but they mark different kinds of wealth – one success in farming and the other success in off-farm economic pursuits – both of which are recognized as necessary for household survival. Being "cash rich" is not considered equivalent to "land rich," and cash cannot replace what agricultural lands provide in terms of healthy food and prestige. Thus, even the most successful entrepreneurs in gold mining seek to identify themselves as successful farmers. Cash incomes from gold mining are, in part, invested in agriculture and rituals that reinforce *comunero* identity within the community. Abundant household supplies and public displays of *misti* food are sources of prestige for families who have them, but only when counterbalanced with adequate supplies of local foods. Thus, the consumption of local foods means much more than simply eating potatoes rather than noodles. It signifies success as a farmer, sufficient landholdings, and good food management skills, all of which are valued today.

My research also has implications for understanding the process of dietary delocalization in rural communities undergoing economic change. The cultural values associated with both local and commercial foods can resist or encourage their use in household diets. Although *misti* food is very much a part of the contemporary Ura Ayllu diet, it would be problematic to assume that its consumption is indicative of an inevitable process toward the displacement and devaluation of local foods. People use local food to identify themselves as *comuneros* who, in contrast to *mistis*, value hard agricultural labor, and who feed their families with food they prefer to eat. From the villagers' perspective, it is logical that *mistis* would express disdain for their peasant food since their lifestyles, social worlds, and health needs are considered to be very different from theirs. Local foods are considered crucial for health and *misti* food, in spite of its prestige value, can make people sick. During times of illness, *misti mikhuy* is rejected in favor of local foods that promote healing and restore strength and, ultimately, health. Thus, the social value placed on *misti* food as a result of the increased importance of cash in the economy has not resulted in a wide-sweeping devaluation of local foods.

Even with the increased importance of gold mining in the Ura Ayllu economy today, people's identities remain closely linked to their land and the production of food. Local foods that are grown on family lands and consumed in traditional ways are highly valued. While the public display of *misti* foods in rituals and cer-emonial meals is indicative of success in mining, a heavy dependence on *misti* foods is not considered an asset but rather a sign of economic vulnerability. Among Ura Ayllinos, households who *need* imported foods, especially lower cost items like wheat flour, to feed themselves are seen as poorer and less well man-aged than those who can selectively use imported foods to supplement local ones. Thus, the characterization of commercial foods as uniformly prestigious masks the multiple symbolic meanings attached to them as well as the complex ways in which people use food to express who they are.

The multiple meanings attached to both local and *misti* foods have important gender dimensions as well. Larme identifies growing gender inequalities in Ura Ayllu as incomes from gold mining have become increasingly important.[20] The increasing importance of money has made *misti* foods a new sign of wealth within the community. Changes in the symbolic value of *misti* and local foods may be related to the economic status of men, the providers of non-farm wealth, relative to that of women, who have a greater role in agriculture. As men's economic roles and self-images have increasingly been defined by mining, women have become the primary food producers who remain in the community throughout the year to manage the household, crops, and animals. In contrast to women, many of whom have never traveled outside the region and who consciously maintain their iden-tity as *comuneros* through clothing and language, Ura Ayllu men must transform their identities when they travel into a social and economic world different from that at home. Men, who earn the cash needed to buy *misti* foods, attach higher social value to commercial foods that mark their hard labor and success in mining. As miners, men shift in and out of their identities as peasants and cash earners in the course of a year and this movement is expressed in the context of food. Although men recognize the importance of local foods like dehydrated tubers for health, they are also aware of the stigma attached to these foods by the larger society. This apparent contradiction in opinion appears to have little to do with taste preferences and much to do with men's shifting, bicultural social identities. The contradictions that men feel toward local and *misti* foods may reflect the ways they think about themselves – as people caught in the midst of socioeconomic transformations in the community.

As Crandon-Malamud showed in her work on medicine, food, and diet can give us a good idea about what is happening in a community. An understanding of the dance of local and commercial food in Ura Ayllu requires unraveling the multiple ways people think about and use those foods and how these views and behaviors reflect broader social and economic conditions within and outside the community. The food dance taking place in Ura Ayllu kitchens is contradictory and dynamic and reveals a social world in flux.

Acknowledgments

I thank Joan Koss, Christine Greenway, Ann V. Millard, Lisa Kealhofer, and Leslie Gray for reading and commenting on a previous version of this chapter. I am, of course, solely responsible for the final product. My research was carried out in conjunction with the "Production, Storage and Exchange in a Terraced Environment on the Eastern Andean Escarpment Research Project," Bruce Winterhalder (Principal Investigator). The PSE project was funded by the National Science Foundation (BNS 8313190). Additional funding for my research was provided by the Center for the Advanced Study of International Development at Michigan State University. My research has benefitted enormously from the support and analyses of my fellow PSE colleagues: Carol Goland, Anne Larme, Jorge Recharte, and Bruce Winterhalder. For help in the field, I am especially grateful to my two research assistants, Herberth Andrade and Virginia Ccapayque. My greatest debt is owed the Ura Ayllu families who welcomed me into their kitchens and lives with a generosity that is difficult to fathom and will be impossible to repay. Both photos in this chapter were taken by the author.

Notes

1 Gretel H. Pelto and Pertii J. Pelto, "Diet and delocalization: dietary changes since 1750," *Journal of Interdisciplinary History*, 1983, XIX: 507–28.
2 Libbet Crandon-Malamud, *From the Fat of Our Souls: Social Change, Political Process, and Medical Pluralism in Bolivia*, University of California Press, 1991.
3 Kathryn G. Dewey, "Nutrition and the commoditization of food systems in Latin America and the Caribbean," *Social Science and Medicine*, 1989, 28: 415–24; William Leonard, "Biosocial responses to seasonal food stress in highland Peru," *Human Biology*, 1989, 61: 65–85; Grace S. Marquis and Kathryn M. Kolasa, "Noodles, rice, and other non locally produced foods in the weaning age child's diet, Pacobamba, Peru," *Ecology of Food and Nutrition*, 1986, 18: 319–29.
4 Benjamin S. Orlove, "Stability and change in highland Andean dietary patterns." In *Food and Evolution: Toward a Theory of Human Food Habits*, Marvin Harris and Eric Ross (eds), Temple University Press, 1987, pp. 481–515.
5 Orlove, "Stability and change," p. 500.
6 Magalí Daltabuit and Thomas L. Leatherman, "The biocultural impact of tourism on Mayan communities." In *Building a New Biocultural Synthesis: Political-Economic Perspectives on Human Biology*, Alan H. Goodman and Thomas L. Leatherman (eds), University of Michigan Press, 1998, pp. 317–37.
7 Orlove, "Stability and change," p. 508.
8 Mary J. Weismantel, "The children cry for bread: hegemony and the transformation of consumption." In *The Social Economy of Consumption*, Henry J. Rutz and Benjamin S. Orlove (eds), University Press of America, 1989, p. 85.
9 Weismantel, "The children cry," p. 85.
10 Jorge Recharte, *Value and Economic Culture among the Peasant Gold Miners of the Cuyo Cuyo District (Northern Puno, Peru)*, PSE Research Project Working Paper No. 3, University of North Carolina, Chapel Hill, Department of Anthropology, 1990, p. 245.
11 Recharte, *Value and Economic Culture*, p. 231.
12 Recharte, *Value and Economic Culture*, p. 45.
13 Carlos Collazos Chiriboga, I. M. Franklin, Y. Bravo de Rueda, A. Castellanos, C. Caceres de Fuentes, A. Roca, and R. B. Bradfield, "La alimentación y el estado de nutrición en el Perú," *Los Anales de la Facultad de Medicina*, 1960, XLIII: 322–27.
14 Collazos, *et al.*, La alimentación, 1960.
15 Collazos, *et al.*, La alimentación, 1960, p. 323.

16 Margaret A. Graham, "Food allocation in rural Peruvian households: concepts and behavior regarding children," *Social Science and Medicine*, 1997, 44: 1697–709.
17 Anne C. Larme, *Work, Reproduction, and Health in Two Andean Communities (Department of Puno, Peru)*, PSE Research Project Working Paper No. 5, University of North Carolina, Chapel Hill, Department of Anthropology, 1993.
18 Larme, *Work, Reproduction, and Health*, p. 97.
19 Larme, *Work, Reproduction, and Health*, p. 98.
20 Anne C. Larme, "Environment, vulnerability, and gender in Andean ethnomedicine," *Social Science and Medicine*, 1998, 47: 1005–15.

References

Collazos Chiriboga, Carlos, I. M. Franklin, Y. Bravo de Rueda, A. Castellanos, C. Caceres de Fuentes, A. Roca, and R. B. Bradfield, "La alimentación y el estado de nutrición en el Perú," *Los Anales de la Facultad de Medicina*, 1960, XLIII (1).

Crandon-Malamud, Libbet, *From the Fat of Our Souls*, University of California Press, 1991.

Daltabuit, Magalí and Thomas L. Leatherman, "The biocultural impact of tourism on Mayan communities." In *Building a New Biocultural Synthesis: Political-economic Perspectives on Human Biology*, Alan H. Goodman and Thomas L. Leatherman (eds), University of Michigan Press, 1998, pp. 317–37.

Dewey, Kathryn G., "Nutrition and the commoditization of food systems in Latin America and the Caribbean," *Social Science and Medicine*, 1989, 28(5): 415–24.

Graham, Margaret, *Dimensions of Malnutrition and Hunger among Children in an Andean Community*, PhD Dissertation, Department of Anthropology, Michigan State University.

——, "Food allocation in rural Peruvian households: concepts and behavior regarding children," *Social Science and Medicine*, 1997, 44(11): 1697–709.

Larme, Anne C., *Work, Reproduction, and Health in Two Andean Communities (Department of Puno, Peru)*, PSE Research Project Working Paper No. 5, Department of Anthropology, The University of North Carolina, 1993.

——, "Environment, vulnerability, and gender in Andean ethnomedicine," *Social Science and Medicine*, 1998, 47(8): 1005–15.

Leonard, William, "Biosocial responses to seasonal food stress in highland Peru," *Human Biology*, 1989, 61(1): 65–85.

Orlove, Benjamin S., "Stability and change in highland Andean dietary patterns." In *Food and Evolution: Toward a Theory of Human Food Habits*, Marvin Harris and Eric Ross, (eds), Temple University Press, 1987, pp. 481–515.

Pelto, Gretel H. and Pertti J. Pelto, "Diet and delocalization: dietary changes since 1750," *Journal of Interdisciplinary History*, 1983, XIX: 507–28.

Recharte, Jorge, *Value and Economic Culture among the Peasant Gold Miners of the Cuyo Cuyo District (Northern Puno, Peru)*, PSE Research Project Working Paper No. 3, Department of Anthropology, The University of North Carolina, 1990.

Weismantel, M. J., "The children cry for bread: hegemony and the transformation of consumption." In *The Social Economy of Consumption* (Monographs in Economic Anthropology, No. 6), Henry J. Rutz and Benjamin S. Orlove (eds), University Press of America, 1989, pp. 85–99.

Chapter 10

Sucking blood or snatching fat

Chagas' disease in Bolivia

Joseph William Bastien

I first learned about Chagas' disease in 1984 when a doctor/epidemiologist and I were visiting Cocapata, a Quechua community, located between snow-crested mountains to the west and the Amazon to the east. We lodged in a peasant's hut of adobe and thatch and slept on llama skins covering the dirt floor. Even though insects bit me, I slept through the night. As the sun came through the tiny window, I arose and asked my companion how he slept.

"I didn't sleep at all," he replied. When I asked why, he continued. "I refused to sleep. I chased *vinchucas* from my body. I didn't want them to bite me!" When I asked what *vinchucas* were, he told me that they caused Chagas' disease. He explained what this disease was, and, for the first time in my life, I questioned the potential price of a good night's sleep. Having lived years in peasants' huts, I realized that I had long been at risk and wondered why no one had advised me about Chagas' disease. Even today, this disease remains relatively unknown. Thus, began my research into this disease, its toll on Andean peoples, and how the suffering and deaths that it causes can be lessened.

How Andeans think about and behave relative to disease was a major concern and contribution of *From the Fat of Our Souls* by Libbet Crandon-Malamud. Aymaras attribute disease to the removal of fluids from the body. For example, *susto* (malaise) is attributed to the loss of *ajayu* (soul),[1] and *kharisiri* (tuberculosis) is caused by the theft of the fat from the kidneys.[2] Aymaras also believe that diseases are caused by objects or fluids entering the body. Bad air causes *aire* (Bell's Palsey),[3] demonic spirits cause *anchanchu*[4] (psychotic behavior), and intrusion of ancestor's bone causes *chullpa* (TB-bone or osteomylitis).[5] These native etiologies have been selected to show how Chagas' disease is understood within a similar Andean ethno-etiology of removing blood and intruding objects or "parasites." As Crandon argued, imagery of foreign intrusion and removal of fluids posits a causality of diseases that encompasses exploitative economic and political relationship. Metaphors of sucking blood and snatching fat are counterposed to Western considerations that disease is exclusively a biological and chemical matter. From a general background to a specific case, I outline the biomedicine, epidemiology, and history of Chagas' disease in the Andes, and then present a case study from Bolivia to illustrate Andean thinking and behavior. Analysis of this case offers the opportunity to contrast diagnosis and treatment from various perspectives of ethnomedicine and biomedicine.

Crawling epidemic

Chagas' disease is an emerging and widespread infectious disease in Latin America, and it is a contemporary public health problem in the Andean region. Chagas' disease is endemic in Bolivia, infecting 60 percent of people in rural areas and developing into a chronic malady in more than a million Bolivians[6] (see Figure 10.1). Its acute attacks frequently kill children, and after it advances to the chronic stage, it is incurable and often fatal in about 13 years. Despite these effects it is a relatively unknown and unrecognized disease because of lack of public knowledge, misinformation, misunderstanding, and denial. Economic and

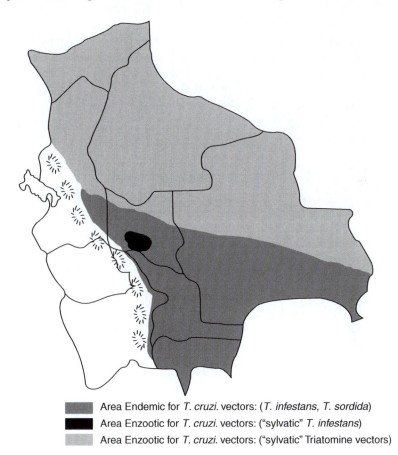

Area Endemic for *T. cruzi*. vectors: (*T. infestans, T. sordida*)
Area Enzootic for *T. cruzi*. vectors: ("sylvatic" *T. infestans*)
Area Enzootic for *T. cruzi*. vectors: ("sylvatic" Triatomine vectors)

Figure 10.1 Areas endemic for *Trypanosoma cruzi* and its vectors in Bolivia.

social costs of Chagas' disease are huge for Bolivians. It is a debilitating disease at all stages, and creates a downward spiral of productivity. It frequently kills young adults, leaving children without mentors and families without bread-winners. Remaining members of the family and community then must assume responsibility for the survivors. When measured by years of life lost adjusted for disability (disability-adjusted life years (DALYs)) (see Figure 10.2), Chagas' dis-ease cheats Latin Americans of 2.7 million years of work.[7] For this reason, it is a major obstacle to development in Bolivia and other countries of Latin America, along with respiratory and diarrheal illnesses, and HIV infection.

Chagas' disease is caused by *Trypanosoma cruzi* (*T. cruzi*), a flagellate para-site, that is transmitted to humans and other mammals by *Triatoma infestans* (*T. infestans*), a small bug similar to a squash bug (see Figure 10.3). These *vinchucas*, as they are known in Bolivia, target sleeping humans with antennae heat sensors and draw blood from their face, defecating shortly after, and deposit-ing an infectious flagellate parasite, that enters the bloodstream and eventually infects neuron muscles of the heart, intestines, and esophagus. *Vinchucas* for-merly fed off forest mammals but with the destruction of forests and fauna, they have descended upon sleeping humans, finding rundown and crowded urban housing a more suitable habitat, and humans a suitable host. Besides infection by contamination, *T. cruzi* is also transmitted through blood transfusions, organ transplants, and from mothers to child in birth and maternal milk.[8]

Chagas is often an unrecognized disease because of its diffuse symptomology. *T. cruzi* parasite causes various and diffuse symptoms, depending upon the

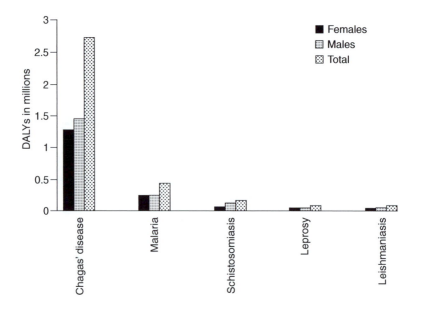

Figure 10.2 Disease burden in Latin America in DALYs from five tropical diseases.

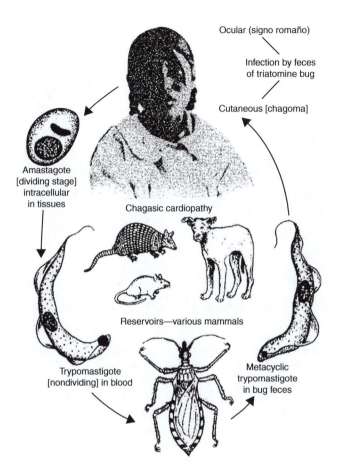

Ocular (signo romaño)

Infection by feces
of triatomine bug

Cutaneous [chagoma]

Amastagote
[dividing stage]
intracellular
in tissues

Chagasic cardiopathy

Reservoirs—various mammals

Trypomastigote
[nondividing] in blood

Metacyclic
trypomastigote
in bug feces

Figure 10.3 Parasitic cycle of *T. cruzi.*

parasite strain (zymodeme), organs where parasites encyst, and victim's immune system.[9] Some characteristic symptoms, though not ubiquitous, are *signo romaño* (a hard boil below the eye), a severe and prolonged acute phase with high infection, chest, throat, intestine, and heart problems.[10] In rare cases, its symptoms may be unnoticeable. While some victims die rapidly in infancy (28 percent mortality during acute phases), others live longer and succumb years later to chronic myocarditis and degeneration of the heart and gastrointestinal system. The majority of people infected with *T. cruzi* never notice the disease until the parasites have sufficiently reproduced and recycled, perhaps ten years after the initial infection (in accord with the old maxim that the parasite does not want to burn down its motel). At this point the host might suddenly die. *Muerto subito*

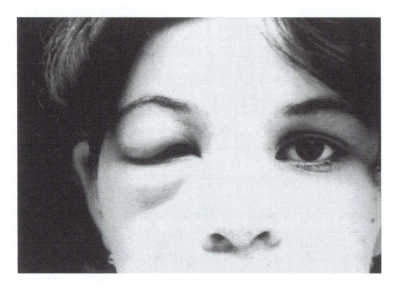

Plate 10.1 Child with *signo romaño*, characteristic of acute phases in some cases.

(sudden death) is highly noticed in Bolivia when an active person suddenly dies from Chagas and a drop of blood falls from his or her nose.[11]

When Crandon did her fieldwork in the 1970s and 1980s, Bolivian doctors and public health officials believed that Chagas' disease did not exist in high altitude communities such as Kachitu. Crandon refers to Chagas' disease in the glossary of *From the Fat of Our Souls* as, "Trypanosomiasis, related to African sleeping sickness, caused by a protozoa carried by the reduviid bug that lives in thatch, and endemic throughout much of the slopes of the Andes. As of 1987 there was no satisfactory treatment, and organ damage was irreversible."[12] She also includes terms that are associated with chronic symptoms of Chagas' disease: *anemia, ataque* (heart attack), *ataques* (attacks), *bocio* (swollen throat), *cólico* (bad stomach), *coto* (goiter), *debil* (debility), *hemoragía de sangre, hinchazon* (swelling), *larpa* (anemia), *mal interior* (intestinal infection), *tullimiento* (debility), and *ventosedad* (colic).[13] Table 12 in her book likewise contains ethnomedical terms that apply to acute Chagas' disease: *aire* (bad air), *ajayu* (soul loss), *fievre* (fever), *hinchazon* (swelling), *infección* (infection), *larpa* (anemia), *negrotewartillo* (fever), *umamausa* (fever), and *ventosidad* (colic). Kachitu medical personnel did not recognize Chagas' disease because it is difficult to diagnose from its symptoms, which vary and are diffuse. Because these locally identified symptoms and illnesses can have multiple causes and can be associated with multiple biomedical disease, it is difficult to make such a diagnosis without corroborative tests.

Although Chagas' disease is both ancient and widespread in the Andes, many Andeans still do not recognize it as a single disease entity, primarily because of its delayed and diffuse symptoms.[14] Recent research[15] shows that *T. infestans* and its parasite *T. cruzi* have infected communities throughout the Andes, and have been spread by migration, transportation, and inadequate and crowded housing. Moreover, as this article shows, Chagas' disease has been found in high altitude communities for centuries.[16] Bolivians became publicly aware of Chagas' disease in 1991, when a conference on Chagas' disease was convened to educate Bolivians about it and to prevent its spread by housing projects.[17] Prevention through spraying and house improvement became a priority in 1991. Chagas' control diminished in 1995, when Public Health Officials emphasized raising overall health statistics, and focused on issues such as child and maternal care which were more recognized by and attractive to international funding agencies. At the same time, capital development discourse in Bolivia projected the country to the world as safe for commerce and travel (especially ecotourism). Hence, Chagas' disease still goes undetected and untreated in Bolivia, and its symptoms are often treated with herbal medicines.[18]

Chagas' disease is referred to as "*La Enfermedad Incógnita*" (The Undetected Disease) in Argentina. It is difficult to detect without tests, and many Andeans resist tests that take fluids from their bodies. Indeed, Crandon pointed out how "fat snatchers" and "shadow catchers" cause illnesses.[19] One unpleasant and seemingly archaic method of testing for Chagas' is xenodiagnosis; still the most prevalent test in Bolivia. Sterile bugs in a jar are placed under the armpits and allowed to draw blood for thirty minutes from the patients. Technicians store the bugs and examining their feces thirty days later to see if they have ingested the parasite. ELISA tests are also used in Bolivia but are not as useful because they only detect Chagas' antibody.[20]

One recent biomedical explanation for the diffuse symptoms of Chagas' disease is that the damage to the body is due more to the immune system over-reacting than to the parasite. The human immune response to *T. cruzi* infection is inadequate and complex, providing at best a partial protective immunity during the chronic phase, and at worst causing a severe immunopathology which may play a significant role in the morbidity and mortality rates of the disease.[21] Even more insidiously, *T. cruzi* immunizes humans to their own antigens so that defensive antibodies become offensive and destroy myocardial and neural cells. As one benefit, *T. cruzi* provides chronically infected patients with immunity from reoccurring acute infections, but only as long as the parasite is present. It is as if to say, "Without me, you're subject to the acute infection from another bite!" This partial immunity is one reason why it may not be wise to destroy the parasite in a patient that has survived an acute phase and who lives in an infested zone, because he or she would be subject to reinfection and the severe and often deadly results of another acute phase.

There are no satisfactory cures for chronic Chagas' disease. Chemotherapeutic agents such as nifurtimox and benznidazole are effective in controlling the acute stage of the disease to prevent damage to vital organs. They claim a cure rate of 85 percent if administered at an early stage and in prescribed dosages. Nifurtimox

(Bayer 2502 and Lampit) was introduced in 1976 and is a 5-nitrofuran derivative with antiprotozoal activity that is also used to treat leishmaniasis and African trypanosomiasis.[22] Nifurtimox is taken three times a day for sixty to ninety days at a daily dose of 8–10 mg per kg for adults and 15–20 mg per kg for children.[23] Benznidazole (Ro7-1051, Radanil, and Rochagan) was introduced in 1978 and consists of a 2-nitroimidazole derivative with antiprotozoal activity.[24] Severe side effects (nausea, vomiting, abdominal pain, peripheral neuropathy, and severe skins reactions), questionable safety, limited availability, and cost (around US$60 a month; about a month's wages) present serious limitations.[25] As one possibility, the new found compound code-named Do870 has been effective against both short- and long-term Chagas' disease.[26]

Ancient symptoms of megasyndrome

In 1992, *T. cruzi* was found in an Inca mummy of a twenty-year-old woman from Cuzco, indicating that Chagas' disease infected people in the Central Andes by the fifteenth century.[27] The mummified heart, esophagus, and colon were abnormally enlarged, suggesting a megavisceral syndrome symptomatic of Chagas' disease. Paleopathologists examined the tissues by means of electronomiscrocopy and immunohistochemistry and discovered round nests of amastigotes of *T. cruzi* within the myocardium and esophagus. *Lancet* published their conclusion: "This Peruvian mummy constitutes an ancient case of chronic Chagas' disease. This is the first demonstration of this disease and agent causing it in South America during the Inca empire."

Long before the fifteenth century in the Central Andes, *T. infestans* (major vector) changed habitats from forests to human communities and houses. Within the Cochabamba valley of Bolivia, *T. infestans* has been found in both forested and residential habitats, suggesting this location as the site of outward radial and selective adaptation to domestic areas. In other parts of the Central Andes, *T. infestans* is exclusively a synanthropic insect that has infested 60 percent of the populated regions. Domiciliary preferences of *T. infestans* enabled them to rapidly reproduce and infect animals and humans, resulting in widespread endemic Chagas' disease. *Vinchuchas* becoming domiciliary was about as devastating to Andeans' health as the domestication of alpacas and llamas was to improving their lives. *Vinchucas* traveled and lived with their herds, spreading *T. cruzi* up and down the Andes and well into the Amazon.

In the Southern Andes, Chagas' disease is reported in mummies dating at 500 AD. Anthropologists discovered mummies of twenty-two Andeans in Quebrada de Tarapacá, Chile.[28] The mummies were 1,500 years old and belonged to an extinct culture called the Wankari. Eleven of the bodies had greatly enlarged hearts, colons, or esophagi. Ten had enlargement of the colon with the nerves of the intestinal walls severely atrophied, perhaps resulting from a long-term disease condition. Modern Andeans from this region, however, suffer milder forms of Chagas' disease than those living in lower regions.[29] This might indicate the long-term adaptation of early Andeans to Chagas disease at Quebrada de Tarapacá. Clinical surveys of chronic Chagas' patients indicate that in the lower Andean region of northern Chile, the infection rate is low, and strong evidence of cardiac involvement is detected by electrocardiograms.[30] This might indicate the effect of altitude on the level of caridac involvement with *T. cruzi* infection.[31] The more benign character of Chagas' disease detected in higher altitudes of Chile is significant because it may relate to the ancient adaptation of the parasite to the human host in the Andean highlands of Quebrada de Tarapacá.[32] It is also possible that the varying severities of Chagas' disease may be due to the unique characteristics of different strains of *T. cruzi* circulating in each area. Individual *T. cruzi* strains and geographic distribution of different strains and their source (sylvatic or domestic) play a role in the wide variety of clinical signs encountered in Chagas' disease.[33]

From fat snatchers to blood vampires

Images of fat-snatching and blood-sucking are used by Andeans to describe causes of sickness. The loss of vital fluids through sucking and the intrusion of fluids/objects are metaphors of processes that inject and dissect the corporeal body related to health and sickness, as well as to Andeans' incorporation into first a colonized and latter a capitalized world. As Crandon-Malamud illustrated in *From the Fat of Our Souls*, Andeans recognize economic and politically exploitative relationships in these images and metaphors.

Andeans believe that fat is a substance of the soul powerfully related to health and sickness, social change, and political process. Fat conveys many meanings for the Aymaras of Kachitu. Llama fat, *llampu*, is always used to feed the earth shrines, to anoint leaders, and to dispel curses. Fat people are considered powerful and the traditional Andeans greeting of *wiraqocha*, translates into "Sea of Fat." Quite naturally so, fat provides warmth to Andeans with scarce resources for heating at night. Fat relates to the culturally constructed illness, *liquichado*, where a *kharisiri* (fat snatcher), doctor, priest, or politician, has snatched the fat from a person. The victim becomes weak and frequently dies; *liquichado* is often used as a cultural construct for tuberculosis. This imagery also refers to foreigners who have asymmetrically parasitized Andean peasants. As energy, fat is a dominant Andean symbol that contains bodily, social, and political meanings; its loss causes sickness, dis-empowerment, and death. As vitality, blood is also a dominant Andean symbol that contains similar meanings.

Bolivians compare parasitic capitalists to *vinchucas* or *T. infestans*. Just as this insect draws blood from sleeping Andeans, so too capitalists have exploited Bolivians by extracting their oil and metals. Chagas' recent endemic spread correlates with inadequate housing, illiteracy, and poverty, which, in turn, correspond to the depletion of land, destruction of flora and fauna, and demographic shifts from rural to urban areas. Destruction of *T. infestans'* forest habitats with its mammalian hosts, immigration of displaced peasants, and clustered settlements of people living in run-down housing provide *T. infestans* with more places to hide and more easily accessible hosts (humans) on which to feed.

Chagas' disease is associated with "vampire bugs" draining Andeans' blood and energy. As Crandon-Malamud noted, diseases manifest themselves in the corporeal body that is related to the environmental, social, and political body. The civic and personal body environmentally interact by intrusion and extraction. Political power is the ability to intrude into the body of the other, modify its humoral balance, and draw blood and fat. It does this through either social or supernatural sanction. The tragic paradox is that both healers and illnesses alike drain the fat and blood for economic and political power. According to Andean body concepts, illness drains fat and blood and, as Crandon-Malamud showed, biomedical and ethnomedical practitioners, sick people, and their families interpret these symbols for economic, social, and political reasons.

Cólico miserere: chagasic megacolon

Cólico miserere (wretched colic) is a common complaint of Andeans. *Cólico miserere*, an enlarged colon, is frequently caused by Chagas' disease. The following case study illustrates how one Bolivian family perceived the symptoms of Chagas' megacolon, how various practitioners interpreted them differently and how they treated these symptoms according to their interpretations. It involves members of the Qolke family (pseudonyms): Yupay Qolke and Isica Qolke are father and mother, Juana is a twenty-one-year-old daughter, Jovita, a thirteen-year-old daughter, and Ramon, a ten-year-old son. Yupay, Isica, and Jovita have Chagas' disease. The medical practitioners involved include a famous *curandera*, Doñ Fonseca, who was ninety-years-old at the time, and five medical doctors: Oscar Velasco (Director of Project Concern in Potosí), Francisco Delgadillo (assistant to Dr Velasco), Pedro Mamani (intern doctor at the regional hospital), Manuel Alvarez (resident doctor at the provincial hospital), and Javier Quispe, surgeon in a private clinic.[34] Juana Qolke is mediator between the family and medical practitioners, as well as between ethnomedical and biomedical practices. Juana works as an auxiliary nurse in Colcha and narrated the following events to Dr Velasco. Her account indicates that Chagas' manifests itself in various ways and illicits different responses among the Qolke family, community, doctors and *curanderos*. Medical pluralism makes dealing with Chagas' disease challenging, but pluralism can also be a route to treat it more effectively, with Andean culture as the semiotic force.

Some ethnographic context is needed to understand the relationship of Chagas' disease to economic, environmental, and social factors. Members of the Qolke family speak Quechua and belong to the Calcha, a traditional Andean ethnic group, located in the Province Nor Chichas, in the northern part of the Department of Potosí. Other local ethnic groups are Chichas, Chara, and Yuras. In spite of concerted influences of European culture, these groups have maintained traditional Andean cultures, especially the Calcha and Yuras, noted for their conservatism and ethnocentrism.

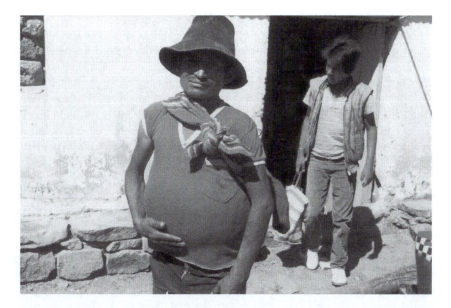

Plate 10.2 Person with chagasic megacolon, who has not defecated for three months. A colostomy was performed in Potosí.

The Department of Potosí is situated in southwest Bolivia, between 18° and 23° latitude and 65° and 69° of longitude. It is the fourth largest department in Bolivia and has 300,000 inhabitants living in a diversity of ecological zones that range from 3,900 m above sea level where there is sparse vegetation, scarce rain, and permafrost, to lower valleys that range from 2,800 to 3,000 m above sea level, where a moderate climate and fertile soil provide many agricultural products and where the majority of the population live. The lower valleys constitute 38 percent of the territory where natives speak Quechua, as a result of Inca expansion, and some Spanish. During the colonial epoch, Spanish conquistadors entered these valleys to produce foods and materials for the mines of Potosí. Spanish families and religious congregations divided the territory under the pretext of establishing adelantamietos (frontier posts), missions, and parishes. They produced apples, apricots, figs, grapes, and vegetables, principally to suit Spanish tastes.

The Qolkes worked for centuries as peasants on vast Spanish estates until the revolution of 1952 destroyed the social structure established by colonialism. Bolivian Agrarian Reform in 1954 allotted them several acres of land. The Reform also made them citizens of Bolivia and provided education and health care. "In much of Bolivia," as Crandon writes, "the very content of ethnic identity and religious affiliation is ambivalent and constantly negotiated."[35] Crandon's research was based on Kachitu, long evangelized by the Methodists, and one can substitute "medical affiliation" for religious affiliation concerning the Calcha. Crandon contends that the Bolivian Indian is not marginalized from the wider system, as Friedlander[36] suggested for Mexican Indians, but is essential to the wider system. Ethnic boundaries are fluid and manipulated for social class in Bolivia, and medical pluralism is one way to symbolize one's cohesion to a particular class or ethnic group. In simple terms, to identify with the Indian group one goes to the *yatiri*, to identify with the *cholo* class one visits the Kallawaya herbalists, and to move into the *mestizo* class one goes to the doctor.

After the Bolivian Agrarian Reform, the ecology of valleys in Northern Potosí changed drastically due to vast deforestation to provide timbers for the mines of Potosí and to the erosive action of rivers, which during the rainy season carried topsoil from plantations and peasant plots to lower regions. Especially devastating were the floods and droughts of the 1980s, followed by hyperinflation, which increased impoverishment and migration among the Calchas and others within these valleys. Morever, the mines had been closed. Privatization of nationalized enterprises (oil, airlines, trains, and utilities) led to layoffs and unemployment. The informal economy of cocaine, smuggling, and money laundering provided a buffer against the crushing formal economy.

These factors made the valleys of Potosí endemic areas for Chagas' disease with *vinchucas* inhabiting every community and infecting more than half the population with *T. cruzi*. People became accustomed to *vinchucas*, which they say are harmless and don't bite. Others believe that their bite only makes them scratch. The fact that their bite causes death is foreign to an etiology of balance and reciprocity, which is more gentle and accomodating to other organisms. Until 1985, Juana Qolke and others of her community thought of *colico miserere* as a backup of fluids. They were unaware of the bioscience of Chagas' disease.

Just as sicknesses cross ethnic and social boundaries, so do practitioners in a medically pluralistic society. Crandon writes that, "medicine restructures social relations outside the medical context."[37] Juana Qolke illustrates how biomedicine provides upward mobility for some persons. Juana is the first Calcha to become a practitioner of biomedicine. She is the first Calcha to translate the biomedical realities of Chagas' disease to the natives of Calcha, informing them that its virulent nature provides scarce hope for *curanderos*. Dr Velasco had educated this community in the early 1980s about assuming responsibility for their health by electing a community health representative. The Calchas elected Juana to be trained as a *Responsable Popular de Salud* (Community Health Worker (CHW)) for their community.[38] Juana participated in several two week courses, where she learned how to provide basic medicine, give advice on health matters, refer cases to primary health posts, and collect health data about the people Calcha. She also educated Calchas about diarrhea control for infants, maternal care, family planning, and how to build a smokeless oven (*horno loreno*). Juana worked for seven years as a CHW in Calcha being so successful that she received financial support to study as an *Auxiliar de Enfermería* (Auxiliar Nurse) in Sucre.

Auxiliary nurses constitute the principal biomedical personnel throughout rural Bolivia. Doctors staff the hospitals in the municipalities and are required to do a year of practice in rural areas (*año de provincia*). Many do this begrudgingly, making little effort to speak native languages and even less effort to understand Andean culture, as shown with Drs Alvarez and Mamani. Their attitudes evoke racial and class superiority to Andeans, which often equates ethnomedicine with lower class and native Indian races. Juana excelled in the six-month course and became the first native nurse among the Calchas, receiving a monthly salary of $50 in 1985. She worked in a *Posta Sanitaria* (Health Post), where she vaccinated people, attended birth deliveries, and administered medicines, and first aid. She educated Calchas in their native language about health. Juana became the pride of her family and community, having established herself as the link between ethnomedicine and biomedicine. She was commended by the *Secretaria Nacional de Salud* for her work in rural Bolivia, and still maintains an important role in the articulation of biomedicine and ethnomedicine among the Calchas.

Juana has ethnic and social ties with the people of Calcha. Dr Velasco trained Juana to be sensitive to their medical beliefs and practices. Under Velasco's tutelage, Juana sensitively translated biomedical beliefs and practices into culturally sensitive concepts. For example, Juana did this by showing her sensitivity to culturally meaningful ailments in Calcha: *las cámaras* (diarrhea), *la congestion* (acute respiratory infections), *las fiebres* (fevers), *las flegmasíasis* (inflammation), *orejo, susto* (soul loss: depression), *tabardillo* (typhus), *las tercianas* (three-day fever), and *cólico miserere* (deadly colic). The Calchas attribute these illnesses to a combination of cultural and biomedical factors: *las cámaras* are due to imbalance of the hot and cold foods and unhygienic conditions; *las tercianas* to bad humors (*mal de aire* or malaria), *susto* to the loss of fluids and social concerns; *la congestion* to the concentration of fluids in the body and respiratory infections. Andean ethno-physiology adheres to an Andean topographic-hydraulic model of body combined with some aspects of a Greek–European humoral theory (balancing the hot and cold, and wet and dry) adapted from the teachings of Spanish missioners (see Figure 10.4). Early missionaries taught humoral theory in medical schools throughout Latin America. Juana treated these ailments with traditional herbs and invited *curanderos* to participate with their rituals. The use of plural medicines was supported by Dr Velasco.

On a slightly different level, Crandon discusses medical ideology in terms of conflicting beliefs that the individual as a conscious actor selects from and uses to accomplish social, economic, and political ends. Kachitu had been affected greatly by Methodist missioners, doctors, and the Agrarian Reform, and was more shaped by racial and social differences than Calcha. Calcha remains a relatively closed, corporate, and traditional community with conservative beliefs and practices. The people of Calcha elected Juana to be the CHW, and she was so successful that they supported her as auxiliary nurse. In her efforts to translate the meanings and benefits of biomedicine into their culture, Juana immersed herself even more into their society. Dimensions of race, class, and ethnicity, while important, fail to include cultural and social distinctions based upon the dependency and exchange of locality and verticality within the Andes, as expressed in

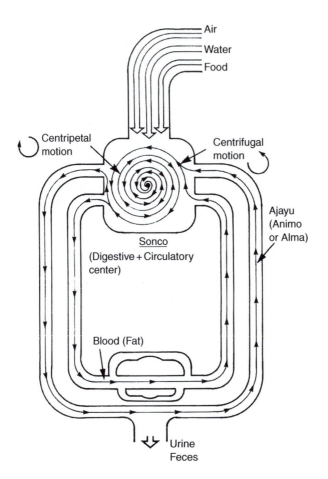

Figure 10.4 Andean ethnophysiology.

the *ayllu*, body metaphors, and earth shrines.[39] By learning how to articulate the ideology of biomedicine with that of ethnomedicine in Calcha, Juana provided a means for residents to participate in both systems, within local Andean ideological constructs and social relations.

Cólico miserere approximates megacolon of Chagas' disease but also refers to *vólvulo* (volvulus), which is the twisting of the bowel upon itself causing obstruction. Volvulus is found among Andeans at high altitudes (13,500 feet) and its predisposing cause is a prolapsed mesentery intestine, which may be caused by *T. cruzi*, although this cause is rarely discussed. Potosinos especially fear *cólico miserere* and *vólvulo* which cannot be cured and causes death. Rather than attributing these problems to a parasite, *cólico miserere* is thought to be caused by eating very fresh or leftover foods that produce gas and swell the stomach. If the person cannot *ventosear* (break wind) or *zurrar* (have a bowel movement) to dispel *cuezcos* (cooked things), the stomach swells more and more until it shuts up the heart and the person dies. Potosinos popularly say "eating pork and drinking cold water brings *cólico miserere*, and if someone does this, don't ask why they died." Eating fresh foods without hot foods also causes *cólico miserere*, and so eating cooked potatoes (a cold food because it grows in the ground) and not chewing coca leaves (a hot food) might cause *cólico miserere*. Potosinos rarely violate these dietary practices, which serve as preventative medicine. Natives consider fat people prone to *cólico miserere*. Signs of the illness are choking, fainting, and indigestion. The afflicted are called *"personas estreñidas"* (constipated, up-tight, and niggardly people) and have a stomach that holds things in and is not in exchange with the outside environment (see Figure 10.1). All classes of Potosinos and other ethnic groups suffer from *cólico miserere*. Juana frequently provided herbal remedies that served as laxatives to treat *cólico miserere*.

Isica becomes muy estreñida and visits a curandera

Isica Qolke showed symptoms of chronic Chagas' disease in 1987 when she complained to Juana that she was *"muy estreñida"* (very constipated) and had not defecated for four days. Juana gave her a herbal laxative that relieved her. A month later, Isica again became constipated, and her husband, Yupay, took Isica to a famous *curandera* of Chalca, Fonseca. Yupay also brought coca leaves and a large white guinea pig that belonged to Isica. Fonseca greeted them with coca leaves and soon began divining the cause of the problem by means of coca leaves and the guinea pig. Fonseca marked the leaves with neat bite marks to designate wind, road, water, and *ajayu* (soul). For more than an hour, Fonseca debated with Yupay and Isica the cause of the constipation. Fonseca then dug her fingers into the belly of the guinea pig, laying bare its intestines, which were bloated with grain. She whispered slowly that Isica was cold in the stomach, most certainly because she had eaten pork and that she had been taken by a *"mal viento"* (bad wind). *Wayra* is the wind deity that brings the rains and the droughts, as well as good and evil.

Isica and Yupay feared Fonseca's diagnosis of *cólico miserere* with its fatalistic omen so they asked the *curandera* to *pichar* (sweep) the *sajjra wayra* (troublesome wind) away from her stomach with a *picharada* ritual. Fonseca mixed fat from a black hen with copal and *hediondilla* (*Cestrum matthewsii* Dun). She stroked Isica's stomach in a dispelling motion, praying in Quechua, *"Sajjra Wayra, puri-jchej"* (Be gone, Troublesome Wind!). Fonseca later left that evening to deposit the ritual items with money attached at the crossroads so that someone would find it and carry the evil to their house.

Isica improved, and the family resumed its daily activities. Towards the end of that year, Jovita, the thirteen-year-old sister of Juana, began complaining of chest pains and such fatigue that she felt like falling asleep even while herding goats. Juana examined her and found nothing abnormal. She gave her injections of vitamin B, saying that this would give her energy. Her grandmother said that Jovita was losing too much blood through menstruation and recommended that she drink fresh blood from a freshly sacrificed hen. These folk remedies were unsuccessful, however, and Jovita had to work sitting down. She complained that her legs were so weak that she couldn't walk and lost her breath at the least exertion. She also still had pains in her chest.

Juana reported Jovita's symptoms to Pedro Mamani, an intern at the regional hospital. Pedro diagnosed the malady as nervousness and prescribed tranquilizers. He also said that she probably had some irritation in the liver or lungs that was causing the pain. He prescribed an injection of magnesium sulfate.

In September, a few months later, a child arrived at the house to inform Isica that Jovita had passed out while harvesting corn. Isica found the girl lying in the *chacra* (field). Jovita was trying to vomit and was grasping for breath. She felt very dizzy. Isica gave her chamomile and rose-hip tea, wrapped her in a blanket and carried her home. After remaining in bed for two days, Jovita again felt "*completo*" (normal).

Around Carnival of the following year, Juana's family celebrated the coming of Lent. They danced, drank, and ate for three days. A week later, Isica complained again that she was unable to defecate for four days. Juana and Jovita rubbed their mother's stomach with the chicken fat and herbs that Fonseca had recommended. A herbalist brought some teas to be used as purgatives.

Two nights later, Isica became extremely nauseated. At first, it seemed like indigestion; she complained about a severe stomachache. Towards morning, Juana massaged her mother with a solution made from burro dung and boiled *hediondilla*. Isica got worse and her stomach enlarged. By sunrise, Isica suffered intense pain and could barely breathe. Her stomach was pushing against her heart.

Juana called a nurse from the neighboring health post, who diagnosed it as *vólvulo*. She prescribed an enema but they couldn't insert it. In desperation, Juana and her father transported Isica in the back of a truck to the provincial hospital in Potosí. The truck traveled for five hours along winding and bumpy roads that agitated the bloated stomach of Isica, causing her to scream in pain.

In the late afternoon Isica arrived at the provincial hospital in Potosí. The resident doctor, Manuel Alvarez, said that he needed to operate and wasn't sure what might happen. Juana said that they didn't want an operation, only some medication to relieve the pain. The doctor then told them to get out and asked the orderly to remove them from the hospital. His parting comments were: "These peasants wait until the last moment to bring their relatives to the hospital, ... they expect miracles, ... if the patient dies, they blame the doctor!" His remarks hurt Juana, who understood Spanish and had served the medical profession for five years. Alvarez' behavior represents an elitist attitude that many Bolivian doctors exhibit in their treatment of peasants. Fortunately, there has been a considerable change in attitude and practice among some physicians in the 1990s, as seen in Drs Velasco and Delgado, who are able to communicate with the peasants and better understand their culture.[40]

Feeling ashamed and rejected, Juana and Yupay transported Isica by taxi to a private clinic. An attending nurse explained that Isica's intestines had become so knotted that she could not pass gas and other matter. She needed an operation to remove the knot or she would die. When Isica screamed to be killed to stop the pain, Juana's father agreed and paid US$200 to have the doctor proceed.

Dr Javier Quispe was the surgeon. When Quispe had finished, he said that he had removed part of the lower colon which was damaged. He showed them a small hole on the left side, a temporary anus (colostomy), to be used until the intestine healed. In several months, he would tie the separated intestines together and Isica could defecate normally.

They were horrified. Yupay told Dr Quispe that he had said nothing about making a hole. They argued, but it was too late and could not be remedied. Dr Quispe was oblivious to what it means for Andeans to have an oriface in the stomach through which waste matter passes. Moreover, he had no idea about the importance of their ideas of ethno-physiology in which fluids come into the body, concentrate according to centripetal motion, and then are distributed by centrifugal motion. In other words, the body is like a distillery, and to have an opening to release the fluids, or to lose one's fat is considered a disaster. When Isica realized she had a colostomy, matters became even worse. A foul odor came from the bandages, and she asked what caused this. Juana explained what happened and Isica said that they should have let her die. She refused to cooperate with the nurses when they tried to help her. They tried to instruct her to use a plastic bag to collect the *qaqa* but she refused. Dr Quispe attributed their shock to ignorance. He explained that he did what was necessary and really wanted to help them.

Perhaps the Qolkes suspected that Dr Quispe was a *kharisiri*, a fat snatcher. A major concern of medical pluralism is how the various systems conceptualize the body. Since the sixteenth century, biomedicine has had surgery as a principal intervention, whereas Andeans were forbidden to trephinate and were encouraged to follow humoral theories of regulation of fluids and systems of correspondence as the principal therapeutic measures.

Juana returned to her community several days later to plant the crops and take care of the cows and chickens. Villagers came in and out of her house, and a neighbor told her in tears that her sister Jovita had died that morning. The night before her sister had complained that the pain had returned to her chest. They had found her dead in her *chacra*, the field she owned, worked, and in which she had her earth shrine. "At least," as Isica said, "she died with *Pachamama*."

After burying her sister, Juana visited her mother in the clinic and told her about the death of her youngest daughter. Isica remained silent for a long while and then screamed, "Why do we have to suffer so much?." The doctor arrived and slowly comforted them. He then told Juana that Jovita had died from Chagas' disease and that Isica was also suffering from it. He suggested that all members of the family be tested for the disease.

Sometime later, Juana, Isica, Yupay, and Ramon, the youngest son, were tested for Chagas' disease. Juana, Isica, and Yupay were found to be infected; Ramon was not infected. Juana had a damaged heart muscle and a slightly enlarged lower intestine. Yupay had severely dilated intestines that were developing into *cólico miserere*. The doctor prescribed nifurtimox for Juana and Yupay to curtail their infection. They discontinued chemotherapy because they were unable to pay the $180 (roughly equivalent to three months' earnings) monthly cost for nifurtimos for all three people.

Dr Oscar Velasco recently spoke with Juana at a conference for auxiliary nurses in Potosí. She still does not believe that *vinchucas* caused the death of her sister and their other illnesses. She said that peasants have always lived in houses with *vinchucas* and they never got sick from their bites. (What has changed is that in the past *vinchucas* were not infected with *T. cruzi* to the degree that they are today.) When Velasco asked her if she had ever seen *vinchucas* suck blood from humans, she said that *vinchucas* suck blood from animals, but not from humans. Certain non-governmental agencies have participated in housing improvement to prevent *vinchucas* in Calcha, but she admits that no one in her community pays much attention to their advice.

Of major concern to doctors and public health officials in Bolivia is that peasants see little connection between severe constipation and *T. cruzi* infection. Constipation is associated with eating improper and unbalanced foods. It is reported that people with megacolon have died from "*dolor de barriga*" (stomach-ache), "*se ha hinchado la barriga*" (swollen stomach), or "*me ha dolido mucho y no he podido hacer qaqa*" (severe stomachache accompanied by the inability to defecate). These frequently reported symptoms all can be attributable to *T. cruzi* parasites, although many Bolivians think they are caused by failing to maintain balance between hot and cold, and wet and dry principles they associate with natural foods and other objects.

As mentioned before (see Figure 10.1), a native Andean understands his/her body as the center of a distillation process that takes in fluids (air, water, and food) and processes them into useful fluids (milk, semen, blood, and fat) and toxic fluids (feces, urine, and sweat) that need to be eliminated. The circulation of fluids is believed to be a process of centripetal (fluids concentrating in distillation) and centrifugal (fluids going to the peripheral) motions. Volvulus (*empacho*) is understood as a stoppage in the centripetal movement. This has cultural signif-icance in that they are unable to connect with the blood and fat outside their bodies, the energy, and life forces of nature.

Conclusions

Juana's history demonstrates the hubris and humility of Chagas' disease and other diseases that at first appear clinically self-evident to scientists. But when serious scholars begin to examine disease pathogens, they discover that the world of microbiology is immersed in environmental, social, and cultural systems. They also come to recognize Libbet Crandon-Malamud's thesis that medical systems are shaped by political and social processes manipulated by practitioners and patients alike. This article supports her thesis on still another dimension, namely that medical systems are discourses about the human body, which they differently control. Libbet recognized this by combining "From The Fat of Our Souls" with "Social Change, Political Process, and Medical Pluralism in Bolivia" in the title of her book. Andean ethnomedicine and Western biomedicine conceptualize the body in entirely different ways. Ethnomedicine is a long-standing folk tradition that places the body within the environment and community as an organically connected part of all-encompassing cultural and social units. Health is a completed exchange between the parts that make up the whole, and sickness is the blockage of this exchange. Symptoms of Chagas' disease, such as *cólico miserere* and *muy estreñida,* are signs of stoppage, disequilibrium, and imbalance, not only within the victim's body but also between that body and the bodies of the community and the land. Conceptually, these concepts parallel the cycle of *T. cruzi*, a parasitic disease facilitated by environmental changes that bring *T. cruzi*, *vinchucas*, and humans into close contact. Humans destroy natural hosts for this parasite and provide habitats for its vector bug. As a result, both parasite and vector have moved to humans.

Biomedicine in Bolivia is a science that interrelates the physiology of the body and pathogens. Its goal is to restore proper functioning to the body by medical and surgical interventions. Bolivian doctors are skilled surgeons and so are referred to as "*kharisiris*" (cutters) by many rural Andeans. Andeans fear that they remove fat, body parts, and make openings, which robs their bodies of vital fluids that connect it to others and to the land. As in the case of Isica, the removal of an intestine and insertion of a tube disturbed a body imaged after the land, with fluids entering, concentrating, and dispersing. The hubris of the scientists who imagine that their uncovering of clinical facts will save people from disease often turns to humility. And Juana, recognizing that she, her sister, and her mother had been bitten by infected *vinchucas* still reverted to folk beliefs about *cólico miserere*. She recognized, as did most other Andean peasants, that biomedical science is only as valuable as its capacity to eradicate disease and heal the sick. This is not a social and economic reality within her family. She and others exhibit cognitive dissonance when it comes to science, because to admit to its curative power is to recognize that positive treatments are available but unattainable.

Moreover, there is no clear agreement among doctors and scientists on the ubiquity and human impact of Chagas' disease in the Andes. Some doctors are hesitant to accept that the high incidence of gastrointestinal problems in some communities is related to chagasic colonopathy. Others contend that *T. cruzi* is the exclusive cause of volvulus in communities where this is clearly not the case. Also, scientists are slow to acknowledge that Chagas' disease exists in higher altitudes of the Altiplano where it is too cold for *vinchucas*, so they attribute gastrointestinal symptoms to other factors. Yet, the evidence shows that Chagas' disease is found in many highland regions and its current spread is reaching many new regions. Thus, when the symptoms of Chagas appear in largely endemic zones of the disease found throughout Bolivia, the best approach is for patients to be tested for Chagas' disease.

Notes

1 Libbet Crandon, *From the Fat of Our Souls: Social Change, Political Process, and Medical Pluralism in Bolivia*, University of California Press, 1991, p. 26.
2 Crandon, From the Fat, p. 248.
3 Crandon, From the Fat, p. 232.
4 Crandon, From the Fat, p. 232.
5 Crandon, From the Fat, p. 233.
6 Joseph W. Bastien, *Kiss of Death: Chagas' Disease in the Americas*, University of Utah Press, 1998. Parts of this article have appeared in this book. End notes provide references for more information on this very complicated disease.
7 World Bank, *World Development Report 1993: Investing in Health*, Oxford University Press, 1993.
8 Bastien, *Kiss of Death*, pp. 58–64, Epidemiology.
9 Bastien, *Kiss of Death*, pp. 170, 163–5, Classification of strains of *T. cruzi*.
10 Bastien, *Kiss of Death*, pp. 196–204, Pathology of acute phase.
11 Bastien, *Kiss of Death*, pp. 78–87, Pathology of chronic phase.
12 Crandon, *From the Fat*, p. 247.
13 Crandon, *From the Fat*, Appendix, Table 12, pp. 231–40.
14 Pathologically, Bolivians suffer differently from Chagas' disease in that the symptoms of Chagas' disease are diffuse, primarily depending upon the person's immune system, the parasitic zymodeme, and the rate of infection(s). Most prevalent is the auto-mimicry theory in that the person's immune system mistakes its own cells for those of the parasite, somewhat similar to rheumatic fever. Basically, the pathology and symptomology of Chagas' disease depends on the organ that *T. cruzi* colonizes, usually the heart, colon, or oesophagus, which varies according to parasite zymodeme and region. In Chuquisaca, there has been high incidence of megacolon or colonapathy, and in La Paz, heart disease. Frequently, these symptoms are not attributed to Chagas' disease. Some Bolivians suffer no symptoms, others suffer severe heart problems.
15 Valencia Tellería, Angel (ed.), *Investigación epidemiologica nacional de la enfermedad de Chagas. La Paz, Bolivia: Ministerio de Previsión y Salud Publica, Secretaria Ejecutiva Pl.-480 Titulo III*, 1990.
16 Bastien, *Kiss of Death*, See pp. 46–64 for epidemiology, Appendix 7 for vector species in the Americas, and Appendix 8 for hosts for *T. cruzi*.
17 Bastien, *Kiss of Death,* See pp. 107 ff. for prevention through housing projects.
18 Joseph W. Bastien, *Healers of the Andes: Kallawaya Herbolists and Their Medicinal Plants*, University of Utah Press, 1987.
19 Crandon, *From the Fat*, p. 26.
20 Bastien, *Kiss of Death*, pp. 217–19, Evaluation of diagnostic tests.
21 Bastien, *Kiss of Death*, pp. 205–16, Immune response.
22 James E. F. Reynolds, "Nifurtimox." In *Martindale: The Extra Pharmacopoeia*, James E.F. Reynolds (ed.), Pharmaceutical Press, 1986, 29, p. 673.
23 Bastien, *Kiss of Death*, pp. 220–1, Nifurtimox chemotherapy.
24 Reynolds, Benznidazole, *Martindale*, p. 660; Bastien, *Kiss of Death*, pp. 220–1, Benznidazole chemotherapy.
25 Bastien, *Kiss of Death*, pp. 220–5, Evaluation of chemotherapy.
26 Julia A. Rubina *et al.*, "Cure of short and long-term experimental Chagas' disease using Do870," *Science*, 1996, 273: 969–71.

27 Gino Fornaciari, Maura Castagna, Paolo Viacava, Adele Tognetti, Generoso Bevilacqua, and Elsa Segura, "Chagas' disease in Peruvian Inca mummy," *The Lancet*, 1992, 339: 128–9.
28 Rothhammer, F. M. J. Allison, L. Nuñez, V. Standen, and B. Arriaza, "Chagas' disease in pre-Columbian South America," *American Journal of Physical Anthropology*, 1985, 68: 495–8.
29 Gonzalez, J. S. Muñoz, S. Ortiz, D. Anacona, S. Salgado, M. Galleguillos, I. Neira, H. Sagua, and A. Solari, "Biochemical, immunological, and biological characterization of *Trypanosoma cruzi* populations of the Andean north of Chile," *Experimental Parasitology*, 1995, 81: 125–35.
30 Arribada, A. W. Apt, X. Aguilera, A. Solari, and J. Sandoval, "Cardiopatia chagasica en la Primera Region de Chiloe. Estudio clinico, epidemiologico y parasitologico," *Revista Medica de Chile*, 1990, 118: 846–54.
31 Villarroel, F. H. Schenone, M. Contrera, A. Rojas, and E. Fernandez, "Enfermedad de Chagas en el Altiplano Chileno. Aspectos epidemiologicos, parasitologicos y clinicos," *Boletin Chileno Parasitologia*, 1991, 46: 61–9.
32 Gonzalez, "Biochemical, immunological, and biological characterization," 81: 132–3; A. Neghme, *La tripanosomiasis americana*, *Creces*, 1982, 3: 23–8.
33 Bastien, *Kiss of Death*, see Appendix 2: Strains of *T. cruzi*, pp. 163–5.
34 Names of people and villages are pseudonyms, as Crandon did for the people of and community of Kachitu. The exceptions are for Drs Oscar Velasco and Francisco Delgadillo, who discussed the case history with me and whose meritorious efforts to articulate Andean ethnomedicine and Western biomedicine deserves recognition (see Bastien, *Kiss of Death*, pp. 134–45).
35 Crandon, *From the Fat*, p. x.
36 Judith Friedlander, *Being Indian in Hueyapan: A Study of Forced Identity in Contemporary Mexico*, St Martin's Press, 1975.
37 Crandon, *From the Fat*, p. 11.
38 Joseph Bastien, *Drum and Stethoscope: Integrating Ethnomedicine and Biomedicine in Bolivia*, University of Utah Press, 1992, pp. 105–6.
39 Joseph Bastien, *Mountain of the Condor: Metaphor and Ritual in an Andean Ayllu*, American Ethnological Society, Monograph 64, West Publishing Company, 1978, reissued in paperback by Waveland Press, 1987.
40 Bastien, *Drum and Stethoscope*, pp. 173–91.

References

Arribada, A., W. Apt, X. Aguilera, A. Solari, and J. Sandoval, "Cardiopatia chagasica en la Primera Region de Chiloe. Estudio clinico, epidemiologico y parasitologico," *Revista Medica de Chile*, 1990, 118: 846–54.
Ault, Steven, Jesse Hobbs, Robert Klein, and Rodrigo Zeledon, "Technical evaluation of USAID CCH-Chagas' disease control project Bolivia – August 1992," *in VBC Report No. 82061*, Vector Biology and Control Project, 1992.
Bastien, Joseph W., *Qollahuaya Rituals: An Ethnographic Account of the Symbolic Relations of Man and Land in an Andean Village*, Cornell Latin American Studies Program, 1973.
——, *Mountain of the Condor: Metaphor and Ritual in an Andean Ayllu*, American Ethnological Society, Monograph 64, West Publishing Company, 1978, Reissued in paperback by Waveland Press in 1987.
——, "Metaphorical relations between sickness, society, and land in a Qollahuaya ritual." In *Health in the Andes*, Joseph W. Bastien and John Donahue (ed.),

Monograph 12. Washington, DC: American Anthropological Association, 1981, pp. 19–37.

Bastien, Joseph W., "Herbal curing by Qollahuaya Andeans," *Journal of Ethnopharmacology*, 1982, 8: 97–111.

——, "Qollahuaya-Andean body concepts: a topographical-hydraulic model of physiology," *American Anthropologist*, 1985, 87: 595–611.

——, *Healers of the Andes: Kallawaya herbalists and their medicinal plants*, University of Utah Press, 1987.

——, "Cross-cultural communication between doctors and peasants in Bolivia," *Social Science and Medicine*, 1987b, 24: 1109–18.

——, "A shamanistic curing ritual of the Bolivian Aymara," *Journal of Latin American Lore*, 1989, 15(1): 73–94.

——, "Community health workers in Bolivia: adapting to traditional roles in the Andean community," *Social Science and Medicine*, 1990, 30: 281–88.

——, *Drum and Stethescope: Integrating Ethnomedicine and Biomedicine in Bolivia*, University of Utah Press, 1992.

——, *The Kiss of Death: Chagas' Disease in Americas*, University of Utah Press, 1998.

Borda Pisterna, Mario, "Breves referencias a la sistemática, bioecología,y morfología externa de los triatomíneos. En especial Triatoma infestans y Triatoma sordida." In *Enfermedad de Chagas*, A. R. Davalos (ed.), Los Amigos Del Libro, 1978, 83–97.

——, Mario, *Conozca El Mal De Chagas*, Centro de Investigaciones Ecologicas del mal de Chagas, Universidad Mayor De San Simon, 1981.

Bottasso, O. A., N. Ingledew, M. Keni, J. Morini, J. F. Pividori, G. A. W. Rook, and J. L. Stanfor, "Cellular immune response to common mycobacterial antigens in subjects seropositive for *Trypanosoma cruzi,*" *The Lancet*, 1994, 344(Dec. 3): 1540–1.

Brener, Zigman, Chemotherapy of *Trypanosoma cruzi* infections, *Advances in Pharmacology and Chemotherapy*, 1975, 13: 1–44.

——, "Present status of chemotherapy and chemoprophylaxis of human trypansomiasis in the western hemisphere," *Pharmacology and Therapeutics*, 1979, 7: 71–90.

——, "The pathogenesis of Chagas' disease: an overview of current theories." In *Chagas' Disease and the Nervous System. Scientific Publication No. 547*, Pan American Health Organization, 1994, pp. 30–46.

Breniere, S. F., M. Bailly, R. Carrasco, and Y. Carlieranti, "Transmission transplacentaire des anti-corps *anti-Trypanosoma cruzi*. Cahier UMR CNRS/ORSTOM (Montepellier, France)," *Entomologie Médecine et Parasitologie*, 1983, 21: 139–40. Also in Spanish in Annuario IBBA, *La Paz*, 1986–87), pp. 207–8.

——, M. F. Bosseno, C. Barnabe, S. Urdaneta-Morales, M. Tibayrenc, "Population genetics of *Trypanosoma cruzi* and *Trypanosoma rangeli*: taxonomical and epidemiological purpose," *Biological Research (BSA)*, 1993, 26(1–2): 27–33.

——, P. Braquemond, A. Solari, J. F. Agnese, and M. Tibayrenc, "An isoenzyme study of naturally occurring clones of *Trypanosoma cruzi* isolated from both sides of the West Andes highland," *Transaction of the Royal Society of Tropical Medicine and Hygiene*, 1991, 85: 62–66.

——, R. Carrasco, S. Revollo, G. Aparicio, P. Desjeux, and M. Tibayrenc, "Chagas's disease in Bolivia: clinical and epidemiological features and zymodeme variability of *Trypanosoma cruzi* strains isolated from patients," *American Journal of Tropical Medicine and Hygiene*, 1989, 41: 521–9.

Breniere, S. F., R. Carrasco, G. Antezana, P. Desjeux, and M. Tibayrenc, "Association between *Trypanosoma cruzi* zymodemes and specific humoral depression in chronic chagasic patients," *Transactions of Royal Society of Tropical Medicine and Hygiene,* 1989, 83(4): 517.

Brenner, Rodolfo R., "General aspects of reduviidae biochemistry." In *Chagas' Disease Vectors. Volume III. Biochemical Aspects and Control,* Rodolfo Brenner and Angel de la Merced Stoka (eds), CRC Press, Inc., 1987, pp. 2–8.

Briceño-León, Roberto, "Housing for control of Chagas' disease in Venezuela," *Parasitology Today,* 1987, 3: 384–7.

——, "Vector control: house improvement and sanitary measures," World Health Organization, unpublished data, 1989.

——, *La Casa Enferma: Sociología de la Enfermedad de Chagas,* Fondo Editorial Acta Cientifica Venezolana Consorcio de Ediciones Capriles C.A., 1990.

Chagas, Carlos, "Nova tripanozomiase humana. Estudos sobre a morfologia e o ciclo evolutivo do *Schizotrypanum cruzi* n. gen. n. sp. Agente etiológico de nova entidade órbida do homen," *Memórias do Instituto Oswaldo Cruz,* 1909, 1: 159–218.

Crandon, Libbet, *From the Fat of Our Souls: Social Change, Political Process, and Medical Pluralism in Bolivia,* University of California Press, 1991.

Fornaciari, Gino, Maura Castagna, Paolo Viacava, Adele Tognetti, Generoso Bevilacqua, and Elsa Segura, "Chagas' disease in Peruvian Inca mummy," *The Lancet,* 1992 (Jan 11), 339: 128–9.

Friedlander, Judith, *Being Indian in Hueyapan: A Study of Forced Identity in Contemporary Mexico,* St Martin's Press, 1975.

Gonzaléz, J., S. Muñoz, S. Ortiz, D. Anacona, S. Salgado, M. Galleguillos, I. Neira, H. Sagua, and A. Solari, "Biochemical, immunological, and biological characterization of *Trypanosoma cruzi* populations of the Andean north of Chile," *Experimental Parasitology,* 1995, 81: 125–35.

Neghme, A., *La tripanosomiasis Americana, Creces, 1982,* 3: 23–8.

Reynolds, James E. F., "Nifurtimox." In *Martindale: The Extra Pharmacopoeia,* James E. F. Reynolds (ed.), The Pharmaceutical Press, 1986, 29: 673.

——, "Benznidazole." In *Martindale: The Extra Pharmacopoeia,* James E. F. Reynolds (ed.), The Pharmaceutical Press, 1986, 29: 673.

——, F. Rothhammer, M. J. Allison, L. Nuñez, V. Standen, and B. Arriaza, "Chagas' disease in pre-Columbian South America," *American Journal of Physical Anthropology,* 1985, 68: 495–8.

Rubina, Julia *et al.,* "Cure of short and long-term experimental Chagas' disease using Do870," *Science,* 1996, 273: 969–71.

Valencia Tellería, Angel (ed.), *Investigación epidemiologica nacional de la enfermedad de Chagas,* La Ministerio de Previsión y Salud Publica, Secretaria Ejecutiva Pl.-480 Titulo III, 1990.

——(ed.), *Estudio de base para control de Chagas,* Chaguaya-Provincia Arce, Tarija., Valencia & Associates, 1990*a,* Vol. RUC 03879931, August– December.

Valencia, Angel, Abraham Jemio, and Ana Maria Aguilar, *Memorias: Taller Sobre La Enfermedad de Chagas en Bolivia,* 13 y 14 Septiembre, Ministerio de Prevision Social y Salud Publica, 1989.

Villarroel, F., H. Schenone, M. Contrera, A. Rojas, and E. Fernandez, "Enfermedad de Chagas en el Altiplano Chileno, Aspectos epidemiologicos, parasitologicos y clinicos," *Boletin Chileno Parasitologia,* 1991, 46: 61–9.

Part IV

Gender, power, and health

Just as we pointed out the stark contrasts and contrasting cycles of opposition that are integral to the Andean social and natural environment, we note the commonality of extremes of class difference among Andean peoples. These differences are linked to extremes in the possession and exercise of power which in turn are linked to access to and control of material resources. These linkages continue toward the potentiality for good health and well being.

These themes run through the chapters in this section but take different turns and phrasing. In a finely detailed description, Larme and Leatherman explain how asymmetrical gender and class relationships are embodied in a widespread, indigenously defined illness. Price's chapter focuses on intrafamilial relationships between the genders and the degree to which men control medical choice for women relatives. In Glass-Coffin's chapter, we encounter a microcosm of power and class differentials in the intense relationship between the ethnographer and her principal participant. The nature of this microcosm appears ubiquitous in relationships that anthropologists form in the field.

Together these chapters raise a number of issues relating to gender and the contested identities that are part and parcel of intimacy between men and women and among men and women. In Peru, according to Larme and Leatherman, women have few avenues other than through use of their bodies for reproduction to obtain power and influence over spouses and other family members, which is the path to the preferred identity as a well-treated woman. The stakes are even higher in the cases detailed by Price in which older women lobby for control in the family and status in the neighborhood, using the currency of their contributions in medical advice and knowledge. Dealing with one's mentor becomes the central issue between Glass-Coffin and her participant but both women lay claim to that role at the moment in time described by the author. Who is superordinate and who is subordinate changes from hour to hour it seems; in this detailed encounter, the stakes, in terms of resources, seem extremely high.

The theme of vulnerability intersects with gender and power in very special ways. Healers in many social settings become highly competitive when their apprentice-clients acquire status as healers themselves. This competition seems especially potent when women are both healer and novitiate because their identity as important people is generally contested. Although this theme is clearly illustrated in Glass-Coffin's chapter, its implications are brought into the other chapters in the discussion of family members of the ill women in Price's case descriptions, and in the bodily "weakness" suffered by Peruvian women as described by Larme and Leatherman.

Chapter 11

Why *sobreparto*?

Women's work, health, and reproduction in two districts in southern Peru

Anne C. Larme and Thomas Leatherman

One of my first clues to the meaning of women's reproductive illnesses in Cuyo Cuyo – only understood after I was back in the States analyzing my data – came from Justina, who arrived on my doorstep one foggy morning shortly after I had arrived. After the initial pleasantries and a gift of fresh herbs and new potatoes, Justina came to the point: She had *madre onqoy* ("womb sickness"). Did I have any medicines for it? Also, what did I know about birth control methods, and could I give her some? She had already had nine children and did not want any more. I later found out that Justina was eight weeks pregnant at the time of this visit.

Anne C. Larme

My first impressions of Nuñoa were as a setting filled with contrasts. It was neither as harsh and bleak nor as culturally exotic as I expected. Over time, I found the juxtaposition of the historic Andes of anthropological literature and the increasing presence of capitalist relations even more marked and contrastive. A prime example was the degree to which historical relations of labor reciprocity (*ayni*) had become eroded in the context of wage labor and how this limited people's options for coping with illness. It became clear that how people classified health states and responded to illness had to do with the myriad of struggles they faced on a daily basis, and the webs of social relations that shaped their reality – just as Crandon-Malamud had so elegantly demonstrated in Kachitu.

Thomas Leatherman

Introduction

Case one: Justina

Justina, a forty-year-old Cuyo Cuyo woman, had given birth nine times. She had gotten *sobreparto* nearly every time due to "cold"[1] entering her lower body when exposed to give birth. Its main symptom was a rash over her entire body. Her husband was frequently away tending their lowland coffee and coca plantings, unable to help with household and subsistence tasks in Cuyo Cuyo. Justina relied on her older children for help, but she bore the major responsibility for agricultural work, collecting firewood, cooking, and childcare. Her *sobreparto* returned during her tenth pregnancy after her feet got wet and cold while working in the fields during rainy season. This time the symptoms were swollen hands and feet and a rash on her face. She continued to complain of *sobreparto* for three months after giving birth, with symptoms of headache, appetite loss, stomachache after eating certain foods, painful urination, and sensitivity to "heat" and "cold" while cooking, washing clothes, or working in the fields.

Sobreparto is a common illness of rural women in southern Peru. Like many other culturally interpreted illnesses throughout the world, it has no biomedical counterpart. Ultimately attributed to childbirth, women's experience of *sobreparto* is intertwined with many aspects of their work and reproductive lives, as Justina's story portrays.

In this chapter we examine women's work, health, and reproduction in two districts in the southern Peruvian highlands. Women in impoverished rural societies are particularly vulnerable to the ways in which high fertility, heavy workloads, and marginal nutrition and living conditions might compromise their health. We explore the illness *sobreparto*, which embodies women's experience of their lives and work. The nexus of work, health, and reproduction allows us to explore the impact of social, political, and economic changes on women. It also provides a context for viewing the negotiation of illness, a process embued with relations of class, gender, ethnicity, and power – a process well recognized in the work of Libbett Crandon-Malamud.[2] In so doing, we join Crandon-Malamud in exploring the "why?" in addition to the "what?" of *sobreparto*.[3] By placing this culturally interpreted illness within its social and political-economic context, we illuminate the multiple dimensions of this women's complaint in the rural Andes.

The data and interpretations in this chapter are derived from two research projects carried out between 1983–8 in the Department of Puno in the southern Peruvian highlands. Leatherman's research[4] in the Nuñoa Project[5] focused on inter-relationships between health and household economy. It was based primarily on survey data from farming and herding households located in three communities with varying degrees of participation in the market economy. Larme's ethnographic study[6] took place in association with a broad ecological and economic study of two communities in the Cuyo Cuyo district,[7] and focused on local interpretations and etiologies of illness, especially in relation to gender and work. During the Nuñoa research, data collected on effects of illness on household work revealed that the leading cause of disruptive illness reported by women was reproduction-associated illness. The most salient category of these illnesses was *sobreparto*, which, interestingly, often manifested in women many years after their last birth. Larme's subsequent ethnomedical research on women's work, reproduction, and health explored the phenomenon of *sobreparto* in more depth. Our approaches, data, interpretations, and insights into *sobreparto* and the conditions of Andean women's lives are complementary. Although our different research designs preclude detailed comparisons of quantitative data, consistency between research strategies and some overlap in methods allow for fruitful comparisons and a more complete picture of women's work, health, and reproduction in the southern Peruvian Andes.

Women's work, health, and reproduction in the developing world

Throughout rural Latin America, agrarian transformations have occurred in response to a host of factors including land reform and capital penetration into rural sectors. These transformations have important implications for health.[8] A picture emerges that has been played out in many contexts in the developing world. Capitalist penetration into rural economies has stimulated the commoditization of goods and labor and has effected a change in household production strategies toward a mix of home food production and wage labor (i.e. semi-proletarianization), in which neither alone is sufficient to meet basic household needs.[9] Women increasingly participate in waged work activities, though often are limited to participating in the informal economy of piecework, for example, weaving others' hammocks, spinning others' wool, and marketing others' goods. In rural Latin America, few wage-earning opportunities are available to women, they regularly receive less pay for the same work, and, in some cases, they are even prevented from owning land. Men work at wage jobs locally and/or migrate in search of work, leaving women to maintain family and home until they return, and often to carry out all agricultural tasks as well as informal cash-earning activities. Indeed, time allocation studies in rural communities throughout the developing world show that women work long days, often longer than men do. Increasingly, women work more "double days" as they intensify their inputs into market work as well as into home food production.[10] In addition, mean completed fertility rates are often high, and women spend much of their adult lives pregnant, lactating, and caring for small children. Biological reproduction can be physically stressful, especially in contexts of high fertility and marginal living conditions.[11] These realities are part of the broader context for our analysis of *sobreparto* in the rural Andes, a diagnosis that illustrates the interrelationship of women's work, health, and reproduction in one region of the developing world.

Research setting

The districts of Nuñoa and Cuyo Cuyo are located at approximately 4,000 and 3,400 m elevation, respectively in the northern part of the Department of Puno (see map of the region, this volume); Nuñoa on the Andean altiplano, and Cuyo Cuyo due east on the Andean escarpment. Both districts are comprised primarily of Quechua-speaking small-scale farming and herding households. Potatoes, and to a lesser degree wheat and barley, as well as the indigenous grains canihua and quinoa, are the locally grown staples in Nuñoa. The primary crops in Cuyo Cuyo are potatoes, other tubers, and broad beans, with limited amounts of corn, coffee, coca, and tropical fruits produced on community lands at lower altitudes.

Alpacas, llamas, and sheep are the primary herd animals. Agropastoral production is supplemented, or in some cases supported, by wage work, small-scale commodity production, and, in the case of Cuyo Cuyo, entrepreneurial gold mining.

Both districts have undergone rapid social and economic change due to the combined effects of agrarian reform policies, the growth of markets, and the commoditization of goods and labor. Cash-generating activities became prevalent in the Nuñoa economy as it became impossible for households to be self-sufficient through farming and herding alone. However, the irregular availability of wage work and extremely low wages (about US $ 1 per day) meant that most wage incomes were insufficient to meet basic needs. Like elsewhere in Latin America, a large semi-proletarian class emerged in Nuñoa, unable to fully meet its basic needs either through agropastoral activities or through wage work.[12] Cuyo Cuyo households have historically met their needs through combining agropastoral activities with entrepreneurial gold mining on community lands above and below Cuyo Cuyo. But during this same time in the 1970s and 1980s, crops were becoming insufficient to feed families, consumer goods held growing allure, and ostentatious spending on fiestas became common. Gold mining, as the most reliable source of cash, gradually took precedence over agriculture as the focus of existence of most families.[13] These shifts in economic strategies in Nuñoa and Cuyo Cuyo had clear implications for the division of labor and gender relations in Andean households.

Division of labor and daily work activities

Men's and women's work in rural Andean households is shaped by farming and herding activities. Although work roles overlap, generally women and children perform most of the herding and day-to-day work in the fields and in processing crops, and most of the household work (e.g. food preparation, child care, obtaining cooking fuel and water, spinning, and weaving). Men do the heavier agricultural work (e.g. plowing, carrying harvested crops), and may also spin wool and weave cloth, and contribute to basic household maintenance.

As Andean households have become more involved in the market economy, the household division of labor has become more differentiated. In general, the more the household is involved in wage work or gold mining, the greater the gender-based division of labor. As Nuñoa men migrated to urban centers in search of work, and Cuyo Cuyo men traveled to mining centers in the lowlands, women and children were left to maintain family and home until the men returned. This meant carrying out agricultural tasks, household maintenance activities, and in many cases a range of low-earning, informal, cash-earning activities.

Time allocation studies were carried out during both projects in the two districts.[14] While the data collection procedures, sample size, and classification of activities differed somewhat in the two studies, comparisons illustrate useful similarities and differences in work in the two regions (Table 11.1).

Men in Nuñoa and Cuyo Cuyo spend slightly less than one-half of their workday (measured as a 10–11-hour-day) in activities related to agropastoral,

Table 11.1 Time allocation in adults from Nuñoa and Cuyo Cuyo

General activity	Nuñoa[a]		Cuyo Cuyo[b]	
	Males (%)	Females (%)	Males (%)	Females (%)
Production Work	47.5	26.5	46.5	35.0
Agropastoral	19.2	9.2	20.0	28.1
Cash-generating	28.3	17.3	26.5	6.9
Household/ family maintenance	32.0	60.7	33.3	50.6
Social/leisure	19.8	12.7	18.8	12.8

Notes
a Based on 10-hour-day.
b Based on 11-hour-day.

communal, or cash-generating production activities. Between 40 and 43 percent of production time is spent in farming–herding activities, the majority being spent in cash-generating activities. Men in both locales spend somewhat less time in household and family maintenance work (32 percent in Nuñoa, 33.3 percent in Cuyo Cuyo), and between 19 and 20 percent of their time in social and leisure activities (Table 11.1).

Women in these two sites spend fewer hours in production activities (26.5 percent in Nuñoa and 35 percent in Cuyo Cuyo) than men, and substantially more time in household and family maintenance activities (61 percent in Nuñoa, and 51 percent in Cuyo Cuyo). They report equivalent amounts of time spent in social and leisure activities (about 12.8 percent), which is 6–7 percent less leisure time than men enjoy. While these aggregate time expenditures are roughly similar in the two regions, Nuñoa women spend more "production" time in cash-generating activities than women in Cuyo Cuyo (65 vs 19.5 percent). This can be explained by the fact that the Cuyo Cuyo women live in rural farming–herding hamlets, and the Nuñoa women in the time allocation sample live in a semi-urban town, many are landless, and many are the single heads of household. Both sets of time allocation data illustrate, however, that women perform a substantial amount of the work involved with agropastoral and cash-generating production activities, as well as the vast majority of daily household tasks. Consequently, they have less social and leisure time, and less respite from work (Table 11.1).

Reproduction, childcare, and stress

In addition to the multiple work roles women perform, women in Nuñoa and Cuyo Cuyo spend much of their adult lives pregnant, lactating, or caring for a small child. Mean completed fertility was 7–8 births by age forty in both groups, although many children (an estimated one in seven in Nuñoa and one in four in

Cuyo Cuyo) die within the first year, and child mortality remains high through age five.[15] On average, women have their first child around age nineteen and cease childbearing by age forty-five. Most women breastfeed their children a minimum of eighteen months. Therefore, an estimated 60 percent of a woman's life between the ages of nineteen and forty-five is spent pregnant and lactating. The care of young children not only complicates work and adds to the length of one's working day, but the added physical costs of childbirth and lactation, in addition to the marginal diets of many households, can precipitate bouts of undernutrition and other physiological stress. Moreover, women's reproductive years coincide with their heaviest work in subsistence and the home, and the most marital stress, which sometimes results in domestic violence.[16] Family planning methods are generally unavailable to rural Andean women, although both women and men desire to limit family size for economic reasons. There is some evidence to suggest that passive infanticide is sometimes used to control family size,[17] a method of family planning with high physiological and emotional costs for Andean women.

Health and illness in Nuñoa and Cuyo Cuyo

One of the main areas of overlap between our two projects was the collection of ethnographic and survey data dealing with household economy, health, reproduction, and demography. The health data from Nuñoa is based on three seasonal surveys of 140, 104, and 79 households from three communities: a semi-urban town, an ayllu, and a herding cooperative. In Cuyo Cuyo, data on household health and illness concepts were collected over one year from twenty households located in two communities emphasizing different subsistence strategies. While sample size and the degree of ethnographic detail sought in our interviews differed between the two projects, we used a similar health survey instrument, one that combined illness event recall and symptomatological assessments. The symptomatology was based on the Cornell Medical Index, but was substantially modified to allow for more open responses and to accommodate local illness concepts.

Local health systems in Nuñoa and Cuyo Cuyo are pluralistic.[18] Most symptoms and illnesses are treated at home by women with herbs and other home remedies. Folk healers and ritual specialists (Qu., *hampikuq*), government *sanitarios* (similar to nurse practitioners), physicians, and pharmacists all operate with relative autonomy, representing traditions with complementary ideologies and treatment regimens. Individuals may utilize one or all treatment regimens in the course of an illness. Decision-making regarding diagnosis and treatment in serious or chronic illness is continually negotiated and renegotiated as the illness progresses, influenced by such factors as gender, production needs, and interpersonal social relations. We explored this negotiation process through key informant interviews, participant observation, and responses to semi-structured health interviews.

Aggregate mortality and morbidity data reveal the marginal health conditions experienced by populations in both research sites. The average mortality rate in the Department of Puno during the period 1940–84 was 17.4 deaths per 1,000, among the highest in Peru and Latin America.[19] During the period of research,

Table 11.2 Prevalence of selected illness symptoms
reported in health surveys (percent of
total symptoms reported, all age and
sex groups)

Illness symptom category	Nuñoa[a]	Cuyo Cuyo[b]
Respiratory	26.3	23.0
Musculoskeletal	16.2	20.5
Gastrointestinal	13.9	16.5
Headaches	11.3	7.6
Dental problems	7.7	6.3
Eye or ear problems	9.2	5.9

Notes
a Based on a subsample of 2,380 symptoms collected
from 550 individuals.
b Based on 1,149 symptoms collected from 107
individuals.

infant mortality rates were calculated at 129 (Nuñoa) and 242 (Cuyo Cuyo)
deaths per 1,000 live births, both higher than the 114 per 1,000 live births for the
Department of Puno, or the 99 for Peru (1986 data). The maternal death rate for
Cuyo Cuyo was estimated at 1,022 per 100,000 live births, nearly twice as high
as the rate for the Department of Puno (543.0) and ten times higher than the rate
for Peru overall (91.9; 1986 figures).[20] High maternal death rates are a sobering
indicator of the very real danger of biological reproduction for Andean women.
Health survey data from Nuñoa and Cuyo Cuyo show that individuals in both
locales report similar types and frequencies of illness symptoms (Table 11.2).
The leading symptom categories in both districts were respiratory (26 and 23 percent in Nuñoa and Cuyo Cuyo), followed by musculoskeletal (16 and 20.5
percent), gastrointestinal (14 and 16.5 percent), headaches (11 and 8 percent),
dental problems (8 and 6 percent), and eye and ear problems (9 and 6 percent).
These categories were roughly the same for men and women in both locales.

Gender, health, and work in Nuñoa

Table 11.3 presents several measures of health for men and women living in
semi-urban and rural settings in the Nuñoa District. These include the percent of
symptoms reported from a condensed list of items from the symptomatological
survey, and the percent of adults reporting work lost due to illness, as well as the
number of work days affected over the two-week recall period. Women reported
about 7 percent more symptoms than men in both rural and semi-urban households. While symptomatological reports showed minor differences between
women and men, larger gender differences were reported in "work days lost" due
to illness. These were accentuated in semi-urban vs rural households. More
women living in rural communities reported work days lost due to illness than did
men (21.6 vs 15.3 percent), and for any given two-week recall period, women
reported losing about 1.5 as many work days as men (1.2 vs 0.8 days). In the

semi-urban town, even more women reported work days lost compared to men (28.9 vs 13.5 percent; $p < 0.10$), and on average lost almost three times more work days due to illness as men (1.4 vs 0.5 days for a given two-week recall period).

Thus, in both rural and semi-urban Nuñoa households, women report more symptoms and more work lost due to illness. Moreover, where we observed the sharpest distinctions in a gendered division of labor (i.e. in the semi-urban households, which were most involved in the cash economy), we also found the greatest gender disparities in work days lost due to illness. More semi-urban women were heads of household (30 percent were single-female headed households), more lacked sufficient land for farming or pasturing animals and were involved in wage work, and more had easily discernible double-days of work.

Heavy work was implicated in much illness, both in respiratory and musculoskeletal complaints. Respiratory problems contributed to 54 percent of the illness cases associated with work lost and to 34 percent of the total days lost to adult men and women (Table 11.4), and musculoskeletal complaints accounted for 15 percent of work lost in adults. Unexpectedly, female reproductive problems constituted 15 percent of the reported cases of work days lost to illness, and 28 percent of work days lost to Nuñoa adults. Nuñoa women reported that approximately 40 percent of their total work days lost due to illness were due to reproduction-related problems, the most common being *sobreparto*, a Spanish term used by Quechua-speakers, which literally means "illness following childbirth." In a number of cases, this term referred to a postpartum infection, associated with pain localized in the lower abdomen, and at times, a fever. However, quite often, *sobreparto* was used in a more general sense, to refer to a group of symptoms that included weakness, general malaise, headaches, and body aches – chronic

Table 11.3 Illness work disruption among adults from a semi-urban town and two rural sites in the Nuñoa district[a]

Illness measure	Semi-urban town		Rural communities	
	Male	Female	Male	Female
Households (N)	43		36	
Individuals (N)	32	53	34	50
Percent symptoms reported	16.8	22.7	18.0	25.1
Percent adults with work lost	13.5	28.9[b]	15.3	21.6
Median days lost/ sick adult	3.6	4.9	5.2	5.4
Days lost/adult/2 weeks	0.5	1.4	0.8	1.2

Notes
a Adapted from Leatherman 1994. Values averaged across three survey periods.
b Male–female differences significant at $p < 0.10$.

Table 11.4 Reported illness categories associated with work days lost in Nuñoa adults

Illness category	Number of cases (%)	Percent of total days lost
Respiratory	54	34
Musculoskeletal	12	15
Reproduction-related	15	28
Gastrointestinal	4	2

complaints that persisted years after the last birth. It was the chronic nature of this illness category that initially caught our interest.

In discussions with Nuñoa women, it became clear that *sobreparto* was an accepted reason for reducing one's workload and for abstaining from sexual relations with husbands. It appeared to be both a convenient folk label used after the fact to make sense of the somatic experience of women, as well as a way for women to negotiate some limited control over their productive and reproductive roles. Beyond this description and partial explanation, no further ethnographic detail on *sobreparto* (or on reproductive illness in general) was collected in Nuñoa. Larme's subsequent ethnographic study in Cuyo Cuyo was able to provide a more detailed explanation – the "why" as well as the "what" – of this illness category in the southern Peruvian Andes.

The experience of reproductive illness in the Andes

Ethnographic data from Cuyo Cuyo helps to understand the phenomenon of *sobreparto* and why Andean women attribute so many of their illness symptoms to childbirth. As in Nuñoa, Cuyo Cuyo women reported high levels of reproductive illness, but this category of illness was more culturally elaborated. Cuyo Cuyo women distinguish three types of reproductive illness – *sobreparto*, *madre*, and *sopla*, although these categories sometimes overlap and are used interchangeably. Eighteen of the twenty women studied intensively reported suffering from one of these illnesses at some point in their adult lives. Twelve out of the twenty had suffered from *sobreparto*. The following examples illustrate the experience of reproductive illness in Cuyo Cuyo.

Case two: Enilda

Although she had escaped reproductive illness with her first three births, Enilda, age thirty-two, became ill with *sobreparto* after her fourth baby. After her fifth, she took special care to rest for two entire weeks in order to avoid its recurrence, but was unsuccessful. She suffered from *sobreparto*, consisting of an itchy rash over her entire body, for three months after giving birth. Enilda also suffered from chronic *madre*, with symptoms of burning pain in her stomach and lower back. It was caused by having too many babies, she explained, and by giving birth alone the first time without receiving proper care. It was also caused by beatings from her husband during the early years of her marriage. Enilda's *madre* recurred whenever she ate, when her stomach was empty, when she ate chile peppers, and especially when she was worried. One episode, for example, was caused by worrying about being alone with the children while her husband was away mining gold, and by worrying about her father's recent death.

Case three: Leonora

Leonora, thirty-one, reported both chronic *madre* and *sobreparto* during her sixth pregnancy and after giving birth, she had had two miscarriages and four live births. Her *madre*, consisting of pain in her abdomen and lower back, had begun after a miscarriage suffered during her second pregnancy. Her husband was away for several weeks working, and, because she had no help and no way to contact him, she had to return to work too soon to take care of their small son. She attributed its recurrence to giving birth, which caused her internal organs to be damaged and which allowed illness to enter when the cold air hit her hot, sweaty body during labor. Other causes were carrying heavy loads while pregnant and returning to hard work too soon after giving birth. Her *sobreparto* had begun after the birth of her first child eight years earlier, and was exacerbated by each subsequent miscarriage and birth. Its symptoms were burning pain in her hands and feet, sensitivity to "cold," sharp lower back pains, abdominal cramps, numbness, and loss of appetite. Leonora was distressed when her old problem returned this time, despite her family's best efforts. Her husband and unmarried aunt had taken care of all the cooking and other household tasks while she rested and cared for the new baby, but she still got sick. Leonora's problems, alternately described as *madre* or *sobreparto*, continued for four months after giving birth.

Enilda, Leonora, and Justina, whose story began this chapter, experienced reproductive illness at the peak of their reproductive years, which in Cuyo Cuyo coincides with heavy responsibilities in childcare and in the home, and strenuous work in the fields. These responsibilities are often carried out without the help of husbands, whose economic activities take them away from home for lengthy periods of time. Family stress and domestic violence are other causes.

But here are the stories of much older women who experienced chronic reproductive illness long after the completion of their childbearing years.

Case four: Seferina

Seferina, forty-seven, had given birth twice and had had one miscarriage. She suffered from chronic *madre*. It had begun after the birth of her son twenty years earlier, when she had not been able to rest properly. It recurred with hard work, walking long distances, and carrying heavy loads, and manifested primarily as pain in her lower back and abdomen. She also suffered from *sopla*, whose underlying cause was childbirth. She explained that the lower back (Qu., *ñañu wasa*) is the most delicate part of a woman's body. It must be protected from childhood on by dressing warmly and not working too hard. Women must be especially careful after giving birth "when every kind of illness enters the body." Because this part of her body was weakened from giving birth, Seferina became ill with *sopla* more than 20 years later when, after boarding a truck, a cold wind hit her when she was still hot and sweaty from walking uphill. The "cold" sweat had entered her weakened *ñañu wasa*, making her ill with shooting pains in her lower back, numbness, and pain in her legs, and heightened sensitivity to "heat" and "cold." For months Seferina treated her symptoms with rest and home remedies, to no avail. She and her husband finally deduced that her *sopla* was actually caused by sorcery because it came in the midst of the legal dispute with another community member and a series of other intractable family and health problems.

Case five: Natalia

Natalia, a fifty-nine-year-old Puna Ayllu woman, had given birth ten times, in addition to three miscarriages. She suffered from chronic *sobreparto*, with symptoms of sensitivity to "heat" and "cold," a rash, headache, poor appetite, burning pain in her abdomen, pain in her lower back, and general weakness. Although Natalia explained that her *sobreparto* had originated from lack of rest and from improper care after childbirth, her first episode did not occur until age 49, years after the birth of her last child. Particular episodes, which she alternately called *sobreparto* or *madre*, were triggered by experiencing "cold," drinking alcohol at fiestas, and hard physical work, such as bending over to cultivate the fields. Natalia and her husband spent considerable time and resources searching for a cure, but although the symptoms sometimes went away temporarily, they were never completely cured.

These examples demonstrate that reproductive illness is sometimes directly related to pregnancy or childbirth, but more often is experienced months or even years later, especially after giving birth multiple times. They also demonstrate how women's complaints about reproductive events are intertwined with many other facets of their work, family, and social lives. Childbirth is perceived to have long-lasting and deleterious effects on a woman's body and health. As one woman explained: "After giving birth, a woman's body is completely *malogrado* (Sp., ruined), just like after a truck accident." Susceptibility to reproductive illness, directly after childbirth or years later, is increased when a woman gives birth alone or does not have proper help at home to allow her to rest in the important weeks following birth.

To prevent reproductive illness, a woman is fed nutritious local foods and family members take over most of her household tasks. She must especially avoid work involving "heat" and "cold," such as cooking and washing clothes, as these are thought to enter the body, which has been opened for childbirth, to cause symptoms. The postpartum period was the only time women were observed to be pampered and taken care of in Cuyo Cuyo. All of these practices are intended to protect a woman's health. Thus, women whose husbands had migrated or who lacked relatives or older children to help out during the critical days and weeks following childbirth were especially at risk for reproductive illness. Postpartum rest is especially important after a woman has already had several children.

Why *sobreparto?*

Why do women in the southern Peruvian Andes emphasize childbearing as a source of symptoms? Why is the image, vocabulary, and bodily experience of childbirth the main idiom through which women communicate their distress? As Browner and Sargent note,[21] "reproductive studies can provide a particularly powerful lens through which to view broader social processes [for reproduction] articulates with a society's patterns of gender role organization and its associated ideological and sociopolitical dynamics."

Reproductive stress and associated illness have been noted by various researchers in the rural Andes and Latin America. Women in the northern Peruvian Andes suffer from an illness they call *debilidad*, with symptoms of chronic malaise, which is associated with reproductive stress.[22] Highland Ecuadorean women frequently suffer from *nervios*, with symptoms of chronic weakness and anxiety, which also appears to be related to high fertility levels.[23] In rural Mexican women, higher numbers of pregnancies and higher levels of reproductive stress (measured as percent of reproductive life spent pregnant and lactating) are associated with more illness symptoms, especially fatigue, malaise, weakness, headaches, backaches, and other body aches.[24] Some of these chronic symptoms and complaints may be associated with aging.[25] However, while reproductive stress and aging provide partial explanations for reproductive illness, they are insufficient. The cultural elaboration of reproductive stress in the southern Peruvian Andes merits further attention.

To understand reproductive illnesses in the Andes, we explore the multiple dimensions of the female body and reproductive illnesses, including the individual biological and phenomenological body, the social body, and the body politic – or control of women's bodies within the current political economy.[26]

Many of the symptoms Andean women group into the illnesses of *sobreparto*, *madre*, and *sopla* can be directly attributed to the biology of reproduction: pregnancy, miscarriage, childbirth, possibly menstruation and menopause, and various problems with reproductive organs. Years of childbearing under conditions of marginal nutrition, hypoxia, hard work, and lack of access to family planning methods deplete women's health, contributing to the cultural construction of reproductive illness.

Andean body concepts add another dimension to women's experience of their bodies. Women's bodies – especially those of married women – are considered to be more *débil* (Sp., weak) than men's bodies.[27] They have an extra orifice, the vagina, where illnesses might enter during childbirth or urination, and they regularly lose blood, which is thought to be irreplaceable, through childbirth and menstruation. Sweating, according to Andean ethnomedical concepts, helps to cleanse the body of illness. So women, who perform "lighter," non-sweat-producing work (Qu., *ruway*) in subsistence and in the home, are thought to be less able to maintain their health than men.[28] Further, all components of a woman's lower body are thought to be damaged and weakened by childbirth, a condition that worsens with age and years of work. These images of women's bodies contribute to the cultural conception of women's bodies as weak, prone to illness, and inherently inferior to men's.

Gender roles and relations are played out on the terrain of women's bodies and reproductive illnesses. Women's heavy workloads and the emotional and physical stresses of juggling their many responsibilities in child rearing, in the home, and in subsistence are represented by reproductive illness symptoms such as lower back pains and those caused by negative emotions. Subordination to husbands, represented by domestic violence, is another factor. These problems may be worsening with social and economic change, which has exaggerated the division of labor and increased the value of, and emphasis on, cash-earning activities by men, and thus shifted the balance of power between husbands and wives.

Within the household, fear of chronic reproductive illness and loss of a woman's labor contribution are major incentives to take good care of a woman after childbirth. However, everyone acknowledges that no matter how well a woman is taken care of, she can still get *sobreparto* or another reproductive illness at any point in her life. Improper care after childbirth becomes a convenient explanation for many symptoms and health problems women experience, whether emotional or physical. Following the concept of the sick role,[29] women may claim reproductive illnesses when their personal stress becomes overwhelming. Reproductive illness gives them limited power to negotiate respite from their heavy workloads and to enlist the support of husbands and other family members.

The behavior surrounding reproductive illnesses also reflects social relations outside of the household. Other community members assign partial blame to husbands for their wives' chronic illnesses. Societal norms for proper husbands include assisting wives after childbirth, avoiding excessive wife beating, and making sure that wives are properly nourished and dressed and do not have to work too hard. Pressures to adhere to these norms by marriage godparents and other community members become an added incentive for husbands to treat their wives well. While the social causes of reproductive illnesses are generally assigned to husbands, in extreme cases chronic reproductive illness may be blamed on social discord in the community. Seferina and her husband, for example, attributed a particularly bad episode of *sopla* to sorcery directed at them by a family with whom they were having a legal dispute.

A final dimension of reproductive illness relates to the body politic and control of women's bodies in Andean society. Foucault,[30] Martin,[31] and feminist biologists such as Birke,[32] Bleier,[33] and Hubbard[34] have discussed the control of bodies, especially women's bodies, in Western culture, science, and biomedicine. But we know little about this process in non-industrial societies. Cultural concepts such as women's *debilidad* (Sp., weakness, vulnerability) and the devaluation of women's labor suggest that power relations are an especially important dimension of reproductive illnesses in the Andes. *Debilidad* explains married women's ill health and also becomes the rationale for limiting women's social and economic roles. Because of their *debilidad*, women perform most of the *ruway* – "light," less-valued work in agriculture, herding, and housework, in contrast to men, who per-form *llank'ay* (Qu.) – heavy, sweat-producing labor, which helps them to maintain their health. In the present economy of Cuyo Cuyo, the "sweat value" of gold min-ing combined with its "cash value" means that it is more highly valued than agri-cultural work, now the domain of women. In other words, whether in Andean or present day economic terms, women's work is valued less than men's work. Female sexual vulnerability also limits Andean women's activities. From the time they are girls, Andean women are taught to be vigilant of their bodies and are limited in where they can travel, lest they be raped or bear children out of wedlock. *Debilidad*, female sexual vulnerability, and women's roles in childbearing and childcare are used by both women and men to explain why women travel less to cities and to gold mining regions to engage in cash-generating activities. These concepts effectively limit women's participation in the cash economy and urban culture of Peru, both of which are increasingly important aspects of life in Andean communities.

Andean beliefs about women's bodies and the effects of childbearing thus play into and reinforce women's subordinate position in present-day Andean society. These beliefs become a rationale to constrain women's roles, reinforcing inequali-ties between men and women. This is ironic, considering that, as time allocation data show, women perform long hours of physically strenuous and tedious work, in addi-tion to the stress of childbearing, during their most economically productive years.

Reproducing illness or reproductive illnesses?

While the basic biological difference between men and women has been used his-torically and cross-culturally to limit women's roles and status, conversely, repro-duction has also served as women's main access to power and status.[35] Childbearing is uniquely feminine and empowering. The capacity to reproduce, which only women possess, is an especially effective locus of women's complaints.

Marriage, childbearing, adult female work roles, and reproductive illnesses coincide in Andean women's lives, as represented by survey and ethnographic data from Nuñoa and Cuyo Cuyo. This is expressed by Andean women them-selves, as they explain the causes of reproductive illness, which are intertwined with the stresses of women's economic activities, social roles, and childbearing.

In addition, Andean women have few outlets for their distress. Unlike men, generally they cannot relieve marital stress by moving to urban areas or other migration sites, or by physically abusing their spouses. They must avoid sexual liaisons with men other than their husbands for fear of pregnancy and retribution from husbands. And negative emotions are proscribed for both health and social reasons in Andean communities. While cultural conceptions of women's bodies are generally employed to women's disadvantage in the southern Peruvian Andes, in the case of reproductive illnesses, women's bodies become a means of power and resistance. Claiming reproductive illness is one of the few acceptable arenas of protest for women, a claim that men and other family members take seriously. Reproductive illness gives women limited power to negotiate respite from their overburdening work and social roles with husbands, family, and community members.

Our analysis of *sobreparto* resonates with the work of Libbet Crandon-Malamud, who demonstrates how the process of illness negotiation emerges from, and recreates, relations of power within the present-day political economy of the Andean region. Reproductive illness in the southern Peruvian Andes is a multidimensional phenomenon, partly biological, but also created, or reproduced by Andean society and culture within the present day political-economic context. *Sobreparto* and other reproductive illnesses embody, literally and symbolically, and give voice and meaning to, the suffering of Andean women, who bear physical, emotional, social, and economic costs of childbearing, in addition to their multiple work and social roles.

Notes

1 "Cold" and "heat" are placed in quotes when discussing Andean ethnomedical concepts because they refer not only to temperatures, but to inherent qualities of environmental features, foods, drinks, and medicines.

2 Libbett Crandon-Malamud, *From the Fat of Our Souls: Social Change, Political Process, and Medical Pluralism in Bolivia* (University of California Press, 1991).

3 Libbett Crandon, "Why *Susto*?," *Ethnology*, 1983, 22: 153–67.

4 Thomas L. Leatherman, *Illness, Work and Social Relations in the Southern Peruvian Highlands*, PhD Dissertation, University of Massachusetts, Amherst, 1987; Leatherman, "Health implications of changing agrarian economies in the Southern Andes," *Human Organization*, 1994, 53(4): 371–80; Leatherman, "A biocultural perspective on health and household economy in Southern Peru," *Medical Anthropology Quarterly*, 1996, 10(4): 476–95.

5 Brooke R. Thomas *et al.*, "Consequences and responses to illness among small scale farmers: a research design." In *Capacity for Work in the Tropics*, K. J. Collins and D. F. Roberts (eds), Cambridge University Press, 1988, pp. 249–76.

6 Anne C. Larme, *Work, Reproduction, and Health in Two Andean Communities (Department of Puno, Peru)*, Working Paper No. 5 from the research project *Production, Storage, and Exchange in a Terraced Environment on the Eastern Andean Escarpment*, Bruce Winterhalder, (series ed.), University of North Carolina at Chapel Hill Department of Anthropology, 1993; Larme, "Child health and selective neglect in rural Peru," *Social Science and Medicine*, 1997, 44(11): 1711–23; Larme, "Environment, vulnerability, and gender in Andean ethnomedicine," *Social Science and Medicine*, 1998, 47(8): 1005–15.

7 *Production, Storage, and Exchange in a Terraced Environment on the Eastern Andean Escarpment*, Bruce Winterhalder, Principal Investigator (National Science Foundation Grant BNS8313190).

8 Thomas L. Leatherman and A. Gordon, "Agrarian transformations and health," *Human Organization* (edited symposium), 1994, 53(4): 371–80.

9 A. de Janvry, *The Agrarian Question and Reformism in Latin America*, The Johns Hopkins University Press, 1981.

10 Carole Browner and Joanne Leslie, "Women, work, and household in the context of development." In *Gender and Health*, Carolyn Sargent and C. Brettell (eds), Prentice Hall, 1994, pp. 260–7.
11 See for example, Browner and Leslie, *Women, Work, and Household in the Context of Development*, pp. 260–7; Magali Daltabuit, *Mayan Women: Work, Nutrition and Child Care*, PhD dissertation, University of Massachusetts, Amherst, 1988; A. J. Harrington, "Nutritional stress and economic responsibility: a study of Nigerian women." In *Women and Poverty in the Third World*, M. Buvinic, M. Lycette, and A. McGreevey (eds), The Johns Hopkins University Press, 1983, pp.130–156; Thomas L. Leatherman, "Gender differences in health and illness among rural populations in Latin America." In *Sex and Gender in Paleopathological Perspective*, A. Grauer and P. Stuart-Macadam (eds), Cambridge University Press, 1998, pp. 114–32.
12 de Janvry, *The Agrarian Question and Reformism in Latin America*.
13 Jorge Recharte, *Value and Economic Culture Among the Peasant Gold Miners of the Cuyo Cuyo District (Northern Puno, Peru)*, Working Paper No. 3 from the research project *Production, Storage, and Exchange in a Terraced Environment on the Eastern Andean Escarpment*, Bruce Winterhalder, (series ed.), University of North Carolina at Chapel Hill Department of Anthropology, 1990.
14 Larme, *Work, Reproduction, and Health in Two Andean Communities*; Leatherman, *Illness, Work and Social Relations in the Southern Peruvian Highlands*; Thomas L. Leatherman, "Illness as lifestyle change," *MASCA Research Papers in Science and Archeology*, 1992, 9: 83–9.
15 Larme, *Work, Reproduction, and Health in Two Andean Communities*; Leatherman, *Illness, Work and Social Relations in the Southern Peruvian Highlands*; Larme, "Child health and selective neglect in rural Peru," *Social Science and Medicine*, 1997, 44(11): 1711–23.
16 Larme, *Work, Reproduction, and Health in Two Andean Communities*; Larme, "Environment, vulnerability, and gender in Andean ethnomedicine," 1005–15.
17 Larme, "Child health and selective neglect," pp. 1711–23.
18 Crandon-Malamud, *From the Fat of Our Souls*; Hans Baer, "Contributions to a critical analysis of medical pluralism: an examination of the work of Libbet Crandon-Malamud," this volume.
19 P. Brito, "Salud, Nutrición, y Población en el Perú." In *Población y Políticas de Desarrollo en el Perú*, Instituto Andino de Estudios en Población y Desarrollo [INANDEP], 1983, pp. 273–379; James Carey, "Social system effects on local level morbidity and adaptation in the rural Peruvian Andes," *Medical Anthropology Quarterly*, 1990, 4: 266–95.
20 Cuyo Cuyo health indicators and official health indicators for Nuñoa, Puno, and Peru are not strictly comparable, because Cuyo Cuyo registries were scrutinized and a number of discrepancies noted. In particular, many deaths of newborns found in death registries had never been recorded in the birth registries. These were unnamed newborns euphemistically termed *fetos* (Sp. fetuses), probably denoting the practice of active or passive infanticide. Thus Cuyo Cuyo indicators appear worse – though they are probably more accurate – than official statistics. See Larme 1993 and 1996 for a more complete discussion of this finding.
21 Carole Browner and Carolyn F. Sargent, "Anthropology and studies of human reproduction." In *Medical Anthropology: Contemporary Theory and Method*, Thomas Johnson and Carolyn Sargent (eds), Praeger Publishers, 1990, p. 215.
22 Kathryn S. Oths, "*Debilidad:* a biocultural asessment of an embodied Andean illness," *Medical Anthropology Quarterly,* 1999, 13(3): 286–315.
23 Ruthbeth Finerman, "Experience and expectation: conflict and change in traditional family health care among the Quichua of Saraguro," *Social Science and Medicine*, 1983, 17: 1291–98.

24 Carole Browner, "Women, household and health in Latin America," *Social Science and Medicine*, 1989, 28: 461–73; Leatherman, "Gender differences in health and illness," pp. 114–32.
25 Finerman, "Experience and expectation," pp. 1291–8.
26 See Nancy Scheper-Hughes and Margaret Lock, "The mindful body: a prolegomenon to future work in medical anthropology," *Medical Anthropology Quarterly*, 1987, 1(1): 6–41.
27 Larme, *Work, Reproduction, and Health in Two Andean Communities*; Larme, "Environment, vulnerability, and gender in Andean ethnomedicine," *Social Science and Medicine*, 1998, 47(8): 1005–15.
28 Larme, *Work, Reproduction, and Health*.
29 Talcott Parsons, *The Social System*, Free Press, 1951.
30 Michel Foucault, *The History of Sexuality Volume 1: An Introduction*, Pantheon, 1978; *Discipline and Punish: The Birth of the Prison*, Vintage, 1979; *Power/Knowledge*, Pantheon, 1980.
31 Emily Martin, *The Woman in the Body*, Beacon Press, 1987.
32 Lynda Birke, *Women, Feminism, and Biology: The Feminist Challenge*, Wheatshelf Books, 1986.
33 Ruth Bleier, *Science and Gender: A Critique of Biology and Its Theories on Women*, Pergamon Press, Inc., 1984.
34 Ruth Hubbard, *The Politics of Women's Biology*, Rutgers University Press, 1990.
35 Browner and Sargent, "Anthropology and studies of human reproduction," pp. 215–29.

References

Birke, Lynda, *Women, Feminism and Biology: The Feminist Challenge*, Wheatshelf Books, Ltd., 1986.
Bleier, Ruth, *Science and Gender: A Critique of Biology and Its Theories on Women*, Pergamon Press, Inc., 1984.
Brito, P., "Salud, Nutrición, y Población en el Perú." In *Población y Politicas de Desarrollo en el Perú*, Instituto Andino de Estudios en Población y Desarrollo [INANDEP], 1983, pp. 273–379.
Browner, Carole, "Women, household and health in Latin America," *Social Science and Medicine*, 1989, 28: 461–73.
——and Joanne Leslie, "Women, work, and household in the context of development." In *Gender and Health*, Carolyn Sargent and C. Brettell (eds), Prentice Hall, 1994, pp. 260–7.
——and Carolyn F. Sargent, "Anthropology and studies of human reproduction." In *Medical Anthropology: Contemporary Theory and Method*, Thomas Johnson and Carolyn Sargent (eds), Praeger Publishers, 1990, pp. 215–29.
Carey, James, "Social system effects on local level morbidity and adaptation in the rural Peruvian Andes," *Medical Anthropology Quarterly*, 1990, 4: 266–95.
Crandon, Libbett, "Why Susto?," *Ethnology*, 1983, 22, pp. 153–67.
Crandon-Malamud, Libbett, *From the Fat of Our Souls: Social Change, Political Process, and Medical Pluralism in Bolivia*, University of California Press, 1991.
Daltabuit, Magali, *Mayan Women: Work, Nutrition and Child Care*, PhD Dissertation, University of Massachusetts, 1988.
De Janvry, A., *The Agrarian Question and Reformism in Latin America*, The Johns Hopkins University Press, 1981.
Finerman, Ruthbeth, "Experience and expectation: conflict and change in traditional family health care among the Quichua of Saraguro," *Social Science and Medicine*, 1983, 17: 1291–8.

Foucault, Michel, *The History of Sexuality, Volume 1: An Introduction*, Pantheon, 1978.
——, *Discipline and Punish: The Birth of the Prison*, Vintage, 1979.
——, *Power/Knowledge*, Colin Gordon (ed.), Pantheon, 1980.
Harrington, A. J., "Nutritional stress and economic responsibility: a study of Nigerian women." In *Women and Poverty in the Third World*, M. Buvinic, M. Lycette, and A. McGreevey (eds), The Johns Hopkins University Press, 1983, pp. 130–156.
Hubbard, Ruth, *The Politics of Women's Biology*, Rutgers University Press, 1990.
Larme, Anne C., *Work, Reproduction and Health in Two Andean Communities*, Working Paper No. 5 from the research project *Production, Storage and Exchange in a Terraced Environment on the Eastern Andean Escarpment*, Bruce Winterhalder (series ed.), University of North Carolina at Chapel Hill Department of Anthropology, 1993.
——, "Child health and selective neglect in rural Peru," *Social Science and Medicine*, 1997 44(11): 1711–23.
——, "Environment, vulnerability, and gender in Andean ethnomedicine," *Social Science and Medicine*, 1998, 47(8): 1005–15.
——, *Illness, Work and Social Relations in the Southern Peruvian Highlands*, PhD Dissertation, University of Massachusetts, 1987.
——, "Illness as lifestyle change," *MASCA Research Papers in Science and Archeology*, 1992, 9: 83–9.
——, "Health implications of changing agrarian economies in the Southern Andes," *Human Organization*, 1994, 53(4): 371–80.
——, "A Biocultural perspective on health and household economy in Southern Peru," *Medical Anthropology Quarterly*, 1996, 10(4): 476–95.
——, Gender differences in health and illness among rural populations in Latin America." In *Sex and Gender in Paleopathological Perspective*, A. Grauer and P. Stuart-Macadam (eds), Cambridge University Press, 1998, 114–32.
—— and A. Gordon, "Agrarian transformations and health," *Human Organization* (edited symposium), 1994, 53(4): 371–80.
Leslie, Joanna and M. Paolisso (eds), *Women, Work and Child Welfare in the Third World*, Westview Press, 1989.
Martin, Emily, *The Woman in the Body*, Beacon Press, 1987.
Oths, Kathryn, *Medical Treatment Choice and Health Outcomes in the Northern Peruvian Andes*, PhD Dissertation, Case Western Reserve University, 1991.
——, "Debilidad: a biocultural assessment of an embodied Andean illness," *Medical Anthropology Quarterly*, 1999, 13(3): 286–315.
Parsons, Talcott, *The Social System*, Free Press, 1951.
Recharte, Jorge, *Value and Economic Culture among the Peasant Gold Miners of the Cuyo Cuyo District (Northern Puno, Peru)*, Working Paper No. 3 from the research project *Production, Storage and Exchange in a Terraced Environment on the Eastern Andean Escarpment*, Bruce Winterhalder (series ed.), University of North Carolina at Chapel Hill Department of Anthropology, 1990.
Scheper-Hughes, Nancy, and Margaret Lock, "The mindful body: a prolegomenon to future work in medical anthropology," *Medical Anthropology Quarterly*, 1987, 1(1): 6–41.
Thomas R. Brooke, *et al.*, "Consequences and responses to illness among small scale farmers: a research design." In *Capacity for Work in the Tropics*, K. J. Collins and D. F. Roberts (eds), Cambridge University Press, 1988, pp. 249–76.
United Nations, *The World Women 1970–1990: Trends and Statistics*, United Nations, 1991.

Chapter 12

Illness management, social alliance, and cultural identity in Quito, Ecuador

Laurie J. Price

Enfolded in emerald-green peaks and hills, Quito, Ecuador is one of the most stunningly beautiful cities in the world. At 9,000 feet, it is also one of the highest. Many newer and poorer neighborhoods sit partway up the mountain ranges that flank the valley of Quito (now a populated strip about 20 miles long, but not very wide). While bus service, health care, phones, potable water, electricity, and garbage pickup are often hard to come by in the aerial *barrios*, views are breathtaking of the city below. "Las Gradas" (a pseudonym) is such a *barrio*, located up the mountain from El Camal, the main outdoor market in south Quito. Las Gradas means "The Stairs": in many places, the hillside is so steep that public streets turn into public staircases. In 1980, I was living in Las Gradas, in the middle of a concrete stairway, climbing a hundred steps to get to the street. Graceful eucalyptus trees and agaves decorated our stairway. But steep drop-offs menaced playing children, and a deep, trash-strewn *quebrada* (gorge) ran alongside. Later, friends told me of the dangers of absorbing fright illness and *mal aire* from the quebrada, especially from eggs and other curing paraphernalia discarded there. On my first visit to Las Gradas in 1980, I noticed many small (home-based) food shops, a soccer field, and a primary school; some residents cultivated corn and herded sheep in the upper reaches. On the main street, a woman vendor dressed in polyester was selling roast pork; next to her, another woman in partly indigenous dress (gathered velvet skirt, bright colored beads) was spinning wool on a hand spinner. This mix of *mestizo* and urbanized indigenous cultures continues today.

In the summer of 1999, I was talking with an Ecuadorian physician about my interest in how different cultures view the mind and the body, and how people manage certain kinds of illness in the family. Tomás said that he formerly did not believe in folk conditions like "fright illness," "anger illness," or "nerves," since in his view, symptoms had to arise from some biological or physical cause.[1] But then he told me a story about his own sons.

Umberto and Jorge, now seven and four, have on multiple occasions become quite ill for no identifiable biomedical reason – they lose their appetite, sometimes have vomiting or diarrhea, and their sleep is restless. As a physician, Tomás has always made certain that all pertinent biomedical tests were conducted; but the results fail to show any physical pathology. The boys' grandmother identifies the problem as *espanto* (fright illness, also known as *susto*). When he first suffered these symptoms, Umberto was about ten months old. His maternal grandmother attributed the "fright illness" to the family's walking past a cemetery at night to arrive at a baptism ceremony.

Young children can contract *espanto* by falling in the street, being threatened by an aggressive dog, or falling out of bed. In vulnerable adults, the illness can come about after a car accident or a walk in the forest. Fear causes the spirit (soul) to separate from a vulnerable person's body, which in turn causes the physical distress. We will return to Umberto and Jorge later in the chapter since this case illustrates how illness management serves social and cultural purposes, in addition to the search for a cure.

Since the early 1980s, my ethnographic work has been among *mestizos* of highland Ecuador. The present analysis draws on three kinds of data collection: participant observation in two working class *barrios* in Quito, Ecuador; semi-structured, open-ended tape recorded interviews with ten informants in these *barrios* (conducted 1997–99); and three extended case studies. The ten semi-structured interviews focus on beliefs about causes, symptoms, treatments, bodily processes, and consequences associated with five emotion-based illnesses. The interviews were tape recorded and will be fully analyzed in a separate publication. Here they are used only to provide general cultural context for three case studies of the management of illness by families. The case studies are based on a combination of observation, interviewing, and recorded narratives.

Belief in emotion-based illnesses is very widespread among *mestizo* Ecuadorians. There are five common culture-bound syndromes in the Andes (they occur in much of Latin America): *espanto/susto* (fright illness), *mal aire* (evil air), *pena* (sadness), *iras/colerín* (anger illness), and *nervios* (stress/worry illness). These illnesses are recognized in varying forms by both *mestizo* and Indian populations.[2] My structured interviews suggest that beliefs about emotion-based illnesses are very common (80–90 percent) among working class urban *mestizos* in Ecuador. *Espanto* and *mal aire* are widely believed to be common causes of children's diarrhea in highland Ecuador.[3] Hess describes *espanto* in highland Ecuador as arising most often in children, but also in women. She writes: "These illnesses never are caused only by dangerous external agents (e.g. the Wind, or mountain spirits), but rather they come from a severe imbalance between the malignant external power, and the vital internal forces of the human being."[4]

Both similarities and differences characterize the questions asked by Libbet Crandon in highland Bolivia, and my own research questions in highland Ecuador. In this chapter, new insights emerge from using Libbet's framework to revisit my fieldwork data. Similarities in our research include a special focus on illness talk as a natural form of discourse, and as part of how people accomplish social purposes, in addition to medical purposes.[5] We both explore medical pluralism in the Andes, and come to the same conclusion: traditional healing meets important social and psychological needs and is not likely to disappear, even if biomedical resources become more available or popular. These needs will be discussed in relation to the case studies below, and in the chapter conclusions. Research methods are another area of similarity: The triangulation of participant observation, extended case study analysis, and structured household interviews is a powerful way to understand the many layers of illness interpretation and management. Last but not least, we both engage in political-economic analysis of illness and treatment, the "critical medical anthropology of medical pluralism."[6] The association of social oppression and poverty with an extra disease burden is well proven, but uncovering the details of this association in specific locales is worthwhile (e.g. Carey's[7] work on gender and age groups that are especially vulnerable to culture-bound illnesses in Southern Peru). Third World countries invest considerable sums in biomedical institutions, money that otherwise could go toward potable water or education. How do poor people experience those expensive biomedical institutions in their own lives? Libbet documents both cooperation and dereliction by biomedical specialists.[8] My work in Quito shows "commerciogenesis" in a health care system that builds hospitals and sells pills but often fails to provide access to caring nurses and doctors.[9]

There are also some differences worth noting in our work. I focus more specifically on emotion-based, culture-bound syndromes in the Andes. These appear to be relatively minor in Kachitu, Bolivia, but constitute some 25 percent of illness episodes in the household morbidity survey I conducted in Quito.[10] Second, my analysis of illness talk focuses not only on its social purposes, but also on the psychological and physical benefits of such talk when people are trying to cope with a serious illness.[11] Such benefits help explain why people make therapy choices that do not always conform to formal "decision models."[12] Third, while Libbet describes the alliances between ethnic groups that people may strengthen or undermine in making their diagnosis and treatment choices, my analysis of illness management has highlighted the extended family network. In this chapter, I explore the salience of ethnic and social class factors in urban illness management, using Libbet's framework as a starting point.

Questions that emerge include the following. Do *mestizo* Ecuadorians forge social alliances outside their extended families through defining illness or pursuing treatment in a particular way? Do they gain access to primary or secondary resources through choosing to manage an illness either biomedically, or with folk medicine? What about the other side of the coin? Do people utilize discourse about illnesses and treatments to more clearly and publically *oppose* one another at times? How do we understand illness and illness management in the context of cultural change in urban Ecuadorian settings? How do ethnic and/or social class identities shape the way people talk about and respond to illness in working class *barrios*, including their experience of biomedical institutions? We need to ask if urban Ecuadorian *mestizos* seem to be suffering the kind of economic and political eclipse, *vis-à-vis* indigenous groups, that is underway in Kachitu. An ongoing theme is the fate of medical pluralism in Andean settings. As Stoner pointed out, there exist a "multiplicity of healing techniques rather than of medical systems."[13]

Alternative healers in urban Ecuador draw on a great variety of healing elements and symbols, and each puts these together in a somewhat unique way. But how available are such healers, now, to urban dwellers? The three case studies presented below help answer these questions. But first, ethnicity and social class in Ecuador must be described. Libbet collected extensive *in situ* evidence that ethnic categories (e.g. Indian, *mestizo*) are not as straightforward as they are sometimes treated in the Andes, either by citizens or social scientists. The next section briefly echoes her labors by trying to sort out the tangle of significant racial, ethnic/cultural, and social class categories in cities like Quito.

Ethnic and social class identities in highland Ecuador

In 1981, Louisa Stark published an account of the complexities of ethnic labeling in highland Ecuador. Referential terms include: *runa* (Quichua term Indians use for themselves), *indigena* (Spanish term for Indian), *natural* (uncultured, uneducated), *cholo* (mix of Indian and *mestizo* attributes), *mestizo* (someone who speaks Spanish, dresses in non-indigenous style), *bien educado* (cultured, educated), *blanco* (white). The choice of term is connected in part with the primary language of the person referred to (Quichua or Spanish), their mode of dress, and level of education. However, the term also depends on who is speaking, to whom they are speaking, the amount of power/prestige and palanca (access to goods, services, and favors) wielded by the person spoken about, the situated social purposes of the speaker in that conversation, and whether the speaker is talking about him/herself, a family member, or someone else. For instance, a person described as *cholo* by people in a nearby town, may identify themselves or a family member as *blanco* – denying that they speak Quichua, and asserting that they are *bien educado*. As Stark notes, the term *educado* in Ecuador refers not just to formal schooling, but also to refined behavior and manners, fashionable clothing and housing, standard Spanish pronunciation, and some degree of access to national public life.[14]

Stark's findings foreshadow Libbet's conclusion in Kachitu, Bolivia, that ethnic and racial labels are a way of labeling social class (wealth, occupation, education) rather than genetic make-up or "blood."[15] In fact, the genetic mingling of European and New World populations in the Andes has been ongoing since the 1500s. All social groups show a mix of physical phenotypes (phenotypic variability is perhaps lowest in indigenous groups.)

In Ecuador, Stark found that people assign ethnic/racial terms most consistently for members of highest and lowest social classes. Elites are always called *blanco* because everyone understands that they have power and prestige and they themselves are not trying to change identity or status. Lower class groups are consistently labeled *runa*, or *indigena*, because they emphasize ethnic identity through appearance and language choices. By doing so, they can enjoy the benefits of ethnic solidarity, for example, traditional reciprocal exchanges of labor and goods and, more recently, indigenous political movements with growing clout.[16]

In the upwardly mobile middle group, ethnic terms and ethnic identities are much more volatile. (Note, this group encompasses the majority of the population, not just the 18 percent or so who are economically "middle class.") Middle groups wish to be identified with the social class above them, and often employ the same ethnic label for their own group as the one above, for example, *blanco* or *bien educado*. The latter term is particularly useful, since it denotes manners and dress rather than physical phenotype, and these are more easily manipulated and amenable to subjective interpretation. Upwardly mobile middle groups tend to clearly separate themselves from the groups below them by assigning distinctive ethnic/racial labels to these lower groups, for example, *natural*. This implies rigid social boundaries between middle and lower social groups (often not the case).

Mestizos comprise some 60–70 percent of Ecuador's population, with an even higher percentage in urban areas. Most *mestizos* have indigenous ancestors on one or both sides of their families. But the process of *mestizaje* (becoming *mestizo*) tends to submerge at least the most overt markers of Indian identity. Stutzman[17] described *mestizaje* in Ecuador as the exchange of ethnic identity for "nation-state identity." Decades ago, when Stutzman wrote about this process, maintaining ethnic identity could be interpreted as a kind of passive resistance to the national culture agenda. This situation has changed, however and indigenous political movements are gaining strength every year. In Ecuador, this began in the eastern lowlands with Amazonian Indian groups, but mobilization proceeded in the highlands as well during the 1980s and 1990s.[18] For instance, in both Quito and Riobamba (capital of Chimborazo province), indigenous movements mobilize attendance by 30,000 or more to protest government or private sector policies that violate indigenous interests.[19] But the government continues to prefer *blanqueamiento* (progressive "whitening" of population in culture and goals): programs to reduce ethnic distinctiveness persist, especially in the cities.

After the Spanish conquest, Ecuador experienced a *mescla de las razas* (mixing of races) especially in urban areas. In the official government view, those who migrate to cities tend to participate in this mixing and are forward-moving, while those who stay in the countryside (the majority of indigenous citizens) are primitive and stuck. As Stutzman notes, the national culture is stratified, urban, and "mixed" (*mestizo*). *mestizo* identity is based on assumption of shared descent; however, the way to affirm participation in the national mainstream is to become ethnically neutral. *mestizos* tend to think of themselves as educated, Catholic or Christian, perhaps as Ecuadorian, but they generally show distaste for the term *mestizo*. This term is used primarily by young people who learned it in school.[20] Terms that refer to indigenous identity are all pejorative, at least in some situations (e.g. *cholo* or *runa* can be insulting if a *mestizo* is talking about or to an Indian). As shown above, ethnic identity and ethnic labels in Ecuador are subjective, situationally variable, and subject to social negotiation. Most people try to avoid using explicit ethnic labels (perhaps because these terms mostly have a history of oppression and insult). In the marginal *barrios* of Quito, people typically identify themselves as Catholic and "poor." My household survey in Las Gradas[21] showed that only 15 percent of residents have a primarily indigenous cultural identity, while another 10 percent maintain some aspects of Indian identity but have switched to Spanish, and abandoned braids, full skirts, and felt hats. In the cities, many institutions discourage the use of Quichua and indigenous dress, and there are penalties for public presentation of the self as "Indian."[22] Formal education (one's own or that of one's children) is the most pervasive of these institutions. Furthermore, while Indians are somewhat insulated from *mestizo* contact in rural villages (especially women, who do not engage in seasonal labor outside the village as much as do men), they interact socially with *mestizos* a great deal in the cities: *mestizos* are their neighbors and landlords. Systems of *compadrazgo* (ritual co-parenthood) often pair indigenous couples with *mestizo* co-parents (who can usually confer more benefits). Urban Indians need to negotiate Spanish-speaking clinics and hospitals, government bureaucracies, and work settings.

Although they abandon many outward symbols of indigenous culture, urban dwellers often maintain ties to the countryside, *mi tierra* (my land, or my home). In this way, many *mestizos* covertly maintain aspects of indigenous identity. This identity is intimately bound up in continuing affiliation with a rural area where the person, or their parents, have ongoing family ties.[23] The tendency to compartmentalize identity into the "urban identity" and "rural identity" reinforces self-presentation as *mestizo* in the city setting. It also supports ongoing links to the countryside: people appear to feel more satisfied if their cultural identity is multidimensional, that is, includes both urban and rural components. This phenomenon helps explain the vigorous migrant associations that exist in many Andean cities,[24] and the dream many Quito residents have of week-end farming on small plots of land outside the city, especially in an area where they have relatives. As seen in the cases below, people often want to use indigenous remedies or healers, but they want to do so without sacrificing their cultural identities as *bien educado* and as good Catholics or Christians. Ongoing affiliation with healing traditions and resources of the countryside is a factor in the case of Umberto and Jorge, to whom we now return.

Fright illness in a privileged family

At the beginning of the chapter, I introduced Umberto and Jorge: these children suffered from vomiting, restless sleep, and diarrhea, but with no biomedical explanation. Theirs is an upper middle class family, living in a wealthy neighborhood in north Quito. It also is a relatively happy and closely knit extended family: their maternal grandmother lives upstairs, while their paternal grandmother lives just a few blocks away and has supper with the family everyday. The boys' parents are highly educated. Tomás has a medical degree and his wife has a Master's degree in public administration; both work as professionals. I first met the family on an all-day train excursion to Mount Cotopaxi, near Quito.

While both parents were born in Quito, the children's maternal grandmother comes from a small town, Cayambe, an hour or two from Quito. Since the grandmother's own mother was a midwife, as a child she learned about herbal remedies and traditional healing. Each time Umberto and Jorge suffer symptoms of *espanto*, and these persist, this grandmother becomes anxious and insistent. Discussing the situation with her daughter, she convinces her that the boys should be treated for *espanto*. But the boys' father, Dr. Tomás, resists a diagnosis of fright illness. To him, *espanto* belief and treatment represent superstition. Thus, treating

Plate 12.1 Espanto healer works to heal young patient.

his sons for this condition might identify his family as less than *bien educado*. The disagreement causes tension between the couple.

After weeks of resistance and biomedical tests,[25] the physician-father agrees to let the boys go through treatment for *espanto*. The healer conducts the ceremonies on Tuesday and Friday, the most auspicious days for healing *espanto*. The boys remove most of their clothing. First, she says the rosary and other prayers over them, blows alcohol over their bodies, and makes crosses with cologne on pulse points. Then, she uses eggs to confirm the diagnosis. The eggs are passed over the body, then broken into a glass of water. If the egg white and yolk are mixed together rather than separate, this is associated with *espanto*. The eggs are also thought to absorb some of the illness out of the body. After this, she "sweeps" their bodies with wild plants, again to absorb some of the illness. The grand mother often invites another older woman (a cousin) to attend the ceremony for moral support and consultation. After each ceremony, according to Dr. Tomás, all his sons' troublesome physical symptoms disappeared.

Illness management can reveal schisms, points of contradiction, and shifting alliances within the community. It also can reveal, or generate, schisms and alliances within extended families. To a lesser extent, illness management also involves a process of social alliance building and cultural identity negotiation in the *compadre* network, and between neighbors in Quito. While most sicknesses are handled in more or less routine ways, according to a standard model of fam- ily roles and responsibility,[26] some illnesses highlight issues of power and agency in the extended family group. Latent tensions between genders, generations, and in some families between competing cultural or social class identities, can come into play.

Gender opposition marks the management of Umberto's and Jorge's illness. After a period of uncertainty, the boys' mother supported the grandmother (her mother) in carrying out treatment for the "folk illness" of *espanto*. This united the two women in opposition to the dominant male, the *jefe* (head, authority) of the household. Dr. Tomás had access to prestige and resources through his profession as a physician, and had not viewed traditional healing in a positive light. In the five or so episodes of *espanto*, the boys' mother had typically taken a "wait- and-see" posture. But, over the course of several weeks, when symptoms continued and biomedical tests failed to yield a diagnosis, she joined her mother's side, at least sufficiently to pursue treatment. She then worked to persuade her husband to allow the curing ceremony.

In this situation, the negotiations around diagnosis and treatment empower the female over the male authority, because they reinforce the alliance between mother and daughter. Another important opposition here is that of generation. Inter-generational conflict is far less evident in Ecuador than in North America, even though (or because) both indigenous and *mestizo* extended families still very frequently share living space, labor, and other resources. There is a greater need to maintain solidarity and to resolve tensions that do arise. Tensions may arise from: sexual license of young women, especially if it results in unmarried pregnancy or divorce, excessive drinking of young men or use of drugs, "uneducated" cultural behaviors of older generations, expectations that parents-in-law have of their children's spouses, or, sometimes, outright rejection by parents-in-law. (In a case reported to me in 1998, an intelligent, pretty woman of thirty-five, mother of three, refused cancer treatment because her husband's parents rejected and disparaged her for having a child in her first marriage, and she could not count on her husband's loyalty in the situation.)

When their grandmother interprets Umberto's and Jorge's symptoms as *espanto*, she risks the family's identity as *bien educado*. As a physician, Dr. Tomás has a marked personal investment in "modern" approaches to health care, and in combating illness "superstitions." He experiences a great deal of ambivalence in finally consenting to the folk treatment, and family members are aware of this. Therefore, the children's grandmother often tells her son-in-law that he does not have the proper attitude of faith to be present at the ceremony; she makes him leave the room. This spatial strategy symbolically highlights the triumph of female over male, older over younger, and family/folk healing over biomedical intervention. Respect for the older generation is expressed as younger family members are persuaded to at least go along with the non-biomedical treatment.[27]

It is typically the case with middle class, educated *mestizo* families, that biomedical approaches are tried first. When biomedical tests fail to yield a satisfactory explanation, there is room to pursue the folk diagnoses and home-based healing. Pockets of resistance to biomedical hegemony in Ecuador often persist or thrive because of equivocal biomedical diagnosis and/or failed treatment. The older generation and females help preserve medical pluralism in Quito partly because it furthers their social standing in the extended family.

Since Precolumbian times, Ecuadorians have had a robust set of home remedies and healers. Specialists include *espanto/mal aire* healers, midwives, herbalists, bonesetters, spiritist healers, and for fifty or more years, pharmacists, nurses, physicians. During the past 15–20 years, commercially packaged natural medicines have become very popular in urban areas, sold retail in small stores identified with medicina natural (natural medicine).[28] Initial responses to illness are usually directed by a process of (extended) family discussion. The terms "self diagnosis" and "self medication" misrepresent these initial stages of illness management in South America. This process is typically profoundly social, as Crandon notes for Bolivia,[29] and the others and I describe in Ecuador.[30] Although some illness management decisions conform to decision-making structures identified by medical anthropologists, for example, hierarchy of resort,[31] and treatment decision models,[32] there are many exceptions. Two kinds of illnesses are likely to be treated on the household level: illnesses perceived as non-life-threatening for which some remedy is known, and illnesses that are defined culturally (e.g. *espanto*), especially if biomedical specialists do not acknowledge the condition as real. Therefore, if family members feel certain about a diagnosis of *espanto* or *mal aire*, the family usually seeks culturally appropriate treatment rather than biomedical assistance. Responses to culture-bound illnesses include: buying appropriate medicinal plants in the market (to make teas, or rub over the body), purchasing pharmaceutical drugs, family-directed rituals, attempts to find/ provide distraction, the patient's attempt at self-control, family support. If these efforts fail and symptoms persist, and especially if they get worse, specialist treatment will be sought.

As evident in the case of Umberto and Jorge described above, the household based healing of *espanto* does not take a long time or highly trained specialists; the healer is often part of the extended family and not a professional. More specialized *espanto* healers are available in the neighborhood and city level for more serious cases, or for people who do not have a practitioner in the family. According to my interviews, most *espanto* healers are women. An important gender difference exists here. Women have the most to gain from true medical pluralism. Female gender in Ecuador is very much tied into family illness management, especially but not only in the home. Females bear the burdens of nursing ill family members and making most of the forays into medical institutions on behalf of family members. Collective female responsibility is a common pattern: in talking about an illness, a mother will often say "we," including her mother, grandmother, aunt, or other adult female kin. As shown in my earlier work,[33] "many illness stories dramatically encode the affective [emotional] proposition that did the right thing ... the more caretaking responsibility a narrator has for the afflicted person, the more pronounced this affective message tends to be ... the 'I did the right thing' proposition appears in its most distilled and dramatic form in stories mothers tell about their children's illnesses." Women's roles in healing the family are reinforced and celebrated through alternative healing in a way that is not possible through biomedical healing. This is partly because biomedicine often dismisses the role of mothers in illness management, appropriating all credit for cure. In contrast, alternative healers often include the mother (or other family care giver) as critical to the outcome. Male family members tend to get more involved when decisions concern biomedical treatment. This often is very costly and men have a great deal of control over such expenses. Finally, it is women who usually have the social networks, time, and knowledge needed to secure alternative treatments. How illness management affects social alliance and cultural identity is further revealed in the case of a middle-aged woman, Sra. Elsa. Living in Las Gradas, she was married to a factory worker, and the mother of nine children.

Chronic, disabling illness in the mother of a family

Elsa was my neighbor in Las Gradas in the early 1980s, and was still living in the neighborhood in 2000. Las Gradas has existed as a *barrio* in Quito for about fifty years; its current population is about 30,000 people. Most residents are not newcomers to the city (the average *barrio* resident has lived in Quito for eight years). Although Las Gradas is not new, it continues to be marginal in economic and political terms. The *barrio* lacked water and transportation services in the 1980s, and while these now have been established in the lower part of the neighborhood, poverty, and underemployment persist. People remark on growing crime in the neighborhood (taxi drivers often warn me about the dangers, or refuse to drive there at all). Men typically work in small-scale cottage industries, or as day laborers. Some young women hold steady jobs (usually service jobs), but most women still work in the informal sector, selling "fast food" out their doors, or peddling some type of merchandise on the street to supplement family income. Extended family is the strongest component of social identity, but Las Gradans also identify themselves as Catholics, "poor people," and "Ecuadorians."

There is a strong pattern of reciprocal exchange between relatives, and sometimes friends/neighbors, in the *barrio*. For instance, extended family members and sometimes *compadres* (co-parents) look after one another's children, help with home remedies or healing ceremonies, accompany one another to consult specialists, loan each other tools, get together to add a second floor to a relative's home, and help construct festive street displays for the "Old Year" celebration. Sharing of food is not continual between households, but not unusual either, particularly when someone has visited the countryside or market and returns with a surplus of some item. The home is the woman's workplace and too many interruptions are frowned on, but visits to share food, information, or help are thought totally appropriate.[34] The importance of extended family bonds and reciprocity in working class Quito is reflected in the residential decisions people make, that is, over a quarter of the households are extended family units. Another 50 percent of households have relatives living in other households in the same *barrio*, that is, within walking distance.[35]

Late on New Year's eve, 1980, members of the Baez family were gathered on the street outside their home for traditional holiday observances with next door neighbors. Some sat on folding chairs inside the traditional *casita* (little house), which extended families build together for the event. Others were standing, taking turns toasting each other with small glasses of hot, spiced rum. Near midnight, a clown appeared, cracking jokes and dancing around with a whip. Everyone present was invited to beat the "Old Year" (a stuffed lifesize dummy) for good luck in the new year. Among the Baez family, however, the mood was one of tears and anger rather than lighthearted clowning. Sra. Elsa, that year, could not stand up unaided; nor could she even manage to hold the whip in her hand for the ritual observance.

The first signs of Elsa's illness appeared in 1977, following a miscarriage. Her legs began to shake and tremble and she suffered severe headaches, and increasing body weakness. Lack of mobility and strength meant increasing inability to carry out her role as mother of the household. Family members associated the illness with Sra. Elsa's miscarriages and *sobreparto* (postpartum weakness), not taking care of herself after pregnancy (e.g. not getting enough rest after childbirth, exposure to cold water in a "hot" state, conceiving another child too soon), her long-existing susceptibility to *iras* (irritability, anger, rage), and a big family fight near the time of the miscarriage. A neighbor pointed to Elsa's recreational activities, her noncompliance with prescribed medical treatments, and her lack of will to get better:

> She went to events like soccer games, outside [al aire] almost unclothed. To dances in that air, can you believe it?? And, on the second or third day after miscarrying [she did the same] ... One should take care of oneself. And the Sra. – note that in one month people say she had three miscarriages, in one month! That is, neither she nor her husband were taking care [of her health] to conceive again right away ... Elsa refuses to take her medicine because she doesn't want it. She's irresponsible. Doesn't it seem that way? If she were responsible, she would try to get better, strive to overcome it. The way I see it, overcoming things in order to keep the home together is the meaning of "mother." And she doesn't do any of that, no. So there it is. And that's why her family doesn't love her.

Larme and Leatherman note (this volume), that Andean women lose many workdays due to reproduction-related health problems. From a biological point of view, such problems are associated with a much higher average number of pregnancies (e.g. Sra. Elsa's miscarriage was her ninth pregnancy). In addition, high fertility takes its toll on the body, so women's morbidity rates are greater than in low-fertility nations. The ethnomedical view presents women as more vulnerable because of the way reproduction opens and weakens their bodies. Sra. Elsa's problems with weakness and balance were attributed to miscarrying, and to her experiences after giving birth. Specifically, she returned to work too soon especially doing laundry in cold water; she went outside at night, exposing herself to *mal aire* (evil air); she conceived too often (in her neighbor's opinion) and experienced too many pregnancies. Where this case differs from Larme and Leatherman, is that at least some individuals blamed the weakness and paralysis on Elsa's own choices, for example, going to a soccer game at night. She failed to claim the sick role, which would have secured family support and temporary respite from heavy labor in the household. Blaming Sra. Elsa for the affliction contrasts with Larme and Leatherman, who report that the husband is generally found responsible for the reproductive illnesses of his wife. Sra. Elsa's illness is not described as mainly her husband's fault by any of the four commentators.

Biomedical help was sought for Elsa early in her illness, consistent with *mestizo* identity. One doctor diagnosed severe arthritis, while another doctor diagnosed Parkinson's disease. The lack of agreement was very confusing to the family. Their frustration with the conflicting diagnoses was reflected in this statement by Sra. Elsa in 1981: "No tengo nada, nada, nada, nada no tengo." ("I don't have anything, anything, anything; I have nothing.")

Within a few months of the biomedical encounters, the family took Elsa to a *curandero* (healer) in El Placer. He diagnosed her problem as due to drinking milk and doing laundry in cold water (during/after pregnancy); this had led to liver damage. The healer prescribed hot medicinal baths. But, according to her daughter, Sra. Elsa insisted on getting up to work the next day while she was still *caliente* (hot): "Because of that, the Cold sat on her and the illness progressed."

Roughly one year later, Sra. Elsa's condition was still deteriorating. Her husband asked his factory for a loan so he could again consult a physician; this time he decided to find out if she was mentally ill (*loca de la cabeza*, or crazy in the head). This doctor told the family that Elsa was definitely not crazy ("*no tiene nada en la cabeza*"), but rather had *nervios*, yet a third biomedical diagnosis.

In 1978, Elsa's husband made her go to the public hospital for an electro-encephalogram (EEG, brain wave study). The family interpreted the testing procedure – attaching electrodes and running current – as a type of treatment to cure the *nervios*. They reported that her symptoms improved this time. However, Sra. Elsa left the hospital before she was supposed to, using money her husband left with her (a mistake on his part, their daughter complained). On arriving home, she announced that she would never go to the hospital again: "I left because it made me afraid ... they said they were sending me downstairs where there are other doctors, so I left." Elsa was afraid she would receive electroshock treatment in the basement of the hospital. Her husband confronted Elsa about her flight. He criticized her for leaving, insisting that the hospital would have made her better.

Within a half year or so, the family took Sra. Elsa to Sangolquí to consult with an alternative healer; she was there for a week. Treatment included vitamin B injections and what sounds like homemade electroshock therapy. Her daughter remembers: "They connected her to a big thing like a tape recorder ... it caught the current ... it extended the legs [twitching]." She believes that the treatment hurt her mother. But then she concludes: "What my mother lacks is bravery; after that, she didn't want to return there [for more treatment]." About this encounter, Elsa said: "They told me that I have to have perseverence (*fuerza de caracter*), but I can't, I can't. I don't know what's happening to me. I want to persevere, but I fall; my body defeats me."

The Baez family faced more medical tragedy in 1979. The events were forecast by a divination specialist they went to see in Tumbaco, another small town outside of Quito. Their neighbor, Mercedes, states that they consulted this healer because of experiences with the biomedical system, especially the doctors' failure to arrive at a clear diagnosis: "When physicians can't cure something, [we say] it's an illness of the Devil. The Devil has been set to work by some enemy that wants to disable them, for example the Sra... When the physician doesn't hit the mark, they go consult with these men who know about that other thing [*saben del mas alla*]."

Mercedes, herself, disclaimed this kind of treatment, emphasizing that she personally had never consulted a healer like this, but only heard about it secondhand. Also, Elsa and her family members avoided discussing this consultation in their long, detailed accounts of therapeutic activity. This kind of therapy is socially disapproved by many *mestizos*. Although they still seek it out in extreme and/or prolonged cases like Sra. Elsa, they try to avoid letting people know about it. This situation is the reverse of those that Libbet describes in Kachitu. That is, rather than building social alliance through choices of diagnosis and treatments, certain healer choices must be kept hidden in order to preserve social alliances and cultural identity.

The Tumbaco specialist was a diviner. He conducted a candlelit seance, a procedure that cost more than a typical doctor visit. His conclusion was that someone stole the Sra.'s underwear and put a spell on her. He forecast that either she or her oldest son would die within a year, and recommended that she undergo medicinal baths in Baños. In fact, within a year, the oldest son did die of cancer at the age of twenty-five. This caused great sadness and trauma in the family and was associated with increasing deterioration in Elsa's condition. Their next healing effort was a week-long trip to the medicinal baths in Baños; Elsa's sister, who lives in Riobamba nearby, came along to assist the family. Little improvement in symptoms was noted, however. A year later, Elsa and the other family members expressed a desire to go to Ipiales, Colombia. They believed this pilgrimage would help despite the failure of the earlier one to Baños. Maybe what they really wanted was a chance to get beyond blame during their quest for a "miracle." Unfortunately, the family failed to secure resources for this trip before Elsa's husband was killed in an accident.

Twenty years after onset, in 1999, Elsa could neither stand, walk, nor talk audibly. About three years ago, Elsa finally went for some more biomedical testing; at this time, she was diagnosed with Parkinson's disease. To have a definite diagnosis was a great relief to the family. However, it was considered too late for medications to alleviate the symptoms. Elsa has been cared for at home during this entire period, first by her daughter Rosa during her late teens and early twenties, and during the past six years or so by her last daughter, Josefina (born two years after Elsa's illness began). Though incapable of speaking, she is carried to major family events, such as her granddaughter's baptism celebration in summer, 1999, and seems to enjoy herself at these.

Illness management in Sra. Elsa's case was complicated by four factors. First, whenever the mother in a household falls seriously or permanently ill, the situation contradicts the standard cultural model of family roles. In Ecuador, the mother of the family is supposed to do everything to help family members who get sick, but not fall sick herself, at least not for very long. When a woman comes down with a chronic incapacitating illness, a "rude awakening" occurs.[36] Like Sra. Elsa, many women with chronic incapacitating conditions may suffer accusations of "irresponsibility" or cowardice in claiming the sick role for an extended period. This complicates both medical and psychosocial management of chronic illness among women.

Second, blame is especially likely when *nervios* or *las iras* are pinpointed as contributing to the illness, as happened with Elsa. With both conditions, the people believe the patient has some responsibility for controlling the disease process. For instance, one informant stated: "[With *nervios*] you have to get yourself out of the house and distract yourself, because in the house, problems concentrate in your nervous system." Another informant discusses *las iras*: "You, yourself, have to control yourself ... If you don't, you can die of *las iras* which lead to *colerin* ... like my father-in-law, who died of *las iras* at sixty." For both *nervios* and *iras/colerin*, the patient is viewed as partly responsible if the affliction becomes chronic.

Third, Elsa and her husband were a strong couple before the illness, having more fun together than average. With nine children, the family was large and close knit. They ignored certain behavioral conventions in the *barrio*, and put less time than average into cementing social alliances with *compadres* and others outside the family (though still having many *compadres* due to nine offspring). Perhaps this explains why some family members and friends held Elsa herself to blame for the paralysis and inability to do household work. Although Elsa greatly resented the idea that she caused her own disability, she needed a solid biomedical diagnosis to effectively counter those who blamed her. But doctors were unable to deliver this firm diagnosis twenty years ago, and this increased Elsa's suffering considerably.

Finally, because Elsa was herself disabled, her husband took an active role in seeking therapy. He solicited advice from many relatives and friends. He arranged the initial medical exams, and, later, the EEG and mental illness exam. He believed in the biomedical system as a way to explain his wife's condition. Had a woman rather than a man been managing the illness, there would possibly have been fewer biomedical visits. Men are more socialized to use modern health care because their jobs often include access to biomedical attention. Additionally, men are less likely to hear stories and other kinds of conversation about non-biomedical healing resources. So they often turn to what is most obvious and most prestigious: doctors, clinics, hospitals.

Unfortunately, physicians disagreed with one another about Elsa's diagnosis and this undermined the family's confidence. In working class populations, people tend to have little patience with drawn-out diagnostic procedures, batteries of lab tests, and trial-and-error approaches to diagnosis and treatment. However, these are all quite common in biomedical management of serious disease. Plus, nurses and doctors did not adequately communicate with Elsa about what they planned to do to her in the hospital: she felt justified in trying to escape what she thought would be painful electroshock therapy.

How important was medical pluralism in this case? In addition to home remedies (especially early in the illness), ethnomedical healing included: herbal baths and spinal manipulation, pharmaceutical injections, divination, pilgrimage to hot baths, homemade electroshock therapy. Most of these options entailed the family traveling outside of Quito. I have found this pattern to be very common. When needed, Quito residents find out how to contact folk healers in nearby locales such as Tumbaco, Chillogallo, Machachi, Ilumán, and Sangolquí, or more distant locales near Latacunga, Ambato, Riobamba, Baños, and Santo Domingo de los Colorados. Patients and their families can reach these destinations in a one-to-three hour bus trip. In some circumstances, the distance may be seen as an advantage, preserving the family's privacy.

Medical pluralism was not an unmitigated boon to the Baez family. By putting Elsa through the homemade electroshock therapy in Sangolqui, the family was (perhaps unconsciously) testing whether she was really malingering. It was a punishing therapy, and reinforced the family's conviction that Elsa lacked "character," because she did not want to comply. Pilgrimage to medicinal baths was an appealing option and the most likely to promote family well being. First, it involved the family in visiting Elsa's sister who lived in another city, thus securing some additional extended family support. Second, it was an experience that Elsa herself could endorse, one that she knew would not cause her undue pain. Finally, pilgrimage served as a public statement of Catholic faith. This the family very much needed in order to counter stigma associated with their neighborhood reputation as "non church goers" and as "people who consult diviners." While medical pluralism can threaten social alliances, for example, consulting diviners, in other circumstances it offers a way to strengthen social bonds. The next case also demonstrates this principle.

Spiritist healing of a crippled child

Susana was a six-year-old who was getting progressively more crippled; I described this case previously[37] but examine it here from a new angle, more explicitly examining medical pluralism and social alliance. Susana's family had lived in Las Gradas about four years at the time of this case study. Susana was the fourth of Maria and Leo's five children. The family was better off economically than the majority of families in the *barrio*. Leo drove his own bus, and the family owned its home in Las Gradas, directly across the stairs from mine. After a while, I became Leo and Maria's *comadre*, and also lived with the family for some months; I thus became very familiar with Susana's situation and their healing efforts. Leo and Maria owned a small mud-walled hut next door, which they rented for extra income. At one point, Maria described the renting family as *medio natural* ("half natural," meaning, "only half civilized" or "Indian"), clearly distinguishing her own cultural identity from theirs. However, she was kind to them, and the interaction constituted a type of patron–client relationship.

Although she distinguished herself emphatically from these Quichua-speaking tenants, Maria's parents lived on a farm and still had a thatched mud hut in addition to a newer block house. Maria's mother wore braids and a kind of *pollera* (full skirt, identified with transitional indigenous identity). Thus, Maria typifies the upwardly mobile middle group in the Andes described by Stark,[38] whose members wish to identify closely with socioeconomic groups above them, while highlighting the distance between themselves and the groups below.

Susana's hip malformation problems began when she was about one, shortly after hospitalization for acute intestinal infection. Maria believed that biomedical treatment caused her daughter's deformity, that is, the hospital injections. Later, when Maria consulted a physician about the child's crippling, he emphatically told her that no cure was possible, that Susana would always be an invalid. The notion of "chronic illness" tends to be uncongenial to people raised in ethnomedical traditions. The doctor's pronouncement was so discouraging that the family stopped seeking treatment for a time.

But then Leo's father died, and the family moved to Quito, into the house his natal family had occupied. Now nearby, Leo's mother pushed Maria and Leo to take Susana to see a surgeon at the public children's hospital, and finally they did so. Physicians operated on both legs. This was followed by casts and then daily rehabilitation sessions. The surgery went well, but after the casts came off, Susana continued to have trouble walking. In addition, rehabilitation therapists criticized Maria for the remedies she was trying at home. For instance, one told her: "'Senora, if you want your daughter to get well, you should not interfere, you should *not* massage her leg.' I said to her, 'Senorita, I [Maria] want to help her, too!!' She [the therapist] said, '*No*, that's what *we're* for!' And that was it." Hospital staff also criticized Maria's use of tonics and unguents to strengthen her daughter's legs (common Ecuadorian remedies for bone/muscle problems).

Susana's legs improved but some disability persisted. It was Leo who discovered Sister Clemencia, a Colombian spiritist healer who visited Quito every few months, holding free clinics for the poor. Sister Clemencia had received her powers through association with a famous deceased Venezuelan healer named Brother Gregorio.[39] Maria was skeptical at first, but then during the consultation her attitude changed: she was moved by the healer's extensive Catholic symbolism and her insistence on providing treatment free of charge. Sister Clemencia diagnosed Susana's problem as *mal operado* (badly operated-on). She told Maria to massage Susana's legs with unguent and say the rosary at a home altar. These activities seemed to improve Susana's condition. After several weeks, Maria decided to go to Pasto, Colombia, to consult Clemencia at her home. She and Susana slept in the chapel next door; Maria had a dream in which she encountered Brother Gregorio. She decided to continue her daughter's treatment with a psychic operation back in Quito. The operation would take place on a designated day in several months. On the designated night, family members perceived windows opening and heard unusual sounds, indicating the healer's presence in the home. Maria recounted these events and sums up her personal, psychological transformation with the words: "From then on, my faith keeps growing. And now, I have tremendous faith indeed."

It is remarkable that Leo and Maria ever considered hospital surgery, after concluding that doctors had caused Susana's paralysis to start with. However, they did avoid biomedical specialists for several years. Leo's family was from a higher economic stratum than Maria's family, and Leo's mother believed very strongly in doctors and hospitals. By pushing the couple to pursue surgery, Leo's mother was asserting her status as a senior therapy manager in the family and asserting her influence over her daughter-in-law. This dynamic was partly due to Maria and Leo's geographic move, which brought them more into the sphere of influence of Leo's family.

Maria and Leo's interactions with biomedical practitioners were not uniformly negative. However, when hospital rehabilitation specialists criticized Maria for participating in Susana's treatment, they alienated her. After several encounters in which practitioners asserted biomedical hegemony and invalidated family-based healing, Maria was open to other healing options. Clemencia was appealing because she celebrated, even expanded, Maria's participation in illness management.

The primary sociocultural benefit of consulting Sister Clemencia was to reinforce the family's cultural identity as devoted Catholics. They, and their neighbors, put this spiritist-based treatment in the category of Catholic miracle. Social class enters into this picture. It was partly because of Leo and Maria's financial standing that they could consult Sister Clemencia without receiving the kind of criticism directed at the Baez family. There is also a difference in symbolism used by the two healers – Sister Clemencia had a Catholic chapel next to her home and used many Catholic symbols and prayers, whereas the diviner consulted by the Baez family did not.

Turning to Clemencia for aid strengthened the bond between Maria and Leo and reinforced their identity as "Catholics." It also re-balanced power relations in the extended family, by countering the dominance Leo's mother asserted when she insisted on surgery for Susana. And, consulting Sister Clemencia did not entail giving up the desired cultural/social class identity of *bien educado*: Catholic-based miracle cures are not disparaged, as are those of diviners or certain other healers. As seen by the Andean poor, by treating patients without charge, alternative healers like Clemencia embody Christian ideology, and live out Jesus' commandments about how to treat the poor. Leo and Maria experienced Susana's recovered ability to walk as their own miracle. (As I observed, she was in fact able to walk almost normally after this treatment sequence.) I do not believe they used this newly affirmed identity to secure any secondary resources in the neighborhood (neither was particularly active in the local church), but collaboration in seeking treatment from Sister Clemencia did strengthen their marital bond for a time.

Discussion and conclusion

Libbet Crandon-Malamud raised very interesting questions about medical pluralism in the Andes, questions that anthropologists will go on exploring and trying to answer for decades. I explore possible parallels between the situation Libbet describes in Kachitu, and that of residents in urban Ecuador, that is, do *mestizos* use certain diagnostic and treatment choices to secure other resources, to build social alliances, or to affirm or change cultural identity? In Quito, it appears that *mestizos* rarely use medical choices as the means to other primary resources. Unlike Kachitu, in Quito, *mestizos* are in the vast majority; and in Ecuador, they continue to wield power both economically and politically. Whereas in Kachitu some *mestizos* now publically endorse indigenous illness concepts and treatments to build alliances with resource-rich Indians, in Quito, *mestizos* usually do not have a great deal to gain from their indigenous friends and neighbors. The flow of resources is more often from *mestizo* to Indian, through formal institutions of *compadrazgo*, and informal institutions of landlord-to-tenant patronage. In many circumstances, social advantage still exists in maintaining a supercilious attitude toward indigenous practices, in order to present one's cultural identity as *bien educado*. *mestizos* may decide to consult Indian healers, especially in desperate or prolonged illnesses. But, depending on the healer, they may keep it quiet.

Ecuadorian *mestizos* do use diagnosis and therapy choices to build social alliances and negotiate cultural identity. This is more visible in the extended family than between "ethnic" (i.e. social class) groups as in Kachitu.[40] In the case of Umberto and Jorge, the children's mother and grandmother reaffirm their bond through collaborating in the diagnosis of *espanto*. This bond was cemented in carrying out home treatments for *espanto*, from which the boys' father was excluded. In the case of Sra. Elsa, consultation with a diviner outside the city was downplayed or concealed to maintain a cultural identity as *educado*, and to preserve alliances with neighbors who frown on such practices. In the case of Susana, husband and wife revitalized their bond by seeking help from Sister Clemencia. Leo and Maria's cultural identity as "Catholic" also was celebrated and enlarged during the course of this treatment. However, this alternative cultural identity did not interfere with the social class identity they preferred, *bien educado*. Access to medical pluralism allowed Susana's parents to counter the power asserted earlier by the grandmother, who pushed for biomedical treatment and looked down on alternative healers.

A second question raised here concerns gender and healing. While generally implicit rather than explicit in Libbet's analysis, her framework lends itself to an examination of how gender affects illness management. She says: "The fundamental issue under negotiation concerned the power to monopolize the construction of the meaning of the illness and hence to define the relationship between the parties engaged in the dialogue."[41] Umberto and Jorge's *espanto* shows how women in an extended family become more closely allied by insisting on alternative (non-biomedical) diagnosis and treatment. A secondary gain is to reassert the importance of the female role in family illness management. *Espanto* healers are almost all women and it is women in the family who usually have the knowledge and connections to diagnose *espanto* and locate an appropriate healer. Two of these cases show the role of the grandmother as crucially important. Their grandchildren's illnesses presented the opportunity to assert their roles as family health monitors and managers. In both cases, their own children sided with them (at least temporarily), causing some tension with the spouse. Home treatment of *espanto* asserted the importance of folk definitions of illness, and also of female-directed, home-based healing, in opposition to biomedical definitions of reality.

Another secondary gain for women, derived from traditions of medical pluralism, is the experience of freedom. In the everyday world, a wife and mother like

Maria could no more travel nine hours on a bus to Colombia with her daughter and a female friend than she could fly. However, to consult a healer this journey was approved of, and in fact, supported by Maria's husband.

Gender roles are important in a different way in Sra. Elsa's case. It is her gender and her role as mother of the family that make especially problematic the lack of a firm biomedical diagnosis. Lack of diagnosis opened the door to "blaming the victim" to a greater extent than would have happened were the patient a man or a child. The blaming attitude can account for some of the punishing "treatments" described above.

A third question concerns illness beliefs as metaphor. Specifically, we might ask why are emotion-based illnesses so common among Ecuadorian *mestizos*? Why these particular illnesses (e.g. *espanto*, *iras*, and *nervios*) rather than more personalized sickness agents? *mestizos* worry more about controlling their emotions and maintaining smooth social interaction than about external oppressors. Urban *mestizos* are not as anxious about being sucked dry by greedy, demanding landlords, as they are about experiencing emotional tidal waves that might overcome them. When personal well being is so tied to extended family cooperation and support, emotional upset can lead to asocial or antisocial behaviors that are believed to sabotage an individual's opportunities, satisfaction, and security in life.

In summary, medical discourse and therapy management are laden with complex social meanings among *mestizo* residents of Ecuador, just as elsewhere in the Andes. Medical decisions are a way to affirm, or sometimes change, cultural identity and negotiate extended family and neighborhood alliances. Medical actions in these three cases reinforce identities of various types. In all cases, management was at least partly biomedical. This identified the families as *bien educado* (cultured, *mestizo*) rather than indigenous, since either money or influence is needed to obtain biomedical treatment. However, experiences with biomedical institutions often were not very satisfying, seeming to undermine the confidence of patients and their families, and at times drive them to seek alternative healers, for example, the Baez family and Susana's parents. But even if biomedical institutions were more accommodating and trustworthy, medical pluralism would survive – it meets important needs, both socially and psychologically. Socially, it provides the means to build alliances within and sometimes between extended families. Psychologically, it contrasts with biomedical treatment in providing patients with more hope (often accompanied by real physical improvements), and in providing caretakers with more affirmation of their efforts to help the patient and manage the illness. Although medical pluralism offers benefits to both men and women, on balance, my analysis suggests that women derive the greater benefit.

In Ecuador, medical pluralism is in flux. Although there are specialists to treat *espanto* and *mal aire*, *parteras* (midwives) are certainly much less available in *barrios* like Las Gradas than they were in the early 1980s. And people often have to journey to the outskirts of Quito to consult alternative healers (e.g. the Baez family went to Tumbaco and Sangolquí). In Quito and other Andean cities, *naturistas* (practitioners of natural medicine) are moving in to fill the gap between the need for alternative therapies and the resources available, with shops that market commercially packaged herbal remedies, superficially based on scientific medicine. However, some of my (*mestizo*) informants report disappointing or even frightening experiences with the treatments they purchased at these shops.

Diagnosis has become more contested. Whereas previously a family-based diagnosis of *espanto* or *colerín* or *nervios* would not be disputed, now some people (not just physicians, but working class informants as well) dismiss such culture-bound syndromes as "superstition." This can cause a struggle in the family over interpretation of symptoms and treatment choices. When urban dwellers make certain therapy choices, they may do so at the expense of their reputation. As with the Baez family, neighbors may gossip about those who consult alternative healers, characterizing them as backward, lower social class, or morally suspect for exploring spirit-based healing. Such criticism is a thinly veiled indictment of indigenous mysticism, as one of the forces that helped shape the modern non-biomedical treatment modalities. In negotiating such therapies, *mestizo* families experience fewer problems if they highlight the Catholic and Christian character of both healer and treatment. But such an assertion works best, as seen in Susana's case, when the family has relatively high social and economic status. Without doubt, socioeconomic factors intersect with cultural identity in the decisions that are made concerning management of illness in *mestizo* urban families. The key factor, however, is negotiation over power and agency in the extended family group. Though rarely acknowledged in studies of formal treatment decision models, in prolonged cases of illness this process often leads to switches in the family member/s who take the lead in managing an illness and, at times, to surprising shifts in the therapies chosen.

Notes

1 All names in this article are pseudonyms.
2 Bastien, Joseph, *Drum and Stethoscope*, University of Utah Press, 1992; Hess, Carmen G., *Enfermedad y moralidad en los Andes Ecuatorianos*. In Salud y Antropologia (*Ediciones* Abya-Yala, 1994), Monograph 29, pp. 47–89; Rubel, Arthur J., O'Nell, Carl W., and Collado, Rolando-Ardón, *Susto: A Folk Illness*, University of California Press, 1984); Stevenson, I. Neill, "*Colerina*: reactions to emotional stress in the Peruvian Andes," *Social Science and Medicine*, 1977, 11: 303–7; Tousignant, Michel, "'Pena' in the Ecuadorian Sierra: A pycho-anthropological analysis of sadness," *Culture, Medicine, and Psychiatry*, 1984, 8: 181–98.
3 McKee, Lauris, "Ethnomedical treatment of children's diarrheal illnesses in the highlands of Ecuador," *Social Science and Medicine*, 1987, 25: 1147–55.
4 Hess, Carmen G., *Enfermedad y moralidad*, p. 71, this author's translation.
5 Crandon-Malamud, Libbet, "Between shamans, doctors and demons: Illness, curing, and cultural identity midst culture change." In *Third World Medicine and Social Change*, John Morgan (ed.), University Press of America, 1983, pp. 69–79; Crandon-Malamud, Libbet, "Changing times and changing symptoms: the effects of modernization on *Mestizo* medicine in rural Bolivia (The case of two sisters)," *Medical Anthropology*, 1989, 10: 255–64; Crandon-Malamud, Libbet, *From the Fat of Our Souls: Social*

Change, Political Process, and Medical Pluralism in Bolivia, University of California Press, 1991*a*; Crandon-Malamud, Libbet, "Phantoms and physicians: social change through medical pluralism." In *The Anthropology of Medicine: From Culture to Method*, Lola Romanucci-Ross, Daniel E. Moerman, and Laurence R. Tancredi (eds), Bergin and Garvey Publishers, 1991*b*, pp. 85–112; Price, Laurie J., *Coping with Illness: Cognitive Models and Conversation in a Marginal Ecuadorian Barrio*, PhD Dissertation, Department of Anthropology, University of North Carolina at Chapel Hill, University Microfilms International, 1986; Price, Laurie J., "Ecuadorian illness stories: cultural knowledge in natural discourse." In *Cultural Models in Language and Thought*, Dorothy Holland and Naomi Quinn (eds), Cambridge University Press, 1987, pp. 314–42; Price, Laurie J., "Life stories of the terminally ill: anthropologic and therapeutic paradigms," *Human Organization*, 1995, 54(4): 462–9.

6 See Baer, this volume; Baer, Hans A., Merrill Singer, and Ida Susser, *Medical Anthropology and the World System: A Critical Perspective*, Bergin and Garvey Pub. 1997.

7 Carey, James, "Distribution of culture-bound illnesses in the southern Peruvian Andes," *Medical Anthropology Quarterly*, 1993, 7(3): 281–300.

8 Crandon, *From the Fat of Our Souls*; Crandon, "Phantoms and physicians."

9 Price, Laurie J., "In the shadow of biomedicine: self medication in two Ecuadorian pharmacies," *Social Science and Medicine*, 1989, 28(9): 905–15; Price, Laurie J., "Metalogue on coping with illness: cases from Ecuador," *Qualitative Health Research*, 1992 2(2): 135–58.

10 Price, "Coping with illness," p. 132.

11 Price, "Metalogue on coping with illness."

12 See Young, James Clay and Linda C. Garro, *Medical Choice in a Mexican Village*, Waveland Press, 1981.

13 Stoner, Bradley P., "Understanding medical systems: traditional, modern, and syncretic health care alternatives in medically pluralistic societies," *Medical Anthropology Quarterly*, 1986, 17(2): 47.

14 Stark, Louisa R., "Folk models of stratification and ethnicity in the highlands of northern Ecuador." In *Cultural Transformations and Ethnicity in Modern Ecuador*, Norman E. Whitten Jr. (ed.), University of Illinois, 1981, pp. 387–401.

15 Crandon-Malamud, *From the Fat of Our Souls*.

16 Meisch, Lynn A., "'We will not dance on the tomb of our grandparents': 500 years of resistance in Ecuador," *The Latin American Anthropology*, 1992, 4(2): 55–74.

17 Stutzman, Ronald, "*El Mestizaje*: an all-inclusive ideology of exclusion." In *Cultural Transformations and Ethnicity in Modern Ecuador*, Norman E. Whitten Jr. (ed.), University of Illinois, 1981, pp. 45–94.

18 Meisch, "We will not dance."

19 *Universo* 10/8/98.

20 Stutzman, "*El Mestizaje*."

21 Price, "Coping with illness."

22 The exception to this is when a young person enrolled in university maintains indigenous dress. I have heard middle class Ecuadorians speak admiringly of this combination of higher education and Indian appearance.

23 Price, "Coping with Illness," p. 93.

24 See, for example, Doughty, Paul, *Life goes on: Revisiting Lima's Migrant Associations. Migrants, Regional Identities and Latin American Cities*. Teofilo Altamirano and Lane Ryo Hirabayashi (eds), Society for Latin American Anthropologoy Publication Series, American Anthropological Association, 1997, 13, pp. 67–96.

25 Tests conducted included: white blood cell counts, fecal tests for bacteria, and amoebas, urine cultures, hepatitis tests.

26 See Price, "Ecuadorian illness stories."

27 I became aware of a new development in this case during summer 2000. It seems that, this past year, Dr. Tomás' own mother came down with the symptoms of *espanto*. Biomedical tests showed nothing. *Espanto* treatment was carried out by his mother-in-law. This time, Tomás was present for the procedure. His attitude toward *espanto* treatment, and toward ethnomedicine in general, now seems more open and positive than in years past.

28 Miles, Ann, "Science, nature, and tradition: the mass-marketing of natural medicine in urban Ecuador," *Medical Anthropology Quarterly*, 1998, 12(2): 206–25.

29 Crandon, *From the Fat of Our Souls*.

30 Finerman, Ruthbeth, "Experience and expectation: conflict and change in traditional family health care among the Quichua of Saraguro," *Social Science and Medicine*, 1983, 17(7): 1291–98; Finerman, Ruthbeth, "The forgotten healers: women as family healers in an Andean Indian community." In *Women as Healers: Cross Cultural Perspectives*, Carol Shepard McClain (ed.), Rutgers University Press, 1989, pp. 24–41; Price, "In the shadow of biomedicine."

31 Romanucci-Ross, Lola, "The hierarchy of resort in curative practices: the Admiralty Islands, Melanesia," *Journal of Health and Social Behavior*, 1969, 10: 201–9.

32 Garro, Linda C., "On the rationality of decision-making studies: Part 1. Decision models of treatment choice," *Medical Anthropology Quarterly*, 1998, 12(3): 319–40; Young and Garro, *Medical Choice in a Mexican Village*.

33 Price, "Ecuadorian illness stories," p. 330.

34 Price, "Coping with illness," p. 96.

35 Price, "Coping with illness," p. 98.

36 As McKee has pointed out for rural Ecuador, women's labor is often invisible and underestimated, both officially and informally in the family. See Lauris McKee, "Women's work in rural Ecuador: multiple resource strategies and the gendered division of labor." In *Women and Economic Change: Andean Perspectives*, Ann Miles and Hans Buechler (eds), Society for Latin American Anthropology Special Publication, 1997, 14: 13–30.

37 Price, "Ecuadorian illness stories"; Price, "Metalogue on coping with illness."

38 Stark, "Folk models of stratification and ethnicity."

39 See Taussig, Michael, *Shamanism, Colonialism, and the Wild Man: A Study in Terror and Healing*, University of Chicago Press, 1987.

40 Crandon, *From the Fat of our Souls*.

41 Crandon, "Phantoms and physicians," p. 88.

References

Baer, Hans A., Merrill Singer, and Ida Susser, *Medical Anthropology and the World System: A Critical Perspective*, Bergin and Garvey Pub., 1997.

Bastien, Joseph, *Drum and Stethoscope*, University of Utah Press, 1992.

Carey, James, "Distribution of culture-bound illnesses in the southern Peruvian Andes," *Medical Anthropology Quarterly*, 1993, 7(3): 281–300.

Crandon-Malamud, Libbet, "Between shamans, doctors and demons: illness, curing, and cultural identity midst culture change." In *Third World Medicine and Social Change*, John Morgan (ed.), University Press of America, 1983, pp. 69–79.

——, "Changing times and changing symptoms: the effects of modernization on *Mestizo* medicine in rural Bolivia (The case of two sisters)," *Medical Anthropology*, 1989, 10: 255–64.

——, *From the Fat of Our Souls: Social Change, Political Process, and Medical Pluralism in Bolivia*, University of California Press, 1991*a*.

Crandon-Malamud, Libbet, "Phantoms and physicians: social change through medical pluralism." In *The Anthropology of Medicine: From Culture to Method*, Lola Romanucci-Ross, Daniel E. Moerman, and Laurence R. Tancredi (eds), Bergin and Garvey Publishers, 1991*b*, pp. 85–112.

Doughty, Paul, *Life Goes On: Revisiting Lima's Migrant Associations. Migrants, Regional Identities and Latin American Cities*, Teofilo Altamirano and Lane Ryo Hirabayashi (eds), Society for Latin American Anthropologoy Publication Series, American Anthropological Association, 1997, 13: 67–96.

Finerman, Ruthbeth, "Experience and expectation: conflict and change in traditional family health care among the Quichua of Saraguro," *Social Science and Medicine*, 1983, 17(7): 1291–8.

——, "The forgotten healers: women as family healers in an Andean Indian community." In *Women as Healers: Cross Cultural Perspectives*, Carol Shepard McClain (ed.), Rutgers University Press, 1989, pp. 24–41.

Garro, Linda C., "On the rationality of decision-making studies: Part 1. Decision models of treatment choice," *Medical Anthropology Quarterly*, 1998, 12(3): 319–40.

Hess, Carmen G., "Enfermedad y moralidad en los Andes Ecuatorianos." In *Salud y Antropologia* (Ediciones Abya-Yala, 1994), Monograph 29, pp. 47–89.

McKee, Lauris, "Folk models of stratification and ethnicity in the highlands of Northern Ecuador." In *Cultural Transformations and Ethnicity in Modern Ecuador*, Norman E. Whitten Jr. (ed.), University of Illinois, 1981, pp. 387–401.

——, "Ethnomedical treatment of children's diarrheal illnesses in the highlands of Ecuador," *Social Science and Medicine*, 1987, 25: 1147–55.

——, "Women's work in rural Ecuador: multiple resource strategies and the gendered division of labor." In *Women and Economic Change: Andean Perspectives*, Ann Miles and Hans Buechler (eds), Society for Latin American Anthropology Special Publication, 1997, 14; 13–30.

Meisch, Lynn A., "'We will not dance on the tomb of our grandparents': 500 years of resistance in Ecuador," *The Latin American Anthropology*, 1992, 4(2): 55–74.

Miles, Ann, "Science, nature, and tradition: the mass-marketing of natural medicine in urban Ecuador," *Medical Anthropology Quarterly*, 1998, 12(2): 206–25.

Price, Laurie J., "Coping with Illness: cognitive models and conversation in a marginal Ecuadorian *barrio*," PhD. Dissertation, Department of Anthropology, University of North Carolina at Chapel Hill, University Microfilms International, 1986.

——, "Ecuadorian illness stories: cultural knowledge in natural discourse." In *Cultural Models in Language and Thought*, Dorothy Holland and Naomi Quinn (eds), Cambridge University Press, 1987, pp. 314–42.

——, "In the shadow of biomedicine: self medication in two Ecuadorian pharmacies," *Social Science and Medicine*, 1989, 28(9): 905–15.

——, "Metalogue on coping with illness: cases from Ecuador," *Qualitative Health Research*, 1992, 2(2): 135–58.

——, "Life stories of the terminally ill: anthropologic and therapeutic paradigms," *Human Organization*, 1995, 54(4): 462–9.

Romanucci-Ross, Lola, "The hierarchy of resort in curative practices: the Admiralty Islands, Melanesia," *Journal of Health and Social Behavior*, 1969, 10: 201–9.

Rubel, Arthur J., O'Nell, Carl W., and Collado-Ardón, Rolando, *Susto: A Folk Illness*, University of California Press, 1984.

Stark, Louisa R., "Folk models of stratification and ethnicity in the highlands of northern Ecuador," In *Cultural Transformations and Ethnicity in Modern Ecuador*, Norman E. Whitten Jr. (ed.), University of Illinois, 1981, pp. 387–401.

Stevenson, I. Neill, "Colerina: reactions to emotional stress in the Peruvian Andes," *Social Science and Medicine*, 1977, 11: 303–7.

Stoner, Bradley P., "Understanding medical systems: traditional, modern, and syncretic health care alternatives in medically pluralistic societies," *Medical Anthropology Quarterly*, 1986, 17(2): 44–8.

Stutzman, Ronald, "El Mestizaje: an all-inclusive ideology of exclusion." In *Cultural Transformations and Ethnicity in Modern Ecuador*, Norman E. Whitten Jr. (ed.), University of Illinois, 1981, pp. 45–94.

Taussig, Michael, *Shamanism, Colonialism, and the Wild Man: A Study in Terror and Healing*, University of Chicago Press, 1987.

Tousignant, Michel, "'Pena' in the Ecuadorian sierra: a psycho-anthropological analysis of sadness," *Culture, Medicine, and Psychiatry*, 1984, 8: 181–98.

Weismantel, Mary J., "Time, work-discipline, and beans: indigenous self-determination in the Northern Andes." In *Women and Economic Change: Andean Perspectives*, Ann Miles and Hans Buechler (eds), Society for Latin American Anthropology Special Publication, 1997, 14: 31–54.

Young, James Clay and Linda C. Garro, *Medical Choice in a Mexican Village*, Waveland Press, 1981.

Chapter 13

Anthropology and Shamanism

Bottom-line considerations in image and practice

Bonnie Glass-Coffin

It is July of 2000 and I am once again in Trujillo. This time, I march in the Plaza and carry the Standard for my Peruvian high school. The announcer bellows as we pass the Tribunal. Twenty-five years since the "gringa" exchange student first traveled to Trujillo and first wore the school uniform.

Since 1975, I have returned to Trujillo again and again – 1982, 1984, 1987, 1988–89, 1996, 1998, 2000. So many images of Trujillo crowd my consciousness that I can barely remember the beginning – before I learned the language, before I became part of a family, before Peru began to shape who I am. But, I remember all the anguish of that first departure. Wrenched away from a new-found identity, leaving was almost unbearable.

During the first several returns, I kept searching for myself reflected in the barren landscape. More recently, I have come to realize how much I stand in two places – a part of Peru and yet a being apart. An identity infused with so much experience, so much belonging and yet so much at the margins. The most recent returns have brought me back, again to myself.

Introduction

Among Libbet Crandon-Malamud's most significant contributions to the study of medical anthropology was the assertion that there exists a dialectical relationship between social and medical processes in societies where medical pluralism is practiced.[1] In the highland Bolivian village that was the focus of her most complete work, asymmetrical social and political relations between *mestizos* and Aymara Indians are not just passively reflected in differing strategies of health-seeking behavior. Instead, medical metaphors are actively appropriated to restructure social relations.[2] Health decision-making behavior is revealed through Crandon-Malamud's research to be *more* than Rational Man looking for medical efficacy.[3] It is also revealed to be the means by which people actively negotiate both their personal identities and their membership in social groups.

As Crandon-Malamud also so deftly detailed, medical systems (and their attendant metaphors) link practitioners and patients within a political and economic context.[4] What appears as "cultural pluralism" (because of the disparate class, religious, or ethnic memberships shared by these constituents) is better understood as a "single complex culture."[5] In fact, Crandon-Malamud's thesis turns on this point. Since practitioners and patients *are* part of the same cultural system, active manipulation of medical choices *can lead to* social transformation. If this were not the case, the ability to actively negotiate identities and even shift membership in social groups through use of medicine as a "primary resource" would have no transformative value for those who make the effort. In fact, her work amply demonstrates the veracity of these two interrelated parts of her thesis.

In this chapter, I will use Crandon-Malamud's key ideas to explore yet another link in the single complex culture of medical ethnography. I refer to the link between anthropologist and medical practitioner – or more specifically to the link between myself and a Peruvian *curandera* or shaman with whom I have worked for almost a dozen years. While considerations of the asymmetrical relationships between ethnographer and informant are certainly not new, neither have the impacts of our research on the lives of those we study been adequately addressed. This is certainly the case in shamanic research. For generations, ethnographies written by anthropologists have introduced popular readers to shamanic images and practices. Our research has served to both exoticize and legitimate these images. Recently, the ambiguous legacy of our research has become all the more problematic as shamanic images and practices have been commodified and co-opted in the service of domestic and international tourism as well as in the promotion of alternative and complementary healing. But, using the lens provided by Crandon-Malamud on this topic, I show in this chapter how shamans and anthropologists are far from passive recipients of these legacies.

Background

In coastal Peru (from Lima north to the border with Ecuador) and in the northern highlands, there exists a centuries-old medical tradition in which shamanic healers, called *curanderos*, conduct all-night healing ceremonies (known as *mesas*) to cure their patients of sorcery-caused illness.[6] Amply reported in the literature,[7] the socio-cultural and politico-economic context in which accusations of sorcery proliferate include the following. First, massive immigration to coastal cities from rural farms has led to both a shift in economic base from subsistence-farming to wage-labor and to an emphasis on the individual (as opposed to the household) as the effective unit of economic production. Second, depressed economies in industrial and service sectors have led to fierce competition for scarce resources and to endemic poverty. The resulting frustrations and anger felt by those who are not successful in the wage-based sectors cannot be directly expressed for several reasons. Most significantly, lack of government infrastructure means absence of state-supported welfare programs. Hence, there is a need to retain "good relations" with peers and family members who have been more successful in order to survive. As many scholars have argued, those who have prospered at the expense of family and friends fear envy, and the retaliation to which it is believed to lead, on a magical plane.

Sorcery is the feared end-result of these inequities. As I have reported elsewhere, sorcery in this setting involves concerted action (a visit to a sorcerer to take out a contract to "do the job") with intent to harm a specific victim. Also significant is that the victim is almost always a close relative or friend rather than a stranger. In short, sorcery is meant to "even the score, [to] remove competitors from the marketplace, or [to] avenge perceived inequities in resource distribution."[8] The actual harm occurs when the contracted sorcerer steals the victim's soul and commends it to an *encanto* (a kind of spirit power) or an *ánima* (a human soul which has not yet ascended to Heaven) where it is imprisoned. To steal the victim's soul, contagious or sympathetic magic is employed. Contagious magic occurs when a body-part (hair or fingernails) or an appurtenance (clothing, jewelry, or even an impression of the victim's footprint) is stolen from the victim, brought to the sorcerer, and used to call the victim's soul away from the body. The sorcerer then "hexes" the soul and commends it to the *encanto* or *ánima* for capture. To complete the hex, the body-part or appurtenance is mixed with a visible manifestation of the *encanto* (soil or water from the enchanted cave or lagoon) or *ánima* (ground-up human bones from the cemetery) and returned to the victim. When the victim unwittingly ingests the potion or wears the clothing, the hex is sealed. Sympathetic magic occurs when a photograph of the victim or a doll created in the victim's likeness is used to trick the victim's soul into leaving the body to inhabit the effigy. The photo or doll is then buried at the site of an *encanto* (a cave, archaeological ruin, spring, lagoon) or an *anima* (in a cemetery). The unnatural separation of body and soul causes the victim to exhibit a variety of symptoms (usually specifically related to the source of the spirit power utilized), and may lead to death unless the soul is restored.

Isabel and the anthropologist: negotiating relations and identities

In 1988, while searching for female *curanderas* on Peru's north coast, I met Isabel C., a forty-year-old *curandera* who heals patients of sorcery-caused illnesses during all-night ceremonies that, in many ways, resemble those where the harm is caused. A Peruvian Anthropologist named Rafael introduced me to Isabel. Rafael was a good friend of the *curandera* and a close friend of mine as well as being a colleague with whom I interacted on almost a daily basis. He knew of my interests in contacting female shamans and suffered through my almost daily requests for an introduction to his friend. He pleaded my case with Isabel for many months before she finally consented to meet me. The reason for her reservations, I was told at one point during my long wait, was that Isabel was afraid of associating with foreigners interested in her ritual-work because of a story she had heard. According to the story, another *curandero* (in this case, a man) had allowed two foreigners to witness his all-night ceremony. During the course of the *mesa*, they had stolen two of the most important objects on his *mesa*. These objects were his defense against attacks from other sorcerers (carried out by means of spirit familiars). During the night he was, in fact, the victim of a spirit attack. Without the objects, he was unable to defend himself and he died. The two foreigners, according to the story, then cut off his hands and removed them to a museum in the United States where they are on display! It was because of this legacy that I spent the better part of a year trying, through my colleague who was Isabel's friend, to gain an interview with this healer.

Isabel finally overcame her reservations and agreed to meet with me. When I told her of my interest in working with female *curanderas* and asked if I might work with her, she replied that she would have to "see my intentions" first. I was subjected to her scrutiny during the first *mesa* in which I participated in October of 1988. At the end of the night she concluded that she would help me because I was "worth the effort" and because I was more in need of a cure than any of her other patients! According to Isabel, I had been made the victim of sorcery while living in Peru many years before.[9] The symptoms of my ailment, as she described them, included my inability to finish my degree, to become a professional anthropologist instead of an "eternal student," and to otherwise get on with my life.[10] Though a more detailed account of my illness is beyond the scope of this paper, I should note that Isabel insisted that my cure would alleviate these problems. According to Isabel, I would find and accept my true identity (which she called my *yo personal*) as a result of her ministrations and as a result of my own efforts to actively participate in the cure. I would then be able to pursue my chosen career as well as to build a life for myself where I belonged, in the University and in the United States, instead of in Peru.

Thus began a long and fruitful association that eventually led to the publication of a book about gender and healing in northern Peru.[11] However, as suggested above, the only way we were able to enter into this relationship was because of my willingness to become Isabel's patient. Unlike the usual "apprentice–healer" relationship that anthropologists acquire, Isabel's insistence on my patient role kept me perpetually subservient. Even when I successfully "mastered" an understanding of her cures, I could do no more than to say I was healed. She always retained the power and the position of the healer. This suited me fine because it helped resolve for me some of the ethical dilemmas with shamanic research.[12] When I read the completed manuscript of my book to her in 1996, she seemed satisfied with this portrayal, and expressed interest that my book would bring other patients to her, as well as bring her money and fame.[13]

Renegotiating relations and identities: Tarapoto

Then, in November of 1998, I was invited to speak at the II International Forum on Indigenous Spirituality held in Tarapoto, Peru. Sponsored by the Inter-American Council on Indigenous Spirituality, the objectives of this event were threefold. First, the forum was to contribute to the interchange of knowledge and experiences between diverse indigenous and *mestizo* groups and their spiritual representatives as well as between academics from diverse disciplines. Second, the event was organized to defend the right to practice religious ceremonies and to use plants and other natural sacred elements as part of these ceremonies without prejudice or persecution from State and Federal bodies. Third, the organizing committee hoped to use the gathering as a mechanism to teach Peruvian and internationally-represented officials, physicians, and health policy makers about the factors that directly affect the spiritual life of indigenous populations. They hoped that future conversations and legislation would be informed by the presentations made at this gathering.

I was at the event for a fourth objective. I wanted to personally introduce Isabel to this international audience of policy-makers, academics, and fellow spiritual leaders. The agendas here were multiple and interrelated. First, I wanted to empower her to present her work at this forum in a way that she would find useful. As the Peruvians say, I wanted to give her *uso de la palabra* or "use of the word." Second, in response to her desire that our work together bring her money as well as notoriety, I wanted to give her an opportunity to widen her circle of contacts with other healers, with academics, and even with potential clients. I hoped that by participating together with her at this event, she would finally be able to speak for herself rather than only being represented by me, the anthropologist, in my books and articles. Third, and more obviously related to my own needs, I wanted her presence to validate the central thesis of many of my writings; namely that gender *is* an important consideration when assessing the illness conceptions and therapeutic strategies used by Peruvian shamans. Fourth, I looked forward to the opportunity of seeing her again after two and a half years. I wanted to take advantage of this visit to give her copies of my book, which was finally in print, as well as copies of an excerpt from the book that had appeared in *The Shaman's Drum* magazine.[14] The article featured a full-page photograph of Isabel, her assistant Olinda, and Isabel's two children that I thought Isabel would find especially pleasing. Finally, I wanted Isabel to see that, as a result of the cure that she had helped me achieve, I had finally "made-it" as a professional. This conference would be the first time that Isabel would see me in the role of professional anthropologist and I hoped that she would be pleased at the success her ministrations had wrought.

During the five days we spent together at this event, all of these goals were met – and more. My formal lecture about gender differences in Peruvian healing set the stage for Isabel's interventions later in the week, and her presentations did lend credibility to my ideas. She was able to express herself in her own words on several occasions, both as part of a round-table discussion in which questions were entertained about gender differences in healing, and as part of an unmoderated forum in which various healers exchanged ideas with one another while the academics listened. She was able to network with both other healers and academics over meals and on excursions. Among the contacts that she made were a Belgian documentary filmmaker, a Peruvian bio-chemist who was on-staff at the country's most prestigious university and a highly-placed political functionary who had co-sponsored the event. She also laid a *mesa* and performed an all-night

Plate 13.1 "Isabel (left), her assistant Olinda (right), and Isabel's two children (seated) pose for my camera at the pilgrimage site of the *Cruz del Chalpon* near Motupe, Peru in 1989. This was the picture that appeared in *The Shaman's Drum* magazine that was 'hexed' upon Isabel and Olinda's return from the Tarapoto forum."

healing ceremony that allowed her to demonstrate her prowess as a healer to conference participants. Finally, like all the other participants at the symposium, Isabel was able to "sample" a wide variety of healing practices during the five days of the symposium. Activities conducive to this end included the daily lectures and round-tables, the informal conversations with other healers, and ample opportunity to participate in the other ritual events – from sweat-lodges to *ayahuasca* and *peyote* ceremonies – that were being offered each evening.

The end result of this event was generally positive with all participants expressing satisfaction at the outcome. Isabel seemed happy to make new contacts, to receive copies of my book, and she seemed pleased to see me in my professional role. But, she was just as troubled as she was pleased by some of the features of the conference. First, she noted that, on several occasions, many of the conference participants seemed to be more motivated by a kind of "surface" mentality than by any honest desire to incorporate the experiences they were having into effective change in their own lives. Second, she lamented that various healing traditions were presented as spectacles for voyeuristic enjoyment of a tourist audience rather than as real or authentic curing events. She predicted that this lack of seriousness on the part of many healers present at the conference would have serious ramifications for patients who were seeking to find a cure for their afflictions.

Finally, she worried about the competition that might ensue among healers present at the conference as they vied for notoriety, potential clients, and money.[15] Specifically, she pointed to one healer who had been invited and who aggressively advertised his healing ceremonies with conference participants. She pointed out that this man was her neighbor in Chiclayo. She told me that he had long envied her success as a healer and that she had a history of problems with him in her neighborhood. On more than one occasion he had even tried to bring down her business by hexing both her and her assistant. At the conference, during one of the round-table discussions that featured Isabel as an invited speaker, this man snapped her picture. Afterwards, when discussing the incident she became visibly alarmed. She worried that he might become even more envious of her reputation as a result of her active participation in the conference and that he might use the picture to do more sorcery when she returned home to Chiclayo. She soon dropped the subject, however. When I left her at the bus station for her trip back to Chiclayo, she seemed elated to have been invited. She was happy to have the book and article copies and to have networked with so many people. We laughingly commented how she had been the "belle of the ball" and how good it was for her (as well as for me) that she had been able to attend. She expressed pleasure at seeing my development as an academic, as an author, and as a conference participant. We made plans to see one another again soon, as I had plans to return to Peru six months hence with a group of students and professionals who would participate in a kind of study-tour that would focus on Isabel's work. Isabel indicated that she was looking forward to the revenue that this opportunity would bring and she was thoroughly in favor of the trip.

The aftermath

During the months following the Tarapoto conference, Isabel and I communicated little. When I tried to call her home I was unsuccessful in reaching her. I had several unexplainable messages on my answering machine, with a recorded operator's voice stating that the caller should "try their call again" but I didn't give these a second thought after noting their peculiarity. Then, one early morning in May, Isabel told me she had been trying to reach me for months. Without giving me details, she told me that her assistant Olinda had been very ill and that I also had been in danger. She declined to comment further, saying that she would give me all the details when we met again in July. For the moment, she needed my advice. Isabel noted that the Belgian filmmaker whom she met in Tarapoto had called to say that she was on her way to Peru. She wanted to film a documentary of Isabel's life and of her work and she wanted me to intercede with the woman on her behalf so that she would be fairly compensated for her efforts. Unfortunately, since the woman had already left for Peru when Isabel finally reached me, Isabel admitted that she would probably go through with the project in any event. Still, she hoped that I could convince the filmmaker to compensate her fairly for her efforts. I agreed to talk with the woman and to share the details of our conversation with Isabel. When the filmmaker and I *did* finally talk by telephone, the conversation was awkward and less than productive. I told her what Isabel was expecting as a fair price. She balked at the figures. I tried to communicate the lack of agreement to Isabel but she was hurried (the ritual she had prepared for the documentary was moments from beginning) and I was left feeling that Isabel had not received adequate counseling to make an informed decision.

I didn't talk with Isabel again until about three weeks later when I arrived in Lima with just one student, bound for Isabel's house in Chiclayo. During the months between my November conversations with Isabel at the Tarapoto conference and my arrival in Peru in mid-July, a series of set-backs had seen the study-tour dwindle from about fourteen participants to that single student. Isabel seemed glad to hear from me. We confirmed the date of our arrival in Chiclayo about a week hence. Almost immediately after our arrival in Lima, though, my student began suffering from the kind of traveler's diarrhea that can put a damper on any visit to a foreign country. As I worried whether or not she would be able to travel to Chiclayo and whether we would be able to keep to our schedule, I began to wonder if traveling with even one student was really such a good idea.

A few days later, my student and I met-up with Rafael (the colleague who had originally introduced me to Isabel) and he decided to accompany us to visit Isabel in Chiclayo. When we arrived at Isabel's house, the reception we received was cool. As I quickly learned, the trip with the Belgian filmmaker had been a disaster and Isabel blamed me. Isabel had received only one quarter of the compensation that I thought had been agreed upon and the filmmaker had apparently convinced her that had stipulated the much-reduced price as being fair. Further, and perhaps more devastating to my ongoing relationship with this healer, the filmmaker and her crew had treated Isabel and her companions poorly during the eight days they had been filming. But, as became apparent in further conversations with Isabel, her sense that I had betrayed her wasn't limited to the difficult experience she had had with the Belgian filmmaker. As the story of her assistant's illness unfolded, she indicated that *all* her misfortunes over the previous months were the direct result of her participation in the Tarapoto Conference.

According to Isabel, the neighbor who had snapped her picture during the Tarapoto event had been consumed by envy and had sought-out a sorcerer much more powerful than he was to harm her once she had returned home. Her likeness in the picture, as well as earth swept from their home, had given him ammunition with which to effect the hex. But the most damage had occurred when the neighbor had managed to steal the copy of *The Shaman's Drum* magazine (which contained my words as author and Isabel and Olinda's pictures) from the "waiting room" where Isabel's clients wait to see her. Apparently, the magazine had been hexed with human excrement and unobtrusively returned to the room. The hex, called a *daño por aire* (air-borne harm) was designed to "bring everything down" and so that "all our projects would end in nothing." Whoever first grabbed the magazine after it had been returned would, via contagious magic, bear the brunt of that hex. As Isabel recounted the story, her assistant Olinda had seen the magazine, covered in filth, and had removed it. By so doing, Olinda absorbed the evil "air" that was intended as the delivery mechanism of the hex and she became very ill with acute gastrointestinal distress. After several weeks of self-treatment, Olinda finally agreed to go to a doctor, who misdiagnosed her ailment.[16] First, she was told that the gastrointestinal distress was most likely the symptomatic reflection of a "really screwed up heart" and that she should worry about an impending heart attack. When tests showed no inflammation, the doctor sent her to a gynecologist. At this point, Isabel suggested that Olinda allow her to lay a *mesa* to see if the cause of her ailment was, in fact, due to sorcery instead of due to the diagnosed conditions that doctors asserted.[17] But, Olinda aggressively declined the invitation, stating that she would follow-up with the doctor's advice. The gynecologist ordered an ultrasound. The results showed ovarian cysts and the physician told her he suspected cancer. Olinda was informed she would need an immediate biopsy if she wanted to save her life. After consulting with her family and determining that she didn't have the money necessary to cover the costs of the operation, Olinda returned home in despair. Coincidentally, the Peruvian biochemist that Isabel and Olinda had met at the Tarapoto Conference came to visit and suggested that she should go to a healer friend of his for a guinea pig cleansing.[18] Olinda agreed. The guinea pig cleansing revealed that she was, in fact, suffering from sorcery. Because of that diagnosis, she finally agreed to have Isabel lay a *mesa* on her behalf. By the time I had arrived, Olinda was well on her way to being cured, thanks to her participation in several restorative *mesa* ceremonies. As Isabel recounted the story of Olinda's distress, she noted that she credits this man with saving Olinda's life because of his interventions at this crucial juncture in the illness episode.

During the next several days of my visit with Isabel – and over the course of two *mesa* ceremonies in which my student and I participated – the scope of misfortunes attributed to the envious healer became apparent. Olinda's gastrointestinal distress and misdiagnosis by the medical community was the most obvious result of the sorcery that had been caused by that envy. But, additionally, Isabel noted that sorcery was also implicated as the reason my study-tour had unraveled (going from fourteen interested clients to just one over a matter of several months). Because I had also absorbed the evil "air" associated with this particular episode, my clients had become disillusioned with the study-tour, my university had declined to support my efforts at organizing the tour, and Isabel had been unable to contact me by telephone to warn me. Furthermore, she blamed the fact that the student traveling with me had become ill since our arrival in Peru on the sorcery. She insisted that I would need to be thoroughly cleansed of the sorcery and that I would need all her power as a healer over the next few days to undo the

Plate 13.2 Isabel's curing altar (*mesa*) as it appeared in 1989.

harm that had been done and to assure my student's speedy recovery. She noted that in all the time I had worked with her on my dissertation, I had never experienced being the victim of sorcery to the degree that I was now suffering. By way of illustration, she performed a guinea pig cleansing for my student and for me. Both guinea pigs died (a sure sign of sorcery) before the ceremony was completed. Furthermore, when Isabel poured a bit of *agua florida*[19] into a portion of the guinea pig's intestinal membrane that she uses as a "lens" to "see" the cause of patient affliction, a horned-framed-face was clearly visible to all of those viewing the pooled liquid. Isabel indicated that this was obvious evidence of the power of this particular sorcery episode, for the sorcerer clearly had a pact with the devil.

As a result of Isabel's diagnosis, I submitted to her ministrations over the next several days. During the second *mesa* ceremony especially, I was made to run, jump, dance, stomp, and otherwise enthusiastically engage in aerobic conditioning from shortly after the *mesa* started (about nine o'clock in the evening) until almost seven o'clock the next morning. On several occasions Isabel chided me for not remembering the most basic elements of the healing ceremony, for not performing adequately or with enough energy, for moving out of place as I jumped and stomped, and for otherwise being a less than adequate patient. None of these actions were really all that out of the ordinary, for, as I have detailed elsewhere, Isabel is not always a very nice person when she is deep in trance and her soul is traveling to other worlds.[20] But, I remember thinking that the unusually rough-treatment at this *mesa* was significant. I wondered to myself (as I struggled to keep up the pace of the aerobics) if she wasn't *really* making me pay for having taken her to the Tarapoto Conference and for all the consequences that had wrought with this rougher than usual treatment. In addition to the two *mesas*, she prescribed two cleansing enemas over as many days for me (and for no one else). If nothing else, I was *certainly* back in the role of "patient in need of a cure," even if I thought I had temporarily left that role behind in the heady days of our meeting, the previous November.[21]

Towards morning, Isabel began to talk specifically about the incidents in Tarapoto that had led to so much suffering. She told me "it would have been nice to interact with other *curanderos* and to share ideas, but, because of envy, competition, this is not possible – instead, someone has to die." She insisted that our actions – mine to invite her and hers to attend the Tarapoto forum – had almost ended in death.

Discussion

I have elsewhere argued that it is our responsibility to give our research subjects their own voice by writing their stories, but even more than this, by empowering them to speak for themselves.[22] This stance requires careful brokering, to be sure, but is more ethical than gate-keeping.[23] It means introducing our research subjects to academics, to other healers, and even to potential clients with the money to pay them richly for their services, if that is their desire. My intent was to empower Isabel and to give her control over the presentation of her image when I invited her to the conference in Tarapoto in November of 1998. But, as I found out six months later, in July of 1999, my best efforts to open doors for Isabel (as she had requested on so many occasions) and to give her control over a future that she would command had backfired. Instead, I had led her into harm's way by bringing her to this event. So, I am left with the following questions: What role(s) should anthropologists play as shamanic healing becomes oriented towards internal and external tourism and towards the profit-motive that consumes the consumer? How do our research programs impact these futures and what responses might we expect from our research subjects as their lives (and images) change as a result of our research?

In thinking about these events, I am struck again by Crandon-Malamud's insights into the ways in which people use medical resources to negotiate identities – both personal and cultural. Through our relationship (and my subsequent writings) Isabel's image was broadcast widely, both internationally and in her own neighborhood. In the intervening years between the time I finished my book manuscript and its publication, I know that Isabel looked forward to the notoriety (and potential future clients) that she would receive as a result. Now, as a result of the publications that were appearing about her, she had become famous enough to field inquiries about further commercialization (from the Belgian filmmaker). She had also become famous in her neighborhood, among clients and enemies alike. However, the public display of her image in *The Shaman's Drum* magazine made her vulnerable in ways that she only recognized after her participation in the Tarapoto conference.

As Michael Brown has also noted, Peruvian shamanism has a dark side of competition, jealousy, envy, and revenge that researchers and seekers refuse to see.[24] Although completely aware of this "dark side,"[25] it seems that I had also been naïve about the effects that competition, envy, and suspicion would have on Isabel as she became more famous in her own community. In part, I blame my naïveté on wishful thinking. In part, I blame it on Isabel's own assertions that, unlike other Peruvian *curanderos* whose lives had changed as a result of anthropological investigations, she could maintain control of the consequences that fame would certainly bring.[26] I labored to make her understand how economic exploitation and image manipulation is an inherent danger in the bottom-line considerations of shamanic empowerment in a profit-driven world. I felt partially redeemed by noting that anthropologists *cannot* be gate-keepers for the consequences of the decisions of the healers with whom we work. Taking a very rationalist and very *Western* perspective, I hid behind the ideology of Isabel's *free agency* and right to choose. Yet, in hindsight, I am left to wonder how I, as a trained anthropologist, could have so discounted the hegemonic ideologies of competition, envy, and suspicion that are so much a part of her social reality.[27]

During the Tarapoto conference and, in a setting in which envy and competition have such negative consequences, Isabel was made vulnerable because of the way her image had been commercialized. *The Shaman's Drum* article had clearly left her feeling "on display" and vulnerable, as became apparent in her assessment of how it had been manipulated and hexed in order to "do us all in." Isabel's discomfort about the consequences of being on display (at the Tarapoto Conference and in publication) is especially significant when related back to her original fears about the consequences of working with foreigners who, sometimes unknowingly, take that which is not theirs and make healers vulnerable to attack. Isabel's response in July was to restructure her relationship with me so that once again she was in control. Putting me in the role of patient served an important purpose because it allowed her to renegotiate her identity in important ways. Not surprisingly, when I asked her that July if she thought she would like to be a part of the XIII International Congress of Traditional Medicine, she responded, "I'll wait and see what Victor says (the Peruvian bio-chemist she credits with having saved Olinda's life). Even though we have known each other a short time, I feel like he is a member of my family and I trust his judgement on these things implicitly. He knows things about the way things work here in Peru that you can't know and I'll let him advise me on whether to participate or not."

After the five days I spent with Isabel July of 1999, I believe the harm (both metaphorical and magical) done as a result of the Tarapoto Conference and *The Shaman's Drum* magazine have been undone. Isabel has once again asserted control over the threats to her image and her identity as a healer that are the result of her continuing association with me as anthropologist and as image-maker. By putting me squarely back in the role of patient, and making me *viscerally* aware of how our relationship must be thus, she has salvaged what she feared lost, and has learned how to domesticate the researcher/shaman dialectic in the process. As evidence of this, I have only a snippet of conversation that I overheard her speak as we prepared to depart from her home at the end of our visit in July. But, the few words I heard speak volumes. As she told Rafael, "you know, now I understand that those two anthropologists didn't cut off the healer's hands and display them in a museum. Now that I've worked with anthropologists, I understand that they don't have that kind of power."

Conclusion

As was painfully obvious in retrospect, my naïve wish to empower Isabel by allowing her to stand-out and to speak-out as an equal in my world was not ethical at all.

Instead, it was at least unconsciously grounded in my desire to cleanse myself of the consequences of my research rather than to protect her in her world. And yet, I still believe that to fully embrace the consequences of shamanic research we must act, jointly, with our shaman subjects to construct scenarios in which control over representation, authenticity, and legitimacy of shamanic practice is actively constructed, rather than passively accepted or left to the whims of market-forces.

The best mechanisms for achieving this empowerment are yet to be determined but these will probably require the kind of coalition-building implicit in the objectives of the Tarapoto gathering. These include a call for dialog among *curanderos* in Peru and throughout the Americas as well as for dialog between healers and academics. Formalization of professional healer-associations that would be empowered to speak on behalf of their members and to sanction the inappropriate commercialization of spiritual traditions has also been proposed. Until healer-associations unite and stand upon a common platform, as has begun to occur in Ecuador but has yet to happen in Peru, envy and suspicion between healers will continue to undermine any possibilities of actively countering the exotic constructions of the image-makers.

Certainly, a critical interpretation of these events requires our consideration of the consequences of our work among shamans from multiple perspectives. Shamans and anthropologists alike are both victims and active agents of the worlds that we construct through our research. The one thing that is certain is that there is no turning back. And moving ahead, as Isabel would agree, we must be prepared to consider the mistakes, as equally valuable lessons in experience.

Notes

1 Libbet Crandon, *From the Fat of Our Souls: Social Change, Political Process, and Medical Pluralism in Bolivia*, University of California Press, 1991, p. 201.
2 Crandon, *From the Fat of Our Souls*, p. 46.
3 Crandon, *From the Fat of Our Souls*, p. 33.
4 Crandon, From *the Fat of Our Souls,* p. 32.
5 Crandon, *From the Fat of Our Souls*, p. 22.
6 Generically known as *daño* or "harm," these hexes are best understood as being part of what George Foster and Barbara Gallatin Anderson have called a "personalistic" rather than a "naturalistic" theory of disease etiology in their 1978 textbook on *Medical Anthropology*, Wiley and Sons, pp. 51–79. In a personalistic system, disease is

believed to come as a result of intentional acts on behalf of a sensate agent. In the case of *daño* as opposed to a spirit-caused ailment, the sensate agent is a sorcerer who, at the request of an enemy of the victim, will perform magical acts to steal the victim's soul. While the *ultimate* cause of illness can be understood in terms of envy and other related socio-pathologies, the *effective* cause of illness is "soul-loss." In the case of *daño* in northern Peru, the *instrumental* cause of harm may either be *daño por boca* (ingestion of a potion that has been "worked" by the sorcerer to facilitate this soul-loss) or *daño por aire* (the hex is received via contagion, absorbed through the skin or breathed-in as an "evil air"). For more on definitions of *daño* and distinctions between *daño por boca* and *daño por aire*, see Bonnie Glass-Coffin, *The Gift of Life: Female Spirituality and Healing in Northern Peru*, University of New Mexico Press, 1998.

7 For more, Douglas Sharon, *Wizard of the Four Winds: A Shaman's Story*, The Free Press, 1978; Donald Joralemon and Douglas Sharon, *Sorcery and Shamanism: Curanderos and Clients in Northern Peru*, University of Utah, 1993; and Glass-Coffin, *The Gift of Life*.

8 Glass-Coffin, *The Gift of Life*, p. 4.

9 I had, in fact, lived in Peru as a high-school exchange student, fallen hopelessly in love with a young Peruvian man, and generally "gone native" to use the terminology of Anthropologists. Since that early trip, I had found it difficult to disengage from the illusion that I could have a Peruvian identity and, according to Isabel, that stance had made it difficult for me to get on with my life in my home-country and in my chosen profession.

10 The story of my first *mesa* with Isabel is recounted in detail in Glass-Coffin, *The Gift of Life*, pp. 81–6.

11 Glass-Coffin, *The Gift of Life*.

12 Bonnie Glass-Coffin, "Anthropology, Shamanism, and the 'New Age,'" *Chronicle of Higher Education*, 15 June 1994, p. A48.

13 While shamanic healers who have been the focus of other anthropological research do not charge for their services (Koss, personal communication) the Peruvians I have worked with *do* charge for their services and view curing as a legitimate, money-making activity. As Donald Joralemon has noted in his article on "The selling of the shaman and the problem of informant legitimacy," *Journal of Anthropological Research*, 1990, 46: 105–18, many Peruvian informants have also been eager to work with anthropologists as a means of increasing their fame and legitimating their power and authority as healers.

14 Bonnie Glass-Coffin, "To stand before Isabel's mesa: female spiritual healing in northern Peru," *The Shaman's Drum: A Journal of Experiential Shamanism*, Spring, 1998, 48: 54–66.

15 Like many of the Peruvian healers I met who work in urban and peri-urban settings, Isabel's healing activities are her sole source of income in a largely cash-based economy. Not surprisingly, Isabel views other healers as competitors for clients (especially clients who can actually afford to pay for their cures). Additionally, a world-view that presumes envy and the intent to cause harm as a logical outcome of economic success influences relationships between healers. During her career as a healer, Isabel has suffered several periods marked by economic downturns and a loss of clientele. Each time this has occurred, she has blamed her misfortune on attacks by other sorcerers. But, in explaining how she is *different* from the other healers I worked with while in Peru, Isabel emphasized that she is incapable of reciprocating their attacks. To engage in negative spiritual actions, she told me, would violate the principles and parameters of her power and God would take away her ability to heal if she succumbed to such vengeance.

16 According to Isabel, *daño por boca* and *daño por aire* leave distinct "markers" or clues as to their origins. While neither kind of sorcery can be cured by a physician or with

the use of biomedicine, the former shows up as "invisible" or as idiopathic when symptoms resulting from it are presented to the medical community. The latter, on the other hand, leaves a diagnostic trail but the diagnosis is always wrong. Thus, Isabel's assertions that Olinda was suffering from a *daño por aire* correlate well with the story of the multiple misdiagnoses that Olinda received.

17 At this point, Isabel reminded me that one of the common consequences of a hex is that the patient is deceived into believing that the problem is *not* the result of sorcery. This has the effect of keeping the patient from looking for a relevant cure until the sorcery is *pasado* (too far gone) to cure via interventions of a healer through use of the *mesa*. The next day, Olinda also noted how powerful the hex must have been to make her blind to its cause. "Especially since Isabel and I *work* in this field, and since we are *always* in danger of being hexed." In short, suffering from a hex is an occupational hazard of working with a healer and Olinda shook her head as she thought back to how stubbornly she had refused Isabel's treatment and to how her stubbornness had almost cost her her life.

18 I should note here the *reason* for this biochemist's attendance at the Tarapoto Conference. While conducting biochemical analyses of the psychoactive cactus that coastal healers use to help them enter into altered states of consciousness and to engage in soul-travel, he had worked with coastal healers, especially those who specialize in guinea-pig diagnosis for several years. Thus, he was well versed in etiologies of sorcery and northern healing traditions.

19 *Agua florida* or florida water is an integral part of Peruvian healing ceremonies. It is, essentially, a very flowery cologne, which is used as both an offering to spirits and as a cleansing agent for sorcery-caused illness. For more on how odors figure in the symbolic systems of sorcery and healing in northern Peru, see Joralemon and Sharon, *Sorcery and Shamanism*, pp. 249–50.

20 Glass-Coffin, *The Gift of Life*.

21 I should note that I was expected to pay for this cure just like any other patient would be expected to pay. I should also note that Isabel's cures are on a kind of sliding-scale – she expects people to pay according to their means (the average rate she charges for upper-class Peruvians in search of her services is $50.00–70.00 for a "private" *mesa* and $10.00–20.00 for participation in a group ceremony). As she often reminds me, this is less than the fees charged by many Peruvian healers and substantially less than sorcerers charge clients who contract with them to do intentional harm. There is no "going rate" than I am aware of for sorcery contracts, but I have heard that some of the more famous sorcerers charge $1000 for their services. Isabel, on the other hand, does much *pro bono* work for people who have no resources. While Isabel has always treated Peruvians of diverse social and economic statuses, one difference in her practice since my work with her has been her increasing access to foreign clients. While I may have been the *first* foreigner Isabel claims to have cured (back in 1988–89), I have certainly not been the last. In the last twelve years, Isabel claims to have cured many foreigners. Some of these are people that she has met through my work (several participants in the Tarapoto conference have since become Isabel's clients). Some are people that she has met through Rafael.

22 Glass-Coffin, "Anthropology, Shamanism, and the 'New Age,'" p. A48.

23 For more on this idea, see Don Joralemon, *The Selling of the Shaman and the Problem of Informant Legitimacy*.

24 Michael F. Brown, "The dark side of the shaman," *Natural History*, November 1989, pp. 8–10.

25 See Bonnie Glass-Coffin, "Discourse *Daño*, and healing in north coastal Peru," *Medical Anthropology*, 1991, 13(1–2): 33–55, as well as Glass-Coffin, *The Gift of Life* and Bonnie Glass-Coffin, "Engendering Peruvian Shamanism through time: insights from ethnohistory and ethnography, *Ethnohistory*, 1999, 46(2): 205–38, for discussion

of the central roles played by envy, suspicion, mistrust, and sorcery in Northern Peruvian Shamanism.

26 For further discussion about the impacts of anthropological investigation on shamanic image and practice, see Joralemon, "The selling of the shaman." The healer that he refers to in his article as having been the object of "New Age" transformations was Eduardo Calderón, a Peruvian healer with whom I had close association over many years. I was also intimately involved in the project that Joralemon refers to in that article and was witness to (as well as a participant in) some of the transformative events in the lives of the other healers referred to in his article. Because of my close association with the topic (I had even been invited to write on this theme by the *Chronicle of Higher Education* in 1994), I had several conversations with Isabel prior to the publication of my book about the possible dangers that might accompany her increased notoriety. I told her she would need to guard against being financially exploited by New Age seekers, documentary filmmakers, or others who would want to market her image for their own ends. She insisted that she could handle the consequences and that, on balance, saw the economic potentials as offsetting any potentially negative outcomes. However, our conversations focused much more on the consequences of capitalization from a rationalist and a humanistic standpoint than on the potential impacts of envy and sorcery attack.

27 See Jacob Pandian, *Anthropology and the Western Tradition: Toward an Authentic Anthropology*, Waveland Press, 1985, for an excellent discussion of how difficult it is to step outside the paradigms that constrain our thinking, even as trained social scientists.

References

Brown, Michael F., "The dark side of the shaman," *Natural History*, 1989, pp. 8–10.

Crandon-Malamud, Libbet, *From the Fat of Our Souls: Social Change, Political Process, and Medical Pluralism in Bolivia*, University of California Press, 1991.

Foster, George and Barbara Gallatin Anderson, *Medical Anthropology*, John Wiley and Sons, 1978.

Glass-Coffin, Bonnie, "Discourse *Daño*, and healing in north coastal Peru," *Medical Anthropology*, 1991, 13(1–2): 33–55.

——, "Anthropology, Shamanism, and the 'New Age,'" *The Chronicle of Higher Education*, 1994, June 15, p. A48.

——, "Male and female healing in northern Peru: metaphors, models and manifestations of difference," *Journal of Ritual Studies*, 1996, 10(1): 63–91.

——, *The Gift of Life: Female Spirituality and Healing in Northern Peru*, University of New Mexico Press, 1998.

——, "To stand before Isabel's mesa: female spiritual healing in northern Peru," *The Shaman's Drum: A Journal of Experiential Shamanism*, 1998, 48: 54–66.

——, "Engendering Peruvian Shamanism through time: insights from ethnohistory and ethnography," *Ethnohistory*, 1999, 46(2): 205–38.

Joralemon, Donald, "The selling of the shaman and the problem of informant legitimacy," *Journal of Anthropological Research*, 1990, 46: 105–18.

—— and Douglas Sharon, *Sorcery and Shamanism: Curanderos and Clients in Northern Peru*, University of Utah Press, 1993.

Pandian, Jacob, *Anthropology and the Western Tradition: Toward an Authentic Anthropology*, Waveland Press, 1985.

Sharon, Douglas, *Wizard of the Four Winds: A Shaman's Story*, The Free Press, 1978.

Index